The man who shook his fist at the Tsar

The man who shook his fist at the Tsar

The story of Alexander Pushkin's epic poem
The Bronze Horseman

With a new translation and background on episodes in
Russian history and Pushkin's life

by Jack Robertson

a Redwords book

The man who shook his fist at the Tsar
The story of Alexander Pushkin's epic poem, '*The Bronze Horseman*'

With a new translation of the poem and background on episodes in Russian history and Pushkin's life by Jack Robertson

Published March 2019

Redwords
ISBN: 978 1 910885 88 8

978 1 910885 96 3 (Kindle)
978 1 910885 97 0 (epub)

Redwords is connected to
Bookmarks: The Socialist Bookshop
1 Bloomsbury Street, London WC1B 3QE

https://bookmarksbookshop.co.uk

Design and production: Roger Huddle
Printed by Short Run Press Ltd, Exeter, Devon

About the author

Born and brought up in Edinburgh, Jack Robertson moved to Manchester in the early 1970s and then to East London a few years later. A lifelong socialist, anti-racist activist and militant trade unionist, he was Secretary of the Joint Shop Stewards Committee at Massey Ferguson, Trafford Park, and edited the shop-floor newsletter of the Joint Combine Committee covering sister plants in Kilmarnock, Coventry and at Perkins Engines, Peterborough. He later edited the national rank-and-file paper for the engineering industry, Engineers Charter. He has been a member of the International Socialists (now SWP) since 1971 and served on its Central Committee between 1976 and 1981, at the time of the Grunwick's strike, the Anti-Nazi League and Rock Against Racism. In the 1980s, he wrote a weekly column for *Socialist Worker* under the pen name Birdy, and in the 1990s, a monthly column for the magazine *Socialist Review*, this time as The Walrus. At the time of the First Gulf War (1990-91) he edited the bulletin of the anti-war campaign group, Media Workers Against the War. He studied Russian Language, Literature and History at Queen Mary & Westfield College, Mile End, and at the School of Slavonic & East European Studies between 1992 and 1996. For most of his adult life he was employed as a journalist, latterly at Thomson Reuters, where he was Father of the NUJ Chapel at its industrial relations subsidiary, Incomes Data Services. He lives in West Ham and is married to a retired East London GP. They have two daughters and two grand-daughters.

Acknowledgements

Special thanks are due to: the most recent of my former editors, Ken Mulkearn, for his regular feedback and editorial advice; to his partner, Katie Griffin, for her unstinting support and expertise with spoken Russian; to my former workmates, Adam Elston, Mick Herron and Lindsay Hutton, for their backing when this project was in its infancy; and to readers Mary Edmondson, Laura Hayes, Paul McSorley, Ida Fairbairn and the Faber Academy, for their always helpful comments and advice. Thanks also to Sally Campbell, David Gilchrist and Colm Bryce at Bookmarks. The expert guidance of Roger Huddle has been invaluable in the final stages of the design and production process, as has the efficient proofreading of Mary Brodbin and Carol Williams. Most of all, thanks to my wife, Dr Mary Edmondson, and to my daughters, Jean and Sarah, for their constant encouragement. Any factual inaccuracies in the book are entirely my fault.

Contents

Notes are at the end of each chapter

8

Note on transliteration and sources

One of the pitfalls of translating to and from Russian is that there are a number of letters in the Cyrillic alphabet which have no direct equivalent in English, some look the same but are pronounced differently and some look different but are pronounced in the same way as their English equivalents.

Although a standardised system of transliteration does exist, in the form of the *Oxford Slavonic Papers,* this is not rigidly adhered to and this can often be especially confusing when it comes to the translation of Russian names: Peter as Pyotr, Evgeny as Yevgeny or Eugene, Elizabeth as Yelizaveta or Elizaveta, and Catherine as Yekaterina, Ekaterina and so on. In this book, I have generally stuck to the convention of naming Russian Tsars and Tsarinas, and Alexander Pushkin, using their anglicised spelling, but this is not always possible - as when a name is spelt differently in a quotation from another author.

The city of St Petersburg, which features prominently in this story, has changed names a number of times since its official foundation by Peter the Great in 1703. It was named after the Tsar's patron saint, Saint Peter, and remained the capital of the Russian empire for the next 200 years, until the Russian Revolution of 1917. The city's name was changed to Petrograd in 1914 and then to Leningrad in 1924. It remained as Leningrad until 1991 when the original name was restored.

On the assumption that it would assist the narrative flow, footnotes appear at the end of each chapter rather than on every page, the bibliography is grouped thematically.

Introduction

> *All that the Tsar, Nicholas I, will ever be remembered*
> *for is that he lived in the time of Pushkin.*
>
> Russian peasant, *Anon*

This book is about *The Bronze Horseman,* an epic poem written by Russia's greatest poet, Alexander Pushkin, in 1833. The title of the poem is a reference to the famous equestrian statue of the Russian Tsar and founder of the city of St Petersburg, Peter the Great. Peter had earned the reputation of being a 'miracle-working' Tsar, not least for having managed to build the city, virtually overnight, in the middle of a mosquito-infested swamp. The monument celebrating his achievements dominates Senate Square in the heart of St Petersburg. It was commissioned half a century after his death by Peter's successor, Catherine the Great, and was designed and constructed by the French sculptor, Etienne Falconet. It is universally known as *The Bronze Horseman,* after Pushkin's poem. In the opinion of the eminent Russian literary historian, Dmitry Svyatopolk-Mirsky: 'It is now a matter of common consent that *The Bronze Horseman* is the greatest work ever penned in Russian verse'.

No visitor to St Petersburg can fail to notice some reference to *The Bronze Horseman.* The monument itself has become emblematic of the city in much the same way as the Statue of Liberty is to New York. Newly married couples go to have their wedding photographs taken against the background of the bronze statue, rearing up on its enormous pink granite base as though it is cresting a wave. Its silhouette appears on everything from Metro maps to chocolate bars and most Russians can effortlessly quote entire passages from Pushkin's poem verbatim.

Not only is *The Bronze Horseman* much loved by ordinary Russians, it is also among the most politically charged of his works. It tells the story of the terrifying retribution unleashed against Pushkin's anti-hero, Evgeny, when he dares to question the 'miracle-working' Tsar's judgement in having chosen such a vulnerable location to construct his new city.

The events described in the poem take place against the backdrop of the Great Flood of 1824, when – not for the first time in its history – St Petersburg was inundated and hundreds of its citizens were swept away by the tumultuous invading waters of the River Neva. In some of the most dramatic passages in his poem, Pushkin vividly describes the devastating impact of the flood. His brother, Leo, had witnessed this first hand and, in an introductory note to the poem, Pushkin assures readers that his account is based on actual events, verifiable from contemporary reports.

Whereas the opening passages of *The Bronze Horseman* praise Peter the Great for his achievement in having created St Petersburg against all the odds in such a forbidding landscape, this enthusiastic endorsement is thrown into doubt after the devastation caused by the flood. All of the hopes and aspirations nurtured by Evgeny are swept away by the floodwaters and he now blames the Tsar for his woes. The dramatic turning point in the poem comes when Evgeny finds himself wandering close to the monument late one evening and suddenly expresses his fury by shaking his fist at the statue and shouting out: 'So be it, miracle worker – just you wait!'. No sooner has he made his protest than the bronze head of the statue appears to swivel round and the entire monument jolts into life.

Both the colossal bronze warhorse and its tyrannical rider then descend from the monument's huge granite base and chase Evgeny remorselessly through the deserted streets of the capital. No longer the 'miracle-working' Tsar, the statue-come-to-life is now described in the poem as a *kumir*, the Russian word for a demi-god, idol or despot. In the concluding section of the poem, Evgeny is found wandering the city half-crazy, until his corpse is discovered and quietly buried on a deserted island. The Great Flood of 1824 takes on additional significance in *The Bronze Horseman,* because it is symbolic of powers which no mere mortal has the capacity to overcome, not even the Tsar of Russia. It can also be decoded as a presentiment of a second calamity which was to shake the capital almost exactly one year after the Great Flood.

This took place in December 1825, when officers in the Imperial Army – subsequently known as the Decembrists – led an attempted uprising against the Tsar on the same day as Nicholas I was due to be inaugurated as the new Tsar. The focal point of this revolt was Senate Square, where the insurgent regiments assembled around the base of *The Bronze Horseman* – before being mown down by grapeshot fired from cannon at close range. This is also the exact same spot where Evgeny makes his protest in the poem and where he is stranded by the floodwaters.

There is no question that Pushkin identified with the Decembrist cause. He was closely involved with many of its leading participants and was universally regarded as its literary flagbearer. In his own verse, Pushkin hailed himself as a 'proud singer of freedom'. In a private interview which took place a few months after the rebellion, Pushkin told the Tsar, Nicholas I, that he would no doubt have taken part in the uprising himself, had he not been exiled, for the second time, to his family estate at Mikhailovskoye at the time it took place.

Much is sometimes made of the fact that Pushkin was never an actual member of any of the Decembrists' secret societies but this overlooks the fact that no other person in Russia was subjected to such an extraordinary degree of surveillance because of his writings. Government spies traced his every move and his mail was routinely intercepted by the police. By the time the uprising took place, Pushkin had already served one period in exile for his writings. It would have been utter madness for any clandestine organisation to recruit such a high profile and mercurial figure as Pushkin to play a role in their conspiracy if they hoped it to remain secret.

Like most of his contemporaries, Pushkin was deeply shocked by the punishments eventually meted out to the Decembrists by Tsar Alexander's successor, his younger brother, Nicholas I. It was a source of some pride among the Russian intelligentsia of his day that, since the time of Catherine the Great (1762-1796), capital punishment was theoretically proscribed in Russia – although that had not prevented her sanctioning the torture of her political opponents and the execution of leaders of the Pugachev Rebellion.

There was widespread revulsion that the reign of Tsar Nicholas I should begin with five leaders of the Decembrist Revolt being sentenced to death and executed, amid great pomp and ceremony, on the ramparts of the Peter and Paul Fortress.

Many more participants in the revolt were exiled to labour camps in Siberia, a fate from which few returned. Pushkin's sketchbooks were littered with doodles of the five ringleaders sent to the gallows and his association with leaders of the revolt was so widely known that he considered himself fortunate to have escaped the noose.

Every word Pushkin wrote between 1826 and 1837, in the last decade of his tragically short life, had to meet with the approval of the Chief of Police, Count Benckendorff, and to satisfy the attention of the Tsar himself. When Pushkin submitted his final manuscript of *The Bronze Horseman* for inspection, it returned with demands for multiple cuts and revisions and was scrawled on every page with red pencil, in the Tsar's own handwriting. Apart from its adulatory prologue, *The Bronze Horseman* was not passed for publication by the official censorship in his own lifetime.

The five leaders of the Decembrist Revolt who were executed on the ramparts of the Peter and Paul Fortress were buried in an unmarked grave on nearby Goloday Island. Despite being low-lying and regularly flooded this island was traditionally used for Lutheran burials. It also fits the description of the place where Evgeny's body is found and where he is finally buried in *The Bronze Horseman.* Shortly after the Russian Revolution of 1917, this island was renamed as Decembrists' Island to commemorate the five leaders of the revolt.

Pushkin's early life

Pushkin was born in Moscow in 1799, two years before the self-proclaimed reforming Tsar Alexander I ascended the throne. Alexander was installed as Tsar shortly after his much-detested father, Paul I, was assassinated by members of the Imperial Guard. Alexander was not directly implicated in the murder but he did know it was about to take place and was in another room of the same building when it happened.

Thanks to his family connections, Pushkin was among the first batch of pupils taken on at the elite academy founded by Alexander, in 1811, on the principles of the French Lycée. The school building was in the grounds of the imperial palace and gardens at Tsarskoe Selo, just outside Petersburg. It was set up, on the Napoleonic model, with the declared aim that it should: 'provide an elite education for aristocratic youths who planned careers in Russia's service'. Alexander insisted that the Lyceum develop a curriculum which would educate students in those areas needed by 19th century administrators. For its time, the ethos of the school was extremely progressive: pupils were provided with a rounded education up to university level, corporal punishment was strictly forbidden, the students were instructed in both French and Russian literature and they were also encouraged to try their hand at poetry.

Pushkin was present at the Lycée's ceremonial opening, which was also attended by the Tsar; by his brother, the Grand Duke Constantine; and by their sister, the Grand Duchess Anna. Before he enrolled, Pushkin had already immersed himself in the classics and in the French poetry and literature which his father had collected in his library. He soon established a reputation as a budding poet and wrote his first poems in the summer of 1813, at the age of 13. When the annual examinations took place, in January 1815, Russia's greatest living poet, Gavrila Derzhavin, was invited to hear the students recite their work.

Derzhavin had been poet laureate at the court of Catherine the Great and Pushkin recalled the event with great pride: 'At last I was called out. I read my '*Recollections in Tsarskoe Selo*' standing two paces away from Derzhavin. I cannot describe the condition of my spirit: when I reached the line where I mention Derzhavin's name, my adolescent voice broke, and my heart beat with intoxicating rapture'. Recognising this exceptional talent, Derzhavin proclaimed: 'Soon, a second Derzhavin will appear in the world; he is Pushkin, who in the Lycée has already outshone all writers'.

Pushkin lived through one of the most tumultuous period in Russian history. Within a year of him starting at the Lycée, Napoleon had invaded Russia. At one point, when it was feared that the Grand Armée might march on St Petersburg, the governor of the school was instructed to prepare for an evacuation of the staff and pupils to a place of safety in Finland. Pushkin's parents were still living in Moscow when the French army reached the capital and his home city was burned to the ground.

Following the Great Fire of Moscow, Pushkin's family decided not to return to their home. Instead, they moved to St Petersburg. Pushkin's mother arrived in the spring of 1814, with her surviving children, Olga and Lev, and rented lodgings on the Fontanka, in the house of Vice-Admiral Klokachev. Pushkin's father, Sergey, arrived later in the year. Pushkin was allowed to visit his family in St Petersburg at Christmas 1816 and Easter 1817. In the aftermath of the war of 1812 and the burning down of Moscow, what one writer described as a form of 'reactionary bacchanalia' descended upon Europe and this was at its worst in Russia.

Alarmed by the growth of liberal ideas among the younger generation, an increasingly reactionary establishment pledged to fight tooth and nail the tide of dangerous ideas coming from the West. Soon, the general clampdown imposed by the combined autocratic forces of Prussia, Austria and Russia was met by an organised 'liberal' opposition which took the form of clandestine organisations such as the *Carbonari,* or charcoal-burners, in Italy and Spain; *Tugenbund* in Germany; and the *Illuminati* in Poland.

Leading the Russian regiments which returned to St Petersburg after Napoleon's defeat were a significant number of officers, recruited from some of the most famous families in Russia, who had been radicalised during the war. Although they were returning home victorious, they resented the fact that they were still being denied some of the basic freedoms they had witnessed being taken for granted elsewhere in Europe. In particular, like Pushkin, they longed to see the abolition of serfdom and an end to autocracy.

Among the returning troops were regiments of the Hussars who quartered at Tsarskoe Selo right next to the Lycée. Influenced by the revolutionaries they had come into contact with abroad, some were founding members of the Union of Welfare, one of the Decembrists' prototype 'secret' societies. Here, Pushkin first met Pyotr Chaadayev, one of the most articulate of the young officers in the Imperial Guard who had been widely expected to become a future *aide de camp* to Alexander I. Chaadayev's ideas and intellect were to have a profound influence on the young Pushkin. According to Yakov Saburov, who knew both men, the effect Chaadayev had on Pushkin was 'astonishing' – he 'thought about that which Pushkin had never thought about', introduced logic into his thought and widened his literary horizons. Such was Chaadayev's influence that, in 1818, Pushkin had addressed a poem to him, the final lines of which read:

Comrade, believe: it will arise
The star of captivating joy
Russia will start from her sleep
And on the ruins of autocracy
Our names shall be inscribed!

When Chaadayev moved to live in one of the most fashionable hotels in St Petersburg in 1817, he was said to receive visitors: 'sitting on a dais, between two laurel bushes in tubs; to the right was a portrait of Napoleon, to the left of Byron and with his own, which was depicted as a genius in chains, opposite'. Like so many of his generation, including Pushkin, Chaadayev soon became deeply disillusioned with the Tsar. Alexander had the habit of agreeing with the last person he had spoken to but, when his supposedly liberal convictions were tested, behaved like any other autocrat.

In 1820, Chaadayev personally witnessed the reprisals taken against officers and men of Alexander's own regiment, the Semenovsky, when they staged a protest against the imposition of corporal punishment by their superiors. This was regarded as a particular affront because Alexander would not have become Tsar in the first place without the support of the Semenovsky. The regiment had been on imperial guard duty the night Alexander's father was strangled in his bedroom, but had done nothing to prevent the assault.

Chaadayev later became renowned for his controversial *Philosophical Letters* – first published, after the defeat of the Decembrists, from exile in France. Chaadayev's main thesis was that Russia had lagged behind the West and had contributed nothing to the world's progress. When Pushkin first read Chaadayev's treatise in Moscow in 1830, he tried unsuccessfully to get it published in Russia. When the first edition was finally published in Russia, in 1836 – a year before Pushkin's death – Chaadayev was declared to be 'clinically insane' by Nicholas

I. The printing press was closed down, and the editor of the magazine, *Telescope,* which had published the letters, was exiled to the far north.

Another extremely important influence on Pushkin during his time at Tsarskoe Selo was Russia's pre-eminent historian, Nikolay Karamzin. Karamzin was not only an important figure in the development of Russian literature, he also played an influential role throughout Pushkin's life. He was Russia's most influential 18th century writer, acknowledged leader of the modernist school in literature and the first official historiographer of the Russian Empire.

Karamzin was also a contemporary of Pushkin's father, Sergey Lvovich, and a close friend of Pushkin's uncle, Vasily Lvovich. In 1816, Karamzin was granted permission by the Tsar to take up residence in the grounds of the Tsarskoe Selo, to complete work on his monumental, 12-volume '*History of the Russian State'.* The palace gardens were landscaped by a Scots Jacobite, Charles Cameron, and a noted gardener from Hackney, suitably named John Bush. Among the buildings in the park were a Chinese pagoda, a granite pyramid built to the memory of Catherine's three favourite whippets, and a marble bridge which is a copy of its Palladian equivalent at Wilton House in England.

During this period, Karamzin welcomed Pushkin to his lodgings and was known to have admired his talent and wit, but not his liberal political opinions or his reckless lifestyle. Pushkin, in turn, did not share Karamzin's conservative view of the world, but he nevertheless was heavily influenced by his writing style, which was regarded as revolutionary for its time. Karamzin was routinely denounced by conservatives, who objected to his contamination of the Old Church Slavonic vocabulary with 'foreign' idioms.

Karamzin had set out to refashion the written language in a way which would be better suited to a more sophisticated and literate audience. For his historical work, he aimed to give an account of Russia's past based on primary sources but which also took inspiration from contemporary French prose writers, and from popular British historians and novelists, notably Sir Walter Scott. Karamzin's linguistic innovations modernised written Russian and provided a template later adopted, with modifications, by Pushkin.

It was through Pushkin that this style was to became the fountainhead of all modern Russian literary prose and the inspiration for the subsequent golden age of 19th century Russian writers, from Gogol, Turgenev and Dostoevsky through to Tolstoy and Chekhov. During his years at Tsarskoe Selo, Pushkin had also established a number of important friendships which he maintained for the rest of his life. The closest of these associations were with Anton Delvig, Wilhelm Küchelbecker, Ivan Pushchin and Kondraty Ryleev.

Delvig would later became the editor of the journal, *Northern Flowers*, to which Pushkin was a regular contributor between 1825 and 1831. Delvig also co-founded, with Pushkin, one of Russia's first weekly newspapers, the *Literaturnaya Gazeta* (Literary Gazette). To this day, the masthead of this paper includes a silhouette of Pushkin's head in the top right-hand corner.

The other three schoolmates – Küchelbecker, Pushchin and Ryleev – all played an active part in the Decembrist Revolt. Pushkin's closest friend at the Lycée, confusingly named Ivan Pushchin, was a leading member of the Decembrists' Northern Society. In fact, he was its Moscow chairman and helped prepare the uprising.

In January 1825, a few months before the Decembrist Revolt, Ivan Pushchin took advantage of a family connection in Pskov to visit Pushkin. By then, he was being held under surveillance by both the state and church authorities at his family estate in nearby Mikhailovskoye. Having ploughed through snowdrifts, Pushchin arrived brandishing three bottles of Veuve Clicquot. According to Pushkin translator, Walter Arndt, the detour he had made was especially risky in view of Pushchin's own active role in the inner circle of the Decembrist conspiracy: 'The friends had a heartwarming reunion, both fearing, correctly, that under the circumstances it might be their last'.

For his part in the rebellion, Pushchin was initially sentenced to death, a punishment which was subsequently commuted to penal servitude for life. When he arrived at the prison camp in Siberia, three years later, he was handed a poem written by Pushkin, which included the following lines:

My oldest friend, companion peerless!
I too blessed fate when, far up north
In my retreat, remote and cheerless
Adrift in dismal snow, so fearless
Your little sleigh bell tinkled forth

During the confrontation which took place on Senate Square, another of Pushkin's close schoolfriends, Wilhelm Küchelbecker, attempted to assassinate the Grand Duke Michael Pavlovich, the youngest brother of Alexander I, but missed – he was a notoriously bad shot. Küchelbecker spent the rest of his life in solitary confinement.

Pushkin's other childhood friend and fellow poet, Kondraty Ryleev, was one of the five Decembrist leaders who were hanged for their part in the uprising. He became the *de facto* leader of the confrontation on Senate Square, when the person appointed to take charge of the rebellion, Prince Sergei Trubetskoy, failed to turn up. Ryleev died clutching a book of poems by Byron.

For a brief period, after leaving the Lycée at Tsarskoe Selo, in June 1817, Pushkin was appointed to the Ministry of Foreign Affairs as a collegial secretary, with a salary of 700 roubles a year – a lowly rank in the imperial bureaucracy very like the one held by the poor clerk, Evgeny, who would later become Pushkin's anti-hero in *The Bronze Horseman*. By this time, the government's security antenna was on high alert to the slightest hint of political opposition or 'liberalism'. Wide-ranging restrictions on press freedom were introduced which not only dictated the nature of topics to be discussed but subjected authors to interminable censorship. It was in this climate that Pushkin's writings soon came under the eager scrutiny of the state.

According to one of the founders of the Decembrist organisation in St Petersburg, Ivan Yakushkin, Pushkin's inflammatory verse – which often included obscene epigrams, some boisterously anti-clerical, others directed at prominent members of the government – had by this time become so popular that 'there was scarcely a more or less literate ensign in the army who did not know them by heart'. Pushkin's 'liberal' poems were distributed in manuscript form throughout the army and eagerly recited by both officers and men.

A self-appointed government spy and informer, Vasily Karazin, was so appalled by the political atmosphere which he met with in St Petersburg and the lack of respect for authority he encountered that he took it upon himself to inform the Tsar of what was going on.

Karazin offered to keep what he described as 'an unsleeping eye' on 'suspicious persons', a list of individuals which included Pushkin's former schoolmates, Küchelbecker and Ryleev, and Pushkin himself. Karazin wrote to the Tsar, expressing his irritation that: 'Some young brat, Pushkin, a pupil of the Lycée – *in gratitude!* – has written a despicable ode, in which the names of the Romanovs are insulted and the Emperor Alexander called a wandering despot!'.

This was a reference to one of Pushkin's verses, *Nöel*, in which he lampoons the Tsar directly, beginning his verse with the lines: *'Hurrah! Here comes the wandering despot, riding through Russia'.* This verse mocks Alexander's liberal pretensions and is written from the point of view of a child asking his mother about the promises being made by the Tsar. It transpires that these supposedly include a commitment to dismiss his Director of Police, put his Censorship Secretary in the madhouse and 'give to the people, the rights of the people'. The boy's mother tells him not to pay any attention to this nonsense, they are all complete 'fairy tales' she tells him.

The Military Governor-General of St Petersburg, General Miloradovich, was instructed to impound Pushkin's writings and, when they were seen by the Tsar, he was not only outraged by their content but also extremely displeased to find that the Lycée he had founded only a few years earlier now appeared to have become a hotbed of sedition. This was not entirely surprising given that Pushkin's French tutor at the Lycée, Monsieur de Boudry, was also the brother of one of the most radical figures in the French revolution, Jean-Paul Marat.

Most of the other professors were likewise of a marked liberal persuasion. The Tsar confronted the director of the Lycée, Egor Engelhardt, and decreed: 'Pushkin must be exiled to Siberia: he has flooded Russia with seditious verses, the entire youth knows them by heart'. The insurrectionary content of what were considered to be three of Pushkin's most incendiary poems were singled out for condemnation by the Tsar. These were his homage to Alexander Radishchev, *Ode to Liberty*; his condemnation of serfdom, *In the Country;* and his 'fairy story' about Alexander's liberal promises, *Nöel.*

It is not difficult to understand why the Tsar might have been so upset by Pushkin. For example, his version of the *Ode to Liberty*, penned in 1817, includes these lines:

> *Autocratic miscreant*
> *Thee, thy throne I abhor*
> *Thy downfall, thy children's death*
> *With cruel joy I see;*
> *The nations read upon thy brow*
> *The stamp of execration*
> *Thou art the horror of the world, the shame of nature*
> *A reproach to God on earth* [2]

In his poem, *In the Country,* Pushkin turns his attention to the iniquities of serfdom:

> *Here, a savage class of squires, without feeling, without law*
> *Has arrogated to itself, with the rod of violence*
> *The labour, property and time of the tiller of the soil*
> *Bent over the soil, humbled to whips*
> *Here an exhausted slavedom plods along the furrows*
> *Of the implacable proprietor*
> *Here all drag on the ponderous yolk unto the tomb*
> *Their souls too crushed to nourish hope or aspiration*
> *Here in their freshness maidens bloom*
> *But for some brute's capricious inclination* [3]

Alexander's initial response was to propose that Pushkin, just coming up to the age of 21, should be transported to the Svyatogorsk Monastery in the frozen north of Russia.

He was only narrowly dissuaded from carrying out this punishment by the intervention of a number of dignitaries on Pushkin's behalf, among them Karamzin and Chaadayev. Karamzin exacted a pledge from Pushkin that he would refrain from writing anti-government verses for two years. This was enough to ensure that, instead of being dispatched to the far north, Pushkin was attached to the Chancellery of General Ivan

Inzov, based in the south of the country, at Ekaterinoslav. This was what Pushkin light-heartedly described as his 'warm exile'.

Explaining the Tsar's decision, the head of the Foreign office, Count Capodistrias, wrote to General Inzov, on 4 May 1820, and said that the young man was being sent because: 'at the Lycée his progress was rapid, his wit was admired, but his character appears to have escaped the vigilance of the tutors'. The letter was signed by the Foreign Minister, Count Nesselrode – who was to become a constant menace in Pushkin's life – and it clarified exactly why Pushkin was seen to be deserving of his punishment:

> 'There is no excess to which this unfortunate young man has not indulged – as there is no perfection he cannot attain through the transcendent superiority of his talents...some pieces of verse and above all an *Ode to Liberty* directed the attention of the government towards Mr Pushkin. Amid the great beauties of conception and style, this latter piece gives evidence of dangerous principles drawn from the ideas of the age, or, more accurately, the system of anarchy dishonestly called the system of the rights of man, of liberty and of independence of nations'.[4]

Pushkin left St Petersburg on 9 May 1820, and arrived in the south just at the time it was becoming the hub of anti-government agitation in the army and the base for what would become the Decembrists' Southern Society. Far from keeping Pushkin out of trouble, he socialised frequently with leading members of the Southern Society, joined the same Masonic Lodge and met their leader, Pavel Pestel. Pushkin expressed great admiration for Pestel who – like his schoolfriend, Ryleev – would be another of the five Decembrists later sent to the gallows.

Pushkin was exiled for the second time, in 1824, when a letter he wrote from Odessa to Moscow was intercepted and read by the police. In it, he said he had been 'taking lessons in pure Atheism' from an Englishman, Dr William Hutchinson, personal physician to the Vorontsov family, which had provided Pushkin with lodgings in their own house. When Alexander I was informed of the contents of the letter, he immediately agreed with the Foreign Minister, Nesselrode, that because of this apostasy (and the charge that Pushkin had been conducting an affair with the Governor's wife) he should be immediately transferred and detained on his parent's estate, at Mikhailovskoye, under the supervision of the local authorities.

Pushkin was under house arrest at Mikhailovskoye when the Decembrist Revolt took place in 1825 and was only granted permission to return, to Moscow in the summer of 1826. He arrived at almost the same time as the Polish national poet, Adam Mickiewicz, who had been exiled to Russia accused of taking part in revolutionary activities at the University of Vilnius. Pushkin and Mickiewicz soon developed a mutual bond of appreciation and respect. The Polish exile rapidly acquired a celebrity status in the literary salons of Moscow, where he was renowned for his impromptu improvisations.

Pushkin translated several of Mickiewicz's poems into Russian and *The Bronze Horseman* was partly written as a rejoinder to one of Mickiewicz's most patriotic works, *Forefathers' Eve*, in which he castigates the Russian autocracy and its pretensions to civilised behaviour. In a passage from the *Digression* of Part Three, Mickiewicz mocks the 'leaden glance' of Nicholas I and ridicules *The Monument to Peter the Great* which he had been to visit in Pushkin's company.

Pushkin lived to witness the defeat of two successive revolutions. The first was the Decembrist Revolt of 1825. The second took place in Poland five years later. The 1830 revolt was again suppressed by Nicholas I, with the aid of his elder brother, the Grand Duke Constantine, in his role as Governor of Poland. Pushkin wrote *The Bronze Horseman,* in 1833, a few years after both rebellions had been crushed. *The Bronze Horseman* was partly written as Pushkin's literary response to Mickiewicz but, according to one of many interpretations, it can also be regarded as an allegory for the Polish Revolt of 1830 and the way that this challenge to the Tsar was dealt with, just as the Decembrists had been five years earlier.

Apart from the obvious parallels which could be made with either of these events – or, for that matter, to any act of rebellion, in any country, at any time – some aspects of the character of Evgeny which appear in *The Bronze Horseman* also reflect the much-reduced personal circumstances in which Pushkin found himself by 1833. Pushkin's family had already been stripped of some of its hereditary status thanks to Peter the Great's reforms. The introduction of his revised Table of Ranks had been meant to establish a less corrupt and more meritocratic society.

Instead it had created a new hierarchy of privilege occupied by *nouveau riche* opportunists and upstarts, regarded by members of some of Russia's oldest aristocratic families with utter disdain. The corollary for some of these older families was that they could no longer rely on their former privileges and many, including the Pushkins, had fallen on hard times. Following his marriage to Natalya Goncharova, in 1831, Pushkin not only faced mounting financial difficulties, he was tormented by the obvious attentions being paid to his wife, both by the dashing French army officer and arch-monarchist, George d'Anthès and by another, more sinister, interloper – Tsar, Nicholas I.

When Pushkin was shot and killed in an entirely one-sided duel with the highly trained crackshot, Baron George d'Anthès, in 1837, at the age of only 38, many ordinary Russians were convinced his voice had been deliberately silenced at the instigation of his numerous foes within the imperial court. The Tsar's entourage typically dismissed Pushkin, in the same breath, as both a radical menace and 'a nobody'. One of Pushkin's contemporaries, the young army officer Mikhail Lermontov, was so outraged at the sympathy expressed in high society for Pushkin's murderous opponent, that he wrote a poem entitled *Death of a Poet,* the last sixteen lines of which are addressed to the 'butchers of freedom'.

Lermontov, who was to become known as the 'heir to Pushkin', directly accused the 'hungry crowd that swarms about the throne' of complicity in Pushkin's death.

Written in a less than a day, in the immediate aftermath of the fatal duel, and circulated by hand in *samizdat* copies, Lermontov's poem caused an absolute furore. Scribbled on the envelope which contained one copy sent by an informant for the attention of the Tsar, were the words '*The Call for Revolution*'. Lermontov was arrested, imprisoned in the Peter and Paul Fortress and then exiled to the Caucasus. When Lermontov was himself shot and killed in a duel a few years later, at the age of 26, the Tsar Nicholas I drily commented: 'A scoundrel's death for a scoundrel'.

Origins of *The Bronze Horseman*

The Bronze Horseman was not written until 1833 and was one of Pushkin's many works which failed to pass the censor during his lifetime. His original intention had been to write a sequel to his commercially successful novel-in-verse, *Evgeny Onegin,* in which the central character – the narcissistic dandy, Evgeny – would seek to acquire some genuine purpose to his life by aligning with the Decembrist cause.

By the time Pushkin came to write the poem, he had already spent seven of his best years in exile and had only been allowed to return to St Petersburg, in 1826, on condition that he submit everything he wrote to the direct supervision of the Tsar. For this reason, when he came to write a 'tenth canto', in which he would continue Evgeny's story, he did so in a form of cryptogram, only fragments of which have survived. When he eventually realised this might get him into even greater trouble, he burned most of the original manuscript.

Pushkin then embarked on an entirely new poem, at the heart of which is the conflict between the hopes and aspirations of his new anti-hero, the 'poor Evgeny', and the demands of the Tsar. This new version became *The Bronze Horseman.* In the autumn of 1833, at the same time as he was writing the poem, Pushkin was unexpectedly granted access to the imperial archives so that he could carry out extensive research on the history of Peter the Great, with a view to writing a biography of the 'miracle-working' Tsar.

Pushkin took advantage of this opportunity to widen his enquiries. He covertly extended his remit to include unauthorised research on the Pugachev Rebellion, one of the most successful of the many armed uprisings against Tsarist rule which took place in 18th century Russia. The information Pushkin gleaned from the archives on this rebellion later provided the background for his novel *The Captain's Daughter* and for his factual account of the revolt, *The History of Pugachev.*

The significance of the Pugachev uprising was that it challenged the authority and legitimacy of Catherine the Great, the German princess whose path to power had come at the expense of her own husband, Peter III – he had been murdered by an assassination squad under command of her lover, Count Grigory Orlov.

What had become increasingly clear to Pushkin during his research on Russian history was that the initial hopes and aspirations that the Russian people habitually placed in their Tsars and Tsarinas had repeatedly been dashed by bitter experience.

As he saw it, Peter the Great's achievements had been immense, but his reign had also been marred by the utmost brutality. Likewise, it was clear that Catherine's early enthusiasm for the ideas of the French Enlightenment had rapidly been abandoned when the heads of her counterparts in Paris began to roll during the French Revolution.

In Pushkin's own lifetime, the same pattern had been repeated when the early promises made by Alexander in the first years of his reign, to introduce a more democratic constitution and abolish serfdom, were soon abandoned after the war with Napoleon and the European revolts of the early 1820s. Similarly, Pushkin's rapport with Alexander's successor, Nicholas I, rapidly deteriorated from guarded loyalty when they first met in 1826, to deep mistrust and mutual loathing.

Throughout his life, Pushkin, had by necessity trodden a very fine line in his conduct towards the Tsars. His education at the elite Imperial Lycée had come about largely thanks to imperial patronage and due to his family's status and contacts within the nobility: on his father's side, Pushkin's ancestry stretched back to the earliest years of Russian history – a pedigree every bit as impressive as that which could be claimed by the Romanovs. By comparison, they were relative newcomers who had only come to power at the beginning of the 17th century, following the cathartic period in Russian history known as the Time of Troubles.

Long before the Romanovs, the Pushkins were prominent within the boyar elite and were in attendance at the coronation of the very first Romanov Tsar, Michael Romanov. In Pushkin's historical drama, *Boris Godunov,* two of the key roles are allotted to ancestors of Pushkin (the play takes place during the Time of Troubles – but was equally intended to be read as a metaphor for the traumatic events of 1825 in Russia). On his mother's side, Pushkin's origins were, if anything, even more remarkable: his great-great-grandfather was an African prince who we now know was born in Logone-Birni, on the border between modern-day Cameroon and Chad.

Named Ibrahim at birth, Pushkin's ancestor was abducted as a child during a raid by a neighbouring sultanate and taken as a hostage from his father's royal residence. From there, he was transported across the Sahara and then by sea to Istanbul. Here, he was taken on as a pageboy in the Topkapi palace, the administrative and political nerve centre of the Ottoman Empire, before being kidnapped for a second time by agents working on behalf of Peter the Great. The Tsar hoped the boy could provide valuable insider information on the Ottoman's internal strife and state of readiness. This time, Ibrahim was smuggled out to Moscow, where he was adopted by the Tsar as his own son before being christened as Abraham Petrovich.

The Tsar's 'black confidant' subsequently accompanied Peter the Great on many of his most important military campaigns during the Great Northern War with Sweden (1700-1721). When he reached adulthood, the Tsar sent his protégé to Paris to train as a specialist in military engineering and siege warfare. After Peter the Great's death, Abraham Petrovich chose the surname Hannibal in imitation of the legendary Carthaginian's reputation as a military commander. In what became an extraordinarily lengthy career, he then went on to serve under a succession of 18th century Tsars and Tsarinas, up to and including Catherine the Great.

Pushkin was extremely proud of his black ancestry and defended it vigorously against repeated slanders from his critics, notably his deadliest opponent – the rival publisher, police spy and informer, Fadey Bulgarin. Soon after he graduated in 1817, Pushkin made regular visits to carry out research on his family history at the family estate of Mikhailovskoye, which had been granted to his great-grandfather by the Empress Elizabeth as a reward for his efforts. Hannibal's biographer, Hugh Barnes, remarks that Pushkin's ancestor had: '…more than repaid his debt to the Tsars. Russian despots, from Catherine the Great to Josef Stalin have owed stout defence to the line of fortifications he built from the Arctic Circle to the frontier with China. To quote Shakespeare on Othello, he had done the state some service and they knew it – or, at any rate, Peter's daughter, the Empress Elizabeth did'.

About this book

On setting out to write this book, my original intention had been solely to attempt a modern, verse translation of *The Bronze Horseman* for an English-speaking audience, many of whom might not be familiar with this work. I first became aware of the poem when I bought a matchbox-sized edition which had been produced to commemorate the 200th anniversary of Pushkin's birth, on a visit to St Petersburg in 1999. Until then, I had no idea of the reverence with which this poem is regarded in Russia.

On a more recent trip to St Petersburg, I was lucky enough to witness this admiration first hand: on 6 June 2017, the anniversary of Pushkin's birthday, excerpts from some of his poems were recited by actors in Artists' Square, at the entrance to the Russian Museum, as part of a nationwide day of celebrations. When the microphone was passed to members of the audience, the first man who spoke recited entire passages of *The Bronze Horseman* from memory, accompanied by a constant murmur from others in the audience, repeating the same lines *sotto voce* by heart.

The bulk of this book deals with the biographical and histor-ical background against which the poem was written. It begins with my new verse translation of *The Bronze Horseman*. This is followed by the chapters on Russian history and Pushkin's life which have been arranged, like the poem itself, in three parts. In *The Bronze Horseman,* these three parts are: Prologue, Part One and Part Two.

This book is likewise subdivided into three main sections. The first of the four chapters which make up the prologue, *Pushkin and Old Russia,* traces Pushkin's ancestry back to the time of the Russian folk hero, Alexander Nevsky, and includes a brief out-line of Russian history before the advent of Peter the Great. The second, *The Miracle-Working Tsar,* explains the importance to Russian history, and to Pushkin, of the reign of Peter the Great, to whom *The Bronze Horseman* is dedicated.

The third chapter, *The Moor of Peter the Great,* outlines the story of Pushkin's black ancestor, Abraham Hannibal, and his remarkable career, first as page boy then engineer and munitions expert to every 18th century Russian Tsar and Tsarina, from the time of Peter the Great, through to the reign of Catherine the

Great. The final chapter in the prologue, *Manufacturing a Myth,* deals with the origins and motives of the Empress who commissioned the monument: Catherine II, Catherine the Great.

Part One traces the history of revolts against Tsarist rule in Russia from the time of the folk hero, Sten'ka Razin, in the middle of the 17th century, through to the Pugachev Rebellion at the time of Catherine the Great and culminating in the Decembrist Revolt of 1825. This section also looks at the important influence on Pushkin of two pioneers of the radical intelligentsia in Russia, Alexander Radishchev and Nikolay Novikov. Both were imprisoned by Catherine the Great for their views and, like Evgeny in Pushkin's poem, paid a terrible price for their opposition.

The chapter headed *The Revolt of the Semenovsky*, deals with the reign of Alexander I and the rebellion in his own regiment which prefigured the Decembrist Revolt. The chapter on the *The Great Flood of 1824* includes contemporaneous, eyewitness accounts and outlines some of the literary precedents which may have influenced Pushkin's description of the flood – from the Bible, Ovid's *Metamorphoses,* Milton's *Paradise Lost* and William Blake's *The Marriage of Heaven and Hell,* through to Mary Shelley's *Frankenstein* and Washington Irving's *Tales of the Alhambra.* The chapters headed *One Tsar Too Many* and *The Revolt of December 1825* detail the preparations made by the Decembrists for their uprising and describe how events unfolded when regiments in the south mounted an armed insurrection and those in the north converged on Senate Square in St Petersburg.

Part Two, investigates the extent of Pushkin's connections with the Decembrists, and the isolated battle he was forced to fight to maintain any semblance of artistic freedom in the aftermath of their defeat. These final chapters outline the myriad of problems accumulating in Pushkin's life following his marriage to Natalya Goncharova – not least the menacing presence of Tsar Nicholas I, the mysterious appearance in Russia of Pushkin's merciless opponent in the duel, George d'Anthès, and the influence of his noxious *eminence grise,* the Dutch ambassador Van Heeckeren.

The chapter on *Pushkin and Mickiewicz* stresses the importance of the genuine friendship which developed between the two national poets and questions the degree to which it was harmed by the long and acrimonious history between Russia and Poland, a history which Pushkin regarded as a matter between the warring 'Slavic brothers', not for the intelligentsia of Europe. This chapter also explains why the relationship between Pushkin and Mickiewicz is so important to an understanding of *The Bronze Horseman.*

The remaining chapters spotlight the extent to which the reactionary society clique led by the dreaded Count and Countess Nesselrode tormented Pushkin, and the constant struggle he was engaged in to have any of his work passed for publication. This brought him repeatedly into conflict with the Tsar's chief of police, Count Alexander Benckendorff, and his Minister of Education and censorship supremo, Sergey Uvarov.

The chapters headed *Despotism Personified, Pushkin's Fatal Gamble* and *Duel at Black River* catalogue the mounting pressures on Pushkin in the months leading up to his duel with d'Anthés. As soon as it was known that Pushkin had been fatally wounded, a police cordon was set up around his house, Benckendorff and Uvarov issued a blanket ban on media coverage of Pushkin's death, and his body was secretly transported overnight to the family estate at Mikhailovskoye, to prevent his burial becoming a focus for discontent among the population of St Petersburg.

The chapter headed *Pushkin's Everlasting Monument*, includes a new translation of his short epigram, *Exegi Monumentum,* in which he accurately forecast that his work would ultimately transcend anything left to us by the two Tsars who had been in power during his lifetime. The *Appendix* examines the history of translations into English of Pushkin's works.

Notes

1   **Pushkin,** by D S Mirsky, introduction by George Siegel, E P Dutton, 1963, p212

2   **To Chaadayev,** in *Pushkin Threefold: Narrative, Lyric, Polemic and Ribald Verse*: the originals with linear and metric translations by Walter Arndt, George Allen & Unwin. 1972, p171

3   Arndt, op. cit. p6

4   Arndt, op. cit., p26

5   **Pushkin: A Biography,** by T J Binyon, Harper Collins, 2002, p100

6   **Gannibal: The Moor of Petersburg** by Hugh Barnes, Profile Books, 2005

The Bronze Horseman
A Petersburg Tale
By Alexander Pushkin

New Verse Translation by Jack Robertson
Illustrations from the 1905 edition, by Alexander Benois

Foreword
This story is based on actual events. Details of the flood are
derived from contemporary reports. For those who wish to
investigate further, see the account given by V N Berkh*

*A Detailed Historical Account Of All The Floods That Occurred In
St. Petersburg, by V N Berkh, St. Petersburg, 1826.

Prologue

On this bleak shoreline, woebegone
Beaten and battered by the sea
Was where our great Tsar Peter once stood
And whereupon, HE – his mind on fire
Fixed his gaze on the far horizon.
There ahead, the river wide
Heaved and surged on every side
While on the upswell, lifted high
A single flimsy craft sped by…

Dotted about on these swamp-infested levels
Lay blackened huts…for some poor devils,
The only shelter to be found.
While the forest, seeming inwardly aglow
As the sun's rays pierced its misty canopy below,
Sighed and murmured all around.

And so, he thought: 'From here indeed
We can no doubt confront the Swede
This is where we shall commence
To make our haughty rivals wince
Our mighty citadel will have them take heed

Here, destiny has on us bequeathed
A Window on Europe[1] whence, godspeed
Our entrance to the world stage we'll proclaim
And here, on *mare incognito* to them

The flags of all nations shall descend
And a fanfare to freedom shall sound out our name

A century passed, till the majestic prospect
of this new northern wonder drew wide respect
From the midst of the forest and boggy mire
It now rose resplendent, for all to admire.
Where a lone Finnish fisherman once might go
One of those ill-fated wretches of yore,
To hurl his threadbare casting nets
From upon the verge of the lower shore
Into those melancholy depths…
Now, all along every bustling quayside
A profusion of villas and mansions take pride
While ships weighed down with the finest of wares
Navigate here from who knows where
Till they jostle the jetties and groan on the tide

Now fully bedecked is the River Neva
With its granite piers, bridges spanning the floe
In between which nestle dark green isles
And hidden gardens now flourish and grow.
Compared to the new-found metropolis
Starry old Moscow now sadly fades
In much the same way as a maiden Tsarina
Casts a faded old dowager into the shade.

I love you, this city that Peter contrived
I love your meticulous, orderly guise
I love your grace, and the Neva's expanse
As along your granite embankments she glides.
I love your ornate, cast-iron railings
How your captivating evenings beguile
Your transparent white nights, your moonless shimmer
Through which I can write and, by the glimmer
Read with no lamp in my room all the while.

I love the sedate, sleepless repertoire
Of your stark, deserted boulevards

THE BRONZE HORSEMAN

The radiant sparkle on the Admiralty spire
Or how the next morning will already arise
Before nightfall cloaks twilight's heavenly glow
And a new dawn soon beckons before our eyes [2]

I love your brutal winter days
Devoid of wind and dusted with frost
When folk come out on the Neva with sleighs
And the cheeks of young girls have that rosy blush
While new debutantes join in with the revels
Inspired by the joy of the festive scene
As the champagne fizzes in every glass
And the punchbowl's blue flames flicker and gleam.

I love the splendour of your martial displays
With their ranks of foot and horse on parade
All bedecked in the grandest attire
And in between each marching array
The tattered remains of their pennants fray
And the glint on bronze helmets ricochet
Some shot through as they'd come under fire.

I love you, warlike metropolis
The smoke and thunder of your guns
Those special days when, in her fine palace

Our Northern tsarina gives birth to a son
Or Russia's mighty battalions loyal
Once more proclaim a victory won
I love the loud crack as the Neva breaks free
Discarding her icy mantle anew
And lifts it impulsively down to the sea
Full of joy now she senses that springtime is due

Flaunt your grandeur, Petropolis
And steadfast be, like the Russia of old
Be magnanimous too, please do not impose
On your vanquished opponents, misfortune untold.
Let bygones be bygones, may I propose
In the waters of Finland may they sink deep
And long may pointless malice no more
Disturb our Tsar Peter's eternal sleep.

It was a terrible time
Of which my memory is undimmed
So, with that, dear friends
My story now begins
And a sorry tale it is going to be…

Part 1

See how the new-born metropolis
With November's brisk autumn breath has been kissed
All along its meticulous, steadfast defences
A great hubbub of the waves commences
The Neva is heaving and swirling ahead
Tossing and turning like a sick man in bed.

It was getting late and already quite dark
When at first the wind and then the rain
Began to raucously lash every window pane
All the while wailing a dreadful refrain.

THE BRONZE HORSEMAN

And just at this time, from a night-out with friends
The young Evgeny homeward wends
(I'll call our hero by that name,
I've already used it once before.
Why bother with a patronym?
It was well enough thought of up to now

Much esteemed by the great Karamzin, no less
But thanks to the gossip, one can but guess
Has seemingly fallen from favour somehow)

Our hero has lodgings in lowly Kolomna
He's a government clerk in an office somewhere
He steers well clear of the upper ranks
And even for his own dear departed
A passing thought he barely can spare.
Now inside his doorway, Evgeny comes to a halt
Takes off his coat, then lies down and dreams
But can't get to sleep; his mind wanders, it seems
Continually turning somersaults.

What on earth could be on his mind?
Poverty, sure, and one suspects
How to escape it, or win any respect.
You never know, God himself might assist?

Either wisdom or cash would not go amiss!
Oh, if only his own life could be so sweet
As it is for the rich, who so often appear
With nothing at all between their ears
But live their lives on easy street
While he's been bound to a desk, the past two years

The weather was clearly growing much worse
The river surged, with enormous force

Pontoons on the Neva were all taken down.
Now it was sure to be two days or more
Till he'd join his Parasha on the opposite shore.
Then, all at once, Evgeny sighed
And with a poet's fading glance
Abruptly sank into a trance:

'Get married? Well…why ever not?
It'd be hard, of course. But then, so what?
No worse than what he's already got.
After all, he's young and resilient
Fit enough to work hard, day and night long
He'd somehow get set up for sure
In a place Parasha would be glad to belong

THE BRONZE HORSEMAN

Humble, cosy and secure.
It might be another year, let's say
Until I get my next step up
During which Parasha would still be here
To manage at home and then, one day
Bring up some little ones who, we'd pray
Would have a good life, with no great fuss
While we'd help out along the way -
Until the day they bury us'.

At least, that's what he thought – in his dismal plight
Praying the wind would stop wailing all night
And the driving rain would not persist
With pounding the windowpanes, like a great fist.
Then, sleepy-eyed, he started to doze
Just as a trace of light from this grim night arose;
A pale new morning's about to ensue
And what a terrible day it would be too...[3]

The Neva had struggled throughout the night
To cope with the onslaught, which never once ceased
And, though she tried with all her might
Could not overpower this mad, raging beast.
Next day, on the quaysides, here and there
Throngs of people came to stare
Spellbound by the mountainous waves in revolt
Whipped up to a frenzy by the raging tumult

Now the force of the tempest from out in the bay
Was too strong for the Neva obstructing its way
Till the river plunged back, boiling with rage
And the islands midstream sank under the waves
Then the weather grew worse, till, from deep down below
The Neva swelled up and let loose a great roar
Boiling up like a cauldron and swirling about
And now like a furious devil – lookout!
Hurled herself down, inundating the town.

In the face of this onslaught, the entire populace fled
No longer so cocky – now in a blind panic instead
The waters poured in to the cellars below
Canals burst their casements and would soon overflow
Till Petropolis appears as an almighty Triton
Around whose waist the waters now tighten.

Beware! Watch out! The malicious cascade
Ploughs in through the windows like thieves on a raid
Boat sterns smash windows, propelled by the squall
Drenched awnings are shredded on street-hawkers' stalls
Next to the goods of these penny-wise vendors
Drift the wreckage and debris of crossbeams and timbers
Even bridges collapse by the force of the flood
While coffins exhumed by the waves from their graves

THE BRONZE HORSEMAN

And lifted aloft through the torrent now scud.
Behold, now bear witness: the Wrath of God
His punishments come at a terrible cost

We must all surely be doomed, for where can we turn?
All is utterly ruined, we're undoubtedly lost!

In this terrible year
The former Tsar, who was then in command,
Was held in respect throughout the land
But there on his balcony, filled with dismay
Even he judged, that, come what may:
"The Tsar too is powerless, in the face of God's might"
So, he merely surveyed the sorrowful sight
Alarmed by the havoc and deeply distraught.

By now, the waters had formed lakes in the town
Down each street and alleyway torrents now surge
And what once were grand palaces of great renown
Now stand out like islands besieged by the flood.

Beholding the scene, the Tsar could but say
His high-ranking generals[4] must, without delay:
'Go out and search both up and down
Through every highway in the town
And though a path through the waters may be fraught
Assure each citizen they must fear not
No matter what…not one of them will be forgot!'.

Around that time, on Senate Square
A grand palazzo had just been built
And here, beneath its lofty façade
Was where two life-like stone lions dwelt
Each with a paw raised as on permanent guard.
Astride one of these beasts now warily sat
Arms clutched to his chest and minus his hat
Our poor Evgeny, believe it or not
Firmly rooted to the spot

He was scared stiff, poor chap – but not for himself
He had no fear at all, though the waters engulfed

THE BRONZE HORSEMAN

And now lapped right up to the soles of his shoes.
Likewise, rain lashed his face to no avail
Nor the fact the wind whistled and howled a gale
And had whipped the cap from his head as it blew.

With a broken-hearted, disconsolate gaze
Fixed on a point somewhere out in the haze
He gazed at the churning, tumultuous waves
Thrown up all around by this mutinous foe
As the storm raged on, hurling wreckage to and fro.

In the name of God, look – there's surely no doubt
Very close to his own place, he now can pick out
A willow tree, an unpainted fence
A ramshackle house…
This must surely be
Where his darling Parasha he so longs to see
Lived with her widowed mum, that makes sense…
Or, had what he'd seen only been in a dream?
Are our lives all for nothing?
A simple illusion? A divine retribution?
An earthly delusion?

And so, he clung on, as though struck by a curse
Tightly hugging the marble and, even worse,
Quite unable to budge.
The turbulent waters, much to his despair
Were all he could see, till becoming aware,
While the unruly waves chopped and churned close by,
Right behind him and looming on high
Reared the infamous idol, on his warhorse of bronze
His arm outstretched…

Part 2

And so, having ransacked and reduced all to naught
And now grown weary of her impudent onslaught
The Neva began to slowly relent
Quite satisfied with the havoc she'd wrought
Discarding her ill-gotten gains as she went
Much as a robber, with his partners in crime
Might beset a small village, with intentions malign
Rampaging, looting, making off with their spoils
Their yells and curses piercing the turmoil
While they offload the haul from their escapade
Afraid it might hamper their getaway
The marauders retreat from their malevolent spree
Strewing sacksful of loot at their heels as they flee

The waters subside, roads re-open at last
Our Evgeny makes haste, his heart sinking fast
And swirling with hope, fear and anguish inside
Only just reaches the riverside.
Still gloating on their wanton foray
The waters still turn in a malevolent way
As though deep below, a great cauldron

Was hidden beneath a carpet of foam
While the Neva gasped and bellowed and brayed
Like a warhorse returning direct from the fray.

Evgeny looked out and there on a bend
A boat hauled into view…what a godsend!

Then he hailed the ferryman for a kopek or so
And off they sped through the swirling waters below
Out there for a while, though the going was tough
The skilful oarsman rode each peak and trough
Even when hidden in furrows in between rows
The boat carried on with its perilous crew
Till at last up onto the far shore it drew

Our unfortunate hero now set off hellbent
To Parasha's lodgings, full of intent:
He took it all in but could not recognise
Any sense to the scene in front of his eyes
Wherever he looked, there was devastation
A trail of destruction…annihilation.
Some homesteads were mangled, others now gone
Carried off by the power unleashed by the storm
It looked just like a battleground
Strewn with corpses, all around.

Evgeny, at first, was confused and perplexed
Being lost in his torment, one suspects
So he rushed over where, next thing he knew
Fate's final verdict would ensue –
His own destiny, in a sealed envelope.
By now, he'd reached a spot that he knew
Where a tumbledown shack came into view
Destroyed by the flood.

What could this be?...
He stopped,
Retraced his steps, then turned around
Checked, carried on … and checked again.

This is the place where her house had once been
Look, there's the willow, but where's the gate?
The house has gone…a dreadful scene
Where can it be? He looks down in despair…
What could have happened? It's no longer there…

Now taken hold by his own cares and woes
He sallies forth and wherever he goes
Rants and raves like a man gone insane
Beating his head, over again

THE BRONZE HORSEMAN

And bursts out laughing…But why? No-one knows.

A nocturnal mist on the city now fell
The townsfolk simply could not sleep, truth to tell
All they had witnessed, they pondered upon
During the horrible day which had just gone.

Next morning, the sky's pale and overcast glow
Cast down shafts of light on the city below
There was barely a trace from the previous day
Of the great misfortune which had come its way.

With an indigo mantle, the mayhem's now veiled
A veneer of normality has once more prevailed
Now folk hurry out on freed-up thoroughfares
Once more calm, nonchalant, without a care.
City pen-pushers from their night-time retreats
Head off to their desks, to cheerfully greet
Stout-hearted vendors, appearing undaunted,
The wares from their ransacked cellars still flaunted
All set to recoup the best recompense –
Insofar as they might – at another's expense
While boats are cleared out from wherever they stood
In courtyards across the neighbourhood.

Alas, our poor soul, Evgeny, now found
His troubled mind could not withstand
The horrors he had witnessed first hand
Overwhelmed by the wind and the terrible sound
Of the din from the Neva that pounded his ears
He now wandered aimlessly, far and near
Tormented by some kind of dream.
A week went by, a month – it seemed
He would never get back to his home, he now feared.
(The landlord meantime, it's no shock
Had rented his empty rooms, ad hoc
To a penniless poet).

Evgeny never came back for his things, struck dumb
A stranger to all was what he'd become
Every day he wandered from place to place
Slept on the quayside and, no disgrace
Begged at kitchen windows for any free crumb.
The clothes on his back were sadly worn
Ripped to shreds, tattered and torn

Street urchins would pelt him with snowballs galore
And the crack of the coachman's whip he'd ignore
When he strayed onto their path in a daze
Not aware they were there as he wandered half-crazed
Absorbed by his own tribulations and woes
A dreary routine we can but suppose:
Neither man nor beast, a mere nondescript
Neither living soul, nor phantom from the crypt.

Once, as he slept on a Neva quayside
And summer days closed to autumn tide
The winds unwound as squally blasts
Dark waves along the embankments lashed
And on their smooth steps muttered and splashed
The waters bold and unabashed
In the way that poor petitioners supplicate
In the face of a cold-hearted magistrate.

THE BRONZE HORSEMAN

Poor Evgeny woke up…darkness prevailed
The rain lashed down, it was blowing a gale
And from somewhere far off, in the dead of night
The watchman called out…causing him such a fright,
Out of nowhere…he jolted upright.

The terrors of yesterday came back too well
He got up like a shot, as if under a spell
Resumed his wanderings…then checked his advance

And turned around quickly as though in a trance
As a wild, fearful look upon his face fell…
Once again he'd arrived at the portico
Of the same mansion house where he'd been once before
Where the lions stood, with paws raised up on the porch
Looking so lifelike, on their perpetual watch
And right there, towering up, in the darkness beyond
High up on the granite platform now reared
Astride the bronze stallion, the image he feared…
The same tyrant once more, with his arm outstretched

Egeny recoiled, deeply troubled to find
He just could not shake off what stuck in his mind:
This was the place where the floodwaters had danced

And where the marauding waves had advanced
Snapping malignly around his feet.

This was the square with stone lions on guard
And there, towering above and motionless
Within the gloom, the graven image, no less
Of the one who by the power of his own hand
Had founded this city at his instant command.

How fearsome he looks in the swirling haze!
Such dread thoughts must lurk behind that gaze!
Such power is forged in this mighty steed!
In this warhorse, a fire is burning indeed!

Where next will you gallop, then, proud steed?
Where next will those hooves be about to swoop down?
Lord and Master of All, is it not so
You alone have raised Russia up from below? [5]
From the very abyss, to such fame and renown
As you do with this warhorse and its harness of iron?

Round the base of the monument, now we find
Poor Evgeny lingers, out of his mind

THE BRONZE HORSEMAN

Shooting wild glances on high, where behind
Looms the face of the ruler of half mankind.
He clutches his breast and presses on
A cold rail with his forehead, whereupon
All at once, at the despot above he gazes
While deep in his heart a fire now blazes
His blood boiling, eyes fixed upon
Directly ahead, the terrible icon.

Gritting his teeth and clenching his fists
Seemingly seized by some unexplained force
He at first starts to tremble, then splutters with hate
'So be it, miracle worker – just you wait!'

Next thing, he was certain, the Tsar on high
Had flown into a rage in the instant gone by
And, somehow, now, without making as sound
The head of the tyrant had wheeled right around…

In that very same instant, on the desolate square
Evgeny took flight and thought he could hear

Behind him, like thunder, ear-splittingly loud
A remorseless clattering, clippety-clopping
Rattling the cobbles, never ceasing, unstopping.

Till, gleaming in the pale moonlight
Arm raised aloft at such a great height
The horseman of bronze loomed still larger
There upon his thundering charger.
And all night long, poor mad Evgeny
Whichever way he tried to flee
Could not shake off the Bronze Horseman behind
The heavy clatter of hooves tormenting his mind.

From that time on, should he…let's suppose
Find himself on Senate Square by mischance
His appearance at once would metamorphose
Until he assumed an unsettled glance

THE BRONZE HORSEMAN

He'd hastily press his hands to his heart
As if to extinguish a torment so great
His worn-out cap would meekly be doffed
His demented gaze no longer held aloft
Edging along, not tempting fate

On this very shore, you can still see the small isle
Where fishermen often alight with their catch
Perhaps a late supper al fresco to snatch
Or office workers go out boating on a Sunday in style
To pull up and land on the shore for a while.

Nothing grows there at all, not a single blade of grass
For this is where the floodwaters, alas
Had washed up a small shack and where its traces
Appeared like a blackened shrub in places
Until it was taken away last spring
And loaded onto a barge one morning
Though it first seemed nothing else was around
This was where, on threshold, poor Evgeny was found
And right there and then, by common accord
They buried his cold body, thank the Lord.

Pushkin's Notes:

Pushkin includes five explanatory notes within the text of *The Bronze Horseman*. These are intended to clarify the following references:

1 The term 'A Window on Europe', quoted here by Pushkin, was first coined by the 18th century Venetian philosopher, poet and essayist, Count Francesco Algarotti. It appears in his correspondence with the English courtier, Lord Hervey, and the Italian writer and critic, Marquis Scippio Maffei. The letters were published in two volumes, in London, in 1769. In an account of his travels, sent from St Petersburg on 30 June 1769, Algarotti writes: 'I am at length going to give you some account of this new city, of the great window lately opened in the north through which Russia looks into Europe'.

2 This credits the influence of a poem written by Pushkin's contemporary and friend, Pyotr Vyazemsky. Entitled *A Conversation on 7 April 1832* it was dedicated to the Countess E M Sadovskaya and contains the following lines in praise of the city (my translation):

Я Петербург люблю, с его красою стройной
С блестящим поясом роскошных островов
С прозрачной ночью – дня соперницей беззнойной
И с свежей зеленью младых его садов

I love Petersburg, the harmonious beauty it displays
With its brilliant garland of exquisite isles
Its translucent nights rivalling sultry days
The refreshing luxuriance of its young gardens beguiles

3 This is a reference to the prediction made in a poem by Adam Mickiewicz, entitled 'Oleszkiewicz'. In one section of the poem, its hero – the Polish painter and mystic, Josef Oleszkiewicz (1777-1825) – measures the level of the River Neva and foretells the Great Flood of 1824. He also prophesies the downfall of tyranny. In his notes to the Bristol Classical Press edition of *The Bronze Horseman*, T E Little comments that: 'Mickiewicz, through Oleszkiewicz, compares the destruction of Russian tyranny to God's humbling of Assyria and Babylon; and perhaps Pushkin, who had suffered as much as the two Poles from the power and pride of Kings, sympathises to some degree with the hope of divine vengeance. Nicholas was keeping him a virtual prisoner in Petersburg, Alexander had exiled him in 1820, and Peter's reign marked the decline of his class and family'.

4 The two high-ranking generals who are sent by the Tsar to assist the citizens of St Petersburg during the Great Flood of 1824 are Count Mikhail Miloradovich and Count Alexander Benckendorff. Miloradovich was Governor General of St Petersburg at the time of the flood and was shot a year later during the Decembrist Revolt on Senate Square. Benckendorff was a constant companion of the Tsar, Nicholas I. As Chief of the Secret Police, Benckendorff was also in overall charge of the Official Censorship and was charged with keeping Pushkin under permanent surveillance.

5 This passage in *The Bronze Horseman* is a direct response to Adam Mickiewicz's sardonic description of The Monument to Peter the Great, from his epic poem *Forefather's Eve: An excerpt*, translated by Waclaw Lednicki, reads:

From Finland's shore they tore this granite mound
Which, when the Empress speaks and waves her hand
Floats o'er the sea and runs across the land
And falls into place at her command.
The mound is ready now, and forth he goes
A Roman toga'd Tsar who rules by blows
His charger gallops on the granite steep
Rearing its body for a mighty leap.

Prologue

One day, in the far future, some hard-working monk
Will find my painstaking, anonymous writings.
He'll light his lamp, as I light mine
He'll shake the dust of centuries from these scrolls
Then he'll copy out, carefully, these true accounts.

Pushkin, Boris Godunov (scene 5)

01 | Pushkin & Old Russia

During the period Pushkin was writing *The Bronze Horseman*, in the early 1830s, different interpretations of Russian history were a hot topic. According to the most influential historian of his day, Karamzin, the starting point in Russian history could be dated precisely, to 862 AD, when a group of Vikings – known by the Byzantine Greeks and Slavs as Varangians – settled in the northernmost outpost of Novgorod, under the leadership of a prince named Riurik. These Vikings were called the Rus', or rowers, because they came by sea and carried their boats between navigable waters. The most vital of the trading routes they established ran north-south along the River Dnieper linking Sweden and the Baltic in the north with the capital of the Byzantine Empire, Constantinople. This was known as the route from the Varangians to the Greeks. A second route, via the River Volga, was called the route from the Varangians to the Arabs.

According to Karamzin, the Finnish and Slavic tribes who lived in the Novgorod region initially resisted Viking rule but relations between the local tribes were so fractious that they eventually wearied of internecine conflict and 'invited' Riurik to come and restore order. With this suspiciously congenial 'Invitation to the Varangians', the Finns and Slavs supposedly pleaded with the Vikings to: 'come to reign and rule over us. Our land is rich and great, but there is no order in it'.[1] Russia's first cities were established in the 9th and 10th centuries along the north-south trading routes established by the Vikings. Twenty years after Rurik's arrival, another member of his family, Oleg, conquered Kiev, on the lower reaches of the River Dnieper and established the state of Kievan Rus', which, over the next century, expanded until it extended from the Baltic to the Black Sea.

During the course of the 10th century, the Rus' were involved in a series of confrontations with the Byzantines over impediments to trade. Partly in an effort to contain this threat, the Byzantines set about the conversion of their new adversaries. It's because this conversion was carried out by representatives of the Eastern – Greek – wing of the Roman Empire, based in Constantinople, that Russia is the only other country in Europe apart from Greece to have adopted Orthodox Christianity. The emissaries sent, Constantine and Methodius, converted the Rus' in 988 and devised a new alphabet for the Slavs.

Constantine and Methodius were two brothers who lived in Thessalonica, an important trading centre. Good at languages, they learned to speak Slavonic through contact with Slav traders. They were asked to devise an alphabet which could represent the spoken word and then be used to translate Orthodox texts. Their first attempt produced an alphabet called Glagolitic, which later developed into Church Slavonic. On becoming a monk, Constantine adopted the name Cyril and the two brothers became known as the Saints Cyril and Methodius, 'Apostles to the Slavs'. Their second attempt produced the alphabet which we now know as Cyrillic.

The ruler who takes the credit for brokering the conversion to Christianity is Vladimir the Great, although there is evidence that many Russians, including his mother Olga, had already been baptised. At the time of his father, Svyatoslav's, death in 972, Vladimir – a Viking – was prince of Novgorod, the wealthiest city in the northern part of Kievan Rus'. Karamzin's main source for his research into Russia's early history was a document called the *Primary Chronicle*, or *Tale of Bygone Years*. This was most likely written by a monk in a Kievan monastery and would have derived mainly from oral tradition and folk legends.

By the time the *Primary Chronicle* was written (the earliest part being in 1116), the Viking names had already been converted, so that Helgi becomes Oleg, Helga turns to Olga, Ingwarr to Igor, and Waldemar into Vladimir. The *Primary Chronicle* also comments upon the multicultural milieu which prevailed in Kievan Rus': 'The Rus', we learn, 'worshipped a pantheon of gods which originated in different cultures – some Iranian, others Slavic, still others Scandinavian – to judge only by the names of Khors, Simargl, Dazhbog, and Perun'.[2] The Kievan Rus' period reached its zenith during the reigns of Vladimir the Great and Yaroslav the Wise but, after the latter's death in 1054, continuous disputes between rivals to the throne reduced the entire country to chaos, with dozens of rival principalities laying claim to the throne.

The collapse of Kievan Rus' was not only due to internal feuding. There was a constant external threat from neighbouring nomadic tribes based on the Steppe, such as the Pechenegs and the Polovtsy. The latter carried out so many raids on the flotillas sailing between Kiev and Constantinople that they eventually brought trade to a complete standstill. A further factor was that trade routes to the east increasingly came to be dominated by merchants from the Mediterranean city states of Venice and Genoa. This was especially so after the Fourth Crusade captured and sacked Constantinople, in 1204, thereby opening up mercantile trade routes to the eastern Mediterranean.

Two important consequences emerged from the disintegration of Kievan Rus'. The first of these, probably barely noticed at the time, was that in the midst of the endless internecine warfare, one of the last of Kiev's Great Princes, Vladimir Monomakh, had sent his son, Yuri Dolgoruky, to govern the Rostov-Susdal province in the north-east of Kievan Rus'. As part of this mission, Dolgoruky founded fortresses in a number of different locations including Tver, Kostroma and Vologda. In 1156, Dolgoruky built a fort at the village of Kuchkovo, on a bend in the Moskva River, which he surrounded with a timber fence and a moat. This was the beginning of what became Moscow.

Although a settlement already existed on the site, Dolgoruky (the name means 'long-armed' in Russian) is nowadays credited as 'The Founder of Moscow' (an enormous equestrian statue of him stands on Tverskaya Square).

The second and much more disastrous consequence of the collapse of Kievan Rus' was that it opened the door to further invasion, both from the east and from the north and west. In 1223, German and Danish members of the Hanseatic League had expanded their interests into the area then known as Livonia, on the eastern shores of the Baltic Sea bordering the Rus' lands. Livonia was inhabited by various Baltic and Finnic tribes, ruled by an upper class of Baltic Germans. Here, the Bishop of Riga founded a military order known as the Livonian Brothers of the Sword, mainly German 'warrior monks', who later merged with the impressively-named Order of Brothers of the German House of Saint Mary in Jerusalem, to become the Teutonic Knights.

With the encouragement of Pope Gregory IX, the primary role of these mightily armed brethren, like their Crusader counterparts, was to bring Christianity to the local pagans, at the point of a sword if necessary. They were instructed to block any incursions into the same territory by the pagan Baltic Russians, ruled over by Kievan Rus' overlords from the neighbouring cities of Pskov and Novgorod. Attempts by the Teutonic Knights to expand their operations into Kievan Rus' failed when they suffered a historic defeat in the legendary Battle on the Ice, on the frozen Lake Peipus, at the hands of Prince Alexander Nevsky of Novgorod and Pskov, in 1242 (memorably depicted in Sergei Eisenstein's anti-Nazi propaganda film, *Alexander Nevsky*, with soundtrack by Prokofiev).

Thanks to Alexander Nevsky, Novgorod also escaped the worst when the Golden Horde invaded Kievan Rus' from the east. After an initial assault in 1223, the invaders mysteriously retreated with the principality at their mercy. But they were to return 13 years later, this time with a much larger host of 35,000 mounted archers commanded by Batu Khan. After a six-day siege at Ryazan, the city was annihilated; Kolomna, Moscow and Vladimir-Suzdal were burned to the ground and another 14 cities were ransacked after their defences had been destroyed by Chinese siege engines. This time, the Horde did not move on. They established a base at Sarai, on the Lower Volga and ruled Russia for the next 250 years. The Mongol Khan became the country's first undisputed personal sovereign and in post-1240

Russian documents he is customarily referred to as the Tsar or Caesar, titles previously reserved for the Emperor of Byzantium.

Though he had distinguished himself in the defence of Novgorod against the Teutonic Knights, Nevsky played a much more questionable role faced with the Mongol invasion. In 1242, after his father's death, he travelled to Sarai to pay homage to the conqueror and to provide assurances that the Russian overlords would keep their own populations under control. His subsequent behaviour fully justified the Mongols' confidence in him. In 1257-9 he stamped out popular uprisings against Mongol census takers which had broken out in Novgorod, and a few years later he did so again in several other cities.

Genghis Khan had successfully united the nomadic tribes which formed the Golden Horde into a formidable war machine but they did not have the necessary resources to administer a country as vast, sparsely populated and poor as Russia. Their census takers and tax collectors were highly unpopular and eventually they concluded the job could best be done by the Russians themselves: 'Nevsky and even more his successors met this need. They assumed on behalf of the Horde the principal administrative and fiscal responsibilities over Russian territories, as compensation for which they gained for their principalities relative freedom from Mongol interference and, for themselves, influence at Sarai'.[3]

The family history archive kept by his uncle, Pyotr, traced the Pushkin ancestry – on his father's side – back to this period, making the Pushkins one of the most ancient families in Russia. Responding to slanderous comments made about Pushkin's ancestry in the newspaper *The Northern Bee* by his bitter adversary, Fadey Bulgarin, Pushkin wrote:

'It was said officially in one newspaper that I am a bourgeois in the nobility. It would be more accurate to say a nobleman in the bourgeoisie. My family is one of the most ancient of the nobility. We descend from the Prussian Radshi, or Rachi, a nobleman (an honourable man, says the chronicler), who came to Russia during the rule of Saint Alexander Yaroslavich Nevsky *(cf. The Russian Chronicler and The History of the Russian State).* The Pushkins, Musin-Pushkins, Bobrishev-Pushkins, Buturlins, Myatlevs, Pvodovs, and others were descended from him'.[4]

Pushkin's ancestors are mentioned in both *The Russian Chronicles* and in Karamzin's *History of the Russian State* and the Pushkins' family estate, at Mikhailovskoye, was located a few miles from Pskov, which – 600 years earlier – had been part of Alexander Nevsky's principality.

Nevsky's calculated policy of collaboration with the Mongols was carried through so successfully by his descendants in Moscow, that the city experienced a period of exponential growth, at the expense of rival centres such as Tver and Novgorod. One of Nevsky's grandsons, Ivan Danilovich – later to become Ivan I of Russia – proved an extraordinarily gifted and unscrupulous political manipulator. By one scholar's estimate, he spent most of his reign 'either at Sarai or *en route* from it...' [5] Ivan, who was given the nickname *Kalita*, meaning 'moneybags', amassed a vast fortune from the tolls which he imposed on travellers and goods crossing his properties, which happened to straddle a number of strategic trade routes.

Following an uprising in the rival city of Tver, which took place in 1327, and in which a high-level Mongol deputation was massacred, Ivan headed a joint Mongol-Russian punitive force which devastated the Tver region. As a reward, Ivan was made Grand Prince and appointed 'Farmer General' of tributes, which not only allowed him to meddle in the affairs of rival courts, but gave him an effective monopoly of access to the Khan. By this means, Moscow gradually isolated its rivals and became the primary intermediary with the Khan. Another advantage was that Moscow could escape the periodic looting raids suffered by other parts of Russia and consequently became an island of relative security in a country otherwise racked by violence.

In a scathing assessment of this period in Russian history, Karl Marx wrote that the Tatar yoke had already lasted 100 years before Muscovy would emerge from its obscurity. The Mongols deliberate policy had been to sow discord among the Russian princes, as a means to secure their servile submission. The strife they encouraged, for the prize of being elevated to the status of Grand Prince, he quotes as being: 'an abject strife – the strife of slaves, whose chief weapon was calumny, and who were always ready to denounce each other to their cruel rulers...on their knees, prostrate and trembling beneath the scimitar of a Tartar, always ready to roll under his feet those servile crowns, and the heads by which they were worn'.[6]

The entire policy of Ivan Kalita was summed up by Marx as follows: '…to play the abject tool of the Khan, thus borrow his power, and then to turn it upon his princely rivals and his own subjects. To attain this end, he had to insinuate himself with the Tartars by dint of cynical adulation, by frequent journeys to the Golden Horde, by humble prayers for the hand of Mongol princesses, by a display of unbounded zeal for the Khan's interest, by the unscrupulous execution of his orders, by atrocious calumnies against his own kinsfolk, by blending in himself the characters of the Tartar's hangman, sycophant and slave-in-chief'.[7]

Gradually, Muscovy became the leading Russian state and the authority of its Grand Duke was immensely strengthened. The first prince of Moscow to openly challenge Mongol authority in Russia was Dmitry Donskoy, son of Ivan II (The Meek). Donskoy reigned as Prince of Moscow from 1359 and Grand Prince of Vladimir from 1363. In this capacity, Donskoy held the Tartar Khan's patent to collect taxes for all of Russia but he also sensed weakness in the Golden Horde, which by that time had become severely weakened by civil war and internal dynastic rivalries.

In one of the most famous victories in Russian history, Donskoy successfully repelled a Mongol assault on Moscow, led by the Mongol general, Mamay, and then routed the Mongol army in the Battle of Kulikovo. Like Nevsky, however, Donskoy was not always the hero: when Mamay was subsequently deposed by a new Khan, Tokhtamysh, Donskoy pledged allegiance and was reinstated as the Mongol's principal tax collector. During the reigns of Ivan III (Ivan the Great) and then under Ivan IV (Ivan the Terrible) Russia progressively gained independence from the Mongol Tartars, stealthily building up a formidable state military apparatus which the nomadic army, by this time riven by its own internal disputes, was unable to match.

Pushkin's take on this entire period in Russian history is outlined in his notes for a work entitled *On the insignificance of Russian Literature*, which he wrote in 1834 but which, like much of the rest of his work, was not published in his own lifetime. It is worth quoting at length:

THE MAN WHO SHOOK HIS FIST AT THE TSAR

'For two dark centuries only the clergy, spared because of the amazing perspicacity of the Tartars, preserved the pale sparks of Byzantine learning. In the silence of the monasteries, monks kept their uninterrupted chronicles…But the inner life of the enslaved people did not develop. The Tartars did not resemble the Moors. Having conquered Russia, they did not give it algebra or Aristotle…'. Meanwhile, by contrast: 'Europe was flooded with an incredible multitude of poems, legends, satires, romances, mysterès, etc., our ancient archives and libraries offer almost no food for the curiosity of researchers except chronicles. The half-expunged characteristics of our nationality were preserved by a few tales and songs which were constantly revised by oral tradition and *The Song of Igor's Campaign* rises up as a solitary monument in the desert of our ancient literature'. [8]

During Ivan the Terrible's childhood, raids on Muscovy continued to be carried out by both the Crimean Tartars and those based in Kazan, a fortress which had originated as a staging post on the Volga trade route between Scandinavia and Baghdad. Ivan and his advisers decided to deal with the Tartar khanates one by one, starting with Kazan. In 1551, Muscovite forces built a fortress at Sviyazhsk on the Volga, about 20 miles above Kazan. This was to serve as a base for the planned attack on the city the following year. In 1552, a successful Russian offensive was launched and this historic victory was celebrated with the construction of one of Russia's most iconic buildings, St Basil's cathedral, the multi-coloured concoction which adorns Red Square in Moscow.

Ivan was not so successful in his struggle with the Swedes. During the first half of his reign, he had made some significant territorial gains but the very existence of Muscovy soon came under renewed threat from the empires of Sweden and Lithuania/Poland. An armistice was reached with the Swedes, after an appeal was made to the Pope to mediate. But the terms of the treaty were humiliating for Ivan, who was forced to give up Livonia, after 25 years of struggle. He then had to concede Ingria, including the mouth of the Neva River, which effectively cut Russia's access to the Gulf of Finland. This gave Sweden the virtual monopoly of sea traffic through the Baltic, which they were to retain throughout the next century, until the time of Peter the Great.

The vast expenditure needed to finance the Livonian war contributed to a monumental internal crisis in Russia. Ivan became convinced of the necessity to take extraordinary measures both for his own personal protection and to increase his control of the army and state administration. Fuelled by his own paranoia, suspicion of the boyars – Russia's land-owning aristocracy – and exacerbated by his wars with Sweden, Lithuania and Poland, Ivan took the extraordinary step of abandoning Moscow and setting up his own private court, called the *oprichnina*, with its own militia, the *oprichnik*i. Granted dictatorial powers by the gentry and lower classes of Moscow to punish the alleged treachery of the boyars, Ivan's personal army was organised along the lines of a monastic brotherhood, primarily made up of members of the lower-class gentry.

The *oprichniki* were easily recognisable: they dressed all in black, rode black horses and wore the emblem of a severed dog's head. Their role was to sniff out treason against the Tsar. Nicknamed the 'Tsar's dogs', the *oprichniki* raided boyar estates, confiscating property with abandon. When a delegation of three hundred boyars requested an audience with the Tsar and pleaded for an end to the persecutions, in 1566, they were all rounded up, imprisoned and tortured. Entire towns were razed to the ground. When the head of the Russian church, Metropolitan Philip, spoke out against the *oprichniki* in his sermons, he was deported to a remote monastery and strangled. In 1570, the whole city of Novgorod, still one of the richest merchant cities in the whole of Russia and an ongoing thorn in the side of Moscow, was once more proscribed and sacked. Ivan IV and a detachment of *oprichniki* instituted a month-long reign of terror known as the Massacre of Novgorod. The *oprichniki* raided the town, conducted executions among all classes and looted ecclesiastical and merchant holdings.

The upshot of this reign of terror was twofold: one was that it created 'a lasting foundation for the growth of Russian absolutism. The old society of semi-independent principalities, on the wane for more than a century, was dealt a blow from which it was never fully to recover'.[9] The second was that it had placed unendurable burdens on ordinary citizens: 'In the last decades of Ivan's rule, serious rioting erupted in central Russia, where bands of peasants and highwaymen attacked monasteries and private estates in search of grain, booty, and revenge'.[10]

Even more alarming was the situation in the borderlands: 'Here the way had been cleared for a full-scale war against the

Muscovite centre. Ivan's expulsion of the boyars, together with the swelling exodus of peasants and townsfolk, had concentrated along the southern frontier a throng of desperate men nursing grievances against the crown and its supporters'.[11] In the view of one of Ivan's contemporaries: 'All the state hath he sundered in twain, as it were with an axe, and this division, methinks, was the forerunner of all the dissensions by which the land is vexed to this day'.[12]

When Ivan the Terrible died, in March 1584, he left two potential heirs. The first was his second son, Feodor – the other, Dmitry, the very young child of his seventh marriage. On his deathbed, Ivan appointed a council of advisers to assist Feodor when he took the throne – he was a weak child, both mentally and physically. This group of leading boyars included three who were to play a critical part in the dynastic power struggle which took place unremittingly over the next two decades, in a period known in Russian history as the Time of Troubles. These were: Boris Godunov, Basil Shuisky and Theodor Romanov. The first two, Godunov and Shuisky – both equally ruthless and conniving – were the first to successfully intrigue their way onto the Russian throne during this period. Godunov oversaw the brief reign of Ivan's son, Feodor, until he died and then ensured that he himself was appointed Tsar.

The alternative to Godunov would have been Feodor's nine-year-old younger brother, Dmitry. Technically, Dmitry had no legitimate claim to the throne, since the Orthodox Church would only recognise the first three of Ivan's eight marriages. Nonetheless, the boyars were taking no chances. Dmitry was found with his throat slit, lying in the courtyard of the royal residence at Uglich. An official commission, headed by Basil Shuisky, concluded that the boy had, incredibly, managed to cut his own throat during an epileptic seizure. The boy's mother, Maria Nagaya (a Romanov), refused to believe this yarn and had no doubt that her son had been murdered by agents sent by Boris Godunov. She was dispatched to a nunnery and forced to take the veil. Many contemporaries and later historians – including Pushkin – were convinced of Godunov's guilt.

Godunov's name first makes an appearance, in 1570, as an archer of the guard in the court of Ivan the Terrible. Soon after, Godunov became a member of Ivan's private militia, the dreaded *oprichniki,* and then, opportunely, married the daughter of his boss – the head of the *oprichniki*, Mulyata Skuratov-Belsky. It was when Ivan chose Godunov's sister, Irina, to be the wife of his second son and eventual heir, Feodor, that Godunov was elevated to the rank of Boyar. Just how much a part of the Kremlin's inner circle Godunov had become is indicated by the fact that he was reportedly present at the notorious scene when Ivan murdered his eldest son – the Crown Prince, Ivan – in a fit of rage.

It was said that when Godunov tried to intervene he also received blows from the Tsar's sceptre. In the course of several years, Godunov managed initially to defeat his rivals at court – not least the rival boyar and second cousin to Feodor, Theodor Romanov. In fact, Godunov orchestrated a purge against the Romanovs because they had an equally legitimate claim to the throne – another of Ivan the Terrible's wives, Anastasia, had been a Romanov. To deal with this threat, Theodor Romanov was banished to a remote monastery and made a monk against his will. Other members of the Romanov family were deported to distant towns in the north.

Dmitry's death had marked the end of the ancient Rurik dynasty and it was the absence of a legitimate heir which contributed to the intense dynastic power struggle during the Time of Troubles. While the infighting continued among the boyar elite in the Kremlin, a number of rival contenders to the throne emerged. A series of three 'False Dmitrys' entered the scene, all claiming to be Ivan's son and to have miraculously survived the assassination. The first to claim legitimacy as the next rightful heir, from the fact that his sister had been married to Feodor, was Godunov. He became the first non-Riurik Tsar of Russia in 1598. He was the descendant of a Tartar Prince who had been converted to Russian Orthodoxy and was renowned for his 'uncanny intelligence and abilities in palace intrigue, diplomacy and statecraft'.[13] Godunov's ill-fated period in power – during which Muscovy was devastated by plague, famine and war – lasted from 1598 to 1605 and provides the backdrop for Pushkin's historical play, *Boris Godunov.*

The first of three successive 'False Dmitrys' made his appearance among the Cossacks of the Dnieper and then in Kiev, which was not part of Muscovy. It belonged to the Kingdom of Poland and Lithuania and had become a refuge for many exiles and émigrés escaping from the impositions introduced by the rulers of Muscovy. In addition to the internal threat posed by pretenders to the throne, an elemental misfortune added to the nation's troubles. Beginning with the summer of 1601, the crops failed three years in succession. More than 100,000 people were estimated to have perished in Moscow alone and 'starving people devoured grass, bark, cadavers of animals and, on occasion, even other human beings'.[14]

All told, in the years between 1584 and 1613, Muscovy underwent a devastating crisis and 'the society suffered a complete political, social, institutional and moral collapse'.[15] During this period, the country was 'at its lowest depths, the Tsar's government had virtually ceased to function, society was in chaos, foreign invaders and native brigands stalked the land ...many of the Tsar's military servitors abandoned their posts and entire regions went their own way, oblivious of Moscow's leadership'.[16]

Between 1601 and 1603, an estimated 127,000 bodies were buried in mass graves in Moscow alone. Widespread starvation is estimated to have killed around two million people in Russia, a third of the population. The most likely cause of this catastrophic crop failure, according to very recent research, is the 'volcanic winter' which spread across the globe in 1600, after the eruption of Huaynaputina volcano in Peru. Harvests were devastated by a gas cloud laced with sulphur dioxide, which blotted out the sunlight, contributing to bitterly cold winters, loss of crops and massive famine, in an arc which spread across Western Europe to China and Japan.

It was at this point that a number of leading boyars decided to incite the nation against the Tsar, Godunov. The most important forces involved in the uprising which now began to develop against Godunov and in support of the False Dmitry were the Cossacks and the vast mass of the urban and rural poor who had been crippled by the exactions imposed from Moscow as well as by famine and war. Eagerly adding fuel to the flames were Polish and West Russian landlords who hoped to benefit by acquiring land and wealth from the disintegration of the Muscovy state.

The precise origins of the first False Dmitry are not known: one version is that he was a former novice of a Moscow monastery, Gregory Otrepiyev; another that he was most likely trained by boyar agents opposed to Godunov, and headed by Basil Shuisky, to assume the role of Dmitry. Either way, the False Dmitry first appeared while in refuge in Galicia, in the castle of a Polish Lord, George Mniszech. Here, he married Mniszech's beautiful and notoriously scheming daughter, Marina – a historical character who fascinated Pushkin.

By the end of the Time of Troubles, Marina had managed to marry two of the three False Dmitrys who appeared on the scene, effortlessly recognising both of them as the genuine article (the Third False Dmitry was her son to another Cossack adventurer, Ivan Zarutsky). Acting as the legitimate claimant to the throne and backed by boyars opposed to Boris Godunov, the First False Dmitry led an army of 1,500 Cossacks, Polish soldiers of fortune and other adventurers to reclaim his assumed rightful status in 1604. And, against all the odds, he succeeded. In April 1605, when the chances of this outcome seemed unlikely, Boris Godunov suddenly died (possibly poisoned), the False Dmitry became Tsar, and Marina Mniszech became Tsarina. Godunov's wife and children were massacred by the people of Moscow.

The First False Dmitry's triumph didn't last long. Within months, opposition to him was being incited by the leader of a new boyar conspiracy, again headed by Basil Shuisky. This time, Shuisky played on the fact that Dmitry was a Catholic. He deliberately incited rumours that Dmitry had been sent by Poland to make Catholicism the official religion in Russia. The anti-Polish sentiment found a willing audience among Muscovites because of the rowdy and arrogant conduct already manifested by Polish troops who had supported Dmitry's claim to the throne and who were notorious for lording it on the streets of Moscow and in the Kremlin.

When the boyars of Moscow saw foreigners, who had come with Dmitry openly preparing to settle down in Moscow, they feared that Polish traders were sure to follow in their wake, with foreign merchandise, which would be sure to deprive the merchants of Moscow of their monopoly. Incited by hatred of the Polish entourage around the new Tsar and his wife, riots were fomented in the city.

Amid the ensuing bedlam, an estimated 500 Polish soldiers were killed and the False Dmitry was shot by a member of the Kremlin guard, or *streltsy*, as he tried to escape through a window. The False Dmitry's body was taken to Red Square and ceremonially burned. His remains were then fired from a cannon in the direction of Poland. In effect, the unexpected arrival and equally sudden departure of the First False Dmitry marked the beginning of a prolonged battle for control of the Muscovite State. Internally, this took the form of rival boyar factions vying for ascendancy and each of these having to seek support for their cause from the lower classes inside Russia and from the Cossacks.

At various stages these rival factions also appealed for military assistance from the neighbouring powers of Sweden, and Poland/Lithuania. Basil Shuisky replaced the First False Dmitry as Tsar in 1606, but, if anything, he had even less popular support than Godunov. The fact that he had taken the throne was regarded as a victory by very few Russians, apart from the Kremlin boyar elite. Opposition to the government continued and outright rebellion took many forms: disorder swept towns on the Volga, the state of Muscovy itself descended into anarchy, with armed bands roaming the countryside, and now there were new rumours that the First False Dmitry had escaped harm and had re-emerged to claim the throne.

In the south, an armed uprising of the lower classes was raised against Moscow by a former slave and captive of the Tartars, Ivan Bolotnikov. Heading a force made up of serfs, peasants, slaves, fugitives and vagabonds, Bolotnikov reached the gates of Moscow in 1606 but he was betrayed by the gentry element in his army who feared what might happen to them if the revolution was successful. As order collapsed and disorganisation spread, more pretenders to the throne emerged. After the defeat of Bolotnikov, the Second False Dmitry appeared and began to rally the forces of social discontent and unrest. He also attracted a very large following especially from Poland and Lithuania, including several famous Polish commanders. Remarkably, he was immediately recognised by Marina Mniszech as her first husband, despite the fact that he had been very publicly shot and fired from a cannon. Heading an army, the core of which consisted of up to 7,000 Polish troops, 10,000 Cossacks and a further 10,000 mercenaries, the Second False Dmitry's army advanced on Moscow and routed the forces of Basil Shuisky, in 1608.

One of the Tsar's prisoners, Theodor Romanov, was raised to the rank of Patriarch. Camped at the village of Tushino, the size of the army grew to more than 100,000 after promises that there would be wholesale confiscation and redistribution of boyar estates drew many commoners to the cause. For a three-year period, from 1607 to 1610, the Second False Dmitry – also known as the Felon of Tushino – became a rival Tsar, with his own court, a boyar duma and his own administration, parallel to Moscow. The court at Tushino even had its own Patriarch, Filaret (formerly Theodor) Romanov, the rival to Godunov who had been banished to a monastery.

This situation of dual power existed for two years. In what is nowadays known as the 'national phase' of the Time of Troubles, the disparate forces of what remained of the Muscovite state finally rallied in opposition to Polish intervention in their affairs and in support of their own Orthodox tradition. In the absence of a Tsar, and because of the impotence of the boyar duma and the rudimentary parliament, or *zemsky sobor,* the church became the sole force apparently capable of mustering an adequate response to the collapse of Mother Russia. Patriarch Hermogenes in Moscow sent manifestos to other towns urging them to raise an army to liberate the capital. In response to this appeal, two consecutive 'national' armies were formed partly from the remnants of the formerly opposing armies of the False Dmitry and Basil Shuisky.

The first of these was defeated by Polish troops in 1611, but the second, led by a Novgorod merchant, Kuzma Minin, and a veteran soldier, Prince Dmitry Pozharsky, besieged Moscow in 1612 and after bitter fighting captured Polish positions in the heart of the city. This historic victory is commemorated

THE MAN WHO SHOOK HIS FIST AT THE TSAR

by the statue to Minin and Pozharsky which today stands in Red Square, between St. Basil's Cathedral and Lenin's Tomb. In 2012, Vladimir Putin introduced a new national holiday, called National Unity Day, to commemorate the 400th anniversary of Minin and Pozharsky's victory in what is now called the Battle of Moscow, when the Polish 'invaders' were driven out of the Kremlin. This holiday takes place every year, on 4 November. The event which marked the end of the Time of Troubles took place in 1613, when the Patriarch appointed by the Second False Dmitri, Filaret Romanov, appointed his own son, Michael, to become the first of the Romanov Tsars.

The Time of Troubles is the backdrop to Pushkin's play *Boris Godunov*, best known in the West in its adaptation as an opera by the Russian composer, Mussorgsky. Explaining his inspiration for the play, Pushkin wrote:

'The study of Shakespeare, Karamzin, and our old chronicles gave me the idea of clothing in dramatic forms one of the most dramatic epochs of modern history. Not disturbed by any other influence, I imitated Shakespeare in his broad and free depiction of characters, in the simple and careless combination of plots; I followed Karamzin in the clear development of events; I tried to guess the way of thinking and the language of the time from the chronicles. Rich sources! Whether I was able to make best use of them, I don't know – but at least my labours were zealous and conscientious'.[17]

In a dedication which appears in the printed version of the play, Pushkin pays tribute to Karamzin, author of the twelve volume *History of the Russian State* from which Pushkin researched the Time of Troubles. Volumes IX to XI of Karamzin's history, covering the period from the reign of Ivan the Terrible's son, Feodor, to the arrival of the first False Dmitry, were published between 1821 and 1824. Another rich source of material for the play came from the Pushkin family papers which were kept on the family estate at Mikhailovskoye, where Pushkin was being held under house arrest in 1825. This is where he worked on *Boris Godunov* and managed to research and write the play in under a year.

Pushkin was immensely proud of the fact that members of the

Pushkin family had played an important role during the Time of Troubles, on both sides of the civil war. Furthermore: 'The exiled poet had no reason to love the reigning Romanov Tsar, Alexander I. But he was at the peak of his poetic fame in the mid-1820s and could only covet the status of national poet-playwright'.[18]

Pushkin sought to emulate the kind of reverence the German people held towards their national poet-playwright, Friedrich Schiller, whose role was to: 'combine in one person the voice of freedom against oppression, an enlightened helpmeet to rulers, and a prophet of their nation's future greatness. Today's readers should be aware that whenever a Pushkin speaks in the play, on either side of the conflict, he voices uncomfortable truths – about serfdom, Boris's reign of terror, support for the Pretender – that are well documented in foreigners' histories and unwelcome as part of the official history endorsed by the House of Romanov'.[19]

Two ancestors of Pushkin are represented in *Boris Godunov*. One of these, Gavrila or Gabriel Pushkin, was a real person who sided with the False Dmitry. Of Gavrila, Pushkin says: 'I have depicted him as I found him in history and in my family papers. He had great talents – man of war, man of court, man of conspiracy above all. It was he and Pleshcheyev who assured the success of the Pretender by an unheard-of audacity. Afterword I have found him again in Moscow – one of the seven chiefs who defended it in 1612, then in 1616 sitting alongside Kozma Minin in the Duma, then as Voevoda of Nizhny, then among the deputies who crowned Romanov, then ambassador'.[20]

Then, as if to emphasise that Gavrila was not entirely a paragon of virtue, Pushkin adds: 'He was everything, even an arsonist, as is proved by an official document which I found in Pogoreloe Gorodishche – the town which he had burned (in order to punish it for I don't know what) in the manner of the proconsuls of the Convention Nationale'[21].

The other Pushkin character in the play, Afanasy, is a composite of two Pushkin brothers who served Boris Godunov. In Scene 10, the duplicitous boyar Shuisky, hotfoot from Poland, enters the Kremlin to inform Godunov about the appearance of the Pretender, False Dmitry. This news, he says, had been given to him in confidence the night before by his trusted lieutenant, Afanasy Pushkin. At which, Tsar Boris mutters: 'Oh, how I loathe this rabid brood of Pushkins!'.[22]

Pushkin regarded *Boris Godunov* as one of his finest achievements. Entirely by design, the events described in the play displayed a remarkable similarity to the confusion which reigned in the final months of 1825 following the death of Alexander I – the rival claims to the throne of his younger brothers, Constantine and Nicholas, and the culmination of this upheaval in the Decembrist Revolt.

The version of the play which Pushkin brought with him from exile, and which had been completed in 1825, is not the same as the 'canonical' version that is most often performed today and which many regard as obscure and indecipherable. That is mainly because of the damaging changes Pushkin was forced to make before the censorship imposed on Pushkin by Count Benckendorff and the Tsar would allow it to be published.

In an article written for *The Russian Review* in 2001, the American academic, Chester Dunning, explains that: 'A very serious weakness in current scholarship about *Boris Godunov* is the fact that relatively little attention has been paid to Pushkin's use of historical sources in writing the play and to the young writer's intense interest in the history of his country and how to interpret that history'. That oversight, Dunning continues: '…is especially regrettable because Pushkin was actually an historian of some note and ability. Indeed, in 1831, Tsar Nicholas appointed him Russia's official historian laureate (or historiographer), only the second one ever, following Karamzin'.[23]

At the time, history and literature were not regarded as separate disciplines and Pushkin was immensely proud of the status granted to him, as the leading literary figure in Russia. The post of historian laureate was not only the same as Karamzin's, it was also the same honour that Louis XV of France had bestowed upon one of Pushkin's literary heroes, Voltaire.

In the original 1825 version of the play, Pushkin moved sharply away from the establishment view – articulated by Karamzin – that, during Russia's Time of Troubles, the pretender Dmitry was an obvious fraud who had simply been the product of a Polish plot to unseat a legitimate Russian Tsar. Instead, Pushkin took a more historically accurate view which was that the Second False Dmitry's successful military campaign against the Tsar had been made possible because of his promise to abolish serfdom. During the 1590s, Godunov – acting as Regent for his predecessor, the Tsar Feodor – had abolished the peasantry's long-held right to leave their lord's service during the two-week period surrounding St George's Day which traditionally took place in late November. Godunov was hated by the peasants for the resulting 'forbidden years' which effectively tied them to the land for the next half-century, until the *Ulozhenie* of 1649.

During the reign of Nicholas I, no other writer had been allowed to publish anything remotely similar concerning popular uprisings in Dmitry's name – and even then, says Chester Dunning, 'the topic was still considered far too dangerous to print by some tsarist censors'. The reason for this reluctance was that *Boris Godunov* touched upon some of the most controversial topics of Nicholas I's own 'time of troubles' – the Decembrist uprising, which challenged his own legitimacy, and serfdom, the abolition of which was one of the Decembrists' primary demands. When Pushkin returned from exile in 1826 and first read aloud the original version of the play to the cream of Russia's intelligentsia, including his former mentor, Pyotr Chaadayev: '… they fully understood it as Shakespearean, revolutionary in form, anti-autocratic, and opposed to serfdom; and they loved it'.[24]

The reception this version of the play received was described by a young Michael Pogodin as follows:

'What effect that reading had on all of us is impossible to convey…we all simply felt as though we were fainting from excitement…We grew hot and cold; one's hair stood on end…The reading ended. We looked at each other for a long time and then threw ourselves at Pushkin. Embraces began, a din arose, laughter broke out, and tears flowed amid the congratulations…Then the champagne appeared'.[25]

One of Pushkin's contemporaries, Ivan Kireevsky, wrote, in 1830, that in Russian literary circles of their day there was a persistent preoccupation with history, partly because of the recent impact of the Napoleonic wars: 'History in our time is at the centre of all intellectual quests and is the most important of all sciences; it is the indispensable condition for all development; historicism embraces *everything*. According to Svetlana Evdokimova, this near obsession with history was not a purely scholarly endeavour, it was above all: '... a deliberate effort to awaken national self-awareness and establish a national identity'.[26]

It is clear from the list of books Pushkin kept in his library and from the many articles and letters that he wrote on historical topics that he had an established preference for periods of political turbulence. In terms of contemporary history in the West, his library included a preponderance of works on the American and French revolution and the Napoleonic era.

Similarly, his writings on Russian history tended to deal with periods of turmoil and drastic change: the Time of Troubles, in *Boris Godunov;* the uprisings of the peasantry and urban poor led Emeliyan Pugachev in *The History of Pugachev* and *The Captain's Daughter* as well as the upheaval caused by the reforms of Peter the Great in his planned biography of the Tsar and in *The Bronze Horseman.*

In all of these works, Pushkin looked at Russian history from a perspective which differed both from his illustrious predecessor, Nikolay Karamzin, and from Karamzin's up-and-coming rival, Nikolay Polevoy. In 1830, Polevoy had caused a storm when he set out to debunk Karamzin's version of Russian history. Pushkin admired Karamzin for the originality of his writing and for the depth of research he had conducted on source material but did not agree with his view that autocracy was the only appropriate form of government in Russia.

Pushkin's standpoint was much more akin to that of the French historian, Alexis de Tocqueville, who had written in his influential *Democracy in America,* that the mistake made by many historians, like Karamzin, was to 'deprive the people themselves of the power of modifying their own condition, and they subject them either to an inflexible Providence or to some blind necessity'.[27]

According to this interpretation of history, de Tocqueville said: '...each nation is indissolubly bound by its position, its origin, its antecedents, and its character to a certain lot that no efforts can ever change... To their minds, it is not enough to show what events have occurred: they wish to show that events could not have occurred otherwise'[28]. When Polevoy's critique was published, not long after Karamzin's death in 1826, Pushkin sprang to Karamzin's defence, not so much because he agreed with his former mentor, more because he disagreed with Polevoy. In his own *History of the Russian People,* Polevoy had relied heavily on what were at that time the very fashionable ideas of French historians such as Thierry and Guizot.

In the introduction to his *Histoire de la Conquête de l'Anglettere par les Normands,* written in 1825, Thierry had maintained that his history of the Norman Conquest was a model of all the histories of the European countries. Likewise, Guizot argued that French history was a model for every other country in Europe: 'I have used the term European civilisation, because it is evident that there is a European civilisation; that a certain unity pervaded the civilisation of the various European states; that, notwithstanding infinite diversities of time, place and circumstance, this civilisation takes its first rise in facts almost wholly similar, proceeds everywhere on the same principles, and tends to produce well-nigh everywhere analogous results'.[29]

Pushkin did not agree with this approach to historical enquiry. 'Providence', he said, 'is not algebra. The human mind, to use an expression from common parlance, is not a prophet, but a conjecturer; it can see a general course of things'.[30] Neither did Pushkin accept that the kind of broad generalisations outlined by Thierry and Guizot were applicable to Russian history. To illustrate the point, Pushkin pointed out more than once that the 'formula' which proclaimed the crucial role played by the 'third estate' (commoners) during the French revolution could not be applied mechanically to Russia, because Russia never had a strong middle class.

Pushkin knew that, elsewhere in Europe, the main challenge to the aristocracy had come from the development of a strong middle class of town dwellers that had grown up as a consequence of the feudal development of cities. In Pushkin's view, the situation in Russia was entirely different. In a characteristically wry comment, he said: 'We never had feudalism; so much the worse'.[31] One consequence of its particular form of historical development was that Russia had emerged with a strong autocratic power which, up to that point in Russian history, had faced no decisive opposition from any other class. Another

– as Pushkin saw it – was that: 'in Russia, due to its specific development, the government was often 'ahead of the people', whereas in Western Europe…it was the other way around'.[32]

Notes

1   **Medieval Russia: A Source Book, 850-1700**, edited by Basil Dmytryshyn, Holt, Rinehart & Winston, 1990 (first published in 1967) p7

2   The Christianisation of Rus According to the Primary Chronicle (978-88)', in **Reinterpreting Russian History: Readings, 860-1860s,** compiled & edited by Daniel H Kaiser and Gary Marker, Oxford University Press, 1994 p63

3   **Russia under the Old Regime**, by Richard Pipes, Weidenfeld & Nicolson, 1974 p60

4   **The Critical Prose of Alexander Pushkin,** with critical essays by four Russian romantic poets, edited and translated by Carl R Proffer, Indiana University Press 1969, p118

5   op cit, Richard Pipes p61

6   **Secret Diplomatic History of the 18th Century**, by Karl Marx, edited by his daughter, Eleanor Marx Aveling, Swan Sonnenschein & Co, London, 1899. Reprinted by Forgotten Books 2015, p78

7   ibid, Marx, p.79

8   **Pushkin on Literature**, selected, translated and edited by Tatiana Wolff, The Athlone Press, 1986, p352

9   **Russian Rebels, 1600-1800**, by Paul Avrich, Allen Lane,, 1972, p11

10   ibid, Avrich, p12

11   ibid, Avrich, p12

12   ibid, Avrich, p12

13   **A History of Russia**, by Nicholas V Riasanovsky, Oxford University Press, fifth edition 1993, p156

14   op.cit, Avrich, p13

15   **The Formation of Muscovy, 1304-1613**, by Robert O Crummey, Longman 1987, chapter eight, *The Time of Troubles* p205

16   ibid, Crummey, p205

17   op cit Wolff, p247

18   op cit, Emerson, pxvi

19   ibid, pxvi

20   op cit, Shaw, p366

21   ibid, p366

22   op cit, Emerson. pxvi

23   **Rethinking the Canonical Text of Pushkin's Boris Godunov**, by Chester Dunning, *The Russian Review*. vol 60, no. 4, October 2001, *http://www.jstor.org/ stable/2679368* p576

24   ibid, Dunning, p581

25   ibid, Dunning, p583

26   **Pushkin's Historical Imagination**, by Svetlana Evdokimova, Yale University Press, 1999, p31

27   Quoted in Evdokimova, ibid p244

28   ibid, Evdokimova p244

29   ibid, Evdokimova, p35

30   ibid, Evdokimova, p38

31   ibid, Evdokimova, p39

32   ibid, Evdokimova, p38

On this bleak shoreline, woebegone
Beaten and battered by the sea
Was where our great Tsar Peter once stood…

Pushkin, *The Bronze Horseman*, 1833[1]

Shall we close our eyes to yet another glaring mistake of
Peter the Great? I mean his founding a new capital on the
northern frontier of the state, amidst muddy billows, in a place
condemned by nature to barrenness and want.

Nikolay Karamzin, *'A Memoir on Ancient and*
Modern Russia', 1836[2]

02 | The Miracle-Working Tsar

No historical figure appeared more prominently in any of Pushkin's writings than Peter the Great: he was the subject of his unfinished *History of Peter* as well as being central to three of his major fictional works: *Poltava, The Blackamoor of Peter the Great,* and *The Bronze Horseman.* According to one of his contemporaries, Vladimir Dal', Pushkin would get 'truly fired up' when speaking about Peter and saw his efforts to portray him both in fiction and non-fiction as one of the great tasks of his life. He had once explained to Dal': 'So far I was unable to comprehend, to grasp the whole of this giant at once; he is too large for us near-sighted people; we are still standing too close to him – we have to step aside for two centuries…'[3]

In an article found in one of his notebooks, Pushkin declared that: 'Russia entered Europe like a ship newly launched – to the sound of hammers and the thunder of guns. But the wars which Peter the Great undertook were beneficent and fruitful. The successful transformation of the whole nation was as a result of the battle of Poltava, and European culture weighed anchor on the shores of the conquered Neva'.[4]

Up to the beginning of the 18th century, the one-time Imperial capital of Russia and birthplace of the Russian Revolution, St Petersburg, did not exist. It was only created, by Peter, after a super-human effort and at an enormous cost in human lives. His aim was to establish, at all costs, a viable mercantile trade route between Russia and the rest of Europe via the Baltic Sea.

To achieve this, he needed to break the blockade on shipping which had been imposed throughout the preceding century by the Swedish Empire, the dominant super-power in the region at the time.

The external threat posed by the Swedish Empire was not Peter's only problem. From the outset, he had faced bitter internal opposition. Before he was confirmed as Tsar, the young Peter had only just survived a bloody episode during which two boyar families – the Naryshkins and the Miloslavskys – had vied for power. Both claimed equal rights to the throne which had become vacant on the death of Tsar Feodor III (1676-1682). Feodor was one of three sons. His mother was Maria Miloslavskaya, the first wife of Tsar Alexey Mikhailovich (1645-1676). A second son, Ivan, was born to Maria Miloslavskaya before she died. Tsar Alexey then remarried, this time to Natalya Naryshkina and she gave birth to another son, Peter. This marked the beginning of bitter feuding between these two families which was to plague the dynastic succession in Russia throughout the next half-century.

In the first of these vendettas, the *streltsy* carried out a massacre of members of Peter's own family, the Naryshkins, inside the walls of the Kremlin. This murderous episode had been instigated by Peter's half-sister, Sofia Alekseyevna. About 40 members of the Naryshkin court were killed including a number of leading boyars and military commanders. Peter was an eyewitness to the murder of two of his uncles, Ivan and Kyrill Naryshkin, who were both dragged from their chambers, thrown from a balcony and hacked to pieces. The outcome of the coup was that Ivan was now installed as 'first' Tsar, while Peter was relegated to a subordinate position, with Sofia acting as regent for both. She was the first woman to have ascended the throne in Russian history. A special, two-seated throne was constructed, which had a hole cut in the back panel, through which Sofia could feed instructions to the child Tsars. This throne is still on display inside the Kremlin Armoury in Moscow.

For the next seven years, Sofia Alekseyevna ruled Russia as regent to Ivan and Peter. During this period, the day-to-day running of her government was carried out by her 'favourite', Prince Vasily Golitsyn, a member of the old Muscovite aristocracy. The young Tsarevich, Peter, meanwhile, lived in a palace on the northern outskirts of Moscow near the village of Preobrazhenskoye. The village was not far from the 'New Foreign' or 'German' quarter of the city which had been established during his father's reign for the training of some Russian infantry regiments on Western lines. It was here that Peter first encountered officers such as the Swiss adventurer, Franz Lefort, and the Scottish soldier of fortune, Patrick Gordon.

While at Preobrazhenskoye, Peter established two 'toy' regiments of his own based on the Western model. By the time he was 14, the estate had been transformed into a virtual military encampment. Alongside the sons of boyars, recruits to his regiments included clerks, stable grooms and serfs. One of these was Alexander Menshikov, who later became the Tsar's closest companion. The soldiers in these 'toy' regiments lived in barracks, trained as soldiers and had soldiers' pay. These first of these regiments was called the Preobrazhenskoye, after the nearby village. This was the first regiment of the Russian Imperial Guard and remained so until 1917. When all the space available at Preobrazhenskoye became occupied, a new barracks was built at Semenovskoye, accommodating the second regiment of the Imperial Guard, the Semenovsky.

The beginning of the end for Sofia came in the aftermath of a disastrous campaign launched by her favourite, Prince Golitsyn, against the Turks. Golitsyn's failure gave the Naryshkin faction at court the chance to force Sofia out. For the first time, Peter felt strong enough to publicly challenge Sofia and tensions between the two camps reached breaking point in August 1689.

Memories of the bloodbath seven years earlier were still fresh in the memory and, initially, Peter was forced to flee to the safety of the Trinity, or Troitsky, monastery of St Sergius. Its walls were between 30 to 50 feet high, 20 feet thick, bristled with cannon and, during the Time of Troubles, had managed to withstand a siege by 30,000 Polish troops whose cannonballs simply rebounded off the monastery walls.

Sofia's apparently strong position was undermined when units of the *streltsy,* including the treacherous Ivan Tsykler, deserted to join Peter's forces. It was further weakened when the Patriarch, who had been sent from the Kremlin to parlay on Sofia's behalf, also defected. Peter's 'toy' regiments were now free to take the Kremlin. Sofia was arrested and banished to the Novodevichy Convent.

For the time being, Peter was now able to focus on removing the obstacles to his ambitions presented by the Swedes. At its high point, in the middle of the 17th century, Sweden had controlled most of Scandinavia and the Baltic region. During the previous century, the Swedes had made important territorial gains along the southern Baltic coastline during the Livonian War with Russia, giving them control of an area which stretched from Nöteberg, at the eastern end of the River Neva where it exits Lake Ladoga, to Riga in the west. For nearly a century, these gains meant that Swedish troops and the Swedish navy dominated the important trade routes operated by the merchants of the Hanseatic League and this allowed them to block Russian trade from their important northern trading centres of Novgorod and Pskov. It was this stranglehold that blocked the Tsar's ambition to provide Russia with its famous 'window on Europe'.

An important element in the strategy adopted by Peter to achieve this aim was first to agree an armistice with its other main rival in the south, the Ottoman Empire. This truce, agreed in 1700 at the Treaty of Constantinople, ended the war which had been waged between Russia and Turkey since 1686.

The armistice recognised gains made by Russia during this period, most importantly its possession of naval bases and fortresses, such as Taganrog and Pavlovsk, at the north-eastern corner of the Sea of Azov, adjoining the Black Sea. But it did not accede to the Russian demand that Black Sea traffic through the Dardanelles be opened up to the Russian fleet. The main point of the truce with the Ottomans was that it allowed Peter to concentrate his forces and prioritise for the battle with his main enemy in the North, Charles XII of Sweden. Peter's objective was to forge a military alliance with other neighbouring powers – Augustus the Strong of Saxony and Poland-Lithuania and Frederick IV of Denmark-Norway – before he had sufficient strength to launch an attack on Sweden.

The first set-piece confrontation between King Charles XII of Sweden and Tsar Peter I of Russia during the Great Northern War took place at Narva in 1700. Charles had only become King three years earlier and was just 18 years old – he must have seemed an unlikely obstacle to Peter's ambitions. In the event, despite being outnumbered four to one, the Swedes routed the 40,000 Russian troops at the first Battle of Narva. Four years later, Russian forces attacked Narva again, laying siege and eventually capturing the fortress, at the expense of more than 3,000 dead on either side.

Peter's victory over Sweden at Narva in 1704 re-established a foothold on the Baltic coast, which had first been won during the reign of Ivan III, or Ivan the Great, in 1492. The fortress Ivan built at that time, on the eastern side of the River Narva, is called Ivangorod, or Ivan's town. It was subsequently taken by Swedish forces in 1581, then won back by Russia in 1590 and lost again in 1612. Together with his successful defeat of Swedish forces at Nöteberg and his establishment of a fortress in the mouth of the River Neva, soon to become Petersburg, Peter was now on the verge of achieving his ambition to crush his Swedish rival.

This is the immediate background against which Pushkin opens his poem *The Bronze Horseman*. The first 10 lines of the poem describe Peter the Great's arrival on the banks of the River Neva, then a mosquito-infested swamp, inhabited by only a few Finnish fisherfolk, eking out a miserable existence in their blackened huts. The Tsar's mind is brimming with plans for the defeat of his 'haughty' Swedish neighbour and to establish a city on this coastline which, by Pushkin's time, a hundred years later, has miraculously become the glorious new mercantile capital of St Petersburg.

The site Peter selected for his new military base was close to the site of the old Swedish fortress of Nyenschantz which stood on the northern bank of the river. Rather than build a new fortress on exactly the same spot, Peter chose as his preferred location the nearby Zayachy (Hare) Island. This is where he constructed the Peter and Paul Fortress, the first building in St Petersburg. According to the legend, known to every Russian, the Tsar took a bayonet, cut out two sods of turf and put one on top of the other in the shape of a cross. During this portentous (but entirely fictitious) ceremony, it was said that an eagle hovered overhead – then came and landed on the Tsar's arm. The church which was then built on the site was named after the apostles, Peter and Paul.

In fact, the construction of the fortress was mainly undertaken by Peter's celebrated companion, Prince Alexander Menshikov, his plans based on a wooden model made by Peter. Initially, the battlements consisted of an earthen mound, topped by wooden palisades and defended by cannon. It was built in one year, 1703, essentially as a defensive battlement against Swedish attack from the West. The formidable granite ramparts and embankments which we see today, and which are mentioned more than once in *The Bronze Horseman* were added between 1706 and 1740.

Although the church in the centre of the fortress is Russian Orthodox, like much of the rest of the city it is built in the Dutch style, with its slender bell tower and needle-like spire. Peter the Great is buried in this church, as are most of the subsequent Russian Tsars and Tsarinas, up to and including Alexander the Third. From about 1720 onwards, the fortress served as the base for the city garrison and was also used for the incarceration of political opponents.

Notoriously, Peter personally supervised the torture, flogging and eventual murder of his own son, the Tzarevich Alexey, in the dungeons of this fortress. The punishment was meted out when Alexey was accused of having tried to subvert his father's plans to modernise and westernise Russia and for plotting to have him assassinated. According to one contemporary observer, the reaction against Peter's plans to westernise Russia – much of it from the hierarchy of the Orthodox Church and the Muscovite old guard – was so intense that: 'It is impossible to express the Consternation which has seized the Russians of the Old Stamp, who look with Abhorrence on Petersbourg, Shipping and Sea Affairs, foreign Customs and Languages'.[5]

At one of the first public show trials ever held in Russia, Peter's son, Alexey, was betrayed by his mistress, Afrosiniya, who claimed to have heard Alexey say that: 'I shall bring back the old people and choose myself new ones according to my will; when I become sovereign I shall live in Moscow and leave St Petersburg simply as any other town; I won't launch any ships; I shall maintain troops only for defence, and won't wage war against anyone; I shall be content with the old domains'.[6]

Later inmates of the Peter and Paul fortress included such outspoken 18th and 19th century opponents of autocracy as Alexander Radishchev and Nikolai Chernyshevsky and then, in the 20th century, Peter Kropotkin, Maxim Gorky and Leon Trotsky. Five of the leaders of the Decembrist Revolt of 1825 were imprisoned here and later hanged on the fortress ramparts. Fyodor Dostoevsky was locked up in its dungeons before being given a death sentence, taken out to the scaffold, granted a last-minute reprieve and then exiled to Siberia.

The second fortress taken by the Russians from the Swedes along this stretch of the River Neva was at Schlüsselburg, east of St Petersburg, at its confluence with Lake Ladoga. Schlüsselburg (also known as Oreshek) was taken at heavy cost by Russian forces in 1702. An estimated 6,000 Russian lives were lost to overcome a fortress defended by only 250 Swedes. The citadel had been named by the Swedes as Nöteborg, or 'nut' fortress, because of its shape. The significance to Peter of the new name, 'key fortress' in Dutch, was that it provided the 'key' to the Swedish Ingrian territories. In later years, Shlüsselberg also became a notorious prison: the Tsar Ivan VI was murdered here in 1764. This is also where Lenin's brother, Alexander Ulyanov, was hanged in 1887, at the age of 21, for his part in the plot to assassinate Tsar Alexander III.

To the west, Peter took Kronstadt, which guards the western-most approaches to the city. The naval base at Kronstadt was founded by Peter the Great after he had driven the Swedes from the island of Kotlin upon which the fortress stands, in 1703. Because the Gulf of Finland is relatively shallow and freezes completely during the winter, foundations were built by filling thousands of oak frames with boulders and then lowering them through holes cut in the ice. Forts were then constructed on top of the new man-made supports, providing cover against enemy access by sea.

Only two narrow navigable channels remained, with the strongest forts guarding them. Pushkin's great-grandfather – Ibrahim Hannibal – played an important role in strengthening the fortifications at both Schlüsselberg and Kronstadt, in his capacity as a specialist in military engineering and trusted adviser to the Tsar. He also oversaw the construction of canals east from Kronstadt and west from Schlüsselberg, which allowed ships to complete their journeys to St Petersburg in calmer waters.

Peter's other challenge to his mercantile ambitions was how to open access to the Black Sea in the south, which allowed entry to and from the Mediterranean. This vital exit and entry point for shipping had hitherto been entirely under the control of the Ottoman Empire. The Turks refused to allow any foreign vessels through the Dardanelles and into the Black Sea. Their unshakable purpose was spelled out in a letter to Peter the Great written on behalf of Sultan Mustafa II and sent by his successor Ahmed III when he was enthroned. This stated that the Black Sea was totally under Ottoman control and that the ships of no other country were allowed to enter its waters. Peter's first attempt to break the Ottoman monopoly began with a series of assaults on the fortress of Azov, guarding the entrance to the Sea of Azov and adjoining the Crimean Peninsula. The first Azov campaign took place in 1695, when Russian forces laid siege to the fortress overland. But they were unable to exert control over other the leeward side, bounded by the River Don.

As a result, the blockade was temporarily lifted but by the end of the year the Russians had prepared a second wave of attacks and this time they built a fleet of ships to block Turkish reinforcements. The fortress was finally taken in July 1696. The success of the Azov campaigns reinforced Peter's determination to create a Russian naval capability. The fleet he went on to build was based at Cape Tagan-Rog, now Taganrog, which is on the coast near Azov. This became the first military base of the Russian navy (and later, incidentally, the birthplace of Chekhov). Despite this breakthrough at Azov, Peter knew Russia was not yet strong enough to tackle the Ottoman Empire without additional assistance.

In 1697, Peter resolved to travel incognito to Europe on an 18-month journey with his version of a 'Grand Embassy'.

Unlike the usual embassy tours, undertaken to absorb the cultural highlights of other capitals, Peter's primary aim was to seek the support of other European monarchs in his war against the Ottomans. His trip included visits to Prussia, the United Provinces (Holland), Great Britain and Vienna. The fact that he had consorted with the Europeans at all was regarded by his internal opponents as a symbolic break with past Muscovite traditions, which were notoriously xenophobic.

Immediately before this expedition got underway, however, two political crises erupted and one of these – the Tsykler-Sokovnin affair – brought to light the first serious manifestation of opposition to the Tsar. It also involved two of Pushkin's ancestors. The main participant in the plot against the Tsar, Ivan Tsykler, was a member of the Duma and former colonel in the musketeers, or *streltsy*, the Kremlin guard which had earned Peter's utmost suspicion due to the murderous role it performed during the period of his own accession to the throne.

Tsykler was among those who had already taken part in the coup which brought Sofia to power in 1682. He also had a long association with the Miloslavskys. But, in 1689, he had switched his allegiance to side with Peter, even informing him of the renewed plot. He had subsequently been rewarded by being put in charge of the construction work undertaken to secure the harbour at Taganrog. This involved building fortresses at the entrance to the Sea of Azov.

Another of the alleged conspirators, Matvey Stepanovich Pushkin, had been appointed by Peter as Governor of Azov. He was an ancestor of Pushkin, as was his son, Fyodor Pushkin. A third of the alleged conspirators, Aleksey Sokovnin, was Fyodor Pushkin's father-in-law. According to one account, by the Russian historian Bushkovitch: 'The Pushkins' main reason for discontent seem to have been real or imagined threats to the family honour, particularly to the boyar, M S Pushkin'.[7]

True or not, Tsykler, Sokovnin and Pushkin believed themselves passed over and consequently joined the plot against the Tsar. Others have seen the conspiracy as a part of the ongoing struggle between the old conservative nobility, of Moscow, and the reforming Tsar. This time Peter was taking no chances: Ivan Tsykler and his co-conspirators were accused of plotting to murder Peter before he embarked on his Grand Embassy. The alleged plot had involved a plan to burn down the Tsar's house while he was still inside.

During the 'investigation' into the affair – which followed the usual course of extracting confessions from the accused by means of beatings and torture personally supervised by the Tsar – Fyodor Pushkin was accused of having said words to the effect that Peter lived carelessly, not like a Christian, and that there was no God or Christianity in him. Pronounced guilty, Tsykler, Sokovnin, Fyodor Pushkin and two others were executed.

To complete the ignominy, Matvey Pushkin lost his rank of boyar and was exiled to Siberia, and property belonging to the sons of Fyodor Pushkin was confiscated. In a particularly gruesome twist (characteristic of Peter) the body of Ivan Miloslavsky – a participant in the earlier plot of 1682 – was exhumed and placed directly below the execution block, so that the blood of the conspirators would fall upon his corpse. The heads of Tsykler and his accomplices, including Fyodor Pushkin, were put on pikes and exhibited in Red Square.

In the event, Peter's attempt to forge an anti-Ottoman alliance via his Grand Embassy fell on deaf ears. France was a traditional ally of the Ottomans and the other European powers were more concerned to deal with a royal succession crisis in Spain. Nevertheless, the journey taught Peter a great deal – in particular about maritime technology in Western Europe.

He studied shipbuilding in Zaandam and Amsterdam in Holland and was given the chance to gain practical experience in what was then the largest shipyard in the world, owned by the Dutch East India Company. During the final phase of his Embassy, in London, Peter spent four months in the shipyards at Greenwich and Deptford, where, according to the historian Ian Grey: 'He did not sign on as a ship's carpenter…as he had done in the Dutch East India Company yards. But he could never stand watching others work, and a journeyman shipwright employed in the yards at the time commented in later years that 'the Tsar of Muscovy worked with his own hands as hard as any man in the yard'.[8] Today, a suitably quirky statue to Peter the Great – with attendant dwarf, two cannons and a throne – is located on the embankment at Deptford Creek.

Only a few months after the Tsykler affair, Peter was forced to break short his expedition in Europe and return to Moscow because of a renewed uprising involving the *streltsy*. Four regiments had mutinied, pledging to destroy all traitors and foreigners and to restore the 'old order', now being systematically dismantled by Peter's reforming zeal. This time Peter's reprisals were merciless: following a six-month trial, during which Peter determined to root out the underlying motives and identify 'accomplices', a total of 1,182 streltsy were executed in Red Square under his personal supervision and a further 601 were flogged and banished from the capital.

As the historian, Lindsey Hughes, recounts: 'The execution of the streltsy became a symbol of Peter's cruelty and ruthless determination to root out opposition'.[9] Men were broken on the wheel, heads were displayed on poles and their corpses were strung up in front of the windows of the convent where Sofia had been incarcerated. One of Peter's first actions on returning to Moscow to deal with the streltsy is the one for which he is perhaps best remembered: leading boyars and government officials were all ordered to cut off their beards, which he regarded as a symbol of the old ways he was determined to consign to the past.

Although the primary aim of the Embassy had been to instigate an alliance against the Turks, it was on the European tour that Peter first considered the possibility of opening a second front against Sweden – encouraged by his success at Azov. After Peter had won control of Zayachy Island, Kotlin and Schlüsselburg, he was able to consolidate his hold on the east Baltic coast as far south as Riga. Important Russian victories against Swedish armies further south at Lesnaya (1708) and Poltava (1709) finally enabled him to contain the Swedish menace. The decisive victory at Poltava (so nearly a disaster) is commemorated in a famous acclamatory poem by Pushkin.

What is now known as the Great Northern War lasted 21 years, from 1700 to 1721. Russia and Sweden were continuously at war during this period, in an arc which stretched all the way from the Baltic ports down to the Ukraine, Crimea and the Black Sea. The war ended with Sweden's defeat and, as part of the Treaty of Nystad in 1721, most of the Swedish dominions were partitioned between the other powers which at various stages had joined forces with Russia.

The first western biography of Peter the Great, was written by the great French enlightenment *philosophe*, Voltaire. In the preface to his *History of the Russian Empire under Peter the Great*, which was published in two volumes, between 1759 and 1763, Voltaire writes: 'When, at the turn of the present century, Czar Peter was laying the foundations of St Petersburg, or rather of his empire, nobody foresaw a happy outcome. Had anyone in those days imagined that a Russian sovereign would be able to send victorious fleets into the Dardanelles, subjugate the Crimea, expel the Turks from four vast provinces, control the Black Sea, found the most brilliant court in Europe, and make all the arts flourish in the midst of war, he would have been considered a mere visionary'.[10]

A few years later, the writer and historian who preceded both Karamzin and Pushkin as official historiographer of Russia, Prince Mikhail Shcherbatov, was commissioned by Catherine the Great to write a narrative history of Russia, from its origins to the reign of Peter the Great. In 1768 he was given special instructions to arrange and catalogue the Peter the Great Archive – which Pushkin would later examine – and, between 1771 and 1774 he published the *Journal of Peter the Great, Notebooks of Peter the Great* and *The Life and Glorious Deeds of Peter the Great.*

In the book for which he is best known, *On the Corruption of Morals in Russia,* Shcherbatov introduces a more equivocal note to his estimation of Peter the Great's legacy, one which is more akin to the stance adopted by Pushkin in *The Bronze Horseman*: 'Now let us consider what changes were brought about in us by the necessary but, perhaps, excessive reformation wrought by Peter the Great, and how, as a result of it, vices began to creep into our hearts…'.[11]

On the plus side, Shcherbatov concludes: '…through the labours and solicitude of the monarch, Russia acquired fame in Europe and influence in affairs. Her troops were organised in a proper fashion, and her fleets covered the White Sea and the Baltic; with these forces she overcame her old enemies and former conquerors, the Poles and the Swedes, and acquired important provinces and sea ports. Sciences, arts and crafts began to flourish there, trade began to enrich her, and the Russians were transformed – from bearded men to clean-shaven men, from long-robed men to short-coated men; they became more sociable, and polite spectacles became known to them'.[12]

On the other hand: '...at the same time true attachment to the faith began to disappear, sacraments began to fall into disrepute, resoluteness diminished, yielding place to brazen, aspiring flattery; luxury and voluptuousness laid the foundation of their power, and hence avarice was also aroused, and, to the ruin of the laws and the detriment of the citizens, began to penetrate the law courts. Such was the condition with regard to morals, in which Russia was left at the death of this great monarch'.[13]

Notes

1   Opening lines of Медный Всадник. А С Пушкин **The Bronze Horseman,** by Alexander Pushkin, main text in Russian,. edited with introduction, notes, bibliography and vocabulary by Michael Basker, Bristol Classical Press, 2003. Translated by the author.

2   **Karamzin's Memoir on Ancient & Modern Russia,** a translation & analysis, by Richard Pipes, The University of Michigan Press, 2008 (first published 1959).

3   **Pushkin,** by T J Binyon, Harper Collins, 2002 p418

4   **On the Insignificance of Russian Literature'**, from **The Critical Prose of Alexander Pushkin,** edited and translated by Carl R Proffer, Indiana University Press, 1969 p163

5   **Russia in the Age of Peter the Great,** by Lindsey Hughes, Yale University Press, 1998 p408

6   ibid, Hughes, p.409

7   **Peter the Great: The Struggle for Power, 1671-1725**, by Paul Bushkovitch, Cambridge University Press, 2001 p194

8   **Russians in London: Peter the Great'**, blogspot by Sarah J Young, Lecturer in Russian at the University of London, School of Slavonic & East European Studies, quotation from Ian Grey 'Peter the Great in England', *History Today* 6.4 (1956), pp.225-234.

http://sarahjyoung.com/site/2010/11/23/russians-in-london-peter-the-great

9   op cit, Hughes, p.454

10   **Russia under Peter the Great,** by Voltaire. Translated by M F O Jenkins. Fairleigh Dickinson University Press. 1983 (first published in two parts, as The History of the Russian Empire under Peter the Great. Part One in 1759 and Part Two in 1763)

11   **On the Corruption of Morals in Russia**, by Prince M M Shcherbatov, edited and translated, with an introduction and notes, by A Lentin. Cambridge at the University Press, 1969 p135

12   ibid, Shcherbatov, p157

13   ibid, Shcherbatov, p157

*Among those young men sent abroad by Peter the Great for the
acquisition of knowledge essential to a country in the process of
reorganisation was his godson, the Moor Ibrahim'.*

Pushkin, *The Moor of Peter the Great,* 1828[1]

03 | The Moor of Peter the Great

Throughout the period of the Great Northern War, Pushkin's
great-great-grandfather, Abraham Hannibal, accompanied
Peter the Great as his personal aide-de-camp. By the end of this
conflict, the Swedish empire had been crushed and subsequently
lost its supremacy in the region. By contrast, Russia had been
transformed into one of the most powerful states in Europe. The
fact that one of Pushkin's grandparents had accompanied Peter
the Great during such a decisive period in Russian history and
had been born the son of an African prince, was a source of
enormous pride for Pushkin. He wrote a partially completed
novel about Hannibal's remarkable life, usually translated into
English as *The Moor of Peter the Great* and included a lengthy
note about his black ancestry in Part One of the first edition of
what is probably his best known work outside of Russia – his
'novel in verse', *Evgeny Onegin.*

The note which appears in *Evgeny Onegin* refers to a passage in
which Pushkin dreamily imagines that the 'hour of my freedom'
will arise when he is able to leave 'this dismal shore' and escape
an environment which, he says, is 'inimical to me'. Instead he
will begin a new course 'under the sky of my Africa' where he
can sigh for 'dreary Russia – where I suffered, where I loved,
where my heart is buried'.[2]

Pushkin's explaining his African ancestry is almost entirely
based on his uncle Pyotr's 'German biography' which is a
manuscript of about 4,000 words. A copy of it is kept at the

Lenin Library in Moscow. The 'biography' consists of a batch of sheets taken from Pushkin's library by police after his death, then sewn together to form a book. Pushkin's synopsis of the biography reads as follows:

'The author, on his mother's side, is of African descent. His great-grandfather, Ibrahim Petrovich Annibal, in his eighth year was kidnapped on the coast of Africa and brought to Constantinople. The Russian envoy, having rescued him, sent him as a gift to Peter the Great, who had him baptised in Vilno. In his wake, his brother arrived, first in Constantinople, and then in St Petersburg, with the offer to ransom him; but Peter I did not consent to return his godchild. Up to an advanced age, Annibal still remembered Africa, the luxurious life of his father and nineteen brothers of whom he was the youngest; he remembered how they used to be led into his father's presence with their hands bound behind their backs, whilst he alone remained free and went swimming under the fountains of the paternal home; he also remembered his beloved sister, Lagan, swimming in the distance, after the ship in which he was receding.

At eighteen, Annibal was sent by the Tsar to France, where he began his military service in the army of the regent; he returned to Russia with a slashed head and the rank of French lieutenant. Thenceforth he remained continually near the person of the Tsar. In the reign of Anna, Annibal, a personal enemy of Bühren, was dispatched, under a specious pretext, to Siberia. Getting bored with an unpeopled place and a harsh climate, he returned to St Petersburg of his own accord and appeared before his friend, Münnich. Münnich was amazed and advised him to go into hiding without delay. Annibal returned to his country estates and dwelled there throughout the reign of Anna, while nominally serving in Siberia.

When Elizabeth ascended the throne, she lavished favours upon him. A P Hannibal lived to see the reign of Catherine II, when, relieved of important duties of office, he ended his days with the rank of general-in-chief, dying in his ninety-second year'.[3] (Note: *Bühren and Münnich were rivals for the attentions of the Empress Anna of Russia*).

In a footnote to this cameo, Pushkin announced his intention to publish in due time his complete biography of Hannibal. He began work on this project in the summer of 1827 and had intended to write a historical novel based on Ibrahim Hannibal's life story. By the spring of 1828 he had completed some drafts but the novel remained unfinished. Its opening passages deal mainly with Hannibal's years in Paris and give a lively description of French high society at the beginning of the 18th century. The main dramatic intrigue emerges when Peter the Great's protégé becomes involved with a French countess: when the countess becomes pregnant and her baby is clearly black, a major scandal is only averted when the black baby is swiftly switched for a white one before her husband finds out.

Only two fragments of this novel were published during Pushkin's lifetime, in the *Northern Star* (1829) and the *Literary Gazette* (1830). The book remained unfinished and the full text was first published after Pushkin's death in 1837 by the editors of *The Contemporary*, a quarterly literary journal which had been founded by Pushkin the previous year. The title they gave Pushkin's novel, in Russian, was *Arap Petrovo Velikovo*. Although the Russian word *Arap* is essentially the same as the English (and Turkish) word Arab, in all the published translations into English, the main character, Ibrahim, is either described as a Moor, Blackamoor, or Negro.

For a while it was believed that Pushkin was descended from an 'Abyssinian'. The legend within the Pushkin family was that his great-great-grandfather, Ibrahim Hannibal, had been an Abyssinian Prince. The late 19th century journalist, Dmitri Anuchin, set out to prove this thesis scientifically, but – as Hugh Barnes points out in his biography of Hannibal – Anuchin had merely succumbed to the then fashionable racist theories: "which distinguished northern Hamitic peoples, such as the Ethiopians, from the 'backward' negroes of sub-Saharan Africa, contrasting the supposedly superior craniology of 'Nilotic' types with the prognathism (*protruding jaw*) and facial angle of 'pure Negroes'".[4]

The entire, racist assumption behind this 'anthropological' explanation for Pushkin's origins was that, since Pushkin was clearly a genius, he could not possibly have also been a negro, because negroes were then regarded by European supremacists as one of the 'lower races' of man.

As Barnes wryly comments, it is an interesting irony that the 18th century German naturalist who first came up with the term Caucasian for white people did so because he thought the Caucasus mountains in the south of Russia produced 'a most beautiful race of men'. Nowadays, by contrast: 'most ordinary Russians take a xenophobic view of the dark-complexioned Muslim peoples of Chechnya and the other north Caucasus republics. Indeed, they are known disparagingly as the *chorniye,* or blacks, of Russia'.[5]

Doubts were first cast on the Abyssinian thesis by the great Russian-American novelist, Vladimir Nabokov, while conducting research for his translation of Pushkin's *Eugene Onegin.* As part of the commentary, Nabokov includes two appendices, the first of which is his '*Notes on Prosody*', a lofty treatise on poetic metres and versification. The second of these appendices is entitled *Ibrahim Hannibal.* This examines the available evidence on the life of Pushkin's ancestor, including the German biography, in forensic detail. Explaining his effort, Nabokov says, with characteristic false modesty: 'It is the outcome of a few odd moments spent in the admirable libraries of Cornell and Harvard universities, and its purpose is mainly to draw attention to the riddles that other workers have either ignored or answered wrongly'.[6]

Nabokov's 'note' on Ibrahim Hannibal runs to over 50 pages and contains some fascinating information but does little to resolve many of the 'riddles' encountered by other workers. This is because, for all his doubts, he persists with the assumption, first specified in the German biography, that Pushkin's forebear must have come from Abyssinia. Even though, as he rightly points out: '...in the 1690s, the period referred to here, no Abyssinian was a vassal of the Ottoman Porte and no Abyssinian prince could have been a Moslem or could have been forced to send any tribute to Constantinople'.[7]

Apart from the German biography, the other primary source of information on Ibrahim Hannibal's birthplace is a petition he himself addressed to the Empress Elizabeth (Peter the Great's daughter) in 1742, applying for a nobleman's diploma and heraldic arms. In this, Hannibal states that he was born on his father's lands 'in the town of Lagone'.

After much sifting about through antique maps of Africa and

the writings of various European travellers to identify the precise location of this town – a search which takes up roughly half of his 'note' and puzzles over every conceivable option of an Abyssinian town or village beginning with the letter 'L' – Nabokov is drawn to this wearied conclusion: 'I am inclined to assume that it was situated in the general region of Northern Abyssinia, where we have been following, through the bibliographic dust, the mules and camels of several adventurous caravans'.[8]

In the conclusion to his note, he is even more adamant: 'It would be a waste of time to conjecture that Ibrahim was not born in Abyssinia at all; that he had been captured by slave traders in a totally different place – say the Lagona region of equatorial Africa, south of Lake Chad, inhabited by Mussulman Negroes; or that he was, as Helbig (1809) affirms, a homeless little Mohr, acquired in Holland by Peter I to serve as a ship's boy'.[9]

As the more recent work conducted both by the Hannibal biographer, Hugh Barnes, and Beninese scholar, Dieudonne Gnammankou, has shown, the Lagona region of equatorial Africa is indeed the more likely location for Hannibal's birthplace. And, if this is correct, it goes a long way to explaining many of the 'riddles' encountered by previous researchers. It concludes that Pushkin's great-great-grandfather was more likely to have been the son of a Central African Sultan, and therefore a Moslem, rather than an Abyssinian Prince. That explains why Hannibal was born as Ibrahim, not Abram, Avram or Abraham.

The evidence suggests that Pushkin's great-great-grandfather was most likely to have been abducted by slave traders from his home in Logone-Birni, a fortified city in Central Africa. It lies on the banks of the River Logone, in an area which is on the border between present-day Chad and Cameroon. Logone was the capital of an African principality of the same name. At the end of the 17th century and the beginning of the 18th, the ruling prince of Logone was the Sultan Brouha. Pushkin's ancestor would have been one of the Sultan's sons, thus confirming that he had been born an African prince – but in a different part of Africa. The boy who later became Abrahim Hannibal was born here between 1690 and 1696.

When the great German explorer, Heinrich Barth, travelled to Logone in the 1850s, he described the Sultan's palace at

Logone-Birni as 'a vast building surrounded by a 14-foot high wall and, to my amazement, I saw two iron cannons in the first courtyard. We were led through a series of long and scrupulously clean courtyards to the audience chamber containing the royal throne…'.[10] Logone's neighbouring sultanates, Bornu and Bagirmi, both had commercial links with the Ottoman Empire and at the time Bornu was the world's fourth most powerful Islamic state. Bornu: 'sold gold, perfumes, leather goods and slaves in exchange for firearms, paper, European imports and even from time to time European slaves. The Sultanate of Bagirmi exported numerous slaves and eunuchs to North Africa, then under Ottoman rule, and Turkey'.[11]

Bornu was also an important source of ivory. In the 17th and 18th centuries, many of the Moslem states of the central Sudan region were involved in the trade of domestic slaves for the royal palaces of the Arab world and the Ottoman Empire, at much the same time as the Christian states of Northern Europe were plundering the coastal regions of Africa in search of slave labour for their plantations in the Caribbean and the Southern States of America.

Throughout Ibrahim Hannibal's childhood, the principality of Logone came under frequent attack from the rival sultanates. Ibrahim would have been among the city's inhabitants who were captured during one of these raids, which took place in 1703. The hostages taken were then sold as slaves to the Ottoman Turks. Ibrahim was eight years old when he was taken from Africa to Constantinople by either Arab, Berber or Persian slave traders who operated a long-distance trade taking their sub-Saharan captives by camel across the desert to the Islamic world.

In a letter he wrote from Odessa in 1824, Pushkin described the Islamic slave route to Constantinople via the Caucasus as 'Turkish slavery'. The Constantinople that the boy arrived in was notorious as a nest of spies, corruption and diplomatic intrigue. In 1703, it was also a time of both internal and external threats: social unrest, economic crisis and a series of revolts convulsed the city. Most often these rebellions were led by the Sultan's own bodyguard, the Janissaries. This armed militia consisted mainly of young men captured as slaves in the Ottoman territories of the Balkans and then trained to protect the Sultan, but – like the

Russian *streltsy* – always liable to rebel against their overlords.

At the time of Ibrahim's capture, the Ottoman Empire controlled the Black Sea and, from it, access to the Mediterranean through the Dardanelles. But Russia, under its new Tsar, Peter the Great, already had designs on the region. To begin with, he was determined to secure Muscovy's southern borders against the threat of constant raids by Crimean Tartars, backed by the Ottoman Empire. Longer term, Peter was equally intent on establishing a foothold on the Black Sea.

Even though the Russians and the Ottomans had just agreed a 30-year truce in hostilities in 1700 – allowing the Russians to concentrate their attentions on Sweden – the Tsar looked to his agents in Constantinople to stir up trouble at every opportunity. His foreign minister and spymaster, Count Feodor Golovin, entrusted the Russian ambassador to Constantinople, Count Pyotr Tolstoy, with the task of gathering as much information as possible about the internal politics of the regime.

Tolstoy was instructed: 'to provide Moscow with analysis of the viziers of power and those most likely to come into power, while also learning what he could about Turkish military and naval tactics and the strength of their fortresses on the Black Sea'.[12] An accomplished intriguer, Tolstoy (an ancestor of the novelist, Leo Tolstoy) had been informed of a dispute between the sultan's daughters and 'was looking for a mole, a source of intelligence and a way of damaging Russia's rivals'.[13]

For this task, Tolstoy employed the assistance of a Black Sea trader – the Croatian, Savva Vladislavich-Raguzinsky – to spy on the Ottomans in the guise as an ordinary merchant. Raguzinsky spoke Turkish, Greek, Albanian, Romanian, French and Russian as well as some Arabic; he also shared a mother tongue – Serbo-Croat – with the Ottoman Court honour guard, the Janissaries, and with the other 'slaves of the Sultan' who had control of the government apparatus.

Tolstoy had also taken the precaution of paying bribes to a particularly corrupt member of the Ottoman bureaucracy who had his own reasons to take revenge on the sultan. This was a Russian-born member of the powerful Koprülu dynasty, called Kavanoz Ahmed Pasha, otherwise known as Koprülu the Corrupt. During the year before Ibrahim Hannibal's arrival in Constantinople, the royal palace was already buzzing with intrigue.

The chief black eunuch of the city, who was one of the most powerful men in the Ottoman Empire, had successfully plotted the overthrow of the Grand Vizier, who happened to be Koprülu the Corrupt's father-in-law. The chief eunuch controlled access to the Sultan by policing his harem and it was in this strategically important inner sanctum that Ibrahim was taken on as a page boy.

Ibrahim was one of several African page boys sent to the harem and, like the others, would have studied Arabic and Persian. It so happened that he was employed at the Topkapi Palace at exactly the same time as the Sultan Mustapha was overthrown by an uprising of the Janissaries. A civil war broke out in the capital, during which Tolstoy's placeman, Koprülu, sensed his opportunity to turn the tables on his opponents. He stoked the rebellion against the Sultan who was immediately replaced by his younger brother. This put Koprülu in an extremely powerful position and it also came as a godsend for Tolstoy, who had struggled to establish a network of informers. Now his priming of Koprülu provided him with the perfect conduit for top-level intelligence on Ottoman plans.

It was at this point that Tolstoy began to plot the abduction of Ibrahim from the Ottoman *seraglio*. In a letter he sent to the Tsar, Ibrahim was described as one of several 'talented African negroes' well-positioned to conduct spying inside the harem. The escape plan was almost immediately foiled when the new Sultan decided that he might be safer without any treacherous rebels inside his court – the chief of police, who had taken part in the uprising against his brother, was thrown into the sea and Koprülu was exiled to Lepanto.

Hearing about the young spies, Peter the Great wrote to Tolstoy with a request that he should try to engineer their escape and send them to Moscow. This was accomplished, with the assistance of the Grand Vizier, and in the summer of 1704, Ibrahim was smuggled out of the harem by Raguzinsky at the start of a journey which took three months, from Constantinople to Moscow, via the Balkans and Bucharest.

In a letter informing the Russian foreign ministry in Moscow of his success, Raguzinsky wrote that there would be 'something extra' in his next delivery of cotton: 'With it there will also be two Negro boys as promised…believe me, my friend, it was a very difficult business to get hold of them and smuggle them out of Turkey'.[14] Hannibal himself later described what had happened, in his petition to the Empress Elizabeth, as follows: 'I left Tsargrad for Russia in the suite of Sava Vladislavich of my own accord at a young age and was brought to Moscow at the house of the Tsar Peter the Great of blissful and eternal memory'.[15]

What happened next in the extraordinary tale of the young Ibrahim is taken up by Pushkin's Lycée French master, Mr Thomas B Shaw. In 1845, he had two articles about Pushkin published in successive issues of *Blackwood's Edinburgh Magazine,* in which he writes that: 'his subsequent career was one of the most romantic that can be imagined. The wonderful Tsar gave his sable protégé, whose name was Annibal, a good education, and admitted him to the marine service of the empire – a service in which he reached (in the reign of Catherine) the rank of admiral. He…died after a long and distinguished career of service having founded, in his new country, the family of Annibalov, of which Pushkin was the most distinguished ornament and of whose origin the poet, both in personal appearance and in mental physiognomy, bore the most unequivocal marks. To the memory of this single progenitor, Pushkin has consecrated more than one of his smaller works, and has frequently alluded to African blood which he inherited from the admiral'.[16]

Ibrahim arrived in Moscow towards the end of 1704. He was first introduced to the Tsar inside the Kremlin on Christmas Day. Peter the Great had just arrived back in Moscow the previous week following his historic victory against Sweden, at a second attempt, in the Battle of Narva. A great ceremony took place on Red Square during which 54 enemy battle flags and around 200 captured Swedish officers were paraded before an immense crowd to much fanfare. Soon after, Ibrahim was adopted as Peter the Great's godson and christened as Pyotr Petrovich Petrov. He was granted permission later to retain the forename he was born with, but in its Christianised form, Abraham. The boy first travelled in the Tsar's entourage from Moscow to Polotsk in the north of the country. It was here that he was baptised as Peter's godson, in the Parakseva church in Vilnius, in July 1705.

At first, he was taken on as a drummer boy in the Tsar's own Preobrazhensky Regiment and took part in the Russian victories over Sweden at Dobroye and Lesnaya, in 1708. In a depiction of the Battle of Lesnaya by the French engraver, Nicolas de Larmessin, the black drummer boy of the regiment can clearly be seen, wearing a white turban. The following year, Abraham was present at one of the most famous battles in Russian military history, the Battle of Poltava, where the Swedish forces were annihilated. Charles XII was forced to flee to safety in Turkey and seek the protection of the Ottomans. Hannibal was also present at the sea Battle of Hangö which took place in the Baltic in 1714. This was the victory which effectively gave the newly built Russian fleet control over the Baltic.

Throughout this period, Hannibal was attached to the Tsar's personal entourage and often slept in the same room as the Tsar. One of the boy's attributes, much appreciated by the Tsar, was that he slept lightly: 'It was a quality that the Tsar required of his close associates. Peter's brain did not rest while he was asleep. He used to wake up regularly to jot down on paper all the ideas that came to him…It was essential for him to have a night secretary to make accurate notes of all his thoughts…Ibrahim therefore had the dual role of aide and night secretary to the Tsar.[17].

In 1716, Hannibal took part in Peter the Great's Embassy to Western Europe, the main aim of which was to conduct research and gain invaluable information on the advances in science and industry developed by the two great mercantile nations of the time, the Dutch and the English. The journey included extensive time spent in the shipyards of Amsterdam and London. The following year, Hannibal was sent to France, at the Tsar's expense, to study artillery and engineering under the duc de Maine, Louis XIV's illegitimate son and Grand Master of the Artillery in the military academy at La Fère. On his return from France, six years later, Hannibal became personal secretary to the Tsar. He was put in charge of the library and technical drawings and worked as a consultant engineer. Trained as an expert in siege engineering, in 1724 he was accorded the title of Lieutenant in the Company of Bombardiers in the Engineering Corps of the Preobrazhensky Regiment. Later, he was put in charge of the construction of the fortress at Kronstadt and on both the Kronstadt and the Ladoga Canals.

Eventually, as Major General Ibrahim Hannibal, he was appointed Head of Technical Management in the Russian Imperial Army, with responsibility for the supervision of work on fortifications throughout the empire. Hannibal was one of many newly qualified young Russians now returning from Europe, having acquired new skills as carpenters, engravers, sailors, fitters, setters, blacksmiths and the like. As the Hannibal biographer, Dieudonné Gnammankou explains: 'This method of integrating the newly qualified experts and craftsmen into Russian society had spectacular results. In a few years, the Russian navy, which had not even existed at the beginning of Peter's reign, was the envy of Europe'.[18]

Hannibal lived to the age of 85 and served under a total of seven 18th century Tsars and Tsarinas: Peter I, Peter the Great (1682-1725); Catherine I (1725-27); Peter II (1728-1730); Anne (1730-1740); Elizabeth (1740-1761); Peter III (1761-1762); and Catherine II, Catherine the Great (1762-1796). By the time he retired from the Directorship of the Engineering Corps, in 1762, he owned two large estates – one at Suyda, outside St Petersburg, where he died in April 1781; the other was at Mikhailovskoye, close to the ancient city of Pskov.

The family estate gifted to Hannibal at Mikhailovskoye is where Pushkin was sent by Tsar Alexander I to spend his second period of enforced exile, which began in 1824. During this time, he wrote the first part of his novel in verse, *Eugene Onegin* and his play *Boris Godunov*. It was also at Mikhailovskoye where Pushkin learned most about his black ancestry from the family records kept by his great-uncle, Pyotr.

In a letter he wrote in August 1825 to his close friend, Praskoviya Osipovo, who lived on a neighbouring estate, Pushkin said: 'I plan to look up my old Negro great-uncle who, I suspect, will die one of these days: I am anxious to obtain from him certain memoirs regarding my great-grandfather'.[19] In the family archive, Pushkin's uncle Pyotr recorded that: 'My father …was a Negro'.[20]

The German historian, H von Helbig, was the primary source of the Pushkin family legend contained in the family's 'German biography'. According to Helbig, Pushkin's great-grandfather was: 'the son of a local ruler, powerful and rich, who traced his descent in a direct line from the house of the famed Hannibal, the terror of Rome'.[21]

Helbig had been the first to offer up the theory that Ibrahim Hannibal came to be in the service of the Tsar after he had been acquired from the skipper of a Dutch vessel in the Russian naval base at Kronstadt 'to serve as a ship's boy'. This false assertion was later used by Pushkin's contemporary and tormentor, Fadey Bulgarin, to justify a nasty, racist attack on Pushkin's ancestry published in Bulgarin's journal, *The Northern Bee*, in August 1830. According to Pushkin's former Lyceé schoolmaster, J Thomas Shaw, Bulgarin was 'the most unsavoury figure in 19th century literary life' and his attack on Pushkin was: 'perhaps the most unsavoury attack of all'.[22] As an agent for the Imperial Secret Police, and cheerleader for the ultra-orthodox policies of Tsar Nicholas I, Bulgarin could count on state protection for his writings. His scurrilous assault on Pushkin, lampooning those 'poets and rhymesters' who, he says 'have taken to emulating Byron', reads as follows:

'Byron's lordship and aristocratic capers, combined with God knows what way of thinking, have driven to frenzy a multitude of poets and rhymesters in various countries: all of them have started talking about their six-hundred-year-old nobility! It is openly related that some poet or other in Spanish America, likewise an imitator of Byron, being of mulatto descent on his father's or (I do not quite remember) his mother's side, began to affirm that one of his ancestors was a Negro prince. A search of the town hall's archives disclosed that in the past there had been a lawsuit between a skipper and his mate on account of that Negro, and that the skipper maintained he had acquired the Negro for a bottle of rum'.[23]

Bulgarin's transparent mockery of Pushkin's ancestry ignited a simmering feud which was to blight the final years of Pushkin's life. The first public manifestation of this was the anonymous attack on Pushkin in the *Northern Bee*. This drew a withering response from Pushkin. It came in the form of a caricature of Bulgarin disguised as Vidocq, a notorious French police spy.

According to Pushkin biographer, Tatiana Wolff, the effect of this 'extra-large cannon-ball' was that the name Vidocq was to stick to Bulgarin 'like a burr'.[24] Pushkin's broadside was published in *Literaturnaya Gazeta*, the newspaper which Pushkin and his close friend and former classmate at the Imperial Lycée, Anton Delvig, had finally won permission to publish, in January 1830, providing its content was kept strictly non-political.

Pushkin's supposedly non-political lampoon of Bulgarin was published, unsigned, in the *Miscellany* section of *Literaturnaya Gazeta*. Pushkin's inner circle all contributed to this new outlet for Pushkin's talents. This group included the poets Pyotr Vyazemsky, who was soon to become Pushkin's best man in his marriage to Natalia Goncharova, as well as Zhukovsky and Baratynsky. Pushkin and Delvig both saw the *Literaturnaya Gazeta*: 'as a platform for attacks both against their old enemies, Bulgarin and Grech, entrenched in the *Northern Bee*, and against the new men who were ever more vociferously expressing resentment at the aristocratic detachment of Pushkin's circle'.[25] Pushkin and his friends 'would prove they had a fight in them' and it was in this context that hostilities with Bulgarin had erupted.

Bulgarin had been born into the Polish nobility and his father had been exiled to Siberia for having assassinated a Russian general during the Polish uprising of 1794. He had managed to fight on both sides during the Napoleonic Wars: after being trained at the St Petersburg military school, Bulgarin fought first in the Russian army but, after being arrested for theft, deserted to join Napoleon's Grande Armeé. He then fought on the side of the French in the Lithuanian campaign of 1812 before being captured and transported to Prussia.

When he next resurfaced in St Petersburg, in 1820, he initially identified with the liberal intelligentsia. The liberal playwright, Griboyedov, was among his acquaintances and Bulgarin wrote for the periodical *Son of the Fatherland* which was edited by the Russian philologist, Nikolay Gretsch. After the Decembrist Revolt had been crushed, both Bulgarin and Gretsch immediately switched their allegiance to become outright apologists for the reactionary policies of the new Tsar, Nicholas I.

At the time Bulgarin wrote his attack on Pushkin, in 1830, he was employed as an agent of the Imperial Secret Police and as a political informer in the service of the state censor,

Alexander Benckendorff – who, in turn, reported directly to the Tsar. According to memoirs written later by Bulgarin's associate, Nikolay Gretsch, he first heard the story of Pushkin's ancestor Hannibal having been sold by a ship's captain 'for a bottle of rum' when it was recounted by Count Sergei Uvarov. Like Bulgarin, Uvarov was highly rated by the Tsar. Nicholas appointed him Minister of Education, with a remit to neutralise the threat of 'foreign ideas' and 'pseudo-knowledge'.

Uvarov was also the person who coined the phrase 'Orthodoxy, Autocracy and Nationality'. This was the official, ultra-conservative doctrine of Official Nationality adopted by Nicholas in direct and diametrical opposition to the French revolution slogans of 'Liberty, Equality and Fraternity'. During Uvarov's time in office, students whose background was not from the nobility were denied access to education, university departments were put under strict government surveillance to identify potential trouble-makers and Uvarov's self-proclaimed mission was to ensure that there would be 'No University Pugachevs' – a reference to the armed rebellion which came perilously close to toppling Nicholas's grandmother, Catherine the Great.

On the advice of some of his closest friends, Pushkin half-heartedly refrained from dignifying Bulgarin's attack with a direct public response, even though it was what the Pushkinologist, Catherine Nepomnyaschy, describes as 'certainly the most notorious, public, racially-charged, journalistic attack on the poet during his lifetime'.[26]

Instead, he composed a poem entitled *My Genealogy*, which combines a rigorous defence of Pushkin's ancestry on both sides of his family, with satirical digs at Bulgarin's own lineage and a few oblique references to the longevity of the Pushkins in Russian history as compared to the Bulgarins, or the Romanovs. This riposte was circulated unofficially but, hardly surprisingly, was not passed for publication either by Benckendorff or by the Tsar.

When Pushkin rashly sent a copy to the Tsar, against Anton Delvig's advice, Nicholas feigned agreement with Delvig and proclaimed that 'such mean and base insults' that had been heaped upon Pushkin: 'dishonour not the one to whom they refer but the one who pronounces them. The only weapon against them is scorn. That's how I would react in his place'.

In Pushkin's poem, Nicholas opined: 'I find wit but even more bile. For the honour of his pen and especially for the honour of his reason, it would be best not to disseminate it'.[27] A more likely explanation for the Tsar's reluctance to see Pushkin's poem in print is less to do with the tenor of Pushkin's response to Bulgarin and more that it begins with an exceptionally well documented account of the Pushkin lineage.

The Pushkin name is cited 21 times in Nikolay Karamzin's monumental *History of the Russian State*. Descendants of Pushkin were around as early as the 12th century (not the 13th, as Pushkin believed) and no less than four Pushkins were in attendance as signatories to the 1613 charter which installed the first Romanov Tsar, Mikhail Fedorovich.

At a time when Pushkin's adversaries – which included the Tsar – were on a mission to bring him down a peg or two, this very timely reminder of the Pushkins' noble credentials was not at all welcome: 'the 'nobility around the throne never forgave him for the first part of the poem, in which he ironically calls himself a descendant of boyars, a 'bourgeois', in contrast to the 'new high nobility' – descendants of cooks, flunkies, foreign renegades, and adventurers. Much of the pain and difficulty of Pushkin's final years can be attributed to this poem – to what provoked it and to Pushkin's response'.[28]

Pushkin most effectively skewers Bulgarin in his 'postscript' to the poem *My Genealogy*. To begin with, he refers to him as *Figliarin*, a nickname coined by Pushkin's friend, Vyazemsky, and derived from the Polish word, *figliar*, which is a kind of spinning top but also means clown or idiot. There is, however, another, more derogatory, meaning: '…the first three letters of the name Pushkin has chosen, or concocted, for his adversary derived from the Russian borrowing *fig*, or *figa*, which is defined in Russian dictionaries as an obscene gesture meaning a clenched fist with a thumb thrust between the closed index and middle fingers' and indicating 'a contemptibly worthless trifle'[29]. Combined with the Russian verb *pokazat*, it means 'to give the fig', and can also mean to be 'not worth a fig', or, to give it an earthier slant (to which Pushkin was not averse): 'up yours' or 'fuck you'.

To cap it all, the *-in* ending in Bulgarin never appears in the

Polish language, but does in the Russian – as in Pushkin, Gagarin, Lenin, Stalin, and Putin. In Russian, the surname Bulgarin would be taken to mean Bulgarian, making Fadey Bulgarin's allusion to some sort of indigenous superiority over Pushkin and Hannibal look increasingly threadbare. The five stanzas of Pushkin's *post scriptum* to *My Genealogy*, read as follows:

Sitting at home, Figliarin thought
That my black grandad, Hannibal
For a jug of rum had been bought
And into the hands of a skipper then fell

But this was the skipper, who, by sheer force
Had once more made our country great
And set upon a powerful course
The rudder of our ship of state

This skipper was my grandfather's friend
Till the (cheap at the price) moor, no knave
Grew up steadfast, upright to the end
The Tsar's trusted confidant, no slave

And he became as a father to Hannibal
Who, in the depths of Chesma Bay, saw revealed
A mass of ships swept up in a fireball
When the fate of Navarin was then first sealed

And so, inspired, Figliarin thought
I'm only a bourgeois among the nobility
But what about him, what's his family got?
Him? He's among the nobility of Meshchansky Street! [30]

As Catherine Nepomnyaschy notes, the 'skipper' Pushkin refers to here was none other than Peter the Great. More important, she argues: '…the issue here is clearly not Gannibal's blackness, which is only tangentially referred to in the original attack, but the slur on Gannibal's social status', which is why, in the next stanza he emphasises the esteem in which Hannibal was held by the Tsar, Peter I. This line also helps to underline the fact that Hannibal was 'The Tsar's trusted confidant, no slave', in total contrast to Bulgarin's utterly servile relationship with the living Tsar, Nicholas I. [31]

The historical references on the second to last stanza of this postscript are to the siege of the Turkish fort at Navarin and the Battle of Chesma, one of the greatest victories in the history of the Russian navy. Pushkin's final dig appears in the final line of his postscript, where he is ridiculing the fact that Bulgarin, for all his lofty ambitions, lives in Meshchansky Street, once a respectable address for the Moscow bourgeoisie but by 1830 a renowned red-light district, where Bulgarin first met his wife, working as a prostitute in one of its brothels.

In the conclusion to his extensive 'note' investigating Pushkin's ancestry, Vladimir Nabokov writes, somewhat dismissively, that, although Pushkin saw Hannibal as a Negro with 'African Passions' and an independent, brilliant personality, actually:

'Pyotr Petrovich Petrov, alias Abram Gannibal, was a sour, grovelling, crotchety, timid, ambitious, and cruel person: a good military engineer, perhaps, but humanistically a nonentity; differing in nothing from a typical career-minded, superficially educated, coarse, wife-flogging Russian of his day, in a brutal and dull world of political intrigue, favouritism, German regimentation, old-fashioned Russian misery, and fat-breasted empresses on despicable thrones'.[32]

Even if all this were true – and it is more than likely that Hannibal was no angel – it entirely misses the point that Hannibal's remarkable career, and his blackness, were both a source of enormous pride for Pushkin and for his uncle Pyotr. Pushkin was a black poet and he was proud of his blackness. But, like Shakespeare's *Othello,* that was an undeniable fact which would have consequences.

Throughout his life, Pushkin used a bronze inkstand in the shape of a young black man leaning on an anchor, to remind him of his black ancestry and to defiantly 'give the fig' to his detractors. The inkwell was a gift from his friend, Pavel Nashchokin, who knew all about Bulgarin's vendetta against Pushkin. In a solidarity note he sent with the gift, Nashchokin wrote: 'I am sending you your ancestor with inkwells that open and reveal him to be a far-sighted person'.[33] Pushkin's African ancestry was an inspiration not only for Pushkin's own sense of identity but also for subsequent generations of black writers and artists. As early as 1847, only a decade after his death, Pushkin was already being elevated to the status of 'black icon' by the

American abolitionist, John Greenleaf Whittier.

In the great man and great woman school of black history, the movement known as *'The Negro can be Elevated'*, Pushkin was depicted as a beacon of hope and shining star in the long dark night of slavery and a 'noble specimen' of Negro achievement.[34]

A century later, Pushkin again held an iconic status for those involved in the Harlem Renaissance, which first emerged in what, by the 1920s, had become the predominantly African-American quarter of Harlem in New York. The intellectual champions of this movement were writers and activists such as Langston Hughes, Paul Robeson, James Weldon Johnson, Claude McKay, Richard Wright, W E B DuBois, Marcus Garvey and, later, James Baldwin. When W E B DuBois was asked to produce an entry for what turned out to be his ill-fated *Encyclopaedia of the Negro,* he chose *'Alexander Pushkin'* for the title of his article.

More recently, the American saxophonist, David Murray, who lives in Paris, wrote what he described as 'a form of jazz opera' entitled *The Blackamoor of Peter the Great* in honour of Pushkin. David Murray's composition was performed, to ecstatic reviews, in two concerts at the Museé de la Culture in Bobigny, in March 2005.

For this production, David Murray collaborated with a Cameroonian film-maker, Blaise N'djehoya, who had written an article on Pushkin for a special edition of the 1999 Pan-African literary journal *Présence Africaine* commemorating the 200th anniversary of Pushkin's birth.

Using quotations from works by Pushkin, including *Ode to Liberty, My Genealogy* and *Eugene Onegin,* Murray's ensemble included actors and musicians from the USA, Russia, France, Cameroon and Angola. The concert was performed in Bantu, English, French and Russian. Explaining the rationale behind his work, David Murray wrote:

'It's difficult not to spot the likeness between the author of *'Boris Godunov'* and Alexander Dumas, who was also of mixed race and figured as a crucial reference for African-American avant-garde writers for a long time. Dumas was knocked off his pedestal by Pushkin by the time the Harlem Renaissance came around. In the hearts and minds of Claude McKay, W E B Dubois, Paul Robeson, Langston Hughes, Richard Wright, and others, Pushkin was the one in whom they could project their desire for freedom, for the freedom to create'.[35]

Notes

1   **The Moor of Peter the Great**, by Alexander Pushkin, included in the Complete Prose Tales of Alexander Sergeyevitch Pushkin, translated from the Russian by Gillon R Aitken, Vintage, 1993 (first published 1966) p3

2   **Eugene Onegin: A Novel in Verse.** by A S Pushkin, translated with an introduction and notes by Stanley Mitchell, Penguin Books, 2008, Chapter 1, Stanza 50 p28

3   **Notes on Prosody & Abram Gannibal,** by Vladimir Nabokov, from the commentary to the author's translation of Pushkin's Eugene Onegin, Bollingen Series, Princeton University Press, 1964 p109

4   **Gannibal: The Moor of Petersburg,** by Hugh Barnes, Profile Books, 2005 p36

5   Ibid. p27

6   op cit, Nabokov, p108

7   op cit, Nabokov, p118

8   op cit, Nabokov, p121

9   op cit, Nabokov, 125

10   **Abraham Hanibal, Prince of Logone: Pushkin's African Ancestor,** by Dieudonne Gnammankou, translated from the French by Edyth Watt, Books of Africa, 2015 (first published in French in 1999)

11   ibid, Gnammankou. p23

12   op cit, Barnes, p64

13   op cit, Barnes, p64

14   op cit, Barnes, p81

15   op cit, Nabokov, p140

16   **Pushkin, the Russian Poet: Sketch of Pushkin's Life and Works** by Thomas B Shaw, Adjunct Professor of English Literature at the Imperial Alexander Lyceum, The Project Gutenberg EBook of Blackwood's Edinburgh magazine. No. 1: Volume 57, No. 356. June 1845. *www.gutenberg.org*

17   op cit, Gnammankou, p57

18   op cit, Gnammankou, p81

19   Letter from Pushkin to Praskoviya Osipova, August 1825, from **The Letters of Alexander Pushkin.** Three Volumes in One. Translated and with an Introduction by J Thomas Shaw. University of Wisconsin Press. 1967. P.241

20   op cit, Nabokov, p117

21   op cit, Nabokov, p117

22   **Under the Sky of My Africa,: Alexander Pushkin and Blackness**, edited by Catherine Nepomnyashchy, Nicole Svobodny and Ludmilla A Trigos, North-western University Press, 2006 p89

23   **Pushkin,** by Henri Troyat, translated from the French by Nancy Amphoux, George, Allen & Unwin. 1974 p385

24   **Pushkin on Literature.** Selected, translated and edited by Tatiana Wolff. The Athlone Press, 1986, p189

25   ibid, Wolff, p189

26   op cit, Nepomnyashchy, p.89

27   op cit, Binyon, p321

28   op cit, Nepomnyashchy, p92

29   **Pushkin's Aestheticized Defence of his African Heritage in his poem 'My Genealogy',** by Sonia I Ketchian, *The Pushkin Review,* Vol 12-13 Symposium. 2009-10. *http://www.pushkiniana.org/index.php?option=com_content&view=article&id=194:ketchian-symposium1213&catid=134&Itemid=257*

30   **My Genealogy,** by A S Pushkin, 1830, translated by the author.

31   op.cit, Nepomnyashchy, op.cit, p91

32   op.cit, Nabokov, p158

33   op.cit, Barnes, p246

34   op.cit, Nepomnyashchy, p252

35   See **Pushkin: The Blackamoor of Peter the Great**. *http://davidmurraymusic.com/pushkin and http://www.presenceafricaine.com*

Catherine abolished torture but the secret police flourished under her patriarchal rule; Catherine loved enlightenment, but Novikov, who was the first to spread its rays, passed through the hands of Sheshkovsky (the timid Catherine's domestic hangman) to prison, where he remained till her death. Radishchev was exiled to Siberia; Knyazhnin was flogged to death; and Fonvizin, whom she feared, would not have escaped a similar fate had he not been so famous.

Pushkin, *Notes on 18th Century Russian History,* 1822[1]

04 | Manufacturing a Myth

The dedication which is inscribed on the base of the monument to Peter the Great – *The Bronze Horseman* – reads on one side in Latin, on the other in Russian: 'To Peter the First, from Catherine the Second, 1782'. Like many of her 18th century predecessors, Catherine came to power following a *coup d'état* and the assassination of her husband, Peter III. The overthrow took place in July 1762, only six months after Peter had been declared Emperor. The removal of her husband was executed by a group of guard's officers under the command of Catherine's lover, Grigory Orlov, who became co-ruler of Russia after the coup. The ascent of this 'petty German princess' to become Empress and Autocrat of All the Russias was even more remarkable because: 'Not one drop of Romanov blood flowed in her veins, and it is more than likely that none flowed in the veins of her son. Nevertheless, she would be remembered as one of the great 'Romanov' autocrats'.[2]

Catherine the Great was born on 2 May 1729 in the Baltic port of Stettin, which at that time was under the dominion of Prussia – in a region known historically as Pomerania, from the Slavic word meaning 'by the sea'. Nowadays, Stettin is called Szczecin and is in north-west Poland, close to the border with Germany. Catherine's father was Prince Christian August of Anhalt-Zerbst, a Prussian general who held the post of Governor in Stettin. Her mother was Princess Johanna Elizabeth of Holstein-Gottorp who had been born in her family's ancestral home just west of Kiel and about 100 miles north of Hamburg in modern-day Germany, on the border with Denmark.

The name given to Catherine at birth was Sophie Friederike August von Anhalt-Zerbst-Dornburg. Anhalt-Zerbst and Holstein-Gottorp were two of the 300 or so tiny sovereign states, or principalities, which, in the 18th century, formed part of the Holy Roman Empire and which covered the area of what is now most of Germany, Switzerland and Northern Italy. The Russian historian, Klyuchevsky, described these endlessly dividing and subdividing states as 'an archaic feudal anthill', within which:

> 'Everyone in these noble families seems to have been related to everyone else, even if only through marriage and at several removes'.[3]

During the Great Northern War of 1700 to 1721, the Dukes of Holstein-Gottorp initially sided with Sweden against Russia. Up to that point, Stettin had been one of the Swedish Empire's most important ports in the southern part of the Baltic Sea. During the campaign, Russian forces under the command of Peter the Great's enforcer and Field Marshal of the Russian Imperial Army, Prince Alexander Menshikov, set siege to Stettin in September 1713. After it fell, Stettin was handed over to Frederick William of Prussia and was formally ceded to Prussia by Sweden in January 1720.

The reigning Duke of Holstein-Gottorp, Charles Frederick, then fled to Sweden, where he had been born. In 1721, Charles Frederick travelled to Russia in secret, in the hope that he might win Peter the Great's backing for his claim to the Swedish throne. This option was ruled out as part of the Treaty of Nystad which brought the Great Northern War to an end. However, when a defensive alliance was signed between Sweden and Russia a few years later, part of the agreement was that pressure would be exerted on Denmark to restore lost territory to Holstein.

Soon after, it was agreed that Charles Frederick would be married to one of Peter the Great's two surviving daughters, the 16-year-old Crown Princess Anna Petrovna. As part of the marriage contract, both Anna and Charles Frederick were obliged to renounce all claims to the Swedish throne. They returned to Holstein where Anna gave birth to a son named Karl Peter Ulrich. The boy was 13 when Anna's younger sister, Elizabeth, was appointed as Empress of Russia in 1741.

Elizabeth eventually served as Empress Elizabeth of All the Russias between 1741 and 1762. As a girl, she had herself been due to marry another member of the Holstein-Gottorp family, Prince Karl Augustus, but he died of smallpox before the marriage could take place. Elizabeth never remarried and, having no legitimate children of her own, subsequently named her nephew, Karl Peter Ulrich, as her heir. He was sent for, received into the Orthodox Church – a prerequisite for becoming Tsar – and given the new title of His Imperial Highness and Grand Duke, Peter Fyodorovich.

The Empress Elizabeth then set about engineering a marriage between the newly installed Grand Duke and the young Sophie Friederike. This involved some complex diplomatic management between the courts of Prussia, Sweden and France. The French particularly resented what they perceived as the Austro-German sympathies of the Russian court. Two of the key players in this intrigue were French diplomats, the Marquis de LaChétardie and the Count de L'Estocq, who had already masterminded the coup d'état which brought Elizabeth to power in 1741. The British Ambassador to Russia during this period and career diplomat, John Carmichael, famously observed that, even though Russian rulers held absolute power over the imperial court, he had never come across one which was so riddled with factions and cabals.

On her marriage to the Grand Duke Peter Fyodorovich, at the age of 16, Sophie enthusiastically took to learning the Russian language and was accepted into the Russian Orthodox Church in June 1744, despite the opposition of her devout Lutheran father. This is the point at which her name was changed to Catherine.

The couple lived at first in the royal palace at Oranienbaum, just outside St Petersburg, but their marriage was not a success. Unlike Catherine, her new Prussian husband made no to attempt to learn Russian, couldn't speak a word of it, hated Russia and remained fixated with Prussia and Prussian militarism.

Catherine's husband was an unprepossessing figure, with a frail physique and a face which had been badly scarred by a bout of smallpox. Plus, he preferred to play with his toy soldiers or get blind drunk with his Prussian military retinue than be with his wife. Despite a series of elaborate manoeuvres designed to encourage Peter to fulfil his marital obligations, it became increasing clear that the marriage was unlikely to be consummated, let alone produce any royal progeny.

And so, the Empress Elizabeth and her close advisor, Bestuzhev, set out to convince the young bride that: 'there are situations in which the honour of a woman requires that she agree to lose that honour for the good of the country'.[4] After five years of marriage, during which Catherine had not produced an heir, a supernumerary was called for and was soon found in the shape of a dashing young count, Sergei Saltykov, a descendant of one of Russia's oldest aristocratic families. He was one of several admirers who had already been paying court to Catherine.

Saltykov was given Elizabeth's blessing to 'have some input' and, after two miscarriages, Catherine eventually gave birth to a son. He was given the name Paul Petrovich (son of Peter). Elizabeth 'regretted that the result would be a bastard who, though titular heir to the crown, would no longer have a single drop of Romanov blood in his veins'.[5]

When the Empress Elizabeth died, in December 1761, Catherine's husband became Emperor Peter III and she became the Empress, Catherine II. At the time, Russia was at war with Prussia. Russian troops and their Austrian allies were already advancing on East Prussia and the destruction of Frederick the Great of Prussia was imminent: 'The road to Berlin was open. Only a miracle could save him – and the death of Elizabeth was just that'.[6]

Peter ordered an immediate cessation of hostilities and began peace talks with the astonished and much-relieved King of Prussia: 'Frederick was willing to offer East Prussia to Russia but even this was not necessary. Instead, Peter prepared to start his own private war against Denmark, to win back Schleswig for his German Duchy of Holstein'.[7]

Opposition to the 'German' Peter as Tsar was swift: in less than six months he alienated most of Russian society by his capricious behaviour, his display of public disrespect at Elizabeth's funeral, his mockery of the Guards regiments as 'Janissaries', his threat to seize the property of the Orthodox church and promotion of Holstein family members to prominent positions: 'His uncle, George-Ludwig of Holstein-Gottorp was appointed member of the Council, colonel-in-chief of the Horse-Guards, and field marshal…Another Holstein prince was named governor-general of St Petersburg and commander of all Russian troops around the Baltic'.[8]

All of this was too much for the imperial regiments, who, in 18th century Russia, had increasingly taken upon themselves the role of prime arbiter when it came to be deciding who would, or would not, be the next Tsar or Tsarina. The period became known to historians as 'The Age of Palace Revolutions'. This was partly down to the confusion brought about as a result of changes to the procedures for dynastic succession introduced by Peter the Great.

Instead of the traditional system of primogeniture – whereby the throne automatically passed from the father to the eldest male relative – Peter proposed that, in future, every Tsar should have the right to choose his own successor. The main purpose of this was to ensure that his eldest son, Alexey Petrovich Romanov, would never ascend the throne. Instead, he had nominated his second wife, Catherine, to be his successor – the first of a series of 18th century Russian rulers who were women.

Elizabeth herself would not have been unable to usurp the throne without the assistance of the Preobrazhensky Guards, the regiment which had first been formed during Peter the Great's adolescence as a 'toy' regiment and was then mobilised to defend his claim to the throne.

Whereas her husband, Peter III, seemed determined to antagonise the regiments at every opportunity, Catherine had wisely cultivated good relations with the imperial guard. So much so that, at the time of Elizabeth's death, Catherine was again pregnant and this time the child's father was her latest *beau* – Count Grigory Orlov, a captain in the Preobrazhensky.

The two most powerful factions within the Russian government at this time were headed by Orlov and Nikita Panin, an influential statesman and former favourite of the Empress Elizabeth. Although they differed much in character and style, both Orlov and Panin agreed that Peter must be deposed. Where they disagreed was on who should be his successor: Orlov favoured Catherine; Panin thought that her first son, Paul, should be the next Tsar.

By now, her drunken and increasingly boorish husband, Peter, was openly boasting that he intended to divorce Catherine, marry his mistress, Elizabeth Vorontsova, and install her as Empress. Peter's fate was sealed when Catherine discovered that the unfolding plot to unseat her husband was in jeopardy. She acted as soon as she heard that some of her co-conspirators, among them one of the active participants, Captain Passek, had been arrested.

Fearing that Passek might be forced by his inquisitors to reveal details of the plot, she immediately set off to the barracks of the Ismailovsky and then to the Semenovsky Regiment to rally their support. In his biography of the Romanovs, W Bruce Lincoln describes how Catherine rushed from the cottage of Monplaisir, in the grounds of the palace at Peterhof, to rouse the guards:

'By the time she reached the Church of Our Lady of Kazan at nine o'clock in the morning, Catherine's entourage, which had numbered a mere two persons when she left Monplaisir, had become a triumphal procession. Not only the Semenovskys and the Izmailovskys but the Preobrazhenskys and the Horse Guards marched in her train. Outside the Church, a number of Russia's senior statesmen assembled to greet her. As she entered, the city's leading churchmen proclaimed her 'Empress and Autocrat Catherine the Second'.[9]

From the Church, she went to the Winter Place, where Russia's leading courtiers, officials, and army officers added their oaths of allegiance. Catherine's next move was to dispatch Grigory Orlov to Orianienbaum to present her husband with a formal ultimatum of abdication for him to sign. With only a handful of Holsteiner troops at his disposal, Peter meekly complied and, as his idol Frederick the Great later wrote, he had 'allowed himself to be overthrown like a child being sent off to bed'.[10]

A few days after Peter's official abdication, on 29 June 1762, the officer in charge of the escort which had held him under house arrest on his estate at Ropsha reported that Catherine's husband had died during what was described as 'an unfortunate scuffle'. Rumours hinted at assassination 'by poison, strangulation, suffocation, beating or shooting'.[11] No one was charged with the murder, but '…even if Peter was not killed on Catherine's explicit orders, his death did not arouse her regret, although at times it came back to haunt her'.[12] News that her husband had been successfully dealt with was conveyed to Catherine by Grigory Orlov's brother, Alexey Orlov, who had been in command of the troops who held Peter in custody at Ropsha.

Despite her denial of complicity, the extent of Catherine's remorse can be gauged by the fact that, three weeks later, Alexey Orlov was promoted to the rank of Major General, awarded for outstanding service to his motherland, and Grigory Orlov was made Lord High Chamberlain. Both were granted gifts of 50,000 roubles and estates holding 800 male serfs. Another young member of the conspiracy, the up-and-coming Grigory Potemkin, was promoted from the rank of sergeant-major to lieutenant in the Horse Guards, together with an estate of 400 hundred male serfs.

Understandably, Catherine denied any involvement in the killing, claiming instead that her husband had unfortunately died from a hitherto little-known fatal combination of haemorrhoids and a violent stomach ache. But she did not attend her husband's funeral and he was not afforded the honour of being buried in the Peter and Paul Fortress as had been the custom with every other 18th century Romanov. Instead, he lay unmourned and unvisited by his wife in the Alexander Nevsky Monastery. His body was said to have shown all the signs of him having been both poisoned and strangled.

In a letter written to another of her lovers, Stanislas Poniatowski, in August 1762, Catherine admitted that plans to oust her husband had been mooted for the past six months. The other serious obstacle to Catherine's ambitions, apart from her husband, was the great-grandson of Peter the Great's half-brother, Ivan V. This was Ivan VI who was to become known as 'the nameless one'. He had been locked up in solitary confinement for 20 years, latterly in the cells at Shlüsselburg, where he was denied any contact with the outside world and driven insane.

In a report sent by the French attaché, Bérenger, to the duc Comte de Choiseul, there was only one conclusion that could be drawn from all of this: 'What a picture, Monseigneur, for the nation once it has returned to its right mind and can judge in cold blood! On the one side, the grandson of Peter I dethroned and put to death; on the other, the grandson of Tsar Ivan languishing in irons, while a Princess of Anhalt-Zerbst usurps the crown, beginning her reign with a regicide'.[13]

Despite her lack of genuine Russian pedigree, Catherine the Great was to become the longest serving of the 'Romanov' autocrats and throughout her long reign missed no opportunity to portray herself as an enlightened thinker who would bring civilisation to Russia. Catherine's monument to Peter the Great – *The Bronze Horseman* – was one of the most dramatic statements of her dedication to enlightenment ideals.

The artist Catherine hired to build the monument, Étienne Falconet, was a prominent French sculptor and former artist-in-residence at the Sèvres porcelain factory in Paris. He was also a close friend of the radical *philosophe*, Diderot, a relationship which began when Falconet responded to a request for an article on sculpture to be published in Diderot's *Encyclopédie*.

Falconet's article, entitled *Réflexions sur la Sculpture,* marked the beginning of a lengthy correspondence between the two men. Eventually, Diderot recommended Falconet to the Russian ambassador in Paris, Prince Golitsyn, as the best choice of sculptor for Catherine's monument to Peter the Great.

Although he had never been granted a commission to carry out any major sculptural work for the French court, Falconet had won the favour of Madame de Pompadour, the most influential of the mistresses of King Louis XV of France. It was on her recommendation that Falconet had been made director of the sculpture workshops at the *Manufacture de Porcelaines de France* at Sèvres, a post he held between 1757 and 1766.

The fact that Catherine eventually chose an artist from outside of Russia to carry out the commission was partly indicative of her own infatuation with all things French and partly because the tradition of sculpture in the round was not well developed in Russia. This was because the Orthodox Church had disapproved of the depiction of 'graven images'.

In 1766, Catherine learned from one of her advisers, Golitsyn, that Diderot was in such dire straits financially, he had been forced to put his entire library for sale. She had already taken an interest in Diderot's *Encyclopédie* and, when its publication was eventually banned in France because it was regarded as seditious and anti-clerical, Catherine offered to continue its publication in Russia. She then pledged to buy Diderot's entire library too, providing that the books remained in his home so long as he was alive. To cap it all, Catherine appointed Diderot as director of his own library and paid him an annual salary, which was to be guaranteed for the next 50 years, in advance.

According to one of Catherine the Great's biographers, Virginia Rounding: 'Diderot was overcome with gratitude and in return he became Catherine's artistic adviser in Paris, searching out great paintings for sale and securing them on her behalf' [14] – the beginnings of the vast collection now held at the Hermitage Museum.

As well as cultivating a relationship with Diderot, Catherine famously befriended the renowned French enlightenment writer and philosopher, Voltaire. In gratitude, Voltaire subsequently wrote a very flattering biography of Peter the Great which was in part intended to cast a positive light on Catherine's own achievements.

However, Pushkin was not one to be impressed by what he called 'the sickening buffoonery' of Catherine's relations with contemporary enlightenment philosophers. Not even the voice 'of the captivated Voltaire' (who he otherwise much admired) would be sufficient 'to shield her glorious memory from the curse of Russia'. In his article *Notes on 18th Century Russian History,* Pushkin summed up the hypocrisy of Catherine's rule as follows:

'Catherine abolished the status (or rather the nomenclature) of slavery, but gave away about a million government peasants (that is, free husbandmen) as gifts, and imposed serfdom in free Malorossia and the Polish Provinces. Catherine abolished torture but the secret police flourished under her patriarchal rule; Catherine loved enlightenment, but Novikov, who was the first to spread its rays, passed through the hands of Sheshkovsky (the timid Catherine's domestic hangman) to prison, where he remained till her death. Radishchev was exiled to Siberia; Knyazhnin was flogged to death; and Fonvizin, whom she feared, would not have escaped a similar fate had he not been so famous'.[15]

Pushkin's assessment of Catherine's reign and on the 'Instructions' she drew up in 1766 for her commission on domestic reform, continues as follows:

'Contemporary foreign writers showered excessive praise on Catherine: it was very natural, they knew her only in correspondence, with Voltaire and by the reports of those whom she allowed to travel…her 'Instructions' were read everywhere and in all languages. This was enough to place her on a level with the Tituses and Trajans of history; but reading over these hypocritical Instructions, it is impossible to restrain one's feelings of righteous indignation. It was pardonable for the philosopher of Ferney *[Voltaire]* to extol the virtues of a Tartuffe in skirts and a crown; he did not, could not, know the truth. But the baseness of Russian writers is beyond my comprehension'.

Up to the time of Peter the Great, despite the prohibition against graven images, wooden statues of religious subjects were permitted in Russia and, in the late 17th century, church interiors were often decorated with high-relief carving in wood and stone. In the early 18th century, though, there was only one sculptor of any note in St Petersburg and he was an Italian, Carlo Bartolomeo Rastrelli. Techniques of deep-chiselling in stone and casting in metal, other than for church bells, were virtually unknown in Muscovite Russia: 'This was probably due not only to a shortage of skills but also to the fact that, in the eyes of the public, not to mention the church, nude figures in marble and bronze looked indecent and 'pagan''.[16]

During the Petrine era, the antipathy to more Western forms of figurative art – like much else in Russia – was soon to be upturned by Peter's reforming zeal. Among the first secular sculptures in the round produced in Russia were: 'wooden figures depicting Mars and Hercules set up on the triumphal gates to honour the victory at Azov in 1696'.[17] Many of the sculptures which can be seen today in the palaces and gardens of St Petersburg were imported during the time of Peter the Great. Marble figures for the summer palace at Peterhof, were commissioned in Rome.

Many of those imported for the Summer Gardens in Petersburg were made in Venetian workshops and those in the famous cascades at Peterhof were made by the Nuremberg artist, Konrad Osner the Elder. The founder of the Russian Academy of Arts, Yuri Kologrivov: 'travelled to Rome, Genoa and Florence, collecting statues, fountains, urns and architectural fittings, including the groups *Venus, Mars* and *Diana with Satyr,* purchased with the help of the Pope's nephew, Cardinal Spinoza'.[18]

The best known of the sculptors hired by Peter the Great was Carlo Bartolomeo Rastrelli, father of the famous architect, Francesco Bartolomeo Rastrelli, who built the Winter Place in St Petersburg and the Catherine Palace at Tsarskoe Selo. Peter had met Rastrelli *père* at Königsberg, in 1716, and immediately invited him to come to Russia where he was commissioned to construct an equestrian statue for the Tsar. It was to be made to commemorate Russian victories over Sweden in the Great Northern War and was intended to be in the style of the famous Roman statue of Marcus Aurelius.

Bronze bas-reliefs which clad the base of this monument would celebrate famous Russian victories over Sweden in the Battle of Poltava and the Battle of Hangö, in Finland, which effectively brought an end to Sweden's ascendancy as the great regional superpower. In the event, work on Rastrelli's monument was only just under way when Peter died. It was not completed until after Rastrelli's death in 1744 and was then stored a warehouse, where it remained for the next 53 years.

The Rastrelli statue was still in storage when Falconet's entirely different monument to Peter the Great was unveiled, in 1782. Whereas the Rastrelli version faithfully mimics the monument to Marcus Aurelius, albeit with additional baroque flourishes, Falconet's memorial is altogether more dynamic. It still takes the form of a bronze equestrian statue, but this time is perched on the pinnacle of an enormous granite plinth, the contours of which could easily be mistaken for a giant wave breaking on the shore. It depicts the Tsar astride a warhorse which rears up from the crest of the rock, with a writhing snake being crushed beneath the horse's hooves.

In Falconet's statue, Peter wears the laurel wreath of a Roman emperor but his figure is otherwise relatively unadorned, dressed only in a doublet and cape. In the Roman statue, the outstretched arm of Marcus Aurelius holds a scroll and is clearly meant to show him as an even-handed lawgiver. In Falconet's statue of Peter, the arm is also outstretched but here the posture appears more ambiguous. Here, there is no scroll and the palm of the hand is ominously turned downwards.

When the French monarchist, Joseph de Maistre, saw Falconet's monument, he described it as follows:

'The equestrian statue of Peter I arises on the shores of the Neva, at one of the borders of the immense Isaac Square. Peter's severe face looks at the river and seems to inspire the navigation created by his genius. Everything that the ear hears and the eye sees on this magnificent stage owes its existence to the thought of this powerful head which made so many splendid monuments emerge from the marshes. On these desolated banks, from which nature seems to have exiled life, Peter set his capital and created subjects for himself. His terrible arm is still extended over their descendants, who press around the august effigy; one looks at it and one does not know whether this bronze hand protects, or whether it menaces'.[19]

Originally, Catherine had also envisaged that her monument would be similar to the one made in honour of Marcus Aurelius, replicated many times over by European monarchs throughout the 18th and 19th centuries. In Pushkin's day, a copy was on display in the St Petersburg Academy of Arts. Instead, Falconet resisted the pressure exerted on him by Catherine to mimic the rather static tribute to Marcus Aurelius.

Pushkin's friend Batyushkov drew attention to the difference in styles when he wrote his reminiscence, *A Walk to the Academy of Arts*. He noted that another of the equestrian statues on display in the gallery, to a different Roman consul, was: '…not very graceful; it is short, with long legs, a fat neck, a head with bulging cheeks and an unpleasant movement to the ears. You will observe the very same thing in another hall, in the horse of Marcus Aurelius. The modern artists are much more successful with horses. We have before our eyes the work of Falconet, this marvellous horse, living, flaming, graceful and so boldly stanced...'[20]

The technical expertise required to ensure that the weight of *The Bronze Horseman* could be carried on its hind legs alone was one of the difficulties faced by Falconet. His solution was the addition of a writhing snake beneath the horse's hooves which helped provide additional stability to the structure, as well as providing a metaphor for obstacles being overcome and enemies vanquished.

Falconet's representation of the horse was greatly admired by contemporaries, so much so that it became the prototype for one of the most famous portraits of *Napoleon Crossing the Alps*, by the French painter Jacques-Louis David. The slab of granite from which the pedestal beneath *The Bronze Horseman* is made – known as 'Thunder Rock' – is estimated to weigh 1,500 tonnes. It took 400 men nine months to move the gigantic boulder from where it was discovered, lodged in a swamp in the Gulf of Finland.

This extraordinary feat was accomplished in two stages. First, it was moved overland by means of a system of pulleys, capstans and a metal sledge on rollers. During the remainder of the journey, by sea, it was attached to a giant barge, supported on either side by two full-size warships. The grand unveiling of the monument took place on 7 August 1782, the centenary of Peter's coronation. The spectacular ceremony was accompanied by remarkable scenes. An enormous crowd of onlookers packed into Senate Square which had been renamed Peter Square to mark the occasion. On the River Neva 'huge masts of imperial warships mingled with the masts of small private boats to form a virtual forest on the water'.[21]

Determined to make the most of the historic event, the Empress arrived for the ceremony by naval launch from her Summer Palace, a mile or so upriver.

As the American academic, Alexander Schenker, explains in his book *The Bronze Horseman: Falconet's Monument to Peter the Great,* the symbolism of this was not lost on the crowd: 'she wished to manifest her devotion to the ideals of the first Tsar who sought to place Russia on an equal footing with the great European powers and who appreciated the importance of the navy in that quest'.[22]

Furthermore: 'Just as Peter's Baltic fleet opened the sea lanes to the North European seaports and beyond, so would Catherine's Black Sea Fleet unlock the Dardanelles and allow Russian ships free passage to the Mediterranean'. Catherine began the inaugural ceremony by raising her hand: 'at which point the screens surrounding the monument dropped to the ground. As soon as the statue loomed into view, the troops presented arms, ships hoisted their flags and the guns of the Admiralty, at the Peter and Paul Fortress and on warships in the Neva gave a triple salute, all accompanied by 'musketry, the throb of drums, martial music and rocket flares'.[23]

From the time of Peter the Great, Russian emperors and empresses emulated Western monarchs, in what the American historian, Richard S Wortman describes as *The European Myth* – one aspect of which is to emphasise, in images of the sovereign, the distance separating the elite from the ruled. In this scenario, rulers appeared 'as heroes coming from without, achieving the transformation or salvation of Russia'.[24] One aspect of this vogue in image creation was the *conquest motif* which set the monarch in a higher realm through symbolic shows of force. However, in the 18th and early 19th centuries, this was accompanied by a utilitarian discourse which also glorified the ruler as triumphant bearer of civilisation and progress: 'The Petrine triumph, Olympian celebrations, imperial parades elevated the sovereign as a saviour redeeming Russia from despotism or ruin'.

An additional advantage, from Catherine's point of view, was that the grand ceremonial which accompanied the unveiling was at its most obvious level intended to instil in the onlooker a realisation of the awe-inspiring wealth and power of its creator. The subtext is that it consciously connects the person who commissioned the work, in this case Catherine, with her illustrious forebear, Peter the Great.

The issue of legitimacy was a continuous impediment for the Romanovs, as it was for all the European monarchies. It was a particular concern for Catherine the Great, because her claim to the throne had been so fragile. By making a direct connection between herself and Peter the Great, via the monument, Catherine sought to validate her status in the eyes of the people and suppress any of the lingering doubts which had accompanied her own accession.

At the unveiling ceremony, Catherine was accompanied by her lifelong favourite, Prince Grigory Potemkin, a constant companion who some historians believe she had secretly married. Potemkin was commander of Russian forces during the late 18th century wars with Turkey. During the first of these conflicts, Potemkin took advantage of the fact that Britain and France were otherwise occupied with the American War of Independence, allowing him to annexe the Crimea.

Potemkin's primary task throughout this period was to mastermind Catherine's Greek Plan, or Greek Project, the ultimate aim of which was to bring about a restoration of the Byzantine Empire centred on Constantinople – and allow Russia unfettered access to the Black Sea. In one of the more celebrated episodes of this campaign, which aimed to spark a Greek uprising against the Turks, a fleet of warships was dispatched, via the Baltic, under the command of Alexey Orlov – prime mover in the assassination of Catherine's husband.

This adventure was not entirely successful but it did culminate in Russia's historic defeat of the Ottoman navy at the Battle of Chesma. Following this victory, Catherine met with the Holy Roman Emperor, Joseph II, and discussed how best to partition the Ottoman Empire jointly between Russia and the Hapsburg Empire. This alliance took place in May 1781, the year before the monument to Peter the Great was unveiled. In the spring of 1787, Catherine made a triumphal tour of her newly acquired territories in the south, which she called New Russia. She was accompanied on this triumphal expedition by her new ally, the Holy Roman Emperor, Joseph II.

Catherine was depicted in commemorative portraits dressed in the military uniforms of Great Britain, which had initially been a willing ally of Russia. This was because of the extensive trade links between the two countries: the requirements of Britain's Industrial Revolution were in part fuelled by wrought iron imported from Russia as well as the long-established trade in raw materials for the Royal Navy such as sailcloth, hemp for ropes and timber, and especially bar iron – which went into the manufacture of wire, nails, horseshoes, bolts, gates and fences. Russian iron bar exports were estimated to be 'by far the greatest direct contribution of Russian commerce to the Industrial

Revolution'.[25]

When it began to look as though that Russian campaign against the Turks was going rather better than they had expected, the British shifted their position: they now began to see Russia as a potential rival for their eastern trade, rather than simply acting as a counterbalance to France, the other major European superpower. The withdrawal of British support left Russia in a superior position in the Black Sea but unable to achieve an absolute victory over the Ottomans. It could do little more than restrict British supply lines and disrupt Turkish trade in the area.

Nowadays, Catherine's Greek Project is largely forgotten but traces remain in the names of the newly founded towns within the territory of New Russia. Many of these were given Greek place names. Odessa, for example, is named after the ancient Greek city of Odessus, which was thought to have been in the same vicinity. Likewise, the cities of Kherson and Sevastopol were both founded close to the site of the former Greek city of Chersonesus; Nikopol is named after the Greek goddess of victory, Nike; and other major towns such as Simferopol and Stavropol are all taken from the Greek word for a city, *polis.*

Several monuments to Catherine's Greek Project can still be seen in St Petersburg.

The first of these is the Sophia Cathedral which stands in the grounds of the Catherine Palace at Tsarskoe Selo. It was designed as a small-scale replica of the Hagia Sophia mosque in Constantinople. There is also a Chesme Column in the grounds at Tsarskoe Selo, and both a Chesme Palace and Chesme Church in St Petersburg – all built by Catherine to commemorate the Russian victory in the Battle of Chesme.

Much grander is the Tauride Palace, named after the Greek word for the Crimea. The Tauride was built by Grigory Potemkin as his city residence and was partly financed by a reward of 100,000 roubles granted by Catherine for his services. After Potemkin's death, in 1791, Catherine bought the Tauride, paid off Potemkin's substantial debts and used the palace as her own summer residence in the city. When Catherine died, her son Paul did his utmost to discredit his mother's association with Potemkin and converted the Tauride Palace into a barracks and stables.

Over a century later, in the immediate aftermath of the

February Revolution of 1917, the Tauride Palace housed the Provisional Government of the Petrograd Soviet. In May 1918, the convention hall inside the palace also housed the 7th Congress of the Bolshevik Party, when it first adopted the name of the Russian Communist Party.

Another important architectural survivor from the time of Catherine's Greek Project is the Cathedral of St Catherine which was built inside the fortress at Kherson, in what is now modern-day Ukraine. This church was one of the first built in New Russia, as a memorial to Russia's conquests during the Russo-Turkish War. It is dedicated to Catherine's patron saint and another Greek, Catherine of Alexandria.

Like the Tauride, it is designed in the classical style and is filled with references to Russia's Byzantine heritage. The dome on the cathedral was built to specifications laid down by Potemkin who wanted it to be the same as the dome on his Tauride Palace. After his death, Potemkin was buried inside the Cathedral of St Catherine.

However, construction of the church was actually undertaken by General Ivan Abramovich Gannibal, who was the son of Pushkin's great-grandfather, Ibrahim Petrovich Hannibal, and therefore Pushkin's great-uncle.

Ivan Gannibal was in command of a detachment of the Russian Mediterranean Expeditionary Force, under the command of Alexey Orlov, which had taken part in two of Russia's greatest victories during the war against the Ottoman Empire: at the great naval Battle of Chesma and during the siege of the Ottoman fortress at Navarino. Just as Pushkin's great-grandfather, Abraham Hannibal, had built an impressive military career during the time of Peter the Great, so too did Ivan Hannibal during the reign of Catherine the Great, rising through the ranks to become commander of artillery for the entire Imperial Navy. In 1777, he was appointed by Catherine to a seat on the Russian Admiralty, the navy's supreme governing body.

After Catherine the Great's death, in 1796, the Rastrelli version of the monument to Peter the Great reappeared in bizarre circumstances. Her son, Paul, rescued it from oblivion and had it re-erected, in 1800, directly in front of St Michael's Castle, the palace-cum-fortress he had built for himself in St Petersburg.

Throughout his adult life, Paul had detested his mother for her part in his father's murder and went out of his way to reject any connection with Catherine. One manifestation of this antipathy was that, whereas Catherine's monument to Peter the Great reads on the base, 'To Peter I, from Catherine II', the Rastrelli statue is inscribed 'To Great Grandfather from Great Grandson'.

Odder still, St. Michael's Castle was built entirely from the ruins of the Pella Palace, the largest imperial residence ever constructed in Russia. It had been conceived by Catherine the Great as a future country residence for her grandson, Alexander. This vast construction was situated on the left bank of the River Neva about 30 kilometres east of St Petersburg and was named after the Greek city of Pella, the capital of Macedonia. The name consciously invoked the memory of Alexander the Great.

Within a week of his mother's death, on 2 November 1796, Paul ordered that the Pella Place be demolished and that the building materials be re-used in the construction of St Michael's Castle, which would henceforth be his principal residence in St Petersburg. He also decreed that the remains of his murdered father, Peter III, be transferred from the Alexander Nevsky Monastery and re-interred inside the cathedral of the Peter and Paul Fortress. A posthumous coronation was re-enacted for his father, who had been assassinated by troops loyal to his mother, and, in a gruesome ceremony held a few weeks later: 'Peter's coffin was disinterred from the vaults of the Alexander Nevsky Monastery and deposited in the Winter Palace, in the hall of columns, beside the coffin of his 'criminal wife'…By order of the Emperor, it was Alexis Orlov, the man chiefly responsible for the murder, who led the procession. Walking bareheaded, with the temperatures below zero, he bore on a gilt cushion the imperial crown of his victim'.[26]

The logic behind Paul I's decision to build a new castle had been that he did not regard the Winter Palace as a safe place for an emperor to live. His new residence was bound by the waters of the Moyka and Fontanka rivers on two sides and by specially dug canals (the Church and Sunday canals) on the other two. Thus, protected on all sides of this artificial island, the castle could only be reached by a drawbridge and was assumed to be impregnable.

Despite these precautions, Paul I was assassinated inside

his new stronghold only 40 days after its completion. The murder was carried out under cover of darkness by members of the Imperial Guard, aided by one of the Tsar's most trusted equerries. His son, Alexander, was in another room of the same building at the time and, although he did not take part, knew of the fate awaiting his father. Paul's assassination was by no means unpopular; when it was announced that his son, Alexander, would now be Tsar: 'In the streets of St Petersburg, people wept with joy and strangers embraced each other…Never had the accession of a Russian sovereign been greeted by such general and heartfelt rejoicing'.[27]

In an article written by Pushkin in 1822, *Notes on 18th Century Russian History*, he said that when Catherine the Great's son, Paul, was made Tsar it proved one thing: '…that Caligulas can be born even in an enlightened age. Russian defenders of autocracy do not agree with this and make of Madame de Staël's famous jest a basis for our constitution: "In Russia, the government is a despotism mitigated by strangulation"'.[28]

Notes

1   **Pushkin on Literature,** selected, translated and edited by Tatiana Wolff, The Athlone Press, 1986 p45

2   **The Romanovs: Autocrats of All the Russias**, by W Bruce Lincoln. Anchor Books, 1981, p214

3   **Catherine the Great: Love, Sex and Power,** by Virginia Rounding, Arrow Books, 2007 p7

4   **Terrible Tsarinas: Five Russian Women in Power**, by Henri Troyat, translated by Andrea Lyn Secara, Algora Publishing, 2001, p196

5   ibid, Troyat, p196

6   **Catherine the Great & Potemkin** - The Imperial Love Affair. By Simon Sebag Montefiore. Weidenfeld & Nicolson. 2016 (first published 2000). P44

7   ibid, Montefiore, p44

8   ibid, Montefiore, p46

9   op cit, Bruce Lincoln, p209

10   op cit, Montefiore, p56

11   **The Romanovs: Ruling Russia 1613-1917**, Lindsey Hughes. Continuum Books, 2008. p104

12   ibid, Hughes, p104

13   op cit, Rounding, p153

14   op cit, Rounding, p.195

15   op cit, Wolff, p.45

16   op cit, Wolf, p45

17   op cit, Wolf, p45

18   **Russia in the Age of Peter the Great,** Lindsey Hughes, Yale University Press, 1998 p228

19   ibid, Hughes, p229

20   ibid, Hughes, p229

21   **Pushkin's Bronze Horseman: The Story of a Masterpiece**, by Waclow Lednicki, Greenwood Press, 1978 reprint of 1955 edition, p36

22   ibid, Lednicki, p34

23   **The Bronze Horseman: Falconet's Monument to Peter the Great**, by Alexander M Schenker, Yale University Pres, 2003, p248

24   ibid, Schenker, p249

25   **Russian Overseas Commerce with Great Britain During the Reign of Catherine II,** by Herbert H Kaplan, American Philosophical Society. Independence Square, Philadelphia, 1995 p55

26   **Alexander of Russia** - Napoleon's Conqueror. By Henri Troyat. Translated by Joan Pinkham. New English Library. 1982 (first published in 1980 as Alexandre I: Le Sphinx du Nord) p33

27   op cit, Bruce Lincoln, p382

28   'Notes on 18th Century Russian History', Pushkin, Kishinev, 2 August 1822, quoted in **Pushkin on Literature'**, Selected, translated and edited by Tatiana Wolff, The Athlone Press, 1986 p5

Part 1

'Thus ended the insurrection that was begun by a handful of dissident Cossacks, that gained strength because of the inexcusable negligence of the authorities, and that shook the state from Siberia to Moscow and from the Kuban to the forests of Murom. Complete order was not achieved for a long time yet'.

Pushkin, *The History of Pugachev*, 1833[1]

05 | Pushkin, Razin & Pugachev

Throughout the period of the Time of Troubles (1598-1613) instability in the country was rife. In addition to endless feuding over the dynastic succession, Russia was devastated by famine and Polish troops eventually occupied the Kremlin. Relative calm was restored for a short period during the reign of the first Romanov, Mikhail, but after his son, Alexey Mikhailovich, came to power in 1645, rebellions again broke out across the country. The most determined of these violent outbreaks were led by rebel 'pretenders' to the throne. During the 17th and 18th centuries it has been estimated that there were a total of 44 pretenders to the crown in Russia. Twenty-six of these appeared during the reign of Catherine the Great. The most important of these rebellions were led by two legendary Russian rebels and folk heroes, Sten'ka Razin in 1669 and Emelian Pugachev in 1773. Pushkin carried out extensive research on the exploits of both desperadoes. He wrote a song cycle praising Razin which was popular among the Decembrists and wrote an extremely impressive and meticulously sourced account of the armed revolt against Catherine, in his *History of Pugachev*. Much of the impetus for these rebellions arose from the fact that, in order to generate sufficient troops and finance for Russia's 16th and 17th century wars with Poland and Sweden, conscription had increased as well as taxes. Many peasants fled to the unruly south of the country to escape these obligations but, in 1658, special officials were appointed by the central government to conduct search operations. These raids amounted to organised manhunts in the black-soil regions of the southern steppe which attracted most of the runaways. In his book, *Russian Rebels 1600-1800* Paul Avrich writes that: 'Landlords who sheltered runaways risked floggings and heavy fines and were made to surrender four peasants of their own for every fugitive found in their possession'.[2]

Another grievance was the decision taken by the Treasury to introduce a universal salt tax as a way of recouping the losses sustained during the Time of Troubles. In 1648, this led to an outbreak of rioting in the streets of Moscow, not least because salted fish formed a staple part of the Russian diet. After this revolt, a commoner was recorded as warning the boyars that more violence was yet to come, because 'the whole world is shaking'. 'The times are bad', he said, 'There is great shaking, and the people are troubled'.[3]

The Moscow Uprising eventually ended when the government made concessions to some of the rioters, while the ringleaders were arrested and executed. But it soon sparked further outbreaks. There were rebellions in the cities of Pskov and Great Novgorod in 1650 and then, in the 1660's, there were two more major outbreaks: the Copper Riots of 1662 followed by the much more serious rebellion led by the Don Cossack, Sten'ka Razin, in 1669.

The first of Razin's many legendary exploits was to attack and plunder a shipping convoy on the Volga. His haul included barges belonging to the Treasury and the Patriarch as well as the wealthy merchants of Moscow. One of the central grievances of the peasantry who supported Sten'ka Razin was that, under the Romanovs, serfdom had become institutionalised. Whereas landowners in the older parts of Russia often had lots of peasants but not that much land, in the newer territories to the south of the country they often had plenty of land but not enough serfs.

There was no longer any such thing as a 'free' peasant: the overwhelming majority were bound to their masters and became their property. As a result, the peasants in this region were worked harder and subjected to harsher treatment by their masters. But they were also in closer contact with the Cossack strongholds of the Don, which remained a law unto themselves, and which the Romanovs were as yet reluctant to confront.

A major cause of this intensification of serfdom was that, in 1649, the Tsar Alexey approved one of the most significant pieces of legislation ever to be promulgated in Russia: this was the Law Code, or *Sobornaya Ulozheniye*, whose primary aim was to enshrine the rights of nobles and wealthy townsfolk to life and property and further enforce the inviolability of autocratic power. In order that they could guarantee a labour force to work the nobles' estates and crown lands, the *Ulozheniye* set out the means by which the peasantry would do the bidding of the state and its nobles. As W Bruce Lincoln explains: 'Peasants were tied to the land, no longer free to leave the estates on which they laboured. Not yet slaves, still their purpose in life was to fulfil their landlords' will'.

Obviously, Russia's peasants did not accept this service status passively, and it is probably no accident that Razin's revolt, the greatest Russia had ever seen, came just two decades after the *Ulozheniye* was promulgated'[4]. After his victory over the merchant fleet, Razin sailed down the Volga with his own convoy of 35 vessels, capturing forts along the way and defeating several detachments of *streltsy*. As they sailed past the city of Simbirsk, they were heard to sing:

We have come to claim our freedom
With our ataman Sten'ka Razin
From wicked judges and officials.[5]

Razin soon earned the reputation as an invincible warrior, credited with supernatural powers and, in June 1670, he finally reached the wealthy city of Astrakhan, known as Moscow's 'window on the East'. Helped by a rebellion of the *streltsy* inside the heavily fortified city walls, Razin gained access to the city where he massacred any opponents, pillaged the bazaars and declared Astrakhan a Cossack Republic.

A general assembly, or *veche*, was appointed from the population and Razin was proclaimed *gosudar*, or sovereign.

Razin's proclaimed intention was to root out all the boyars and establish a realm committed to the Cossack ideal of absolute equality, throughout Muscovy. Unfortunately for Razin, another important consequence of the ending of Russia's long-running war with Poland was that there was no longer any shortage of experienced troops, armed with up-to-date weaponry and equipment on the government side. Dragoons sent to suppress the revolt at Tambov, for example, were trained 'in the German manner' and equipped with 'thirty pairs of pistols with holsters and thirty carbines with slings and hooks' all the latest European design[6]. Regiments were assembled from across the land to facilitate the task of repression until a force of 60,000 men was paraded before the Tsar in a field outside Moscow before being sent to suppress the rebellion.

In the Russian folk memory, Sten'ka Razin retains the legendary status of a Robin Hood to this day. More songs and legends are written about him than any other popular hero in Russia. Long after his death he was regarded as a sorcerer endowed with mystical powers: 'bullets could do him no harm, he could cast a spell over snakes, open locks by magic, and escape from prison merely by drawing a boat on the wall with charcoal or chalk and sailing away'.[7] Tsarist authorities did their utmost to combat the cult of celebrity associated with Sten'ka Razin but his reputation as a champion of the oppressed lived on: in August 1918, he was named as one of the revolutionaries who should be commemorated with a statue by the new Soviet Republic. This monument was unveiled by Lenin on May Day, 1919.

Drinking songs extolling the daring of Sten'ka Razin were part of the regular repertoire of the young officers who conspired to overthrow Tsarism during the Decembrist uprising of 1825; and, when Pushkin wrote a mischievous cycle entitled *The Songs of Sten'ka Razin*, publication of some verses were banned because they clearly glorified the outlaw's actions. Sten'ka Razin's exploits provided the immediate inspiration for two further explosions of popular discontent which took place in the 18th century. The first of these was led by Kondraty Bulavin, early in the reign of Peter the Great.

Peter's new regional bureaucracy and his highly trained and experienced westernised troops quickly proved more than a match for Bulavin's rebel force. But this did not prevent sporadic outbreaks recurring: towards the end of Peter's reign, a series of riots flared up because of poor harvests and the introduction of a universal Poll Tax.

Later, during the reign of Catherine the Great, official accounts recorded around 40 outbreaks of rural violence between 1762 and 1772 in the Russian provinces and, according to the historian Jerome Blum, 'it is certain there were many more'. Blum estimated that: 'Between 1764 and 1769, in Moscow *guberniia* alone, thirty proprietors – nine of them women – were slain by their peasants and five others had attempts made on their lives'.[8]

It was against this background that, in 1773, after a short period of relative calm, the entire south of the country erupted, and: '... for a few unbelievable months it seemed possible that rebelling peasants might overthrow the established order'.[9] This revolt, led by Emelian Pugachev, involved the greatest numbers of any uprising in 18th century Europe prior to the French Revolution.

Pugachev was a Don Cossack who had served in the Russian army in Prussia and rallied support by claiming to be the true Tsar. He said he was Peter III, Catherine the Great's husband, who had not been murdered by Alexey Orlov as everyone had been told but instead had miraculously escaped, then fled to Egypt and then Constantinople before returning to Russia. Pugachev led an army pledged to the abolition of serfdom and the overthrow of the person they regarded as the true imposter, Catherine the Great.

In a manifesto he issued in July 1774, Pugachev's appeal was directed to every disaffected group in Russian society, including the Old Believers – religious dissidents who had refused to accept reforms to the Orthodox liturgy introduced by the Patriarch Nikon in the 1650s. Pugachev's revolt attracted a wide assortment of peasants, Cossacks, the urban poor and workers from the iron foundries which had been established by Peter the Great in and around the Ural mountains. These ironworks had been set up to manufacture cannon and musketry for Peter's wars but during the uprising access to this artillery gave the rebels an initial advantage over government forces.

For more than a year, Pugachev's rebel force successfully

outfought the Imperial Russian army, freeing serfs and executing members of the upper classes on the way. From its initial base in the Ukrainian territories, the Pugachev Revolt grew exponentially until it numbered up to 25,000 men and controlled vast tracts in the south of the country. Had his army been more decisive, Pugachev might feasibly have taken

Moscow. Instead, he eventually suffered a crushing defeat in an engagement with superior imperial troops led by Colonel Aleksandr Bibikov and was finally delivered up to the Empress in a metal cage. Pugachev was decapitated and quartered in Bolotnaya Square outside the Kremlin in January 1775.

Pushkin's historical novel, *The Captain's Daughter,* is a fictionalised account of the Pugachev Revolt. In the introduction to their translation of this work, Robert and Elizabeth Chandler note that: 'Pushkin would have known that peasants on his father's family estate in Boldino took part in the rebellion, and he had been interested for a long time both in Pugachev and in Sten'ka Razin...In a letter written in November 1824, he asked his brother to send him a book entitled *Life of Emelian Pugachev*; in another letter he asked his brother to provide him with 'the historical, dry information about Sten'ka Razin, the only poetic figure in Russian history'.[10]

Razin is mentioned again in a letter Pushkin wrote to his friend, Alexander Turgenev, a decade later, in September 1834. In this, Pushkin promises Turgenev that he will be the first to see a copy of his *History of Pugachev,* as soon as it has been published. In a footnote, he says: 'In 1671, Simbirsk held out against Sten'ka Razin, the Pugachev of that time'.

In his three-volume collection of Pushkin's letters, the American Pushkinologist, J Thomas Shaw, notes that Pushkin's various mentions of Sten'ka Razin indicate that: 'Pushkin was very much interested in the uprising, in the seventeenth century, as well as that of Pugachev, in the eighteenth, and the Decembrist Revolt, in the nineteenth'.[11] Pushkin began to pay increasing attention to these episodes in Russian history at the time he was writing *The Bronze Horseman*. In particular, Thomas Shaw argues that Pushkin developed a fascination for two different types of revolutionary: one was Peter the Great, who had introduced changes 'from above'; the other, Pugachev, who had fought for them 'from below'.[12]

Furthermore: 'Nor was Pushkin's interest confined to Russia. He managed, through his own and friends' connections with foreign diplomats in Petersburg, to obtain foreign journals and books on the French Revolution of 1789 and on contemporary European upheavals'.[13] In her book, *Pushkin and Literature,* Tatiana Wolff includes a catalogue of the foreign (non-Russian) books Pushkin kept in his extensive library.[14] Commenting on Pushkin's reading habits, Wolff remarks that two special collections in the library highlight Pushkin's fascination with periods of political unrest. The first of these is a collection of a dozen books on the Civil War in England and the other a collection of three dozen on the French Revolution.

On the English Civil War, his collection includes 12 separate volumes of memoires and historical analysis, all published in French. The collection dealing with the French Revolution is even more extensive: it runs to 34 volumes which are again all in French. It is also worth noting that, without exception, all the books on the French Revolution have publication dates from 1821 to 1825.

In the early 1830s, Pushkin had petitioned the Tsar, Nicholas I, for permission to carry out historical research in the state archives, ostensibly to unearth material for a history of Peter the Great. Much to his surprise, this request was granted and, in November 1831, he was officially enrolled in government service with a modest salary to do historical research. As Pushkin worked on the archive, the focus of his attention shifted from the time of Peter the Great to the reign of Catherine the Great and to the Pugachev Revolt.

In a letter Pushkin wrote to the Adjutant General, Count Alexander Chernyshev, in February 1833, he formally requested permission to work in the archives of the Ministry of War. Pushkin made out that he merely hoped to compile a biography of Count Alexander Suvorov, Russia's most decorated military commander. Pushkin asked for permission to see the official reports on Suvorov's campaigns of 1794 in Poland and against the French revolutionary armies in Italy, in 1799. But he also included a request to see 'the dossier of the investigation regarding Pugachev'.

Pushkin may also have wanted to see the files relating to suppression of the Polish uprising of 1794, led by Kosciusko. During this campaign, Suvorov's forces had stormed Warsaw, captured the borough of Praga and carried out a massacre of approximately 20,000 civilians. The more recent suppression of the Polish Revolt of 1830 was still raw in the memory and had

soured Pushkin's relationship with Adam Mickiewicz, Poland's national poet.

At the time Pushkin was conducting this research, the suppression of both the Decembrist Revolt and the Polish Revolt were still extremely sensitive topics. In his introduction to a paperback version of *The History of Pugachev,* the historian Orlando Figes points out that Pushkin wrote his book at a time when he was under attack for having allegedly renounced his past connections with former friends who had taken part in the Decembrist Revolt. Figes writes that, to the contrary: 'In many ways the history is a courageous book – a fearless warning to the Tsar at the height of the repression of the 1830s, when Russia's police state came into force, the prisons were all filled with dissidents, and no one else but poets dared to speak about the subject of the people's liberty. Church, state and gentry were haunted by the spectre of the Pugachev Revolt, and censorship was such that Pushkin's account of its history remained the most complete until 1917'.[15]

In the autumn of 1833, Pushkin travelled to those parts of the country where the Pugachev uprising had been most intense, in and around the Ural mountains. In a letter written to his wife, in August 1833, Pushkin describes one of these visits:

'In the village of Berdy, where Pugachev was encamped for six months, I had *une bonne fortune* – I found a seventy-five-year-old Cossack woman who remembers that time as well as you and I remember 1830'.[16]

The Cossack woman sang three songs about Pugachev for Pushkin and showed him the hut where the rebel leader had lived.

On his way back to Petersburg, Pushkin stopped off at the family estate of Boldino which had been granted to another of Pushkin's ancestors, Fyodor Pushkin, for his services in the recapture of Moscow from the Poles in 1612.

Boldino is where, in late summer of 1830, Pushkin had

effectively been marooned and unable to travel due to quarantine regulations introduced during a cholera epidemic in Moscow. It turned out to be one of his most productive periods, now known as the first 'Boldino autumn', when, among other things, he completed work on *Evgeny Onegin*. Now, in his second Boldino autumn, Pushkin again worked intensively on his history of Peter the Great, on his factual historical account of the Pugachev Revolt, *History of Pugachev,* and on his historical novel, *The Captain's Daughter,* his fictional account of Pugachev which is heavily influenced by the style of Sir Walter Scott.

It was also during this period that Pushkin wrote *The Bronze Horseman.* Just as Pushkin begins *The Bronze Horseman* with a 'foreword' emphasising the fact that his account of the 1824 Flood in St Petersburg is based on verifiable fact, so he opens his *History of Pugachev* with a similar preface, which reads as follows:

'This historical fragment comprised part of a work which I left unfinished. I have brought together in it everything that the government has published regarding Pugachev, as well as whatever appeared to be reliable in those foreign authors who wrote of him. I also had the opportunity to make use of several manuscripts, of traditions, and of the testimony of still-living witnesses. The Pugachev file, still sealed to this day, was located in the state archives of St Petersburg, together with other important papers, which were once state secrets and have now become historical materials. His Majesty the Emperor, upon his accession to the throne, had them put in order.

These treasures were thereupon removed from the cellars, where several floods had visited them and nearly destroyed them. The future historian who is allowed to unseal the Pugachev file will find it easy to correct and amplify my work, which is of course imperfect, but conscientious. A page of history on which the names of Catherine, Rumyantsov, the two Panins, Bibikov, Mikhelson, Voltaire and Derzhavin meet should not be lost to posterity'.[17]

Pushkin's graphic account of the uprising is assembled from his travels in the region, from eyewitness accounts and from the official record. In the opening chapter, he describes the territory occupied by the Yaik Cossacks, and bordering the Yaik river, as follows:

'...to the left spread dreary deserts where there wander hordes of wild tribes, whom we know as the Kirghiz-Kaisaks. Its current is swift; its turbid waters are full of fish; its banks are for the most part un-forested clay and sand, but the flood plains are convenient for cattle raising. Near the mouth the banks are covered with tall reeds, where wild boars and tigers lurk'[18].

Pushkin was already well acquainted with this part of Russia – he had been exiled here in 1820 and this is where he found inspiration for his suite of 'Southern' poems: *The Prisoner of the Caucasus, The Gypsies* and *The Fountain at Bakhchisarai*. But his account of the region is not only based on first-hand experience, he also went to considerable lengths to verify his descriptions. On the origins of the Yaik Cossacks, for example, he says that we should not pay too much attention to 'that which foreigners have written about them' because 'the larger part of such writings is based on conjectures which lack any proof, and which are often absurd and contrary to the truth'.[19]

Pushkin preferred to place his trust, more authoritative sources, beginning with a report given by a Yaik village ataman, Fedor Rukavishnikov, to the Ministry of Foreign Affairs, in 1720. Others reports he had been able to examine included:

'1) The report of the Orenburg governor Nepliuev to the War Ministry, November 22, 1748.

2) Rychkov's *History of Orenburg*.

3) Rychkov's *Topography of Orenberg*.

4) A rather interesting manuscript journal of Ivan Akutin, a former Yaik military ataman.

5) Several more recent documents which are preserved in the archives of the Ural Military Chancellery and of the Orenburg Border Commission'.[20]

These, Pushkin says, are the best and almost the only reliable sources for the history of the Ural Cossacks. The most satisfactory study of the original settlement of Yaik Cossacks, he concludes, can be found in A I Levshin's *A Historical and Statistical Survey of the Ural Cossacks*. This, study, Pushkin says, 'like all of this author's works, is distinguished by true erudition and common sense'.[21]

In the first chapter of his history of the rebellion, Pushkin makes clear that part of the explanation for the outbreak was that it came as a reaction to what they regarded as unwarranted interference by successive Tsars. The Cossacks of the Urals, or Yaik Cossacks, had for years carried out military service under orders from Moscow.

In return, they paid no taxes to the central government and maintained their original form of government at home.

The key principles of the Cossack culture were: 'Absolute equality; the atamans and the elders elected by the people as the temporary administrators of popular decisions; the circles, that is, meetings at which every Cossack had a free voice on all public affairs were decided by majority vote; no written decrees; 'in a sack and into the river' for treason, cowardice, murder and theft: such were the main features of this government'.[22]

In the 17th century, Don Cossacks had first provided military service for the Romanov Tsars, in return for allowing them to 'make their living as a free people'. But, by the beginning of the 18th century, Cossack control of the region and their incessant raiding began to be a threat. Peter the Great was the first to take measures to integrate the Yaik Cossacks into the general political system. This triggered the revolt of 1720, which was soon put down, and subsequently the Emperor himself appointed the military ataman.

During the reigns of the Empresses Anna and Elizabeth, plans were drawn up to restructure the internal administration of the Yaik Cossacks but these were not implemented until Catherine II came to the throne. In the very first year of her reign, the more rebellious elements in the Cossack army began to complain that the actions of government officials were deliberately violating their ancient rights. There were several minor revolts and an investigative commission was set up to consider these complaints but when the Cossacks attempted to bring their grievances directly to the Empress, their envoys were arrested in Petersburg, put in irons and punished as rebels.

After a further revolt, the instigators were subjected to the lash and about 140 were exiled to Siberia. For a short time, there was 'an uncertain calm' but among the mutineers the word was: 'That's just the beginning. We'll give Moscow a real shaking yet'. As Pushkin explains: 'The Cossacks were still divided into two factions: the assenting and dissenting (or, as the War Ministry quite accurately translated those words, the obedient and the disobedient). Secret conclaves were held in the inns of the steppes and in remote farmhouses. Everything promised a new mutiny. Only a leader was lacking. A leader was found'.[23] When Emelian Pugachev issued his proclamation in July 1774, it was calculated to appeal to all those groups disaffected by the impositions of central government and hostile to the German princess who had come to power after deposing her own husband, the grandson of Peter the Great:

'By God's grace, We, Peter III, Emperor and Autocrat of all the Russias... grant by this personal *ukaz* to all who were previously peasants and subjects of the landlords to be true and loyal servants of our throne, and we reward them with the ancient cross and the prayer, with bearded heads, with liberty and freedom and to be forever Cossacks, demanding neither recruit enlistment, poll tax, nor other money dues, and we award them the ownership of the land, of forests, hay meadows, and fishing grounds, and with salt lakes, without purchase and without dues in money or in kind, and we release peasants and all the people from the taxes and burdens which were previously imposed by the wicked nobles and mercenary urban judges'.[24]

In the copious notes which Pushkin appended to his history of the rebellion, he writes that: 'Pugachev's first seditious appeal to the Yaik Cossacks is an astonishing example of popular eloquence, for all its faults of grammar'. It was all the more effective since the pronouncements made by his adversary, Reinsdorf, the Governor of Orenburg: 'were written in a style that was as feeble as it was incorrect'.[25]

Pushkin's admiration for Pugachev's eloquence did not prevent him from communicating the realities of the uprising in the most graphic detail. Here is his description of what happened when rebel forces reached the fortress at Tatishcheva in the district of Orenburg, about 1,000 miles south-east of Moscow. First, they appealed to soldiers of the garrison to disobey their nobles. When this failed, they set fire to haystacks next to the wooden fortifications and when the soldiers rushed to put out the flames:

'Pugachev, taking advantage of the confusion, attacked from the other side. The Cossacks in the fort went over to him…At length the rebels burst into the smoking ruins. The commanders were captured. (*Brigadier General*) Bilov was beheaded. Elagin, a stout man, was skinned; the villains extracted the fat from him and smeared their wounds with it. His wife was hacked to pieces. Their daughter, Kharlov's wife, so recently widowed, was brought before the victor as he was ordering the execution of her parents. Pugachev was struck by her beauty, and made the poor girl his mistress, sparing her seven-year-old brother for her sake. Major Velovsky's widow, who had fled from Rassypnaya, was also at Tatishcheva; she was strangled. All the officers were hanged. Several soldiers and Bashkirs were taken out in the field and executed with canister-shot. The rest had their heads shaved in the Cossack fashion and were impressed into the rebel forces. Thirteen cannon fell to the victor'.[26]

During the course of the rebellion, Pugachev burned the city of Kazan to the ground and by the time his army reached Nizhny Novgorod, the governor of the city, General Stupishin, wrote to the head of the Imperial army, Prince Volkonsky, to warn that he foresaw Kazan's fate for Nizhny 'and that he couldn't even answer for Moscow'.[27] In the event, Pugachev was no longer planning on taking Moscow. More than a year after the uprising began, government troops were in hot pursuit and he could no longer trust his own confederates. They had come to realise the writing was on the wall and one of them, Perfilev, had already sent an envoy to Petersburg with a proposal to hand Pugachev over to the authorities. Pugachev managed to avoid capture for several more weeks but was eventually hunted down by government troops under the supreme command of Suvorov. To escape their clutches, he crossed the Volga in four boats with a force of no more than 30 Cossacks and with the Imperial Cavalry in hot pursuit. He was now out in the open on the vast steppe and in the final hours before his eventual capture, as Pushkin describes it:

'Pugachev was roaming the same steppe. Troops surrounded him on every side; Mellin and Mufel, who had also crossed the Volga, cut off his road to the north; a light field detachment was moving to meet him from Astrakhan; Prince Golitsyn and Mansurov were blocking his way to the Yaik; Dundukov was roving the steppe with Kalmyks; patrols were set up from Gurev to Saratov and from Chorny Yar to Krasny Yar. There was no way for Pugachev to get out of the nets that were closing in on him. His confederates, seeing on one side inevitable ruin and on the other – a hope for pardon, agreed among themselves to hand him over to the government'.[28]

When Pugachev was brought to Red Square to face his execution, the event was witnessed by a 14-year-old boy, Ivan Dmitriev, who later became an eminent statesman and served as Minister of Justice under Alexander I. Dmitriev had been a family friend of Pushkin's parents and Pushkin's account of Pugachev's execution, at the Bolotnaya (or marsh) on Red Square, is almost entirely based on Dmitriev's memoirs, which were unpublished at the time Pushkin was writing. Dmitriev describes how, on the morning of 10 January 1775, his mother reluctantly allowed him to go with his elder brother to join the spectators:

'...at eight or nine in the morning we arrived at the Boloto: in the middle of it stood a scaffold, or place of execution, around which army regiments were drawn up. The commanders and officers had their insignia and their scarves on over their fur coats, because of the biting cold...On the highest part, or platform, of the scaffold, I saw executioners for the first time: a repugnant sight. Behind the troops, the whole expanse of the marsh, or better say hollow, and the roofs of the houses and shops on the rises on both sides of it were strewn with people of both sexes and various classes'.[29]

Pugachev was brought to the scaffold sitting on top of a sleigh 'of uncommon height'.

According to Dmitriev: 'Pugachev, hatless, bowed to both sides as he rode. I did not notice anything ferocious in his features. He looked about forty years old, was of medium height, his dark-complexioned face was pale, his eyes flashed; his nose was rather bulbous, his hair, as I recall, was black, and his beard small and pointed'.[30]

Pugachev was beheaded, as was his former second-in-command, Perfilev, who had betrayed him. The details of the execution, Pushkin notes, were strikingly similar to the execution of another Don Cossack 'who rampaged a hundred years before Pugachev in the same regions and with the same terrible success'.

To find out more about this, he recommends the account given in: '*Relation des particularites de la rebellion de Stenko-Razin contre le Grand Duc de Moscovie*' translated from the English by the Frenchman C. Desmares. This book, says Pushkin, 'is very rare; I saw one copy of it in A S Norov's library, which now belongs to Prince N I Trubetskoy'.[31]

In the conclusion to his history of the Pugachev revolt, Pushkin writes:

'Thus ended the insurrection that was begun by a handful of dissident Cossacks, that gained strength because of the inexcusable negligence of the authorities, and that shook the state from Siberia to Moscow and from the Kuban to the forests of Murom. Complete order was not achieved for a long time yet. Panin and Suvorov remained in the pacified provinces an entire year, re-establishing their weakened administrations, restoring cities and forts, and eradicating the last remnants of the suppressed rebellion. A general amnesty was announced at the end of 1775, and the order was given to consign the whole episode to eternal oblivion…But the name of the fearsome rebel still rings in the regions where he rampaged. The people still remember that bloody time, which they have dubbed – so expressively – *Pugachevshchina*'.[32]

In February of 1835, Pushkin wrote to Dmitriev, to apologise for his delay in sending a copy of his book, the *History of Pugachev*. The reason for this delay, he explained, was: '…because I have been momentarily expecting the portrait of Emilian Ivanovich (Pugachev) which is being engraved in Paris; I have wanted to present my book to you in perfect condition'.[33] As a footnote, soon after Pugachev's execution, yet another pretender appeared on the scene. Her name was Princess Tarakonava and she claimed to be another child of the relationship between Catherine's predecessor, the Empress Elizabeth, and her court favourite, Alexey Razumovsky. Since she was their daughter,

Tarakanova claimed, this made her the legitimate sister of Peter III and therefore rightful heir to the throne.

Just as she had relied upon the Orlov brothers to deal with her husband, Catherine once more dispatched Grigory Orlov's brother, Alexey, to take care of the latest 'pretender': he travelled to Livorno in Italy, seduced Tarakonova (who, at different times, was also known as Princess Elizabeth of Vladimir, Fräulein Frank and Madame Tremouille) and then took her prisoner. She was escorted back to St Petersburg and locked up in the Peter and Paul Fortress, where she died a few months later, probably of tuberculosis. However, there was also another legend that the Princess Tarakanova had drowned inside the fortress, at the time of the flood which inundated St Petersburg in 1777. A painting of this imagined scene, by the artist Konstantin Flavitsky, hangs in Moscow's Tretyakov art gallery.

Notes

1 **The History of Pugachev,** by Alexander Pushkin, translated by Earl Sampson, introduction by Orlando Figes, Phoenix Press 2001 (Russian edition first published in 1833). p108

2 **Russian Rebels, 1600-1800,** by Paul Avrich, Allen Lane, The Penguin Press., 1972, p54

3 Avrich, Ibid. p.55

4 **The Romanovs: Autocrats of All the Russias**, by W Bruce Lincoln, Anchor Books, 1981, p126

5 Avrich, op.cit. p99

6 Avrich, op.cit. p106

7 Avrich, op.cit. p121

8 **Lord and Peasant in Russia: From the Ninth to the Nineteenth Century**, by Jerome Blum, Princeton University Press, 1961, pp554-555

9 Blum, Ibid. p555

10 **The Letters of Alexander Pushkin,** Three Volumes in One, translated and with an introduction by J Thomas Shaw, University of Wisconsin Press, 1967, p189

11 Shaw, Ibid. p694

12 Shaw, Ibid.p38

13 Shaw, Ibid.p38

14 Published as an Appendix in: **Pushkin on Literature,** selected, translated and edited by Tatiana Wolff, The Athlone Press, 1986, pp485-522. The catalogue was originally compiled by the Russian researcher, B L Modzalevsky, and was first published in **Pushkin and his Contemporaries**, 1910.

15 Pushkin on Pugachev, op.cit. p8

16 Shaw, op.cit. p.613

17 Pushkin, on Pugachev, op.cit. p10

18 Pushkin, on Pugachev, op.cit. p11

19 Pushkin, on Pugachev, op.cit. p111

20 Pushkin, on Pugachev, op.cit. p111

21 Pushkin, on Pugachev op.cit. p111

22 Pushkin, on Pugachev op.cit. p13

23 Pushkin, on Pugachev op.cit. p17

24 From a supplementary essay on 'Pushkin and History' in **The Captain's Daughter,** By Alexander Pushkin, translated by Robert Chandler and Elizabeth Chandler, NYRB Classics, 2014, p136

25 Chandler, ibid. p.140

26 Pushkin, on Pugachev op.cit. p27

27 Pushkin, on Pugachev op.cit. p94

28 Pushkin, on Pugachev op.cit. p103

29 Pushkin, on Pugachev op.cit. p153

30 Pushkin, on Pugachev op.cit. p153

31 Pushkin, on Pugachev op.cit. p154

32 Pushkin, on Pugachev op.cit. pp152-153

33 Shaw, op.cit. p704

How is it possible, in an article on Russian literature, to forget
Radishchev? Whom, then, should we remember?
Pushkin, *Letter to Alexander Bestuzhev*, 1823[1]

Pages 350 to 369 contain, in the guise of a discussion on
prosody, an ode most clearly, manifestly revolutionary, in which
the Tsars are threatened with the block. Cromwell's example is
cited and praised. These pages are of criminal intent, completely
revolutionary.
Catherine II, Notes on Radishchev's *Liberty: An Ode*[2]

06 | Pushkin, Radishchev & Novikov

Among the landed aristocracy and serf-owners, a few were astute enough to realise that the revolt led by Pugachev might not be the last. One of these was Alexander Radishchev, who grew up on his father's estate in the province of Saratov, in the heart of the territory where the Pugachev Revolt had taken place. Radishchev was one of the very few people in Russia who not only realised why the peasantry would be prepared to join such a rebellion but also to warn that a far worse fate awaited the landowners unless urgent reforms were introduced. His ideas were articulated in one of the landmark manuscripts in the development of Russian thought: a book called *A Journey from St Petersburg to Moscow.* When it was published – anonymously – in 1790, this work was instantly banned by Catherine who ordered the arrest and imprisonment of both the author and the publisher. The other outstanding opponent of autocratic rule to emerge during the reign of Catherine the Great was Nikolay Novikov, an inspirational satirist and publisher who would suffer much the same fate as Radishchev. These two figures were the pioneers of a radical literary tradition in Russia which is either unknown in the West or is consciously ignored.

Until the time of the Pugachev Revolt, there was little in Radishchev's upbringing to suggest that he might be seen as a threat to the established order. His father was a well-educated landowner who was elected marshal of the gentry for the district of Kuznetsk, in Saratov province. Radishchev had been one of 12 Russian students privileged enough to have been sent to study at the University of Leipzig, in 1766 (at the same time as Goethe). On his return from Germany, he entered the civil service as a clerk to the Senate and was then transferred to military service, from which he emerged with an honourable discharge and the rank of second major. When he resigned from the military in 1775, after the war with Turkey had been won and the Pugachev Revolt was over, Radishchev took a journey from St Petersburg to his family estate, to seek his parents' assent to marry.

This trip was to provide much of the inspiration for Radishchev's *Journey from St Petersburg to Moscow*: 'On the way, he travelled through some of the country ravaged by the Pugachev Revolt in the past two years. When he reached home, he was told how his father's peasants had helped his father hide out safely in the woods and had disguised his younger brothers and sisters as peasant children while Pugachev's men were near their estate. But he also heard of things that had happened to many another landlord, less enlightened and less generous to the peasants than his father'.[3] Because he appears to have been liked and trusted by the peasants on his own estate, they protected him during the Revolt, whereas many other peasants happily murdered their proprietors.

Radishchev repeatedly warns his fellow serf-owners that unless there are immediate and significant reforms, including the abolition of serfdom, another revolution was inevitable. According to the American scholar, Roderick Page Thaler: 'Radishchev was not a revolutionary, nor a prophet of revolution in the usual sense. He did predict revolution, if a whole series of liberal reforms were not made and made in time. But he wanted the reforms, not the revolution'.[4] Radishchev worked on his *Journey* over the course of a decade, beginning around 1780. The whole point of the book was to identify problems he had witnessed in Russian society and to suggest measures to improve education and introduce trial by jury. He also favoured complete religious toleration, emancipation for the manorial serfs, freedom of the press and an end to the Table of Ranks. Many of these were the kind of reforms which the reigning Empress, Catherine the Great, purported to support.

By the time he submitted his book to the censors, Radishchev was a respected member of St Petersburg society and had only just been appointed by the Empress herself as administrator-in-chief of the St Petersburg Custom House, an extremely important post at a time when overseas commerce between Russia and Britain was at a peak. By a stroke of bad fortune, by the time his book was eventually published, Catherine's attitude towards enlightenment ideals had flipped dramatically from enthusiasm to revulsion. The impact of the French Revolution of 1789 – the alarming consequence of Enlightenment ideals – had sent shock waves throughout Europe. Closer to home, in the newly partitioned Russian territory of Poland, a group of revolutionaries known as the 'Patriots' had mounted an armed revolt and had taken control of Warsaw.

According to one biographer of Catherine: 'The French and Polish Revolutions changed the atmosphere at Catherine's court as well as her foreign policy. She was alarmed by the spread of French ideas – or 'poison' as she called them – and was determined to suppress them in Russia'.[5] Pushkin's opinion was very similar: 'If we imagine ourselves back in 1791, if we call to mind the power of our government and of our laws, which had not changed since the times of Peter I, and their severity …then Radishchev's offense will appear to be the act of a madman. A petty official, a man without any power, without any prop, dares to take arms against the established order, against autocracy, against Catherine!'[6] On the other hand, when Pushkin – much later – wrote his own famous poem, *Exegi Monumentum* (after the Roman poet, Horace) he said, in one variant, that he would always be remembered: 'because, following in the footsteps of Radishchev, I sang the praises of liberty'.[7]

When Radishchev submitted his completed manuscript to the censor (an institution he compared to the Inquisition), substantial parts were cut out. Undeterred, Radishchev went ahead and printed the entire document anonymously, on a printing press he had acquired on credit. When the book was resubmitted for clearance, the censors unwisely gave it the final stamp of approval without reading it again. It had never occurred to them that anyone would dare to print anything they had cut out. Radishchev published 650 copies, claiming to have secured 'the permission of the Department of Public Morals'. He then calmly distributed them to friends, bookstores and leading lights in the literary establishment. Somewhat naively, one copy was sent to the poet Derzhavin, who was fiercely loyal to the Empress.

What happened next is explained by Pushkin in an essay he wrote on *Alexander Radishchev*, in April 1836, for his literary journal *The Contemporary:*

'...his book, at first unnoticed – probably because the first pages are extremely boring and tedious – soon caused an uproar. It reached the Empress. Catherine was powerfully struck. For several days in a row she read these bitter, outrageous satires. "He's a Martinist" she said to Khrapovitsky (*her private secretary*), "he's worse than Pugachev; he praises Franklin'.[8]

As Puskhin notes, the final remark, about Benjamin Franklin, one of the leading figures in the American War of Independence, was: 'a profoundly notable statement: the monarch who was striving for the unification of all the heterogeneous parts of the state could not see the colonies tearing away from the dominion of England and remain indifferent'.[9]

Catherine was so incensed by what Radishchev had written that she wrote ten closely printed pages of notes on Radishchev's *Journey.* She regarded it as an incitement to revolution. 'The purpose of this book', she wrote: 'is clear on every page: its author, infected and full of the French madness, is trying in every possible way to break down respect for authority and for the authorities, to stir up in the people indignation against their superiors and against the government'.[10] Catherine was particularly infuriated by the content of a poem entitled *Liberty: An Ode,* which Radishchev had incorporated into his *Journey,* not least because it praised such celebrated regicides as Brutus and Oliver Cromwell.

Radishchev introduces the poem in the course of an imaginary conversation which takes place between two diners at a restaurant in Tver. Following a discussion on prosody and a comparison of contemporary Russian poets such as Sumarakov and Lomonosov with Virgil and Homer, Radishchev's traveller announces that he too had written a poem but, he says, there is only one copy left of the whole lot, the reason being that: 'the rest were consumed in a fire, and the same fate that met its fellows awaits this one'.[11]

Explaining why this might be the likely outcome, the traveller says that: 'In Moscow they did not want to print it for two reasons: first, because the meaning of the verses was not clear and many verses were clumsy; second because the subject of the verses was not suitable for our country'.[12]

The traveller then tells his companion that he is on his way to St Petersburg to petition for its publication, although he does admit that the title alone *Liberty: An Ode* had been enough to prevent its publication in Moscow. Now that Catherine had introduced her *Instruction for the Composition of a New Code of Laws* which – she claimed – would guarantee every citizen the same liberty under the law, he caustically remarks that it must now be 'permissible among us to speak of liberty'.[13]

To give just one example of the tenor of the *Ode,* here is how the traveller describes what stands in the way of his freedom, 'crowned with an olive branch, seated upon a hard stone, dispassionate and cold, a deaf divinity…'[14]

Behold a horrible monster, hydra-like, with a hundred heads!
It looks mild and its eyes are ever full of tears, but its jaws are full
    of venom.
It tramples upon the earthly powers, and stretches it head up
    toward heaven
Which it claims as its native home.
It sows false phantoms and darkness everywhere,
And commands all to believe blindly.[15]

The poem continues in this vein until the traveller foresees the day when 'the voice of freedom' resounds on all sides, and: 'The whole nation streams to the assembly; it destroys the iron throne, and, as Samson did of yore, it pulls down the perfidious palace. It builds the citadel of nature on the foundation of the law. Thou art great, aye great indeed, Spirit of Liberty; creative as God himself'.[16] His verses culminate with a 'prophesy about the future fate of our country':

'When it comes, then, the heavy fetters of night will break.
Even in its death throes, stubborn Power will set up a guard
  against free speech,
And gather all its strength for its expiring effort to crush rising
  freedom…
But humanity will roar in its fetters
And, moved by the hope of freedom and the indestructible law
  of nature
Will push on…and tyranny will be dismayed.
Then the united force of all despotism, of all oppressive power
Will in a moment be dispersed. O Chosen of days!…
The dark citadel totters, and liberty shines forth with a glorious
  radiance.[17]

It is not difficult to see why Catherine might have been horrified by what Radishchev describes as his 'new-fangled' poet's sentiments. Less than three weeks after the book was published, Radishchev was arrested and imprisoned at the Peter and Paul Fortress. Catherine ordered that every copy that could be found be collected up and burned.

It is estimated that about 18 copies of the original are extant in Russia and one of these belonged to Pushkin. In August 1790, Radishchev was sentenced to death, a punishment which was subsequently commuted to banishment to Siberia. According to one account, the death sentence was rescinded only after the intervention of Catherine's favourite, Grigory Potemkin.

Pushkin kept a copy of Radishchev's own edition of the *Journey* in his library: 'He made a great many marginal notes in it and knew it through and through. In 1826, in a poetical epistle to his friend Sobolevsky, he told him where to go and what to see on a journey from Moscow to St Petersburg, all of it based on Radishchev's journey: 'The most amusing part of it is where he tells him to be sure not to miss certain delicacies in Valday – the very delicacies that Radishchev' had not missed when he was there'.[18]

Ten years later, at the time Pushkin was working on his *History of Pugachev* and *The Bronze Horseman,* he was also working intermittently on his own travelogue, *A Journey from*

Moscow to St Petersburg, in effect doing the same journey as Radishchev but in reverse. Like the original, Pushkin's tale is narrated by a traveller who meets other travellers and comments on the various cities he passes through. Pushkin's version has 12 chapters, named after the topics chosen by Radishchev for the chapters of his book.

Although Pushkin is often critical of Radishchev, this is often more to do with his style than with what he is saying – and Pushkin could not have missed that Radishchev repeatedly makes the same, mock self-deprecating comments about himself. Pushkin agreed with many of Radishchev's ideas but thought the way he expressed them was clumsy: 'The *Journey* tends to be repetitious. Landlord after landlord, with monotonous consistency, is cruel, wicked, grasping, brutal and rapacious'.[19]

The language Radishchev used included a great deal of Church Slavonic, which would have sounded archaic and heavy to Pushkin's ear. Nonetheless: 'At the time Radishchev wrote, it should be remembered, the Russian literary language as used by the great writers of the nineteenth century had yet to be developed…By the time Pushkin wrote his criticism of Radishchev's style in 1836, the language, thanks to the work of Karamzin and Pushkin himself, had become an incomparably richer and greater literary vehicle'.[20]

Later Russian critics took Pushkin to task for his reluctance to express anything but admiration for Radishchev's style. Because Radishchev had been brave enough to challenge the old order, any note of disapproval could be seen as disloyal, a betrayal of the cause. In fact, the very opposite was the case: 'From what we have already said, of course, it is sufficiently clear that Pushkin was thoroughly loyal to the ideals of Radishchev. He was, in fact, so loyal that he wished Radishchev had expressed them more effectively'.[21]

Pushkin was quite consistent in his admiration for Radishchev throughout his life. His exile to the South of the country by Alexander I had been triggered by three of his poems: *In the Country, Nöel,* and *Ode to Liberty,* the last of which was Pushkin's own take on Radishchev's *Liberty: An Ode.* One of the reasons Pushkin's version of the *Ode to Liberty* had been regarded as seditious was that one of its final stanzas includes a reference to the brutal assassination of Alexander I's own father 'by hands of mercenary treason' – a coup which Alexander had been implicated in and which haunted him for the rest of his life. Pushkin's *Ode to Liberty* also includes the following stanza, the penultimate lines of which foreshadow those which appear a year later in *The Bronze Horseman:*

> *The tyrant's lonely statue roaming,*
> *Its ominous torpor in the gloaming…'* [22]

In 1822, Pushkin directly refers to Radishchev in his poem *Message to the Censor,* celebrating the fact that: 'Radishchev, slavery's foe, got around the censor'.[23] Pushkin came by his own, elicit copy of Radishchev's *Journey*, while in exile. As he wrote triumphantly on the title page, it had cost him 200 roubles, a third of his salary as a nominal official on the Board of Protection of Foreign Colonists in South Russia.

The copy that Pushkin owned was an especially good one: '… bound in red morocco, with marbled end-papers and gilded fore-edge'.[24] However, its real value lay in its association, it was the one which: '…had been used by the Secret Chancery to indict Radishchev and contained numerous notes made in red pencil made by Catherine II'.[25]

At much the same time, he had written to his friend Alexander Bestuzhev, from exile in Kishinev, thanking him for sending a copy of *The Polar Star* in which Bestuzhev had written an article *Glance at Old and New Literature in Russia.* Pushkin had only one criticism to make: 'For the time being I complain to you about one thing: how could you forget Radishchev in an article on Russian literature? Just who are we going to remember? The failure to mention him is unforgivable both to you and Grech (*the editor*) – and I did not expect it of you'.[26]

This is a little bit harsh because the omission may have been due to the censorship: it was a risky business even to mention Radishchev's name in print and Pushkin himself never obtained permission to publish an article on Radishchev during his lifetime, even though he went to considerable lengths to do so in 1836. His unpublished article, *Alexander Radishchev,* begins with a quote from Karamzin: *'Il ne faut pas qu'un honnête homme mérite d'être pendu'* – 'it is no good thing that an honest man should be hung'.[27]

Pushkin had intended to publish his article on Radishchev in the third edition of his literary magazine, *The Contemporary*. The article was written in August 1836, a few months before his death, but was blocked by the Tsar's devoted subordinate and Minister of Education, S S Uvarov. The censor's verdict was that: 'the article in itself is not a bad one and could, with a few alterations, be passed. On the other hand, I find it both inconvenient and absolutely unnecessary to revive the memory of a writer and of a book, which have been completely and rightly forgotten'. [28]

Part of the reason why Radishchev's name has been airbrushed from history is that the treatment meted out to him is so much at variance with the image which has been created of the supposedly 'enlightened' Empress, Catherine the Great. During Radishchev's incarceration, Catherine ordered that Radishchev be subjected to interrogation by her witch-finder general, Stepan Sheshkovsky, Chief Secretary of the Chancellery for Secret Investigations.

Sheshkovsky was a notorious sadist who had also been in charge of the torture and interrogation of Pugachev before his execution a few years earlier. He supervised the special investigating commissions which were set up at the scene of the uprising and which had sentenced over 20,000 accused of having taken part in the rebellion to flogging, exile and death. According to author, Ronald Hingley, in his history of *The Russian Secret Police,* Sheshkovsky had a particularly sinister reputation: 'He captured the imagination of contemporaries to a greater extent than any other eighteenth century Russian head of political police, and many tales were told about his methods of interrogation':

> 'His inquisitions often took place in a room festooned with icons, where the groans of knouted victims would mingle with the prayers of the Orthodox Church as chanted by their chief tormentor with a piety which recalls two earlier and more august torturers: Ivan the Terrible and Peter the Great'. [29]

Describing himself as a faithful hound of the Empress, Sheshkovsky remained in constant touch with her, receiving detailed instructions in respect of the many political cases in which she maintained an interest. When irritated on one occasion by some misdemeanour of a Madame Kozhin, a Major-General's wife, the Empress told Sheshkhovsky to abduct her from a masked ball she was known to be attending and to take her off to the Secret Bureau for a whipping before returning her to the ballroom with due courtesy'.[30] Sheshkovsky's distinctive interrogation techniques are explained in a 19th century biography of Catherine II, *The Romance of an Empress,* by the Polish émigré writer, Kazimierz Waliszewski:

'A legend has been formed about this mysterious functionary, whom Catherine was never without. The reality…was doubtless of a kind to cast some shadow on the reputation that the friend of the philosophers desired to preserve in Europe. In her hands, the department of police was a cunning and hypocritical machine of state. Sheshkovsky had neither official titles corresponding with his position nor apparent organisation of his inquisitorial work. But his hand and eye were everywhere. He seemed to possess the gift of ubiquity. He never arrested anyone: he sent out an invitation to dinner, which no one dared refuse. After dinner, there was conversation, and the walls of the comfortable and discreet abode betrayed none of the secrets of these conversations. A particular chair was, it seems, set aside for the guest, whom a word, amiable but significant, had induced to cross the formidable threshold. Suddenly the chair, in which he had politely been motioned to be seated, tightened upon him, and descended with him to the floor below, in such a manner, however, that the head and shoulders of the personage remained above. The victim thus preserved his incognito from the assistants of Chechkofski, who subjected his body to more or less rigorous treatment…The performance finished, and the chair restored to its place, the host turned about and smilingly took up the conversation at the point where it had been interrupted by this little surprise'.[31]

In the event, Radishchev appears to have escaped torture, mainly because he made an immediate confession and, in a term which was to become notorious in subsequent Russian show trials during the Stalin era, expressed regret for having written this 'insane' book. Radishchev was banished to Ilimsk in Eastern Siberia for 10 years and deprived of his status as a member of the gentry, of his rank in the service and of his status as Knight of the Order of St Vladimir. When Catherine the Great died, her successor Paul – who detested everything his mother had stood for – summonsed Radishchev back from exile and made him promise not to write anything against the spirit of the government, which he did.

In fact, as Pushkin explains: 'During the entire reign of Emperor Pavel I he didn't write a single line'.[32] When Alexander I ascended the throne, he appointed Radishchev to the Commission he had established for *Compiling a New Code of Laws*. Carried away by the apparent trust Alexander had placed in him, Radishchev set about repackaging the reforms he had championed in his youth.

When he then presented his plans to the authorities, Pushkin recorded that another of Catherine's 'favourites', Count Pyotr Zavadovsky: '…was surprised by the youth of his grey hairs and said to him, as a friendly reproach: "Eh, Alexander Nikolayevich, you've got a hankering to prate in the old way! Or wasn't Siberia enough for you?. Radishchev saw these words as a threat. Chagrined and frightened, he returned home, remembered the friend of his youth, the Leipzig student who once gave him the first idea of suicide, and…poisoned himself. The end which he had long foreseen and which he had prophesied for himself'.[33]

Some critics have suggested that the central character, Evgeny, in *The Bronze Horseman* might have been inspired by Radishchev, with both having been driven insane following a futile revolt against a despotic state. The first edition of Radishchev's *Journey* to be published after his first edition was banned in 1790, appeared in London in 1858. Its publication was championed by Alexander Herzen. In the preface to this edition, Herzen wrote that Radishchev: 'sympathises with the suffering of the masses, he talks with coachmen, serfs and recruits, and in his every word we find hatred of arbitrary power and a sturdy protest against serfdom'.[34]

Concluding a sketch on Radishchev's life, which is based on Pushkin's version, Herzen asked: 'How can the memory of this martyr be anything but dear to our hearts?'.[35] Radishchev's *Liberty: An Ode* was not published in full until after the 1905 revolution in Russia. Pushkin's version of the *Journey* was not published during his lifetime and did not appear in full until 1880 when it was included in the Efremov edition of his collected works, to coincide with the unveiling of the Pushkin monument in Moscow.

The other outstanding opponent of autocratic rule to emerge during the reign of Catherine the Great was Nikolay Novikov.

In his history of Russian literature, D S Mirsky wrote that Novikov was one of the most remarkable men of his generation: 'He edited the *Drone* (1769-70) and the *Painter* (1772-73) … but instead of making his papers, as his fellow journalists did, and as Catherine wanted them to do, a collection of harmless jokes at the expense of old-fashioned prejudice, he tried to make them a weapon of serious satire. He aimed his blows at the very core of contemporary society – the system of serfdom'.[36]

For a short period, Catherine the Great had toyed with the establishment of a free press in Russia. At one point she had even produced her own satirical magazine *Vsyakaya Vsyachina* – which roughly translates as 'Bits and Pieces', or 'This and That' and installed herself as editor-in-chief. The idea that a magazine edited by the head of an autocratic state could be genuinely satirical was, of course, preposterous, and Novikov was not afraid to say so. Far from mounting any challenge to the status quo, its main focus was to attack any sign of opposition within society, the main target being the genuinely satirical magazines produced by Novikov

Soon, Novikov's 'witty and earnest attacks on serfdom' were curtailed when Catherine decided that enough was enough and all the satirical journals in existence were closed down. Novikov made a second, highly successful, career as a publisher and, between 1775 and 1789, he turned out a greater number of books than had been published in Russia since the beginning of printing. In a review he wrote for the *Literary Gazette* in 1830, Pushkin said that:

'Novikov did not spread love for the sciences and desire to read among us – he created it. Before him, according to Karamzin, there were two bookstores in Moscow which sold 10,000 roubles worth yearly; within a few years there were twenty, and they sold 200,000 roubles worth of books. Besides that, Novikov started bookstores in other Russian cities – the most remote ones; the works he considered especially important he distributed almost for nothing; he had useful books translated, he expanded the number of participants in his activity, and soon not only all European Russia, but even Siberia began to read. Then our fatherland, though not for long, was a witness of an event almost singular in the annals of our enlightenment: the birth of public opinion'.[37]

However, like Radishchev, Novikov soon became another victim of Catherine's aversion to the French 'poison'. In 1791, Novikov's printing press was closed down, he was arrested on Catherine's orders and, when he was brought before Sheshkovsky, was presented with a written questionnaire. He dutifully answered all 75 questions but refused to renounce his convictions. For this, he was sentenced to 15 year's imprisonment at the Schlüsselburg Fortress accused of being a Freemason and a publisher of works which contradicted the tenets of Orthodox Christianity. Like Radishchev, after four years in the dungeons, Novikov was released from captivity when Paul came to power in 1796, but by then he was a broken man and never returned to active life.

Notes

1   **The Letters of Alexander Pushkin,** 3 Volumes in 1, translated and with an introduction by J Thomas Shaw, University of Wisconsin Press, 1967, p114

2   **The Empress Catherine II's Notes on the *Journey,*** published in Wiener/Thaler. These notes were first published by Osip Bodyansky in 1865 and reprinted in Radishchev's *Complete Works,* as edited by Borozdin, Lapshin and Shchegolev, pp239-249.

3   **A Journey from St Petersburg to Moscow,** by Aleksandr Nikolayevich Radishchev, translation by Leo Wiener, edited with and introduction and notes by Roderick Page Thaler, Harvard University Press. 1958, p7

4   Thaler, ibid p7

5   **Catherine the Great & Potemkin: The Imperial Love Affair,** by Simon Sebag Montefiore, Weidenfeld & Nicolson, 2016 (first published 2000), p490

6   **Pushkin on Literature,** selected, translated and edited by Tatiana Wolff, The Athlone Press, 1986, p387

7   Thaler, op.cit. p36

8   Pushkin quoted in Wolff, op.cit. p388

9   Wolff, op.cit. p388

10   Thaler, op.cit. p239

11   Thaler, op.cit. p193

12   Thaler, op.cit. p193

13   Thaler, op.cit. p194

14   Thaler, op.cit. p195

15   Thaler op.cit. p196

16   Thaler, op.cit. p200

17   Thaler, op.cit. p201

18   Thaler, op.cit. p35

19   Thaler, op.cit. p30

20   Thaler, op.cit. p32

21   Thaler, op.cit. p37

22   **Pushkin Threefold: Narrative, Lyric, Polemic & Ribald Verse**, the originals, with linear and metric translations by Walter Arndt, includes a verse translation of *The Bronze Horseman,* Allen&Unwin, 1972, p5

23   **Message to the Censor,** Poem by Pushkin, Collected Works. Volume I.

24   **Pushkin,** by T J Binyon, Harper Collins, 2002, p86

25   Binyon, ibid. p486

26   Shaw, op.cit. p114

27   Wolff, op. cit. p385

28 Wolff, op. cit. p391

29 **The Russian Secret Police: Muscovite, Imperial Russian and Soviet Political Security Operations**, by Ronald Hingley, Simon and Schuster, 197, p19

30 Hingley, ibid. p19

31 **The Romance of an Empress: Catherine II of Russia,** by Kazimierz Waliszewski, first published from the French, by William Heinemann, London. 1895. Classic Reprint Series by Forgotten Books. 2015, pp295-6

32 Wolff, op.cit. p388

33 Wolff, op.cit. p389

34 Thaler, op.cit. p36

35 Thaler, op.cit. p36

36 **A History of Russian Literature,** by D S Mirsky, edited and abridged by Francis J Whitfield, Routledge & Kegan Paul, 1949, p56

37 **The Critical Prose of Alexander Pushkin,** with critical essays by four Russian romantic poets, edited and translated by Carl R Proffer, Indiana University Press, 1969, p86

'A weak and cunning ruler
A balding fop, and enemy of endeavour
Fortuitously favoured by fame
Reigned over us then'.

Pushkin, Canto X of *Eugene Onegin* [1]

07 | The Tsar Liberator

Catherine the Great fully intended that she would be succeeded by her grandsons, Alexander and Constantine, and not by her son, Paul. There were two main reasons behind her determination to circumvent Paul's expectation that he would succeed her as Tsar. The first was his determined opposition to everything she represented. He was an enthusiast for Prussian militarism, not French high culture. His virulent opposition threatened to undo what his mother regarded as all the great achievements of her reign. The second was that she had long envisaged that her armies would overcome Turkish resistance and eventually retake Constantinople from the Ottomans. The crowning glory of her Greek Project would be to elevate her grandsons, Alexander and Constantine, to the throne and place Russia at the heart of a new Orthodox Empire.

Alexander and Constantine were the first two sons from her son, Paul's, marriage to Maria Feodorovna, Empress Consort of All the Russias. Like Paul's grandmother, Catherine, Maria had been born in Stettin, as the Duchess of Württemberg, and grew up in the ancestral castle of Montbéliard. Three months after the birth of Maria's first child, in December 1777, Catherine stepped in to take charge of the upbringing of the baby. This grandchild was named after the Greek commander, Alexander the Great.

As soon as he was born, the baby was taken from his mother

and raised according to the dictates of his grandmother, not his parents. When their second son was born two years later, Catherine again commandeered the child's upbringing. The second boy was named Constantine after the Byzantine emperor who gave his name to the capital city Constantinople. The boys' parents, Paul and Maria Feodorovna, were only allowed weekly visits and were packed off to their new home, the Palace of Pavlovsk, where they nursed their resentment, but not their new baby. Much the same had been inflicted on Catherine herself when her son Paul was born in September 1754.

Like Catherine's husband, Peter, her son Paul was a great fan of Prussian militarism – as were all four of his sons: the future Tsars Alexander I, Constantine (for one month), Nicholas I and their younger brother, the Grand Duke Michael. In the final years of Catherine's reign, Paul had been excluded from the Imperial court in St Petersburg and spent most of his time on his own private estates at Gatchina, where he was granted a battalion of troops to guard his family and his miniature empire of 6,000 serfs from the bands of brigands who infested the neighbourhood.

He spent most of his time instructing this private army in the performance of Prussian drill exercises. He learned how to marshal these troops from the Baron von Steinwehr, a disciplinarian 'thoroughly schooled in the automaton-like' parade-ground techniques of Frederick the Great's drill sergeants'.[2] Although these methods were already obsolete, Paul viewed them as the height of military efficiency.

Unfortunately for Catherine, her succession plans were thwarted when she suffered a stroke in 1796 and died, somewhat ignominiously, while on the toilet in her bedchamber. Knowing of his mother's intention to skip a generation and nominate Alexander to be the next Tsar, Paul intervened swiftly after Catherine's death. His very first instinct was to search out any evidence of a testament naming Alexander as her successor and have it destroyed.

As soon as his own appointment as Tsar was confirmed, he re-introduced the hereditary principle of primogeniture which had been abolished at the beginning of the 18th century by Peter the Great. One notable consequence of this decree was that, whereas a procession of Empresses had come to the throne during the palace coups of the 18th century, all the subsequent Russian monarchs were male.

Despite the many precautions taken by Paul to consolidate his own position and ensure the safety of himself and his family, his reign did not last. In his first few months, he took a series of decisions which indicated that he might not be quite as tyrannical as had often been feared – such as releasing Alexander Radishchev, Nikolay Novikov and the Polish rebel Tadeusz Kosciusko from jail. But, like many of Paul's actions, these were primarily gestures intended to spite his mother's record rather than indications of a less tyrannical regime.

The more general trend was that Paul's behaviour became increasingly intemperate. He became notorious for unpredictable, capricious behaviour and often humiliating treatment of subordinates, tearing strips from respected officers for the slightest costume malfunction on the parade ground. Even more objectionable was his idolisation of Frederick the Great of Prussia, with whom Russia had been at war for the past seven years. Many of the troops he berated would have very recently fought in this war and detested the sight of a Prussian uniform, which Peter now decided should be the model for his own regiments.

At the forefront of opposition to Paul were supporters of Platon Zubov, the 22-year old who had established himself as lover of Paul's 60-year old mother, Catherine, during the last few years of her life. Like her favourites Menshikov, Biron, Orlov and Potemkin before him, Zubov had used his VIP status to vastly aggrandise his own personal fortune. Much of this wealth was accumulated through the plundering of landed estates assimilated by Russia during the carve-up of Poland.

The mastermind behind the plot to get rid of Paul, however, was Count Peter Pahlen, who bore a serious grudge after being dismissed by Paul as Governor of Riga earlier in his reign. Although Pahlen had returned to pre-eminence by 1799, when he was restored as Military Governor of St Petersburg, Riga and the Baltic Provinces, he was more than ready to join the plot which was brewing against the Tsar. The other two most prominent conspirators were Count Nikita Panin, the Russian Vice-Chancellor, and José de Ribas, the Vice-Admiral. There is more than a hint that both Charles Whitworth, the British Ambassador, and

Count Cobenzl, the Austrian Ambassador, were also involved. These two latter figures were removed from the scene towards the end of 1800, when, clearly under suspicion, they were both declared *persona non grata* and expelled from the country.

A few months later, the number of available plotters diminished further when Panin was disgraced by the Tsar and de Ribas died suddenly. Despite these losses, Pahlen's support was boosted at the end of the year when an amnesty was ill-advisedly granted to Platon Zubov and his brothers Nikolay and Valerian. The Zubov brothers had been sent into exile by Paul on suspicion of having encouraged Catherine to put Alexander on the throne instead of himself.

As Military Governor-General of New Russia, Pahlen was extremely well placed to lead the conspiracy. As well as being in supreme command of the military his responsibilities also made him chief of Paul's military police, and in charge of the postal service and the foreign office. By February 1801, the conspiracy against Paul included a number of Russia's leading generals and statesmen. According to W Bruce Lincoln: '…there were more than 50 men, including all three of the Zubov brothers, five Senators, the Commanders of the Preobrazhensky and Semenovsky Guards, and two of Paul's aides-de-camps'.[3]

On the night of 11 March 1801, the plot reached its culmination. The conspirators made their way to the Mikhailovsky Castle, the supposedly impregnable fortress built by Paul only a few months earlier. The assassination squad sent to deal with Paul was led by Platon Zubov and an army general, Count von Benningsen. They were able to cross the drawbridge easily because they had with them General Peter Argamakov, the less than loyal aide-de-camp whose official duty was to warn the Tsar of any danger. Paul was found hiding behind a curtain in his bedroom, dragged out and felled by a blow to the head from a heavy gold snuffbox. He was then strangled with a scarf belonging to one of his assailants.

During the melee, Paul glimpsed a red uniform, worn at the time by the officers of the cavalry guard, and he presumed that one of the assassins must be his son, Constantine, who was a colonel in that regiment. In fact, Constantine knew nothing about the plot. By contrast, Alexander did know that his father was about to be deposed but had either failed to grasp the full implications or had convinced himself that there would be no need for violence. According to the person who was to become Alexander's closest friend and adviser during the early years of his reign, Adam Czartoryski: 'Although everybody sympathised with the conspiracy, nothing was done until Alexander had given his consent to his father's disposition'.[4]

In his version of the events which followed the assassination, from the memoirs he wrote in 1832, Czartoryski said:

'I will now describe what happened during this terrible night in the part of the palace which was inhabited by the Imperial family. The Grand-Duke Alexander knew that his father would in a few hours be called upon to abdicate, and without undressing he threw himself on his bed full of anxiety and doubt. About one o'clock he heard a knock at his door, and saw Count Nicholas Zuboff, his dress in disorder, and his face flushed with wine and the excitement of the murder which had just been committed. He came up to Alexander who was sitting on his bed and said in a hoarse voice: 'All is over'. 'What is over?' asked Alexander in consternation'.[5]

When Alexander eventually realised what Zubov meant, Czartoryski describes him as being: 'prostrated with grief and despair…the idea of having caused the death of his father filled him with horror, and he felt that his reputation had received a stain which could never be effaced'. [6] The reaction of Alexander's mother, the Empress Maria Feodorovna, was not quite so distraught: '…directly the news reached her, she rushed out of her apartments with cries of despair and rage. Perceiving some grenadiers, she said to them repeatedly: 'As your Emperor has died a victim of treason, I am your Empress, I alone am your legitimate sovereign; follow me and protect me'.[7]

According to Czartoryski: 'At first she seemed determined at all risks to seize the reins of government and avenge her husband's murder'.[8] However, this did not have the desired effect: 'Her appeals to the soldiers (which were perhaps rendered somewhat ridiculous by her German accent) produced no effect, and she retired in confusion, vexed at having uselessly disclosed her ambitious views'.[9]

Although Alexander always claimed to have been horrified at

his father's assassination, he was conveniently located in another room of the palace at the time it took place and, after he had been informed of his father's death, meekly complied with Pahlen's instruction to accept the crown. Urged on by Pahlen, Alexander emerged from the palace to address a detachment of the Semenovsky Guards who were on duty at the Mikhailovsky Castle.

To this audience, he announced: 'My father has died from an apoplectic seizure. During my reign, everything will be as it was during the time of my grandmother'.[10] In his memoirs, Czartoryski provides a convincing impression of the hesitancy and indecision which engulfed Alexander after the murder and which was to characterise most of his reign. Pushkin once described Alexander as a 'harlequin' because of his chequered responses to difficult decisions. On the night of the murder, the only member of the royal household to have retained her composure was Alexander's young wife, now the Empress Elizabeth. Czartoryski recounts that she alone: '… exercised a mediatory influence between her husband, her mother-in-law, and the conspirators'.[11]

During the first few months of his reign, Alexander was said to have feared being at the mercy of the assassins himself but, as he saw it, he was prevented from exacting any punishment for their actions, because:

'He knew that there was general sympathy for the objects of the conspiracy, and that those who had personally taken part…had only decided to do so when they were assured of his consent. It would have been difficult in the circumstances to distinguish between degrees of guilt: every member of the society of St Petersburg was more or less an accomplice in the fatal deed, for those who wished Paul to be deposed must have known that his deposition, if resisted, might have involved his death. If the assassins alone had been brought to trial, they would certainly have accused the other conspirators and have referred to Alexander's consent in justification of their action, though the crime had been committed against his express wish'.[12]

Immediately after the murder, Count Pahlen took the reins of State into his own hands: in addition to his role as Military Governor of St Petersburg, he also became Secretary of State for

Foreign Affairs. Within a week of Paul's assassination, the British Fleet, under the command of Admiral Nelson, had entered the waters of the Baltic, had defeated the Danish Fleet at the Battle of Copenhagen and was menacing Russian positions along the Baltic coast, at Riga, Reval and Kronstadt. Proclamations issued at the time were all signed by Pahlen; nothing could be done 'except through him and with his consent'.[13] The effect of all this on the young Tsar was that he was 'overcome with sadness and despair'.[14]

After the murder, it took him several days to persuade his mother to relinquish her claim to the throne and it was reported that, for some time afterwards, whenever her son came to visit, the Dowager Empress 'would place a casket between them containing the bloodstained nightshirt that Paul was wearing at the time of his murder, as a silent reproach'.[15] Maria Feodorovna also introduced the precedent of assuming the highest female position at court, so that during public ceremonies, she often took the emperor's arm, while his wife, the Empress Elizabeth, was made to walk behind. The assassination of Paul is referred to by Pushkin in his poem *Ode to Liberty*. This was written in 1817, at a time when the impact of events elsewhere in Europe were beginning to have an important impact in Russia.

In his history, *The Road to Revolution,* Avram Yarmolisky writes that: 'The uprisings in Spain and Portugal, the Carbonarist insurrections in Naples and Piedmont, the Greek Rebellion, were so many object lessons to malcontents in Petersburg and Moscow. Several writers, notably a young scapegrace with a golden tongue in his head by the name of Pushkin, wrote saucy epigrams against those in power and lyrics celebrating liberty and tyrannicide'.[16]

In one of the final stanzas of his *Ode to Liberty*, one of a number of poems which earned Pushkin his first period of exile, he describes the conspirators who carried out the murder, as: 'The clandestine assassins, huddled with brazen brow and wolfish heart':

And silenced is the faithless guard,
The drawbridge downed at midnight season,
In secrecy, the gate unbarred
By hands of mercenary treason.

Oh shame! Of horror newly found!
The janissars burst in, appalling
Like beasts, the impious blows are falling…
And slaughtered lies the miscreant crowned'

Trans: Walter Arndt[17]

During his adolescence, the most powerful influences on the moulding of Alexander's character had been the education he received from his Swiss republican tutor, Frédérick-César de La Harpe, and from the parade-ground mania instilled in him by his father during his visits to Gatchina. These were opposite poles of attraction but, as W Bruce Lincoln observes:

'Anxious to please both grandmother and father, Alexander lived two completely different lives as an adolescent. Yet the worlds of Catherine and Paul were so contradictory that neither permitted compromise with the other. Alexander therefore developed two different personalities but never integrated them into what might be called a 'real' Alexander. In Catherine's presence, he was Alexander the enlightened prince, the sensitive and charming youth, steeped in the writings of the Enlightenment and early sentimentalism. At Gatchina, he became the parade-ground commander, a part of that raw militarism of jackbooted officers and sharp, brusque commands that his father so adored'.[18]

This duality in Alexander's nature was to become all too evident during the years of his reign. In his book, *The Twilight of Imperial Russia,* the author Richard Charques writes that: 'If, during the two centuries which divide the Russia of Peter the Great from the Bolshevik Revolution, there was any period in which the spell of the authoritarian past might have been overcome, the forms of state liberalised in a constitution, and the course of the Russian development merged with the historic currents of the west, it is the earlier part of the reign of Alexander I. Or so, for a moment, one is tempted to think'.[19]

Because of his enlightenment education, one half of Alexander was tempted to bring about major reforms in Russia and, initially at least, he did begin to take some steps in this direction. But, like his grandmother, Catherine, his other half was just as horrified by the logical outcome of these enlightenment ideas, in the French Revolution of 1789. The aftermath of the French

Revolution still reverberated around Europe when Alexander ascended the throne, in 1801. The entire period from 1789 to 1848 became known as *The Age of Revolution* and, as the Marxist historian, Eric Hobsbawm writes, the inspiration of the French Revolution was such that:

'France provided the vocabulary and the issues of liberal and radical-democratic politics for most of the world. France provided the first great example, the concept and the vocabulary of nationalism. France provided the code of laws, the model of scientific and technical organisation, and the metric system of measurement for most countries. The ideology of the modern world first penetrated the ancient civilisations which had hitherto resisted European ideas through French influence. One of the direct consequences of the revolution was that between 1792 and 1815, there was almost uninterrupted war in Europe, during the course of which the role of France was to appeal to the 'liberals' in other countries to overthrow tyranny and embrace liberty. Meanwhile, the forces of the monarchy and conservatism mustered everything in their power to oppose these ideas'.[20]

According to Hobsbawm: '...virtually every person of education, talent and enlightenment sympathised with the revolution, at all events until the Jacobin dictatorship, and often for much longer. (It was not until Napoleon had made himself Emperor that Beethoven revoked the dedication of the Eroica Symphony to him)'.[21]

The list of European talent and genius which supported the revolution in France included the poets Wordsworth, Blake, Coleridge and Robert Burns in Britain. It also inspired the birth of the very first organisations set up to represent the interests of the labouring classes in Britain, the *Corresponding Societies,* and it was supported enthusiastically by the radical, Tom Paine, whose book in defence of the French revolution, *The Rights of Man,* sold an estimated one million copies.

In his poem, *Eugene Onegin,* the heroine Tatyana, finds that, like Pushkin's contemporary, the philosopher Pyotr Chaadaev, Onegin decorates his office with a portrait of Byron on the wall and a cast-iron statuette of Napoleon: '...on a little column standing, arms crossed...with gloomy forehead and a hat'.[22]

In Central and Eastern Europe, the influence of French 'Jacobinism' was most profound in Poland. As Eric Hobsbawm explains: 'France had long been the chief foreign power in whom Poles hoped to find backing against the joint greed of the Prussians, Russians and Austrians, who had already annexed vast areas of the country and were soon to divide it among themselves entirely. France also provided a model of the kind of profound internal reform which, as all thinking Poles agreed, could alone enable their country to resist its butchers'.[23]

When Napoleon's revolutionary Grande Armée (consisting of volunteer infantry, not conscripts) first advanced on the rest of Europe, its success was instantaneous and the rival monarchical powers of Austria, Prussia and Russia were thrown into confusion. Against the advice of his chief advisor, Adam Czartoryski, Alexander now took the very rash decision to put himself at the head of the Russian army, the first Russian ruler to do so since the time of Peter the Great.

With Alexander in command, the combined forces of Russia and Austria were routed by Napoleon at the Battle of Austerlitz on 2 December 1805. Virtually half of the allied army of about 60,000 men were killed in the battle, to French losses of no more than 9,000. As the historian, Janet Hartley, writes: 'The defeat was all the more shaming for Alexander since he had personally contributed to it. Not only had he put himself at the head of the armed forces, but he had deliberately ignored the advice of his experienced commander-in-chief, Kutusov, who wished to delay giving battle until the arrival of enforcements'. When Kutosov asked to see a plan of march for the armies, Alexander reportedly replied: 'This does not concern you'.[24]

When Napoleon offered an armistice (probably as a ploy), Alexander made this impossible by sending as his emissary Prince Peter Dolgoruky, who made the mistake of addressing Napoleon '...as he would have done to a boyar he wished to send to Siberia'.[25] Instead of returning from the battle as a hero, Alexander came close to being captured by the French and on the evening of the Russian retreat, found himself curled up quivering on the floor of a peasant's hut suffering from violent stomach cramps.

Napoleon celebrated his victory at Austerlitz by commissioning the construction of a monument, the Vendôme Column, centrepiece of the Place Vendôme in Paris. Modelled on Trajan's Column in Rome, the spiralling bas-relief is made of bronze plates, melted down from the Russian and Austrian cannon captured at Austerlitz.

Alexander's confidence in his own abilities took a shattering blow after this defeat. The Sardinian diplomat, Joseph de Maistre, wrote that: 'The Emperor believes himself to be no use to his people, because he is not in the position of commander of his armies and this is very shaming for him…He had been more defeated than his army at Austerlitz'.[26]

After a further defeat at the Battle of Friedland, in June 1807, when Russia lost another 10,000 men, with 15,000 wounded, pressure was put on the Tsar both by his generals and by his brother, Constantine, to agree a pact with Napoleon. A summit meeting between Napoleon and Alexander took place, famously, on a raft in the middle of the River Nieman, which at that time flowed into Baltic along the border between Russia and Prussia (now between Lithuania and Russia).

In talks which culminated in the Treaty of Tilsit, named after a nearby village, Alexander characteristically lurched from despair to brazen effrontery, instructing his General, Lobanov-Rostovsky, to address Napoleon as follows:

'You tell him that this union between France and Russia
has constantly been the object of my desires and that I have
the conviction that this alone will ensure the happiness and
tranquillity of the world'.[27]

Frederick William of Prussia, supposedly Russia's ally, was excluded from the talks, whose main purpose was to determine the fate of his country after it had been over-run by Napoleon's Grande Armée. The talks are reported to have started with Alexander telling Napoleon: 'Sire, I hate the English no less than you do and I am ready to assist you in any enterprise against them'.[28]

This rash assertion was confidently given despite the fact that Russia had long-standing trade arrangements with Britain. The British cabinet was furious at the possibility of a Franco-Russian alliance which would destroy this vital relationship, strengthen Napoleon's Continental Blockade of English trade and increase his dominance of the rest of Europe. As Janet Hartley explains: 'Napoleon had presented the Tilsit peace as an alliance between Russia and France but it was clear that Russia was the junior partner. The reality was that Napoleon now dominated the continent. Prussia and Austria had been defeated and Russia had been neutralised, so allowing the emperor to concentrate his efforts on the struggle with Britain'.[29]

As much as he tried to dress it up, the terms of the Treaty agreed at Tilsit were regarded as a humiliation by most Russians and Alexander's popularity slumped. There was even talk of a plot against Alexander's life. The Irish traveller, Martha Wilmot, recalled that: 'In St Petersburg, even in Moscow, in all the places in Russia most touched by education, the Tilsit peace made the saddest impression; in these places they knew that the alliance with Napoleon could be nothing other than enslavement to him'.[30] The irony was that although Russian high society was in thrall to French cuisine, couture and culture, Martha Wilmot could also see that '…there is no one who does not blaspheme against Bonaparte and lament Lord Nelson'.[31]

In his memoirs, Adam Czartorysky writes that, in order to understand the political movements of that time and the animosity with which all Europe wanted to fight Napoleon, it was necessary to take account of the state of public opinion in Europe:

'Those who had become enthusiastic at the outbreak of the French Revolution had looked upon Bonaparte as the hero of liberalism; he seemed to them destined, by Providence to make the cause of justice triumph and to remove by great actions and immense successes the innumerable obstacles presented by facts to the oppressed nations. When they saw that Napoleon did not fulfil their expectations, their enthusiasm diminished…each of his actions and words showed that he would act only by force of bayonets and of numbers. By ceasing to be the champion of justice and the hope of oppressed peoples, he lost one of the strongest elements of the power of the French Republic, and descended to the class of ambitious tyrants, with immense talents it is true, but with motives as mean as theirs'.[32]

Within a few years of the agreement at Tilsit being signed, it began to fall apart, not least because of Alexander's collusion with Austria and Prussia. When hostilities with Russia eventually resumed, in 1812, Napoleon mobilised an army of around 500,000 men which crossed the River Niemen into Russian territory and headed eastwards.

Napoleon hoped to win a quick and decisive victory, force Russia to comply with the terms agreed at Tilsit and, in the process, isolate and defeat Napoleon's real enemy, Britain. Despite his overwhelming superiority in numbers, Alexander's uncertainty on how to deal with the new offensive forced a retreat. The Russian forces were not even able to save the sacred city of Smolensk: it was set on fire by its own inhabitants. After two days of fighting Russian forces abandoned the city and withdrew even further towards the interior of Russia. Napoleon described watching Smolensk in flames as being like the spectacle an eruption of Mount Vesuvius offered the inhabitants of Naples.

This dreadful defeat was greeted with horror in Russia but it also created immense problems for the French. Napoleon had wanted to have secured victory by the time he reached Smolensk. Now, one of their officers, Lieutenant Vossler, wrote:

'…we were embarked on a strenuous campaign entailing frequent forced marches, along abominable roads, either smothered in sand or knee-deep in mud and frequently pitted with precipitous gulleys, under skies alternately unbearably hot and pouring forth freezing rain…many regiments had no more than three days' supply of rations which, because of the total devastation of the countryside, could never be adequately replenished…within two or three days of crossing the Niemen the army, and particularly the infantry, was being ravaged by a variety of diseases, chief among them dysentery, ague and typhus…inexorably, the whole host seemed to be moving ponderously to disaster'.[33]

When the Russian retreat had reached as far as Borodino, about 72 miles west of Moscow, the Russian commander Kutuzov had no choice but to make a stand. By this time the French forces were already massively depleted by illness and they had been forced to abandon much of their artillery. In the ensuing battle, the largest in world history to that date (7 September 1812), Napoleon is estimated to have lost 40,000 men, including 14 lieutenant-generals, 33 major-generals, 32 staff-officers,

86 aides-de-camp and 37 regimental colonels. The Russians losses were even greater: and estimated 50,000 men, many of whom were mere cannon fodder.[34] A French participant in the battle, Phillipe-Paul de Ségur, wrote that the Russian infantry:

'...advanced in compact masses in which our cannon balls cut wide and deep swathes...Those inert masses simply let themselves be mowed down for two long hours, without any motion other than that of falling. The massacre was frightful: and our artillerymen, knowing the value of bravery, admired the blind, motionless, resigned courage of their enemies'.[35]

Napoleon finally reached Moscow, only to find that the city had been abandoned by its inhabitants and then set ablaze; he faced an unenviable dilemma. He had reached the heart of Russia but had no means of forcing Alexander to sue for peace. It was at this point that Napoleon considered marching on St Petersburg but was unable to do so because his army was so depleted and supply lines had been cut. One option which Napoleon seriously considered was to proclaim the abolition of serfdom as a way of undermining the Tsar and winning the support of the Russian peasantry.

While in Moscow, Napoleon ordered that all material available on the Pugachev Revolt be brought to him from archives and public libraries. In the event, the Russian government had already pre-empted the possibility of a rural uprising by stationing additional troops in the provinces to cope with such an eventuality. Napoleon's entry into Moscow was a catastrophe for Alexander.

When he attended a service at the Kazan cathedral in St Petersburg at the end of September, he was advised to travel in a closed carriage rather than on horseback, to avoid public hostility. When the royal party entered the church, the crowd fell silent.

On 19 October 1812, faced with the onset of a Russian winter and constantly harassed by partisan groups, the Grande Armée was forced to abandon Moscow. Less than 40,000 men survived the journey back to France, from an army of over 400,000, a blow from which Napoleon never recovered.

Alexander, one the other hand, was now lauded as the Tsar Liberator and soon: '...the French invasion, and his own religious experience, had convinced him that he had a mission to save Europe and Europe's oppressed people (including the French) from the tyranny of Napoleon'.[36] A new alliance was forged with Prussia and shortly afterwards the Austrian Chancellor, Clemens von Metternich, despite reservations, agreed to join the coalition.

In June 1813, at Alexander's headquarters in Reichenbach, the three continental monarchies agreed terms for the restoration of all Prussian and Austrian territories lost to the French, to recreate independent German states and to formally dissolve the Duchy of Warsaw, the buffer state created by Napoleon on former Polish territory. The alliance was supported by the British but, like Metternich, they nevertheless feared the consequences of a Russian victory and what this might mean for Alexander's ambitions in Poland and the Balkans.

Over the coming months the combined forces of Russia and Prussia pursued the remnants of the Grand Armée back to France and, on 31 March 1814, Russian troops entered Paris, with Alexander leading the troops on horseback. The Tsar followed up his triumphal arrival in Paris with ceremonial visits to England and Holland, where he was greeted as a popular hero. In the following months, he was also heavily involved in negotiations on the terms under which his cousin, the Bourbon candidate Louis XVIII, would be restored as King. These talks are important because it was through Alexander's insistence that Louis was returned to the throne not as an absolute monarch but as a constitutional monarch. That the same should happen in Russia was to become one of the central demands of the liberal opposition in Russia in the coming years. The new French constitution enshrined the principle of equality before the law and religious toleration and retained Napoleon's Civil Code.

Alexander also played an important role in the establishment of a constitution for Switzerland, the birthplace of his tutor de La Harpe. And he approved the establishment of a new German Confederation of 38 states, with a Federal Diet, or parliament, at Frankfurt. When it came to the tricky question of Poland, however, there were major obstacles to an agreed constitutional settlement:

'The Russians had no reason to feel generous. Napoleon had hoped that the Polish and Lithuanian nobility within the

Russian Empire would rally to the French cause in 1812. Although this did not happen to any significant degree, approximately 100,000 Poles from the Duchy of Warsaw had joined the invasion of Russia. Many of them envisaged a restored Poland which would include at least the lands acquired by Russia as a result of the Partitions and possibly absorb part of the Ukraine. The popular perception of the behaviour of Polish troops in Russia (Russian memoirists consistently put the blame for most atrocities in Western Russia on the Poles rather than the French or other nationalities in Napoleon's multinational army) further inflamed Russian popular opinion against the Poles'.[37]

One of Alexander's defining characteristics was that he could express a viewpoint to one person which he would diametrically contradict with another. He was, in other words, entirely two-faced. In May 1814, he wrote to the Polish rebel leader, Tadeusz Koskiusko – who had led the rebellion against Catherine the Great's Second Partition of Poland, in 1794 – promising that:

'With the assistance of the All-Powerful, I hope to effect the regeneration of the brave and respectable nation which you belong to…a little more time, and with a wise course, and the Poles will recover their true name and I will have the pleasure of convincing them that the man who they believed to be their enemy will, having forgotten the past, fulfil all their desires. How much it will please me, General, to have your assistance in these beneficial labours!' [38]

However, when Adam Czartoryski, a member of one of the oldest and wealthiest families in Poland, came up with a proposal for the creation of an enlarged kingdom of Poland to be ruled by Alexander's younger brother, Michael, Alexander ruled it to be 'impractical at this stage'. He also told Czartoryski that he regarded the lands acquired by Russia as a result of the Partitions as permanent possessions.

In their younger days, both Czartoryski and Alexander had been members of an inner circle of reformers known as the Unofficial Committee. Three of the members of this secretive cabal – Czartoryski himself, Nicolay Novosiltsev and Victor Kochubey – had been forced to leave Russia during the reign of Alexander's father, Paul, but were allowed back after his death.

The declared purpose of the Unofficial Committee was to come up with proposals for reform of Russia's state institutions and all of its members were known to be 'filled with French and Polish constitutional spirit'.[39]

Now, as a result of peace talks which took place during 1814-15, a new Congress Kingdom of Poland was created, with its own constitution. However, the Polish constitution also bound Poland to Russia, through the person of the Tsar, who became King of Poland. The constitution permitted the election of a lower house of parliament, or *Sejm,* but it only had limited powers: it had no authority to initiate legislation and relied entirely on the king to decide when it should be called and whether or not its decisions should be implemented.

To cap it all, the person Alexander appointed to the most authoritative post in the government, that of Viceroy, was his brother Constantine. As one of Alexander's chief advisers on constitutional change, Mikhail Speransky once said, in an unguarded moment: 'You know the suspicious character of the Emperor. Whatever he does, he does by halves. He is too feeble to reign and too strong to be governed'.[40]

The reforms Alexander introduced for Poland created contradictory signals which were to have important consequences for the history of both Poland and Russia in the next two decades. The Poles regarded the powers granted to them under the new constitution to be weaker than those which had been enshrined in the Polish Constitution of 1791, while the liberal voices of Russia wanted to know why Poland could have its constitution but not Russia?

The outcome was that: 'Alexander demonstrated yet again his stubbornness by his determination to proceed with this plan against the advice of his diplomats and advisers; these feared that his actions would only increase Polish ambitions and that the constitution would be a dangerous inspiration for Russian youth'.[41] The widespread enthusiasm for constitutional change, especially among the young, alarmed many of the older generation.

When Alexander gave a speech to the Polish *Sejm* in 1818, he expressed the hope that the Polish constitution would 'extend a beneficial influence over all the countries which Providence had committed to my care'.[42] This type of talk alarmed many conservatives in Russia. One member of the General Staff was heard to say that Alexander's speech could have terrifying consequences. And when Pushkin's former mentor, the staunchly conservative, Nikolay Karamzin, heard that the Tsar had appointed Nikolay Novosiltsev to draw up a constitution for Russia, he told

Alexander that: '…to give Russia a constitution…is to dress up some respected man in a dunce's cap'. To emphasise the point, he later added: 'Russia is not England, autocracy is its soul'.[43]

At about this time, Pushkin had just arrived in St Petersburg, at the age of 18, and paid a number of visits to the home of Karamzin, but his relationship with him became increasingly strained, partly because of Pushkin's reckless behaviour and partly because of Karamzin's conservatism. Pushkin wrote a damning epigram ridiculing Karamzin's stance:

'In his 'History' elegance and simplicity
Disinterestedly demonstrate to us
The necessity for autocracy
And the charms of the knout'.[44]

By the end of 1819, a report in a Paris newspaper, *Le Constitutionnel,* announced that Novosiltsev's constitutional proposals had been completed and that: 'The Emperor Alexander is going to lay the foundations of representative government in his vast empire, by giving a constitution to Russia'. [45] But, when the draft of his proposals was finally released, it emerged that although there was to be an elected lower house, or *duma,* similar to the Polish *Sejm,* members of the upper chamber would be appointed by Alexander. Furthermore, Article 12 of the document stated very clearly: 'The sovereign is the only source of all authority (*pouvoirs)* in the Empire'.[46]

In the event, none of Novosilstev's proposals were ever implemented, mainly because of troubling developments at home and abroad. Despite the constitutional concessions Alexander believed he had made to Poland, in both 1818 and 1820 there was uproar in the public galleries of the parliament when gangs of students and journalists thronged the galleries and applauded obstructive speeches.

The French constitution had not prevented the revival of revolutionary sentiments and uprisings of the '*carbonari*' in Spain and Italy alarmed the Tsar and his advisers. They became increasingly convinced of the existence of a European-wide revolutionary conspiracy. One of those who went to great lengths to convince the Tsar of the necessity to ditch his infatuation with liberalism was his meddlesome younger sister, the Grand Duchess Catherine of Russia. She approached the official historiographer, Nikolay Karamzin, with the proposition that he should write a historical summary, hoping that his conservative influence would help to discourage her brother's notion of pursuing liberal reforms in Russia. Despite misgivings, Karamzin duly obliged and produced a short treatise called '*Memoir on Ancient and Modern Russia*'.

In the event, the Grand Duchess's ploy backfired: although Karamzin's 'memoir' argued in favour of an autocratic form of government for Russia as a guiding principle, in his introductory section on 'bygone reigns' his portraits of the Romanovs who had preceded Alexander were shockingly forthright for their day and often scathing in their estimation of previous Tsars and Tsarinas. Speaking of what happened during the mid-18th century reigns of the Empresses Anne and Elizabeth, for example, he said:

'Russia stayed on the course which had been charted for her by the hand of Peter, departing ever further from her ancient customs and coming closer to those of Europe. Secular tastes made rapid strides. The Russian court dazzled with splendour, and, having spoken German for several years, now turned to French. In matters of dress, carriage equipment, service, our lords vied with Paris, London and Vienna. But the terrors of autocracy still frightened the minds of the people; they looked about whenever the name of the most gentle Elizabeth or a powerful minister came up; tortures and the Secret Chancery continued to exist'.[47]

Karamzin expressed great admiration for Catherine the Great. In his view, she had: 'cleansed autocracy of the stains of tyranny…this calmed men's hearts and led to the development of secular pleasures, knowledge and reason'.[48] On the other hand, 'we must admit that the most brilliant reign of Catherine was not without its dark side'.[49]

THE MAN WHO SHOOK HIS FIST AT THE TSAR

Citing violation of the cannons of morality, depravity and 'foibles' which would make a person 'blush for mankind', Karamzin also notes that justice 'did not flourish at that time' and that the political institutions devised by Catherine 'reveal more sparkle than substance'.[50] This was all strong stuff to put before any Tsar, let alone Alexander, who was Catherine's grandson. When it came to Alexander's own achievements, Karamzin's judgement was even more damning. Here, he admitted, 'I need spiritual fortitude to speak the truth'. Russia, he says: 'is seething with dissatisfaction. Complaints are heard in the palaces and in the cottages; the people lack confidence as well as enthusiasm for the government and condemn strongly its aims and policies'.[51]

Usually, Karamzin argues, the successor to a cruel monarch (such as Alexander's father, Paul) should easily win general acceptance when he takes a softer approach. But it had been quite the opposite with Alexander: 'How then shall we explain this woeful condition of public opinion among the people who have been calmed by Alexander's gentleness, whom he had freed from the threat of unjust persecution by the Secret Chancellery and Siberian exile, and to whom he has given the freedom to enjoy all the pleasures permissible in civil societies?'.[52]

The answer, Karamzin went on to argue, lay in a series of catastrophic misjudgements in Alexander's dealings with Napoleon. These failures had led to the humiliating defeat for the Russian army at the Battle of Austerlitz and the unfavourable settlement with Napoleon at Tilsit. This, in turn, had led to the abandonment of Russia's special relationship with Napoleon's sworn enemy, England, and had culminated in the consolidation of French hegemony throughout Europe. It had made Russia, through the newly created Duchy of Warsaw 'the neighbours of Napoleon'.[53]

Karamzin was every bit as uncharitable about Alexander's attempted reforms of political institutions and for his having 'developed a fancy to introduce novelties into the principal organs of royal authority'.[54] He poured scorn on Alexander's attempts to reform the education system in Russia; and opposed the abolition of serfdom and the creation of a form of Code Napoleon which would afford political rights to Russian citizens.

Hardly surprisingly that when Karamzin met with Alexander at his sister's residence in Tver, hoping to discuss his memoir, it met with a frosty response. So frosty, that the original manuscript never saw the light of day until 25 years later, when it was unearthed among the papers of Alexander's chief policy adviser, Aleksey Arakcheyev. and a copy came into the possession of Pushkin's friend, the poet Zhukovsky. When Karamzin died, in 1826, Zhukovsky had a transcript of the memoir made for Karamzin's widow and another was made for Pushkin.

Pushkin kept this copy and was in the process of having a part of Karamzin's *memoir* published in the edition of his journal *The Contemporary* (*Sovremennik*), shortly before the duel in which he died. Pushkin deliberately submitted to the censors only the first part, which contained the historical introduction, not the hefty critique of the Romanov's track record, but even this was severely cut. When the text came back from the censors, Pushkin attached to it a brief foreword, which read:

'In the Second Number of *Sovremennik* (for 1836) we made reference to an unpublished work of the late Karamzin. We consider ourselves fortunate to be able to present to our readers at least an excerpt from the precious manuscript. In it they will hear, if not the whole speech of our great compatriot, then at least the sound of his silenced voice'.[55]

Pushkin then issued instructions to have the memoir published in the following issue, scheduled for early 1837, but was shot and killed before it went to the printers. Despite a further attempt by the censors to block publication of the memoir after Pushkin's death, a severely truncated version did finally appear, with Pushkin's foreword. This version stopped at the time of Peter the Great but here again, it was only a bowdlerised version from which 'all hostile or even mildly critical remarks had been expurgated'. [56]

After the censors had done their job, the entire emphasis of Karamzin's original text was now quite different: 'Instead of an impassioned critique of Russia's past and particularly Russia's present, the public read a paean in honour of all previous tsars and a grand eulogy of the course of Russian history'.[57]

Nevertheless, handwritten copies of the full text did circulate clandestinely in Moscow and St Petersburg and excerpts were published by the Decembrist, Nicholas Turgenev, from exile in Paris. By the time the truncated memoir was published, Alexander I was no longer Tsar. His brother, Nicholas I, who replaced Alexander in 1826 after the Decembrist uprising, would not have been any more impressed by what the *memoir* had to say about the Romanov family's record.

In particular, Nicholas might well have baulked at Karamzin's description of Nicholas's father, Paul, who, like Nicholas himself: 'took to ruling by means of general terror, obeying no law save his own whim. He treated us not as his subjects but as his slaves. He executed the innocent and rewarded the worthless. His actions robbed capital punishment of the stigma of disgrace…In the regiments, he stamped out the noble spirit of war…substituting for it the spirit of martinetism. Heroes, accustomed to victories, he taught to parade'.[58]

Another aspect of Karamzin's memoir, is that it has a particular relevance to *The Bronze Horseman,* which Pushkin was working on at this time. This emerges in the historical passages which deal with Peter the Great's decision to build his new capital city in the midst of a swamp – the exploit which is roundly praised in the prologue and then held up to question in the body of the poem.

Karamzin bluntly questions the wisdom of this move and asks: 'Shall we close our eyes to yet another glaring mistake of Peter the Great? I mean his founding a new capital on the northern frontier of the state, amidst muddy billows, in a place condemned by nature to barrenness and want'.[59] Furthermore, Karamzin continues:

'He might have founded on the shores of the Neva a commercial city for the import and export of merchandise; but the idea of establishing there the residence of our sovereigns was, is, and will remain, a *pernicious* one. How many people perished, how much money and labour was expended to carry out his intent? Truly, Petersburg is founded *on tears and corpses…* This is the residence of the Russian sovereigns who must strive to the utmost to keep the courtiers and guards from starving to death, as well as make good the annual loss of inhabitants with newcomers, future victims of premature death! Man shall not overcome nature!'.[60]

Pushkin draws much the same conclusion in *The Bronze Horseman*, in that part of the poem where the Tsar, Alexander I, watches helpless from his balcony as the waters from the Great

Flood of 1824 invade the city. When Pushkin's play about the Time of Troubles, *Boris Godunov*, was finally published, after much interference from the Tsar, the dedication which appeared in the preface read: 'To the memory, precious to Russians, of Nikolay Mikhailovich Karamzin, this work, inspired by his genius, with reverence and gratitude is dedicated'.[61]

Pushkin's estimation of Alexander was less generous: when he went to see the marble bust of Alexander made by the much-sought-after Danish sculptor, Bertel Thorvaldsen, Pushkin wrote:

To the Bust of a Conqueror

'Look here, there must have been a slip:
The artist's hand encapsulates
A smile upon these marble lips,
But a frown upon that cold, shiny pate.
That he looks two-faced must surely be meant
That's what you'd expect from this sovereign
In the habit of mixed-up sentiments
In his face, as in life, a harlequin'.

Notes

1 Pushkin. Canto X of *Eugene Onegin.* Quoted in **Pushkin,** by T J Binyon, Harper Collins, 2002, p42

2   **The Romanovs: Autocrats of All the Russias**, by W Bruce Lincoln, Anchor Books, 1981, p370

3   Bruce-Lincoln, ibid. p379

4   **Memoirs of Prince Adam Czartoryski and His Correspondence with Alexander I** (Volume 1), by Adam Jerzy Czartoryski, with documents relative to the Prince's negotiation with Pitt Fox and Brougham and an account of his conversations with Lord Palmerston and other English Statesmen in London in 1832, First published 1888, reprinted by Gyan Books (Facsimile Publisher), 2015, p235

5   Czartoryski, ibid. p245

6   Czartoryski, ibid. p245

7   Czartoryski, ibid. p246

8   Czartoryski, ibid. p246

9   Czartoryski, ibid. p246

10   Bruce-Lincoln, op.cit., p381

11   Czartoryski, op.cit. p247

12   Czartoryski, op.cit. p247

13   Czartoryski, op.cit. p249

14   Czartoryski, op.cit. p249

15   Empress Maria Feodorovna (Sophie Dorothea of Württemberg). See Wikipedia entry (paragraph on Dowager Empress).

16   **Road to Revolution: A Century of Russian Radicalism**, by Avrahm Yarmolinsky, Collier Books, New York, 1962, p21

17   **Pushkin Threefold: Narrative, Lyric, Polemic & Ribald Verse**, the originals, with linear and metric translations by Walter Arndt, includes a verse translation of *The Bronze Horseman,* Allen & Unwin, 1972, p3

18   Bruce-Lincoln, opcit. p384

19   Quoted in **A History of Russia,** by Nicholas V Riasanovsky, Oxford University Press, Fifth edition, 1993, p300

20   **The Age of Revolution: Europe 1789-1848**, by Eric Hobsbawm, Abacus, 2014 (first published 1962), p73

21   Hobsbawm, ibid. p102

22   **Eugene Onegin: A Novel in Verse,** by A S Pushkin, translated with an introduction and notes by Stanley Mitchell, Penguin Books, 2008, Ch.VII, Verse 19, p151

23   Hobsbawm, op.cit. p104

24   **Alexander I,** by Janet M Hartley, Longman, 1994, p73

25   Hartley, ibid. p73

26   Hartley, ibid. p74

27   Hartley, ibid. p74

28   Hartley, ibid. p77

29 Hartley, ibid. pp77-78

30 Hartley, ibid. p79

31 Hartley, ibid. p79

32 **Memoirs of Prince Adam Czartoryski and His Correspondence with Alexander I** (Volume 1), by Adam Jerzy Czartoryski, with documents relative to the Prince's negotiation with Pitt Fox and Brougham and an account of his conversations with Lord Palmerston and other English Statesmen in London in 1832, First published 1888, reprinted by Gyan Books (Facsimile Publisher), 2015. p85

33 Hartley, op.cit. p113

34 Hartley, op.cit. p115

35 Hartley, op.cit. p115

36 Hartley, op.cit. p121

37 Hartley, op.cit. p130

38 Hartley, op.cit. p130

39 Hartley, op.cit. p32

40 Hartley, op.cit. p91

41 Hartley, op.cit. p133

42 Hartley, op.cit. p166

43 Hartley, op.cit. p168

44 Binyon, op.cit p83

45 Hartley, op.cit. p170

46 Hartley, op.cit. p172

47 **Karamzin's Memoir on Ancient & Modern Russia.** A Translation & Analysis. By Richard Pipes. The University of Michigan Press. 2008 (first published 1959). p130

48 Karamzin, ibid. p131

49 Karamzin, ibid. p133

50 Karamzin, ibid. p133

51 Karamzin, ibid. p140

52 Karamzin, ibid. p140

53 Karamzin, ibid. p145

54 Karamzin, ibid. p147

55 Karamzin, ibid. p96

56 Karamzin, ibid. p97

57 Karamzin, ibid. p97

58 Karamzin, ibid. p135

59 Karamzin, ibid. p126

60 Karamzin, ibid. p127

61 **Boris Godunov and other Dramatic Works,** translated with notes by James E Falen, introduction by Caryl Emerson, Oxford World Classics, Oxford University Press, 2009, Historical introduction, p1.

'Reared as he was to drum and banner
Our Tsar was such a bold commander;
At Austerlitz, he ran
In 1812, he trembled...'

Pushkin, On Alexander I, 1825[1]

08 | Revolt of the Semenovsky

In October 1820, Alexander's 'own' regiment, the Semenovksy, refused to accept orders from their officers. The mutiny of the Semenovsky marked a critical turning point in Alexander's reign. This was one of the two oldest and most prestigious regiments in Russia. The other was the Preobrazhensky. Both had been created by Peter the Great and had served in the Great Northern War before being appointed to the elite status of Palace Guard. During the 18th century, the Semenovsky had played an instrumental role in bringing Catherine the Great to power and had also been on guard duty when the assassination of Alexander's father took place. Throughout the wars with Napoleon, the Semenovsky had carried the initiative in Alexander's campaigns and provided the equestrian escort for the Tsar when he entered Paris in 1814. 'The Preobrazhensky Regiment is a royal regiment', Alexander once remarked, 'but the Semenovsky is my own'.[2] Precisely because of its special status, the revolt of the regiment was all the more shocking.

The underlying factor behind the revolt was the way in which discontent had been steadily growing among officers and men returning from Paris after Napoleon's defeat. How could it be that they, the victors, were coming back to a country where fundamental human rights were non-existent and where serfdom underpinned the entire society?

In an article on the mutiny of the Semenovsky, written for *The*

Russian Review in 1970, Joseph Wyszynski writes that: 'By 1820 liberalism was common among Russian officers, and discontent was common among the lower ranks'. One observer reported having witnessed a group of Russian officers carousing in a Petersburg restaurant, apparently oblivious of the consternation they were causing among other diners, and singing a Russian version of a French revolutionary song:

> *'Our fatherland is suffering*
> *Under the yoke, villain!*
> *If despotism oppresses us*
> *We shall topple throne and Tsars'.*[3]

Officers of the Semenovsky Regiment were hand-picked from the best-known families of the Russian nobility and were granted privileges that no other unit would have received. Many of them had received the highest military honours and because of this were exempted from corporal punishment. The first indications that this privileged existence was about to come under threat manifested itself when Alexander announced that a club the officers had formed must be abolished. Alexander's attitude towards any symptom of potential 'liberalism' had hardened significantly since the Congress of Vienna in 1815, during which the Triple Alliance of Austria, Prussia and Russia had determined to stamp out revolutionary tendencies in Europe.

Eager to encourage him in this view were the Austrian Foreign Minister, Metternich, and Alexander's own chief adviser, Count Alexis Arakcheev, a rigid disciplinarian who had risen to power after the dismissal of the more moderate Speransky.

Metternich warned the Tsar that the revolt of the Semenovsky was most probably attributable to the work of secret societies operating within Russia. Arakcheev was increasingly influential in the Tsar's entourage and, after Russia's defeat at Austerlitz, had become a fanatical advocate of strict military discipline. This view was shared by Alexander's youngest brother, the Grand Prince Michael Pavlovich, who, in July 1819, was appointed to be commander of the First Guards Infantry Brigade, which comprised the Semenovsky, Preobrazhensky and Egersky regiments. It was an opinion also shared by Alexander's second youngest brother, the Grand Duke Nicholas Pavlovich, who was later to become Emperor Nicholas I.

Nicholas already commanded two brigades of the Guards and had been heard to complain that the Guards only ever conducted themselves in a proper military manner on the battlefield. Alexander's brother, Michael, was appalled at the privileges extended to the Semenovsky and began to urge the Emperor to exert greater discipline on the regiment. This meant replacing the existing commander, the much-respected General Potemkin. Arakcheev then proposed his own candidate for the position, another fanatical disciplinarian called Colonel Schwartz. He would be the ideal man 'to knock the nonsense out of the heads of those dandies'.[4]

Schwartz was widely regarded as a 'tactless and brutal martinet', whose appointment to replace Potemkin was greeted with despair by the officers of the Semenovsky. They were right to be concerned. Schwartz immediately insisted on the introduction of daily drills and inspections, during which 'the new commander acted like a man possessed. Screaming, shouting and throwing his cap in rage, Schwartz constantly berated and abused his charges'.[5] Against all the traditions of the regiment, Schwartz began to administer corporal punishment for even the most minor infractions of discipline, execution of orders and cleanliness. The final ignominy came when Schwartz took to spitting in the faces of perceived offenders and ordered men in the ranks to do likewise.

When he extended this treatment to the lower ranks and ordered that they pay for worn-out and damaged equipment from their own pockets, this proved too much. The regiment mutinied. In the middle of the night of 17 October 1820, the enlisted men of the 'the Emperor's own' First Company called their company commander and informed him they would no longer serve under Schwartz. He fled the compound, apparently fearing for his life. The commander of the Guards, General Vasilchikov, then assembled the entire regiment on the parade ground, drawn up between two double ranks from the Pavlovsky regiment. The officers and men of the First Company were accused of treason and mutiny and the entire force was marched off, under guard, to the dungeons of the Peter and Paul Fortress. The other 11 companies of the regiment then began to congregate in the barracks and when commanded to disperse, they demanded that either Schwartz be dismissed or they should be taken to the fortress as well. Vasilchikov's response was to agree to the second request and march the remainder of the regiment to the prison.

The revolt of the Semenovsky created immediate alarm in the upper echelons of the government and the military: 'The incident struck most of these men as a clear indication that the revolutionary unrest flaring throughout Europe had at last reached Russia; many decided that a radical movement had already been formed on Russian soil, with the mutiny as its first fruit'.[6] This view was more than confirmed when a written proclamation was discovered soon after, in the courtyard of the Preobrazhensky Regiment. The flyer made no mention of Schwartz but it did condemn the entire political and social structure of the Russian state and described Alexander himself as a 'powerful brigand'.

Written as an appeal to fellow soldiers, the leaflet proclaimed that the Semenovsky had been reduced to a pitiful state by its brutal commander 'and now was at the mercy of a tyrannical sovereign and his cruel nobility; that Alexander was a tyrant, who had been placed on the throne by the murderers of his father, Paul, and had then forced the people of Russia to swear allegiance to him or face punishment'.[7]

The note concluded with a call for representative government and for troops to be able to elect their own commanders and citizens free to choose their own officials.

As Wyszynski notes, this proclamation, and a second which followed soon after: '…can be regarded as the first truly seditious literature to appear in Russia'.[8] In the clampdown which followed its discovery, Alexander increasingly came under the influence of Metternich who warned that unless the Tsar implemented more repressive domestic policies, Russia would face revolutionary upheavals, just like the rest of Europe. The closing years of Alexander's reign were marked by ultra-conservatism verging on obscurantism and any prospect of reform was forgotten.

News of the mutiny of the Semenovsky Regiment first reached Alexander while he was attending a conference of the Quintuple Alliance being held at Troppau in Austria, in October 1820.

The main purpose of this gathering, which had been called at the request of Alexander, was to discuss the measures necessary to suppress the revolutionary wave sweeping Europe that year. This pandemic had already included revolutions in Spain, Portugal and Italy calling for the introduction of constitutional monarchies and, in Greece, for the overthrow of Ottoman rule.

In Britain, in the same year, the establishment was up in arms over 'the mania of wild liberty ...which is spreading in Britain'. There had been a series of outbreaks in different parts of the country since the end of the war against Napoleon, at the Battle of Waterloo, in 1815. These confrontations had culminated, in August 1819, with the Peterloo Massacre, when a peaceful demonstration of 60,000 in St Peter's Square, Manchester, was attacked by sabre-wielding cavalry. Eighteen people were killed in the ensuing bloodbath and over 700 men, women and children received serious injuries. Such was the insurrectionary climate throughout Britain in 1820 that, in a contemporary pamphlet, entitled *A Warning Letter to His Royal Highness the Prince Regent,* the author, the Reverend Lionel Berguer, a complete reactionary, warned:

'The people are entirely changed: loyalty and religion are not only exploded, but *laughed at,* and the most undisguised *hatred* of the government and *expectation* of its downfall are nightly expressed in almost every ale-house in the metropolis. Even the very beggars in the streets are growing insolent at the prospect...Dustmen and porters read and discuss politics'.[9]

Against this background of unrest across Europe, the most immediate issue being discussed by the European powers assembled at Troppau was how to deal with the revolution of 1820 which had erupted in Sicily and Naples. Inspired by the uprisings which had already taken place the same year in Cadiz, the revolt in Southern Italy had forced King Ferdinand I of the Two Sicilies to make concessions, which included the promise of a constitutional monarchy and the adoption of a parliament.

Encouraged by this apparent success, the revolt then spread to Northern Italy. It was led by members of the *carbonari*, or 'charcoal burners'. The fact that organisations like the *carbonari* appeared to be springing up all over caused increasing alarm among the crowned heads of Europe. When, in early 1821, the *carbonari* marched on Turin, then the capital of the Kingdom of Sardinia, they again won assurances that there would be substantial 'liberal' reforms and the introduction of a constitutional monarchy.

The Holy Alliance had no intention of allowing any such compromises and resolved to despatch an army to crush the rebellion in the south of Italy. This set out in February 1821 and by early April a Hapsburg army had defeated the rebels. Later that year, Pope Pious VII condemned the *carbonari* as a secret society of Freemasons and excommunicated their members.

The person who delivered the communiqué, bringing Alexander news of the Semenovsky Revolt from St Petersburg to Troppau, was Pyotr Chaadayev, one of the group of officers who had been stationed at Tsarskoe Selo during Pushkin's final years at the Imperial Lycée and had greatly influenced Pushkin. When the news arrived of the refusal of his 'own' regiment to obey orders, Alexander became convinced that the mutiny must be part of a wider movement which, if it was not rooted out and immediately suppressed, could threaten the government of Russia. In a letter to Arakcheev, he wrote:

'No one in this world, I tell you, will convince me that this incident was thought up by the soldiers or that it happened, as has been testified, because of their cruel treatment by Colonel Schwartz. He has always been known as a good and careful officer and has commanded his regiment with honour. Why should he suddenly become a barbarian? It is my belief that other causes are at the bottom of it'.[10]

To make sure there would be no repeat of the Semenovsky Revolt, the entire regiment was disbanded and the officers assigned to regular units. A military court was held at which 220 soldiers of the regiment, including most of the First Company, were found guilty of treasonous behaviour. Initially, all 220 were sentenced to death, but after one of Alexander's generals had intervened, this sentence was commuted to 50 lashes and imprisonment with hard labour.

Thinking that this concession was too lenient, Arakcheev recommended that each man be made to run the gauntlet through a battalion, six times each, and then be committed to the Siberian mines. Arakcheev described his recommendations as 'the most humane measures it was possible for me to take' even though they meant that each man would receive as many as 6,000 blows. In 1821, Alexander decreed further reprisals against the families of the mutineers which withdrew permission allowing the wives of former Semenovsky soldiers to be resident either in St Petersburg or Moscow. In addition:

'Their children were barred from military service and were kept under surveillance, lest their parents' traits appeared in their progeny. A secret police organisation was instituted in the Guards to determine whether other units were deserving of similar attentions. This then, was the fate of the proud regiment that had six years earlier borne the Russian flag through the heart of Europe and brought Russia a military renown and recognition unique in her history'.[11]

As Alexander must have known, from the reports he received from his secret police in the years prior to the revolt, the first signs of an active underground opposition to the Russian autocracy were already evident. Several years earlier, in February 1816, six young officers had met up to form the secret society which came to be known as the Union of Salvation or Society of True and Faithful Sons of the Fatherland. All of these officers had served in the campaigns against Napoleon and all but one were freemasons. Most were also officers in the Semenovsky which possibly explains the real reason Schwartz had been sent to take command of the regiment.

The more that the outbreaks of rebellion in Europe weakened Alexander's enthusiasm for reform, the more they inspired the more radical intelligentsia: 'The Russian periodical press kept educated Russians informed of events in the Iberian and Italian peninsulas. Nikolay Turgenev wrote of that time that "we breathed European news"'. The outbreak of revolt filled educated Russians with the optimism that this was a Europe-wide process in which Russia would share and which would bring liberties to all European peoples, including themselves'.[12]

The Spanish revolt, against Napoleon, had a particularly strong influence: one future Decembrist, A P Beliayev, had witnessed the crushing of the Spanish revolt while serving as a naval officer aboard a Russian frigate in 1824. Rather than being discouraged by this defeat, the Spanish example had inspired 'more enthusiasm for freedom' and the method of revolt was of particular interest: '...in that the initial success was bloodless and was achieved by a small number of soldiers. This pattern could only appeal to the Russian military, especially as there were precedents in Russia for the army spearheading *coups d'état* against Tsars in the 18th century'.[13]

Another lesson acquired from the events in Spain was to have observed the actions of the Spanish king, Ferdinand VII. He had, initially, agreed to introduce the form of constitution demanded by the rebels: '...and then, three years later, reneged on his agreement and crushed the rebels by force with the assistance of French troops'.[14]

This convinced Russia's future Decembrists that rulers were not to be trusted, a conclusion which was strengthened by Alexander's role in the Spanish revolt: 'In 1812, he had recognised the very constitution which the rebels demanded in 1820; but now he sided with Ferdinand and ultimately approved of the French invasion'.[15]

One of the five Decembrists who were to be hanged for their part in the uprising, Pyotr Kakhovsky, concluded that: 'The breach of the constitution in France and its complete destruction in Spain were the reasons which compelled me to agree to the extermination of the imperial family'.[16] Portraits of Rafael del Riego and Antonio Quiroga, the leaders of the Spanish revolt, were displayed in a bookshop in St Petersburg during the abortive December Uprising.[17]

The first meeting of the Union of Salvation took place in a room of the officers' quarters belonging to the Semenovsky Life Guards on Zagorodny Prospect in St Petersburg. In attendance were six young officers, all aged between 21 and 26. They had all served abroad and their names were: Alexander and Nikita Muravyev, Prince Sergei Trubetskoy, Ivan Yakushkin and the brothers, Matvey and Sergei Muravyev-Apostol.[18] This group would form the nucleus of what would later become the Decembrist Revolt of 1825.

In its infancy, the Union of Salvation had about 30 members and was a form of dining club. According to one of the founders, Ivan Yakushkin, during these get-togethers, officers would read aloud foreign newspapers reporting on events in Europe. The primary aims of the Union were for the abolition of serfdom and the introduction of a constitution in Russia. Beyond this, there was not a great deal of unanimity on how these objectives could be achieved.

One member of the society, who had kept a dagger with which he hoped to murder Napoleon, proposed that he could now use it to kill Alexander instead. He suggested that the Tsar could easily be ambushed and assassinated by a band of masked men on his way to Tsarskoe Selo. Others were horrified at any suggestion of regicide and within a short space of time the organisation folded. But it was soon superseded by another secret society known as the Union of Welfare. This was formed in 1818 and grew to more than 200 members. In its early stages, the leadership of the Union of Welfare believed that the freedoms they hoped for in Russia would come about as a result of the reforms promised by Alexander.

As time passed, it became increasingly clear that, as Lenin later said, Alexander had only been 'playing at Liberalism'. There was a growing conviction that the whole system was rotten and that change was unlikely to happen without more decisive action. The most resolute advocate of a complete revolution and, if necessary, the use of force, was Colonel Pavel Pestel, a veteran of the Battle of Borodino and of the European campaigns against Napoleon.

Until his promotion to the command of a regiment of infantry at Vyatka, Pestel had been aide-de-camp to General Wittgenstein, General-in-Chief of the Second Army of the South. Pestel was the most determined activist in the branch of the Union of Welfare which was based at the headquarters of the Russian southern army at Tulchin, in present-day Ukraine.

In the immediate aftermath of the Semenovsky Revolt, membership of an organisation like Union of Welfare would have been an extremely hazardous pursuit. In effect, the organisation split, in part because of an emerging difference in emphasis between proponents of a campaign of 'moral force', mainly based in St Petersburg, and those in favour of 'physical force', headed by Pestel and based in the South. At a special conference of delegates held in 1821 it was agreed that it would be a wise move for the Union to temporarily dissolve itself.

Meantime, the core membership of the society, based in St Petersburg, would carry on in secret as the Northern Society, while the branches in the Ukraine, which refused to disband, assumed a quasi-independent status and adopted the name the Southern Society. A contemporary of Pestel, the French historian Jean Henri Schnitzler, wrote in his *Secret History of the Court and Government of Russia* that the real strength of the conspiracy was in the south:

> '...there were its men of action; there it formed as it were
> a vast net, the meshes of which, only a few months before,
> had been held by able and powerful hands. They had not
> wasted their time in making theories, but everything had been
> prepared for a general rising with arms in their hands; at the
> first signal, more than ten commanders of regiments would
> have been ready to march. The somewhat tardy vigilance
> of the government had, it is true, dissolved this formidable
> organisation; but despair gave added strength to its scattered
> remnants'.[19]

Schnitzler, who was employed as a tutor in Russia at the time, estimated that, if irregular troops were included, there was a total of more than 800,000 soldiers in the Russian army, of whom between 30,000 and 40,000 were in the Imperial Guard.

The sheer size of the army and what do with it after the wars with Napoleon had been one of the pressing concerns of the Russian government and had in fact been the primary reason for the creation of Arakcheev's much-detested 'military settlements' – outposts where under-utilised troops would be bivouacked with villagers, forcibly subjected to military discipline.

Despite its huge size, and because Russia's borders covered such a vast area, the army was nevertheless unevenly distributed around the country. The Imperial Guard and the Grenadiers formed the reserve force, and they were based in St Petersburg. The army proper, however: '...was being mustered in different points, either to keep a watch on Europe, ever agitated by ideas of progress and emancipation; or for the purposes of menacing Turkey, with which it had not been possible to come to any satisfactory arrangement since the rupture of 1821; or to repel the mountaineers of the Caucasus, who, though reduced to order in 1823, were again taking up arms; or, lastly, to guard Finland or other points on the frontier and the wilderness of Siberia'.[20]

The task of keeping a watch on Europe fell to the Lithuanian Corps and this was to prove extremely important factor during the events which were unfolded in 1825. In the vanguard of the Lithuanian Corps was the army of Poland, which, since 1822, was under the command of Alexander's younger brother, the Grand-Duke Constantine. Constantine had at his disposal a total of around 80,000 men; in the Second Army of the south, based at Tulchin, there were nearer 120,000; and, in the First Army, based at Kiev, an estimated 150,000.[21]

According to Schnitzler, what was common to all of these 'great bodies' – and the smaller concentrations which were stationed in Finland, Orenberg, Novgorod and Ekaterinburg – was that they all contained 'the nucleus of a military conspiracy': 'almost every corps was infected with it, and the idea had already been conceived of disaffecting the third corps of the Second Army, which was composed of two divisions of infantry, of one division of hussars, and of the artillery belonging to those divisions'. [22]

Not only were the majority of officers in favour of a revolt but 'an attempt had even been made to win the subalterns and soldiers, by insinuating that the time had come to rid themselves of the tyranny of their German chiefs, as the guards of the Semenoff (Semenovsky) had formerly done'.[23] In evidence given to the Report of the Commission of Enquiry, which later followed the Decembrist Revolt, a Captain Kornilovich maintained that 100,000 men in the Second Army of the south were prepared to join the revolt.

As if to add a match to this tinderbox, the government decided to send many of the lower ranks of the Semenovsky Regiment and some of the officers who had taken part in the revolt of 1821 to join the Third Corps of the Russian southern armies. As Joseph Wyszynski remarks, their appearance must have come as 'something of a godsend' to the conspirators in the Southern Society: '...their outraged sense of justice could easily foster a spirit of dissatisfaction in the lower ranks that would parallel the desire for reform felt by the upper ranks and facilitate co-operation between the two...The officers who had served in the old Semenovsky Regiment at the time of its mutiny could mediate between the common soldiers and the strategists of the Southern Society of Decembrists and prepare the ranks for insurrection'.[24]

Both the Northern and Southern Societies pinned their hopes on a purely military campaign, believing that they could secure the command of enough regiments to mount a successful military coup. Their inspiration had been the revolt led by the Spanish General, Rafael del Riego, which had started in Cadiz in January 1820 and then spread to the rest of the country, forcing the King of Spain to agree the restoration of the former constitution of 1812.

None of the leaders of the planned revolt in Russia envisaged the possibility of a popular uprising. On the contrary, they were nearly all members of the nobility and most of them believed they had every bit as much to fear from the townsfolk and the peasantry as they had from their tyrannical government. For some, the rebellion was necessary precisely to avoid the bloodbath which was likely if nothing was going to change in Russia. What would happen if a popular uprising turned into a Frankenstein monster?

In a letter to one of his co-conspirators, a member of the Southern Society wrote: 'Let us suppose that it is easy to bring the axe of revolution into play, but are you certain that you will be able to stop it afterwards?'[25] Baron Steinheil, of the Northern Society, voiced similar concerns. In Moscow alone, he said, there were 90,000 serfs ready to seize knives, and the first victims, he predicted, would be their own sisters, aunts and grandmothers.

Pestel, along with the majority of the rebels in the south, favoured the establishment of a republican regime in Russia, modelled on the constitution introduced in America following its battle for independence from Britain. He outlined his proposals in great detail in a book called the *Russkaya Pravda* (Russian Truth). Pestel also believed that, to ensure its success, the *coup* would need to assassinate the Emperor and, indeed, the entire royal family. He conceived the idea of a 'lost cohort', a form of suicide squad which would be prepared to act as regicides on orders from the Society. One retired captain in the Society was said to have come up with the novel idea that a cost-effective way of dealing with the imperial family would be to construct an 'economy gallows' tall enough to accommodate the Tsar as well as all the Grand Dukes, hanging each one vertically from the feet of the next.

One of the most active members of the Union of Salvation in the North had been Pushkin's close friend at the Lycée, Ivan Pushchin. He joined the Union in the summer of 1817 while he was an ensign in the Life Guards Horse Artillery. Pushchin later wrote that he had thought of introducing Pushkin to membership of the society, because 'we always thought alike about the *res publica*' but had ultimately decided against it. The reason he gave was that 'when I thought of carrying out this idea, I could not bring myself to entrust a secret to him, which was not mine alone, where the slightest carelessness could be fatal to the whole affair'.[26]

Despite Pushchin's vigilance, just a few months before the mutiny of the Semenovsky Regiment took place, Pushkin had been sent by Alexander to his 'warm exile' in the south. His journey to the south began in May 1820. This meant that, by the time he arrived in the Ukraine, in November – about a month after the Semenovsky Revolt – he soon found himself in the company of the Union of Salvation.

The Davydova estate in Kamenka was where leading members of the Southern Society would meet and was its *de facto* headquarters. Pushkin stayed here between September and November 1820. The owner of the estate, Ekaterina Davydova, was a niece of Catherine the Great's favourite, Grigory Potemkin. She was an extremely wealthy *grande dame* and owned a number of substantial estates in the south. Kamenka itself was enormous, with an artificial grotto, a billiard room, a library and its own serf orchestra. One of Davydova's sons, Basil, was a war hero and an influential member of the Southern Society. In his biography of Pushkin, Henri Troyat writes that all the local revolutionaries met at Kamenka: 'On November 24, his mother's birthday, every liberal for miles around assembled at Kamenka, ostensibly to wish the chatelaine many happy returns of the day. On that occasion, Pushkin met the future Decembrists Yakushkin and Okhotnikov, and the very remarkable General Orlov, a rabid conspirator and author of a petition demanding the abolition of serfdom'.[27]

As well as these individuals, there was a:

'swarm of military men, too, both active and retired, but all of them inspired by the same hatred of the government and the same dream of social reform. These informed plotters were actually meeting to prepare a vast secret assembly which was to take place in Moscow in January 1821…Their idea was not to start a people's revolution but to overthrow the tsarist regime by a military coup, and then, once the country was liberated, to establish a constitutional government of their choice. The Spanish revolution, the Neapolitan Revolution of July 1820, the Portuguese Revolution of August 1820 had all been preceded by military *coups d'etat;* they would follow the example of these pioneers of independence'.[28]

During his time at Kamenka, Pushkin had taken part in a lively and supposedly theoretical discussion for and against the establishment of a society like the Union of Salvation. According to one of those present, the revolutionary Yakushkin, Pushkin had 'heatedly demonstrated all the advantages that a secret society could bring Russia'.[29] When Yakushkin ribbed Pushkin by asking if such a secret society already existed, would he join it, Pushkin replied that he certainly would and was infuriated when told they had only been teasing.

Clearly upset at being made to look a fool, Yakushkin recorded Pushkin as saying: 'I have never been so unhappy as now; I already saw my life ennobled and a sublime goal before me, and all this was only a malicious joke'.[30] At each stage on his journey, from St Petersburg to Kamenka and then from Kamenka to Kishinev, Pushkin encountered 'the same atmosphere of demagogical debate and conspiracy'.[31] He even met with the leader of the Southern Society, Pavel Pestel, another of the five who was to die on the scaffold for his part in the conspiracy against the Tsar.

On April 9 Pushkin wrote in his diary: 'Spent the morning with Pestel; a man of wit in every sense. My heart is materialist, he said, but my reason rebels against it. We had a metaphysical, political, moral etc. conversation. He is one of the most original minds I know…'[32] By the time Pushkin arrived at Kishinev (now known as Chisinau, capital of Moldova) it was March 1821 and an insurrection had broken out in Greece: 'Serbs, Romanians, Albanians, Bulgarians and Greeks flooded the town with their strongboxes, their harlots and their portable patriotism'.[33] Pushkin was said to be 'in transports of enthusiasm and impatience. That struggle for freedom he had talked about so often with the officer conspirators of St Petersburg and Kamenka was suddenly becoming a reality, here on the outposts of the empire'.[34]

In May, Pushkin asked a young Frenchman who was setting off to join the Greek rebellion, if he would carry a letter from him addressed to the leader of the revolt, Prince Alexander Ypsilanti, requesting that he too be allowed to join the ranks of the resistance. While in Kishinev, he joined a Masonic Lodge, known as 'Ovid No 25,' where he 'participated joyfully in its political discussions and plans to change the face of Europe'.[35] Soon after, the local Commander, General Insov, received a letter from St Petersburg wanting to know how Pushkin had been behaving and why Insov 'had not seen fit to remark upon his activities in the Masonic order'.[36]

By this stage, Pushkin was under constant surveillance by the police. As far away as St Petersburg, it was already widely known that Pushkin was 'publicly, and even in cafes, maligning not only the military administration, but the government as well'.[37]

As the Pushkin biographer, T J Binyon, comments:
'Considered objectively, it is difficult to imagine why any serious conspirator belonging to an organisation which had the aim of overthrowing an absolute monarchy would wish to enlist a crackbrained, giddy, intemperate and dissolute young rake, whose heart and sentiments – as his poetry demonstrated – might have been in the right place, but whose reason often seemed too absent. How could any conspiracy remain secret which had as one of its members someone who, in a theatre swarming with police spies, paid and amateur, was capable of parading round the stalls carrying a portrait of the French saddler, Louvel, who assassinated Charles, duc de Berry, in 1820, inscribed with the words 'A Lesson to Tsars?'[38]

On another occasion, again at the theatre and in full view of the rest of the audience, Pushkin had shouted out: 'Now is the safest time – the ice is coming down the Neva'.[39] By this he meant that a surprise revolt would not face any problem dealing with troops from the fortress because they would be unable to cross the river. Pushkin is also believed to have written at this time an adaptation of the famous lines by Diderot:

'We will amuse the good citizens, And in the pillory
With the guts of the last priest, will strangle the last Tsar'.

Notes

1 **Pushkin Threefold: Narrative, Lyric, Polemic & Ribald Verse**. The originals, with linear and metric translations by Walter Arndt, includes a verse translation of *The Bronze Horseman*, Allen & Unwin, 1972, pp23, 203

2 **The Mutiny of the Semenovsky Regiment in 1820,** by Joseph L Wyszynski, *The Russian Review*, Vol. 29, No. 2 (April 1970). p167

3 Wyszynski, ibid. p169

4 Wyszynski, p170

5 Wyszynski, p170

6 Wyszynski, p172

7 Wyszynski, p172

8 Wyszynski, p173

9 **Poetry and Popular Protest: Peterloo, Cato Street and the Queen Caroline Controversy**, by John Gardner, Palgrave Macmillan, 2011, p6

10 Wyszynski, p177

11 Wyszynski, p178

12 **Alexander I,** by Janet M Hartley, Longman, 1994, p213

13 Hartley, ibid. p214

14 Hartley, p214

15 Hartley, p214

16 Hartley, p214

17 Hartley, p215

18 **Pushkin,** by T J Binyon, Harper Collins, 2002, p56

19 **Secret History of the Court and Government of Russia,** Volume 2: *Under the Emperors Alexander and Nicholas*, by Johann Heinrich Schnitzler, Kessinger Legacy Reprints, First published 1847, p3

20 Schnitzler, ibid. p4

21 Schnitzler, ibid. p5

22 Schnitzler, ibid. p9

23 Schnitzler, ibid. p10

24 Wyszynski, op/cit. p178

25 **Road to Revolution: A Century of Russian Radicalism**, by Avrahm Yarmolinsky, Princeton University Press, 1986, p28

26 Binyon, op.cit. p57

27 **Pushkin,** by Henri Troyat, translated from the French by Nancy Amphoux, George, Allen & Unwin, 1974, p165

28 Troyat, ibid. pp165-66

29 Troyat, ibid. p167

30 Troyat, ibid. p167

31 Troyat, ibid. p177

32 Troyat, ibid. p177

33 Troyat, ibid. p177

34 Troyat, ibid. p177

35 Troyat, ibid. p179

36 Troyat, ibid. p179

37 Troyat, ibid. p179

38 Binyon, op.cit. p59

39 Binyon, op.cit. p59

*'This story is based on actual events. Details of the flood are
derived from contemporary reports. For those who wish to
investigate further, see the account given by V N Berkh'.*

Pushkin, Foreword to *The Bronze Horseman,* 1833[1]

09 | The Great Flood of 1824

One of the unforeseen consequences of Peter's plans for his new capital city was that, throughout its history, St Petersburg was vulnerable to widespread flooding. The floods were driven in at regular intervals by winter storms driving eastwards from the Baltic Sea. The winds would force the natural east-west flow of the Neva into reverse and the build-up would then inundate the city. The worst of these storms broke on the evening of 6 November 1824, an event which takes centre stage in *The Bronze Horseman*. The Great Flood of 1824 was the most devastating in the history of the city. Several hundred people are thought to have drowned in the floodwaters, roads were destroyed and raw sewage flowed onto the streets, exacerbating already poor sanitary conditions. It took more than a decade for the city to recover fully from the impact of the flood and its aftermath contributed to the subsequent cholera epidemic which struck in 1831.

After the Great Storm, a special study was commissioned by the Admiralty to examine the frequency of these floods. In the subsequent report – which was published in 1826 and which is referred to by Pushkin in the preface to *The Bronze Horseman* – the author, V N Berkh, documents a total of 11 major floods in St Petersburg between 1721 and 1824. All except one of these took place either in September, October or November and each lifted the waters engulfing the city by up to 16 feet above their normal level.[2]

An eye witness account of the 1824 flood was written by an English physician who was resident in St Petersburg when it happened. His account is reproduced in the memoir written by a colleague, Robert Lee MD:

'The autumnal equinoctial gales most generally prevail at St Petersburg from the south-west, by which the waters of the Gulf of Finland and Neva are much increased. So it was in 1824; and for some weeks the wind continued from nearly the same quarter. The night of the 18th of November was very stormy; and at daylight of the 19th it blew a hurricane from WSW, by which the stream of the river – the upper part at least – was reversed, and the waters, running higher than ever remembered, soon caused the lower parts of the city …to be inundated. At nine o'clock in the morning I attempted to cross the Voskresenskoy Bridge of boats, on my way to the General Naval Hospital in the Wyborside, but was unable owing to the great elevation…From this time the rise was rapid ; and at half-past eleven, when I returned to my house, in the Great Millione, the water was gushing upwards through the gratings of the sewers, filling the streets and courtyards with which every house is provided…The wind now blew in awful gusts; and the noise of the tempest with the cries of the people in the streets was terrific. It was not long ere boats were seen in the streets, with vast quantities of firewood and other articles floating about…Now and then a horse was seen swimming across from one pavement to another…'[3]

Robert Lee was one of a number of English doctors who attended to the Tsar, Alexander I, when he took ill unexpectedly the following year, when on a trip to Taganrog in the Crimea. In his memoir, which is called *The Last days of Alexander and the First Days of Nicholas (Emperors of Russia),* Dr Lee records that: 'the effects of this calamity were still visible more than a year after, when I visited St Petersburgh subsequent to the death of the Emperor Alexander. The red painted lines to the houses still remained to mark the height to which the water had risen'.[4]

Another eye witness account of the flood was written by an African-American traveller, anti-slavery campaigner and proto-feminist, Nancy Gardner Prince, who was in Russia during the Great Flood as well as during the succession crisis and Decembrist Revolt of the following year. Nancy Gardner had married an older man, called Nero Prince, who was among a small number of black domestic staff employed in the Russian court since the time of Peter the Great. He was most likely taken on because of his seafaring connections.

In a narrative account of her travels, '*A Black Woman's Odyssey through Russia and Jamaica*', Nancy Prince writes: 'St Petersburg was inundated October 9th, 1824. The water rose 16 feet in most parts of the city; many of the inhabitants were drowned. An island between the city and Cronstadt, containing five hundred inhabitants, was inundated, and all were drowned, and great damage was done at Cronstadt. The morning of this day was fair; there was a high wind. Mr Prince went early to the palace, as it was his turn to serve; our children boarders were gone to school; our servant had gone of an errand. I heard a cry, and to my astonishment, when I looked to see what was the matter, the waters covered the earth. I had not then learned the language but I beckoned to the people to come in…'[5]

Nancy Prince's recollection continues:

'…at four o'clock in the afternoon, there was darkness that might be felt, such as I have never seen before. My situation was the more painful being alone and not being able to speak. I waited until ten in the evening; I then took a lantern, and started to go to a neighbour's, whose children went to the same school with my boarders. I made my way through a long yard, over the bodies of men and beasts, and when opposite their gate I sunk; I made one grasp, and the earth gave way; I grasped again, and fortunately got hold of the leg of a horse, that had been drowned. I drew myself up, covered with mire, and made my way a little further, when I was knocked down by striking against a boat, that had been washed up and left by the retiring waters; and as I had lost my lantern, I was obliged to grope my way as I could, and feeling along the walk, I at last found the door that I aimed at…At 12 o'clock, Mr Prince came home, as no one was permitted to leave the palace, till his majesty had viewed the city'.[6]

In *The Bronze Horseman*, Pushkin's solitary hero, Evgeny, falls victim to this flood. We find him stranded by its waters and cling-

THE MAN WHO SHOOK HIS FIST AT THE TSAR

ing to one of the two stone lions which adorn the entrance to the former Lobanov-Rostovsky Residence, on the southern edge of Senate Square. By the time *The Bronze Horseman* was written, this building had been acquired by the State Treasury for one million roubles. It is now the very upmarket Four Seasons Lion Palace Hotel. The two stone lions are copies of the 16th-century sculptures which guarded the entrance to the Medici palace in Rome and then the Loggia dei Lanzi in Florence. In Russia, they are more instantly recognised for being the spot where Evgeny sought refuge from the flood in *The Bronze Horseman.*

When Evgeny raises his fist to the statue and curses the Tsar in Pushkin's poem, he is voicing the thoughts of many ordinary Russians who were well aware of Peter's tyrannical excesses, and continued to doubt the genius of successive leaders in subsequent generations. In his own day, Peter was regarded by many Russians not as a miracle-worker but more of an Anti-Christ. Thousands had fled to the borderlands and to the forest to escape his reach.

In his history of Peter the Great, the American historian Robert Massie recounts that: 'On one occasion, a peasant who disliked being forced to live in St Petersburg prophesied that the following September the Neva would flood so high that it would cover an ancient, lofty ash tree which stood near a church. People immediately began to move themselves and their belongings to higher ground. Peter, furious at this interruption of his plans for the city, ordered the tree cut down and the peasant imprisoned until September. At the end of that month, when no sign of the threatened inundation had appeared, the population was summoned to the site of the tree stump, on which a scaffold had been built. The rustic seer was brought, lifted onto the scaffold and given fifty lashes with the knout while the crowd was lectured on the foolhardiness of listening to false prophets'.[7]

Almost exactly one year after the Great Flood of 1824, in December 1825, Senate Square witnessed one of the most momentous events in Russian history. This was the first great revolt against tsarist rule in Russia, led by officers of some of the most illustrious regiments in the Russian army. Now known as the Decembrist Revolt, this rebellion took place on 14 December 1825, as a set-piece confrontation between rebel army battalions and forces loyal to the new Tsar, Nicholas I. The cannon which fired on the rebels were stationed on exactly the same steps as those occupied by the stone lions, in the same place where Evgeny sought refuge from the floodwaters.

Apart from Berkh's contemporary account of the Great Flood of 1824, Pushkin took part of his inspiration for the flood from more literary sources. One of these is the description which appears in the epic poem *Metamorphosis* by the Roman poet, Ovid. Pushkin felt a particular identity with Ovid because he was not only a poet like himself but he too had been exiled by a Tsar – in his case by Augustus Caesar. Like Pushkin, Ovid had been banished when the content of some of his writings offended the Emperor. One poem in particular, called *Ars Amatoria*, or *The Art of Love* – was taken to be a satire on recent laws introduced by Augustus which had been intended to reform the supposedly degenerate morals of the Roman populace.

Not only had Ovid been sent into exile in an attempt to silence his pen, like Pushkin, their place of exile was almost identical. Ovid was banished to the city of Tomis which at the time was an eastern outpost in Byzantine Greek territory, on the north-western coast of the Black Sea. In Ovid's day, this region was predominantly inhabited – outside of the city – by Scythians, a Eurasian tribe of steppe nomads. Tomis is now called Constanța and is the oldest continually inhabited city in Romania. What Pushkin called his 'warm exile' was spent in much the same area, on the northern coast of the Black Sea and then in Odessa. In what is probably Ovid's most famous work, *Metamorphoses,* he includes a dramatic section called *The Flood* which has very obvious echoes with the biblical story of Noah and the Ark, and equally with Pushkin's description of the St Petersburg Flood of 1824:

> *Neptune the sea god deployed his waters to aid his brother*
> *He summoned the rivers and when they'd arrived at their*
> *   master's palace*
> *He spoke to the meeting: 'No need for a lengthy harangue', he*
> *   said*
> *'Pour forth in the strength that is yours – it is needed!'*
> *'Open the floodgates, down with the barriers,*
> *Give full rein to the steeds of your streams!'*

He had spoken. The rivers returned to relax the curbs on their
      sources
And then they rolled down to the ocean flats in unbridled career.
Neptune himself now struck the earth with his trident
It trembled under the blow and a raging torrent gushed from the
      chasm.
Bursting their confines, the rivers engulfed the plains and the
      valleys.
The orchards along with their crops, and the cattle along with the
      people
Houses and shrines with their sacred possessions were swept to
      oblivion.
Dwellings which stood their ground and were able to face such an
      onslaught untoppled
Were still submerged from above by an overwhelming,
      mountainous wave
Which levelled their pinnacles deep in the flood-tide.
And now no more could the land and sea be clearly
      distinguished… '[8]

In Greek mythology, the first King and Queen of Northern Greece – in the region now known as Thessaly – were named Deukalion and Pyrrha. Deukalion was the son of Prometheus, the creator of mankind, while Pyrrha was the daughter of Pandora, the first woman. According to the ancient Greek tradition, Prometheus had incurred the anger of Zeus because of the rebellious nature of his creation – the Bronze Race of Man, the first to include both men and women. By his creation, Prometheus had triggered a fateful conflict between the gods and mankind. In revenge, Zeus set out to destroy humanity by unleashing a Great Deluge, The Flood of Thessaly.

In 1823, a year before the Great Flood of St Petersburg, a little-known English poet and dramatist called Bryan Waller Proctor – who went by the pseudonym Barry Cornwall – published a volume of verses which included one entitled *The Flood of Thessaly.* In a foreword to the poem, Cornwall is at pains to stress that what he has written is '*a sketch only* of the great event which desolated the earlier world'.[9] Pushkin was a great fan of Cornwall, so much so that, in January 1837 he wrote to his friend, Alexandra Ishimov, a well-known children's author and translator, to say that he wanted to introduce the works of Barry Cornwall to the Russian public and to ask if she would translate a few of his dramatic sketches. On 27 January 1837, the day he was shot in a duel, he again wrote to Ishimov, apologising that he would not be able to meet her as planned – because of his other, ultimately fatal engagement. He enclosed a copy of *The Poetical Works of Milman, Bowles, Wilson and Barry Cornwall.* The letter was the last Pushkin ever wrote.

Cornwall's description of *The Flood of Thessaly* includes this passage:

'Still the rain fell:
No pity, no relapse, no hope: – The world
Was vanishing like a dream. Lightning and storm,
Thunder and deluging rain now vexed the air
To madness, and the riotous winds laughed out
Like Bacchanals, whose cups some God has charmed.
Beneath the headlong torrents towns and towers
Fell down, temples all stone, and brazen shrines;
And piles of marble, palace and pyramid
(King's homes or towering graves) in a breath were swept
Crumbling away'.[10]

In Ovid's description, the waves are finally pacified when Poseidon calls upon the 'azure Triton' and at his command: 'Triton arose above the waving seas, his shoulders mailed in purple shells. He bade the Triton blow, blow in his sounding shell…and as it touched his lips, wet with the brine beneath his dripping beard, sounded retreat: and all the waters of the land and sea obeyed'.[11] Likewise, in Pushkin's poem, the city Peter had built now appears like '…an almighty Triton, around whose waist the waters now tighten'.[12]

One of the founders of Greek tragedy, Aeschylus, adapted the story of man's conflict with the gods for his play *Prometheus Bound.* According to Aeschylus, Prometheus is himself an immortal god but he is also the friend of the human race who had provided them with fire, was an inventor of the arts and could foresee the future. Prometheus is overcome by the superior power of Zeus but will not bend to his inflexible will; he becomes a heroic sufferer who deprives humanity of their knowledge of the future but gives them hope instead and knowledge of science, metal-working, architecture, astronomy, mathematics, medicine and the art of writing. This portrayal of Prometheus as a hero and the saviour of man comes almost entirely from *Prometheus Bound,* where he is punished by Zeus by being chained to a mountain crag, and is subjected to a never-ending torture by having his eyes and liver pecked out by an eagle.

The location for this punishment is the Caucasus, in the land of the Scythians, close to where both Ovid and Pushkin had been exiled. In a chapter of his book on *The Byronic Hero,* the author of an article on *Satan and Prometheus,* Peter Thorslev, writes that it is in Aeschylus that Prometheus: '…becomes completely transformed into a titanic hero and saviour of man, and it is in this form that he has captured the imagination of poets ever since'.[13]

In this incarnation: 'he is not only the bringer of light and fire to man…but a benefactor in many other ways: he has taught man the sciences of astronomy and mathematics and the rudiments of physics. He has initiated the culture of the soil and the building of cities; he has taught man the means of locomotion on land and on sea, and he has even introduced the art of music. In doing all this for man…he has incurred the wrath of Zeus, and for this he has to suffer eternal punishment'.[14]

In the Christian version of this conflict between god and man, the parts played by the Greek rulers, Deukalion and Pyrrha, are replaced by Adam and Eve, who defy God by eating an apple from the tree of knowledge of good and evil. Over 1,500 years after Aeschylus, at the time of the English Civil War, the great English poet, John Milton, returned to the theme of the Fall of Man in his epic poem, *Paradise Lost.* Written in 1667, this poem also includes a vivid description of the biblical flood (Book XI. Line 738):

Meanwhile the south wind rose, and with black wings
Wide hovering, all the clouds together drove
From under heav'n; the hills to their supply
Vapour, and exhalation dusk and moist,
Set up a-main; and now the thickened sky
Like a dark ceiling stood; down rushed the rain

Impetuous, and continued till the earth
No more was seen; the floating vessel swum
Uplifted; and secure with beaked prow
Rode tilting o'er the waves, all dwellings else
Flood overwhelmed, and them with all their pomp
Deep under water rolled, sea covered sea,
Sea without shore, and in their palaces
Where luxury late reigned, sea-monsters whelped
And stabled; of mankind, so numerous late
All left, in one small bottom swum embarked.[15]

The most controversial aspect of Milton's *Paradise Lost* is that the equivalent part to Prometheus in the Greek legend is played in the Bible by the rebel angel, Lucifer, otherwise known as Satan or the Devil. Even more troubling in Milton's story is that God rather than Satan is the character who is repeatedly portrayed as a merciless tyrant, 'every inch a king'. Pushkin kept in his library copies of *The Poetical Works of John Milton* in English and a French edition of *Le Paradis Perdu,* translated from the English by Chateaubriand.

A century after Milton, at the time of the French Revolution, the great English radical and visionary, William Blake, published a book of illuminated illustrations entitled *The Marriage of Heaven and Hell* in which he too embraces Milton's interpretation of the Bible story. In this manuscript, published in 1790, Blake – who wore a Phrygian cap in solidarity with the revolutionaries in Paris – not only reverses traditional notions of Good and Evil, Angels and Devils and Heaven and Hell but celebrates the tensions produced by these 'contraries'.

For Blake, there was no other God than the human imagination. In a note to the chapter headed *The Voice of the Devil,* Blake says: 'The reason Milton wrote in fetters when he wrote of Angels & God, and at liberty when of Devils & Hell, is because he was a true Poet and of the Devil's party without knowing it'.[16] Describing the Infinite Abyss, Blake conjures much of the imagery we have already encountered from the story of the Great Deluge:

'But now...a cloud and fire burst and rolled thro' the deep, blackening all beneath, so that the nether deep grew black as a sea & rolled with terrible noise; beneath us was nothing now to be seen but a black tempest, till looking east between the clouds & the waves, we saw a cataract of blood mixed with fire, and not many stones throw from us appear'd and sunk again the scaly fold of a monstrous serpent; at last to the east, distant about three degrees appear'd a fiery crest above the waves; slowly it reared like a ridge of golden rocks till we dicover'd two globes of crimson fire, from which the sea fled away in clouds of smoke, and now we saw, it was the head of Leviathan; his forehead was divided into streaks of green and purple like those on a tygers forehead; soon we saw his mouth and red gills hang just above the raging foam tinging the black deep with beams of blood, advancing towards us w*ith all the fury of a spiritual existence*'.[17]

In his last finished work, *Witness against the Beast: William Blake and the Moral Law,* the Marxist historian, E P Thompson, highlights how far Blake was inspired by dissident religious ideas rooted in the thinking of the most radical opponents of the monarchy during the English Civil War. Blake was a close friend and associate of William Godwin, another English radical who was a confirmed atheist and believed that the monarchy was 'a species of government unavoidably corrupt'.

Godwin married Mary Wollstonecraft and their daughter, Mary Godwin, became Mary Shelley on her marriage to Percy Bysshe Shelley. As we know from Modalevsky's catalogue of non-Russian books kept by Pushkin in his library, there were copies of two books written by Godwin.[18] These were a French translation of his three-volume political novel *Things as They Are; or, The Adventures of Caleb Williams,* published in Lausanne in 1796, and an English edition of *Lives of the Necromancers* – a book which has the subtitle *'..or an account of the eminent persons in successive ages, who have claimed for themselves, or to whom has been imputed by others, the exercise of magical powers'.*

Godwin's book on 'necromancy' – the form of ritual incantation, or witchcraft, used in many societies to summon up the dead, often as a prelude to foretelling the future – is a *tour de force* explaining the development of such beliefs in ancient societies and how 'this faith in extraordinary events, and superstitious fear of what is supernatural, has diffused itself through every climate of the world, in a certain stage of human intellect, and while refinement had not yet got the better of barbarism'.[19] In the section of his book which deals with the deities of ancient Greece, Godwin describes the magical powers Prometheus was endowed with as follows:

'Prometheus, one of the race of giants, was particularly distinguished for his proficiency in the arts. Among other extraordinary productions he formed a man of clay, of such exquisite workmanship, as to have wanted nothing but a living soul to cause him to be acknowledged as the paragon of the world. Minerva (*the Goddess of Wisdom*) beheld the performance of Prometheus with approbation and offered him her assistance. She conducted him to heaven, where he watched his opportunity to carry off on the tip of his wand a portion of celestial fire from the chariot of the sun. With this he animated his image: and the man of Prometheus moved, and thought and spoke, and became everything that the fondest wish of his creator could ask'.[20]

Mary Shelley famously wrote her novel *Frankenstein* at the age of 18, while on holiday with Shelley at Byron's residence in Italy. The book is subtitled: '…*or, The Modern Prometheus*' followed by a quotation, from John Milton's *Paradise Lost:*

Did I request thee, Maker, from my clay
To mould me man? Did I solicit thee
From darkness to promote me?[21]

Mary Shelley dedicated *Frankenstein* to her father. The frontispiece to the first edition reads: 'To William Godwin, author of *Political Justice, Caleb Williams etc* these volumes are respectfully inscribed'.[22] According to the literary critic, Gay Clifford, Mary Shelley read both of her father's books mentioned in this tribute in 1814 and again in 1816, the year she wrote *Frankenstein.*[23]

In her novel, the name of the scientist who develops a secret technique to bring to life inanimate matter is Victor Frankenstein. Mary Shelley is thought to have chosen the name Victor because the name Milton gives to God in *Paradise Lost* is 'the Victor'. The name is appropriate because Mary Shelley sees Victor as playing God by creating life. In addition, Shelley's portrayal of the monster owes much to the character of Satan in *Paradise Lost*.

At one point in the book, the monster actually reads Milton's poem and afterwards announces that he empathizes with Satan's role in the story. The first edition of *Frankenstein* was published, anonymously, in London in 1818. Two years later, Percy Bysshe Shelley returned to the Greek legend in his four-act play, *Prometheus Unbound*. This time, Shelley differs from Aeschylus in that he steadfastly refuses to resolve the conflict between Zeus and Prometheus at the end of his tale because: '…in truth, I was averse from a catastrophe so feeble as that of reconciling the Champion with the Oppressor of mankind'.[24] The way Shelley sees Prometheus, he is more than just a rebel. In his biography *Red Shelley*, Paul Foot explains:

'He represents cultured, intellectual man; scientific man who has made discoveries which can change the world. He represents, in short, Shelley as he imagined himself. He is wise, kind, brave. But he is also a god, a Titan, born, bred and educated as Jupiter himself. Though his spirit is unbroken by the torture, he cannot do anything to free himself. There is a sort of stalemate between Prometheus on his rock, representing the idea of progress but unable to put it into effect, and Jupiter in heaven, able to contain Prometheus but unable to break his spirit or destroy his knowledge'.[25]

In the first chapter of the Old Testament, the *Book of Genesis*, God creates the world, along with the first humans and all the animals in the Garden of Eden. When Adam and Eve are tricked by a serpent to disobey God's instruction not to eat from the tree of knowledge, they are banished from paradise and he destroys his own creation, through the Flood. In the first book of the Bible written in verse, the *Book of Job*, man's obedience to divine justice is again questioned, when God and the angel Satan engage in a battle of wills to put Job's virtue to the test. God robs Job of his family and his property, Satan afflicts Job's body with boils and he is made to suffer in sackcloth and ashes.

The dominant theme of the *Book of Job* is the difficulty of understanding why an all-powerful God would allow the virtuous to experience such agonies. In a series of dialogues with his friends, Job is told that the sufferings imposed on him must be because he has sinned. But because Job is convinced of his own righteousness, he refuses to accept this explanation and demands an answer from God. In a passage of the poem, entitled *Hymn to Wisdom*, Job challenges God to explain his suffering but the response is uncompromising:

'Then the Lord answered Job from out of the whirlwind, and said:

Who is this that darkeneth counsel by words without knowledge?

Gird up now thy loins like a man; for I will demand of thee, and answer thou me.

Where wast' when I laid the foundations of the earth? Declare if thou hast understanding.

Who hath laid the measures thereof, if thou knowest? Or hath stretched the line upon it?

Whereupon are the foundations thereof fastened? Or who laid the cornerstone thereof?

When the morning stars sang together, and all the sons of God shouted for joy?

Or who shut up the sea with doors, when it brake forth, as if it had issued out of the womb?

When I made the cloud a garment thereof, and thick darkness a swaddling band for it,

And brake up for it my decreed place, and set bars and doors, and said:

Hitherto shalt thou come, but no further: and here shall the proud waves be stayed? [26]

Not one to belittle his own achievements, God goes on to expand at great length on the multitude of miracles he has created: from the wind and stars and clouds in the sky, to the ice, rain and snow, darkness and light. He also boasts of his creation of the two terrifying chaos monsters, Behemoth and Leviathan, who he alone can control. Behemoth is the primal monster of the land, with bones as strong as brass or bars of iron and a tail like a cedar. He lives in the invisible desert, east of the Garden of Eden. The Leviathan is the primeval monster of the sea who dwells in the Abyss. In apocalyptic literature, which envisages the end of time, Leviathan is identified with God's adversary, the Devil, and subsequently became a metaphor for any powerful entity, such as capitalism or state oppression. At the time of the English Civil War, it was the term used by the writer, Thomas Hobbes, to justify the need for absolute monarchy. When God replies to Job, in Verse 41 of the *Book of Job*, he asks:

'Canst thou draw out Leviathan with a hook? Or his tongue with a cord which thou lettest down? Canst thou put a hook into his nose? Or bore his jaw through with a thorn?'.

The Leviathan has such enormous strength that he 'esteemeth iron as straw, and brass as rotten wood'. Sparks of fire leap from his mouth, smoke belches from his nostrils and he fears no weapon: arrows 'cannot make him flee', he 'laugheth at the shaking of a spear' and darts 'are counted as stubble'.[27]

And, within this abyss:

'He maketh the deep to boil like a pot: he maketh the sea like a pot of ointment

He maketh a path to shine after him; one would think the deep to be hoary.

Upon the earth there is not his like, who is made without fear.

He beholdeth all high things: he is a king over all the children of pride'.[28]

In our day, most of these biblical references may seem somewhat extraneous. But this was far from the case at the beginning of the 19th century, either in England or in Russia. In March 1811, Shelley was expelled from the University of Oxford, six months into his course, for having written a tract, *The Necessity of Atheism,* which rejects the Bible version of history. Pushkin's second period of exile was ensured, in 1824, when a letter he wrote from Odessa was intercepted and read by the police.

In this letter, Pushkin said he had been 'taking lessons in pure Atheism' from an Englishman, Dr William Hutchinson, personal physician to the Vorontsov family, Pushkin's host during his first period of exile in the South of the country. Pushkin described Hutchinson, who was much the same age as himself, as 'the only intelligent Atheist I have met'. And, although it had taken the doctor 'over 1,000 pages' to prove that there was no such thing as a supreme creator of mankind, Pushkin nevertheless concluded: 'This system, though not as comforting as is usually thought, is unfortunately most likely to be true'.[29]

When Alexander I was informed of the contents of the letter, he immediately agreed with the Foreign Minister, Nesselrode, that because of this apostasy (together with the unfortunate subsidiary charge that he had been conducting an affair with the Governor's wife) Pushkin should be immediately transferred to his parent's estate, at Mikhailovskoye, to be detained under the supervision of the local authorities.

Explaining the Tsar's decision, Nesselrode wrote: 'Unfortunately, everything indicates that he (Pushkin) is too imbued with the harmful principles which expressed themselves so perniciously at his first steps in a public profession. The attached letter will convince you of this: the Moscow police learnt of it because it was going from hand to hand and became widely known. In consequence, his majesty, as a lawful punishment, has ordered me to exclude him from the list of officials of the Foreign Ministry for his bad conduct; moreover, his majesty does not wish to leave him completely without supervision, for the reason that, making use of his independent position, he will, without doubt, disseminate more and more widely those harmful ideas which he holds and will oblige the authorities to employ against him the most severe measures'.[30]

When the 19th century Russian literary scholar, P V Annenkov came to write a biography of Shelley in 1874, at the height of Shelley's popularity in Russia, he speculated that Dr William Hutchinson was: 'in all probability a passionate admirer of Shelley, who taught our poet (*Pushkin*) the philosophy of atheism and made himself into an unintentional instrument of his second catastrophe'.[31]

In a more recent article on *The Reception of Shelley in Russia*, the English author and specialist on Russian cultural history, Rachel Polonsky, notes that Pushkin was aware of Shelley's verse and had taken some interest in his life story. Pushkin's library included an edition of *The Poetical Works of Coleridge, Shelley and Keats*, published in Paris in 1829 and a memoir by Thomas Medwin called *The Shelley Papers*. Medwin was a 19th century poet and translator, a cousin of Shelley and a close friend of Byron. Pushkin also kept in his library a two-volume set entitled *Lord Byron and Some of His Contemporaries: with recollections of the author's life and of his visit to Italy*. This was written by Leigh

Hunt, a radical journalist who was one of the most important figures in the radical artistic circle which included the poets Shelley, Byron and Keats. Leigh-Hunt and his brother, John, were both jailed in 1813 for having published a series of attacks on the reigning Prince Regent, the Prince of Wales, in their liberal journal, *The Examiner.* One of Leigh-Hunt's erstwhile friends, the painter Benjamin Haydon, became convinced that Hunt, Byron, Shelley and Godwin were all 'co-conspirators in a plot to bring revolution to Britain'.[32]

When Leigh-Hunt was incarcerated at Surrey Gaol in Southwark, one of the most notorious prisons in England, Byron was one of Leigh Hunt's most high-profile visitors. Like Pushkin, Leigh-Hunt's ancestors on his father's side were black. His father, Isaac Hunt, was a refugee from Philadelphia, and his parents were West Indian. In her book about the 'tangled lives' of the *Young Romantics,* which included Shelley and Byron, the writer Daisy Hay notes that, throughout his life, Leigh-Hunt's adversaries would seize upon his black ancestry; 'commenting in sly asides on his swarthy complexion, dark hair and thick lips',[33] insults which were all too familiar to Pushkin.

By the time Pushkin came to write *The Bronze Horseman* in the 1830s, the new Tsar, Nicholas I, had introduced a creed known as the Official Nationality. Under this doctrine, the three pillars of Autocracy, Orthodoxy and Nationality were made the guiding principles of the political system of Russia. The law of the land declared: 'The Tsar of all the Russias is an autocrat and absolute monarch. God Himself commands us to obey the Tsar's supreme authority, not from fear alone, but as a point of conscience'.[34]

As the Russian historian, Nicholas Riasanovsky, points out, these principles were reinforced by Article 20 of the military statutes which dated back to the time of Peter the Great. This stated: 'Whoever utters blasphemous words against the person of His Majesty, whoever deprecates his intentions and His actions and discusses them in an unseemly manner, he will be deprived of life by decapitation. For His Majesty is an autocratic monarch Who need answer to no one in the world for His actions, but Who possesses power and authority to govern His states and His lands, as a Christian ruler, according to His will and judgment'.[35] In the final analysis, Riasanovsky says: 'God provided the foundation for the authority of the Tsar'.[36]

Even in 21st century Russia, it is not unknown for artists to be accused of performing the work of the devil. In February 2012, five female members of the punk collective, *Pussy Riot,* were arrested for staging a deliberately provocative happening over abortion rights inside Moscow's Cathedral of Christ the Saviour. Wearing multi-coloured balaclavas, the group performed and filmed a video entitled: *'Punk Prayer – Mother of God, Chase Putin Away!'*.

The response of the Russian President, Vladimir Putin, was that the band had 'undermined the moral foundations of the nation' and, when two of its members – Nadezhda Tolokonnikova and Maria Alyokhina – were sentenced to two year's imprisonment for 'hooliganism motivated by religious hatred', he said they had 'got what they asked for'.[37]

According to Tolokonnikova, *Pussy Riot* is a collective which regards itself as part of the global anti-capitalist movement: '*Pussy Riot's* performances can either be called dissident art or political action that engages art forms. Either way, our performances are a kind of civic activity amidst the repressions of a corporate political system that directs its power against basic human rights and civil and political liberties'.[38]

The band referred to the Russian Orthodox Patriarch, Kirill I, as a *suka* (bitch) and a regular target of their protests has been what they regard as the growing ties between the Orthodox Church hierarchy and Vladimir Putin – a man they see as being 'as far as can be from God's truth'. The Patriarch openly supported Putin's 2012 election campaign calling him 'a miracle from God' who had 'rectified the crooked path of history'.[39]

In the introduction to his play, *Prometheus Unbound,* Shelley wrote that: 'We owe the great writers of the golden age of our literature to that fervid awakening of the public mind which shook to dust the oldest and most oppressive forms of the Christian religion. We owe to Milton the progress and development of the same spirit: the sacred Milton was, let it ever be remembered, a republican, and a bold inquirer into morals and religion. The great writers of our own age are, we have reason to suppose, the companions and forerunners of some unimagined change in our social condition or the opinions which cement it'.[40]

In the same introduction, Shelley writes: 'Poets, not otherwise than philosophers, painters, sculptors and musicians, are, in one sense, the creators, and, in another, the creations of their age. From this subjection, the loftiest do not escape'. [41] In a similar vein, in a footnote to one of the illustrated chapters in *The Marriage of Heaven and Hell*, entitled *Proverbs of Hell*, William Blake writes: 'The ancient Poets animated all sensible objects with Gods or Geniuses, calling them by names and adorning them with the properties of woods, rivers, mountains, lakes, cities, nations, and whatever their enlarged & numerous senses could perceive. And particularly they studied the genius of each city & country, placing it under its mental deity. Till a system was formed, which some took advantage of & enslaved the vulgar by attempting to realize or abstract the mental deities from their objects: thus began Priesthood. Choosing forms of worship from poetic tales. And at length they pronounced that the Gods had ordered such things. Thus men forgot that All deities reside in the human breast'.[42]

Notes

1   **The Bronze Horseman,** by Alexander Pushkin, main text in Russian, edited with introduction, notes and vocabulary by T E Little, Bristol Classical Press, 1974

2   **A Detailed Historical Account of all the floods that Occurred in St. Petersburg**, published on the instruction of the State Admiralty Department. by V N Berkh, St. Petersburg, 1826.

3   **The Last Days of Alexander: And the First Days of Nicholas (Emperors of Russia),** by Robert Lee, reprinted by Ulan Press in 2012, first published by Harrison & Sons in 1854, p3

4   Lee, op.cit. p8

5   **A Black Woman's Odyssey through Russia and Jamaica,** *The Narrative of Nancy Prince*, Markus Wiener Publishers, Princeton, 1990 (first published 1850), p20

6   Prince, ibid. p21

7   **Peter the Great: His Life and His World**. By Robert K Massie. Abacus. 1993 (first published by Victor Gollancz in 1981). p.787

8   **Metamorphoses.** By Ovid. A new verse translation by David Raeburn, with an introduction by Denis Feeney. Book I - The Flood, p.19

9   **The Flood of Thessaly, the Girl of Provence and other Poems.** By Barry Cornwall (pseudonym of Bryan Waller Procter). Henry Colburn & Co. London. 1823. Reprinted from the British Library Historical Collection 2015.

10   Cornwall, ibid., p.29

11   Ovid, op.cit., pp. 21-22

12   See *The Bronze Horseman,* Part One, Lines 92-93

13   **Satan and Prometheus.** By Peter L Thorslev. From *The Byronic Hero.* University of Minnesota Press. 1962. http://www.jstor.org/stable/10.5749/j.ctttsh8q.11 . P.113

14   Thorslev, ibid., p.113

15   **Paradise Lost.** By John Milton. Edited with an introduction and notes by John Leonard. Penguin Books. 2000 (first published in 1667). p.266

16   **The Marriage of Heaven and Hell.** By William Blake. Dover Publications. 1994. p.30

17   Blake, ibid., p.38

18   See Appendix to **Pushkin on Literature.** Selected, translated and edited by Tatiana Wolff. The Athlone Press. 1986. Short-Title Catalogue of the Foreign (Non-Russian) Books in Pushkin's Library. Compiled by B L Modalevsky. 1910. pp. 485-522

19   **Lives of the Necromancers,** or An Account of the Most Eminent Persons in Successive Ages Who Have Claimed for Themselves or to Whom has been Imputed by Others, the Exercise of Magical Power. By William Godwin. Echo Library. 2006 (first published 1834). P.13

20   Godwin, ibid., p.37

21   Introduction to first edition of **Frankenstein,** or **The Modern Prometheus.** In Three Volumes. By Mary Wollstonecraft Shelley. First published 1818 by Lackington, Hughes, Harding, Mavor & Jones. This edition: Penguin Classics. 2003

22   Shelley, ibid., frontispiece to first edition.

23 *Caleb Williams* and *Frankenstein:* First-person Narratives and 'Things as They Are'. By Gay Clifford. From the Pennsylvania inline edition of *Frankenstein – The Modern Prometheus.* http://knarf.english.upenn.edu/

24 **Prometheus Unbound.** A Lyrical Drama in Four Acts. By Percy Bysshe Shelley. Edited by Thomas Hutchinson MA. First published 1820. p.4

25 **Red Shelley.** By Paul Foot. Bookmarks. 1984. p.179

26 From the Old Testament Book of Job, Verse 38 (King James Edition of The Holy Bible)

27 The Bible, ibid. Book of Job. Verse 41

28 The Bible, ibid. Book of Job. Verse 41

29 **Pushkin.** By T J Binyon. Harper Collins. 2002, p.175

30 Binyon, ibid., p.190

31 **The Reception of P B Shelley in Europe.** Edited by Susanne Schmid and Michael Rossington. Continuum.2008. See chapter: *Revolutionary Etudes: The Reception of Shelley in Russia* by Rachel Polonsky. p.231

32 **Young Romantics.** The Shelleys, Byron and Other Tangled Lives. By Daisy Hay. Bloomsbury. 2010. p.97

33 Hay, ibid., p.5

34 **Some Comments on the Role of the Intelligentsia in the Reign of Nicholas I of Russia, 1822-1855.** By Nicholas V Riasanovsky. *The Slavic and East European Journal,* Vol. I, No. 3. Autumn 1957. www.jstor.org/stable/304154. p.164

35 Riasanovsky, ibid., p.164

36 Riasanovsky, p.164

37   See: https://en.wikipedia.org/wiki/Pussy_Riot

38 See: https://en.wikipedia.org/wiki/Pussy_Riot

39 See: https://en.wikipedia.org/wiki/Pussy_Riot

40 Prometheus Unbound, ibid. p.3

41 Prometheus Unbound, ibid. p.7

42 Blake, op.cit., p.34

Comrade, have faith, the day will arrive
When our joyful star lights up the sky
Russia from her slumber will arise
And on the ruins of autocracy
Our legend shall be inscribed!

Pushkin, *To Chaadaev,* 1818[1]

10 | One Tsar Too Many

When news of Alexander's death first circulated, his eldest younger brother, the Grand Duke Constantine, was Viceroy of Poland. His official residence was the Belvedere Palace in Warsaw. His younger brother, Nicholas, was based more than 700 miles away, at the Winter Palace in St Petersburg. Under the existing rules of primogeniture, restored by their father, Paul I, Constantine should have been the automatic next-in-line to the throne. An oath of allegiance was in fact taken to him both in Moscow and St Petersburg. Commemorative coins were minted which had Constantine's profile on one side and posters depicting the new Tsar went on display in shop windows, declaring; 'Constantine I, Emperor and Autocrat of All the Russias'. What most people did not know was that Constantine was said to have already conceded, in a secret agreement with Alexander, that the next Tsar would be Nicholas, not himself. For more than three weeks, correspondence on how best to deal with this monumental quandary passed back and forth between Warsaw and St Petersburg. A correspondent writing for the *The Times* of London noted that Russia was now 'in the strange predicament of having two self-denying emperors, and no active ruler'.

Confusion over the succession was such that: 'On 27 November 1825, the day that the news of Alexander's death reached Petersburg, the entire Imperial Guard, including

Nicholas and officers of state institutions, took the oath of allegiance to Constantine and three days later in Moscow similar action was taken'.

For most of the 18th century, Russian autocrats had the right, established by Peter the Great, to nominate their own heirs. The main purpose of this change was to ensure that Peter's son, Alexey, would never become Tsar. This precedent changed dramatically in 1797, when Catherine's successor - her son, the Emperor Paul I – took the throne. Determined in every way to spite his mother, Paul decreed that future succession to the throne should be hereditary in the male line, as it had been in the past. What the majority of Russian were unaware of was the steps which had already been taken by Alexander and his inner circle to secretly reverse his father's policy, to ensure that Constantine did not succeed him as Tsar.

One explanation for the hostility to Constantine was that, since 1815, he had been in a relationship with a Polish noblewoman, and Catholic, Joanna Grudzińska. This match did not meet either with the approval of his brothers - Alexander, Nicholas and Michael - nor of their mother, the Empress Maria Feodorovna. The first difficulty was that Constantine was already married. His German wife, Anna, had fled their arranged marriage at the first opportunity and had not set foot in Russia since 1801. She had made her getaway at exactly the same time as the newly restored rule of primogeniture introduced by Paul was being fast-tracked to skip a generation and while the imperial guard stood by as the Emperor was being assassinated.

Constantine had come up against considerable opposition from the rest of his family when he initially requested consent for a divorce from Anna Feodorovna, which would allow him to marry Joanna Grudzińska. Anna had developed a close friendship with Alexander's wife, Princess Louise of Baden (soon to be the Empress Elizabeth). When Alexander finally did grant permission, he included an important caveat: Constantine would be expected to forego his right to succeed Alexander.

In effect, Constantine's marriage to Grudzińska seemed to provide the opportunity to resolve Russia's perennial problem of the imperial succession. The reason was that, though Constantine had fathered three children - Pavel, Constantine and Constansia

- from previous relationships with a series of mistresses, he had no legitimate offspring. And any children born in future would be the product of a 'morganatic' marriage - in other words, via marriage to a commoner and a Polish catholic at that.

This was a prospect which the imperial court in St Petersburg could not tolerate. The problem was that, in the same way as his grand-mother, Catherine, had been obliged to keep quiet about her preference for her grandson, Alexander, over her own son, Paul, - Alexander could not have openly declared for Nicholas. Under the rule of primogeniture re-introduced by his father, he had no legal right to nominate a successor.

The decisive factor which changed the thinking of the rest of the royal family was that, on 29 April 1818, Constantine's younger brother, Nicholas, immensely improved his own claim to the throne when his wife, Charlotte of Prussia, gave birth to a son. This was especially significant because it meant that only Nicholas had a legal successor to himself. Alexander still had no sons and the one Constantine had was illegitimate. Following much internal politicking, an agreement was eventually reached between the brothers and, in special *ukaz* issued on 20 March 1820, the day after the dissolution of Constantine's first marriage, the rights to accession were amended to include the wording:

'...if any person of the Imperial Family enters into a marriage with a person of a status unequal to his, that is, not belonging to any Royal or Ruling House, in such a case the person of the Imperial Family cannot pass on to the other person the rights which belong to Members of the Imperial Family, and the children issuing from such a marriage have no right of succession to the Throne'.[2]

Most Russians knew nothing about the special 'manifesto' which Alexander subsequently signed two years later, on 16 August 1823, and which had then been sealed, with the authorisation: 'Not to be opened until after my death'. What the testament said was that Constantine had formally renounced his right to the throne, thereby placing his younger brother, Nicholas, next in the line of succession. Sealed copies of this testament were deposited in the Uspensky Cathedral in Moscow and in the Senate, the Holy Synod and State Council in St Petersburg. Alexander's enforcer, Arakcheev, had ordered the Archbishop

Filaret of Moscow that the existence of the document should be kept secret but Alexander himself 'indirectly mentioned its contents to a number of associates, including Karamzin, Arakcheev and some foreign members of royalty, for example, Wilhelm, Prince of Prussia'.[3]

During the period of vacillation over the competing claims of Constantine and Nicholas, the sarcastic question doing the rounds on every street corner, was: 'When will the sheep finally be sold?'. To add to the confusion, Alexander had said nothing about the succession on his deathbed. And, when he died, the two adjutants-general who were present, Prince Volkonsky and General Ivan Diebitsch, who knew nothing about the secret manifesto, immediately sent a dispatch to Warsaw, addressed to His Majesty, the Emperor Constantine, requesting his instructions.

The primary function Constantine had been expected to perform in Poland was to root out any sign of 'liberalism', particularly in the armed forces. To achieve this, Constantine had effectively been made Commander-in-Chief of two armies, with supreme authority over the 30,000 Russian troops stationed in the Congress Poland as well those in the newly formed Polish army. When he first took charge, in November 1815, Constantine proclaimed an order of the day, stating that: 'Tsar and King wishes all rules applicable in the Russian army to be applicable in the Polish Army'.[4]

What this meant in practice, was that: '...not only Russian military regulations, but also Russian penalties, such as corporal punishment, which up to that time was unknown in the Polish Army, were to become operative. Further, Russian models of administration and accounting, Russian arms and equipment and even Russian music were introduced into the Polish army'.[5]

Much more of a military man than his brother, Constantine's method of achieving the required standardisation of the troops based in Poland is vividly described in a memoir written by a German officer cadet, Harro Harring, who served in the Lancer Regiment of the Grand Duke Constantine's Imperial Russian Body Guard. 'Just as Rome and the Pope are two inseparable ideas', wrote Harring, 'so are Warsaw and the Grand-Duke Constantine. The infallibility of the one corresponds with the despotism of the other. The clergy form the highest and most powerful rank in Rome, so do the military in Warsaw. What the convents are in Rome, the barracks are in the Polish capital'. [6]

Following in the Prussian tradition of his murdered father, Constantine was a fanatical adherent of parade ground discipline, so much so that: 'the most remarkable thing in Warsaw is the Parade, on the Saxon Square, fronting the Brühl Palace... This square owes its present spacious size to the Grand Duke Constantine, who ordered the pulling down of all the buildings which formerly limited its extent'.[7]

For the 15 years that Constantine remained in command in Poland, military parades were conducted daily and, according to another cadet, Ignace Komorowski, the recruits were expected to perform like a 'group of marionettes'.[8]

Brutal punishments were exacted for the slightest infraction, such as a missing button on a uniform, or a collar at the wrong height. Officers were routinely humiliated and subjected to violent abuse in the presence of their own peers. As a result: 'the officers hated Constantine personally as a temperamental and arbitrary tyrant who had a mania for outmoded military and disciplinary forms'.

Quoting the Russian historian, Nikolai Karamzin, Harring notes: 'The investigator of history knows not which to wonder at most, the unlimited and barbarous despotism of the tyrant, or the patience and forbearance of the people by whom he was tolerated'.[9]

Apart from the army, Constantine's other major pre-occupation was the secret police and especially his secret military police whose role was to keep him informed about everything that might be going on in the army. He had five secret police divisions under his command, each of which spied on the other and scrupulously controlled military courts and punishments. His spy network was so efficient that he often knew what was happening in any given regiment before its own officers.

Constantine's spies would glide about on the parade ground, without knowing each other, and were trained to 'keep their eyes on the officers, whom they watch as narrowly as a jealous old guardian watches a pair of lovers making an assignation... They do not concern themselves much about the uniforms, for the Grand Duke is to be on the parade and will himself see that all the buttons and button-holes are in good order'. [10]

At the same time as Alexander had appointed his brother to take charge of the army in Poland, he had appointed his own aide, Nikolai Novosiltsev, to run the council of state and to head the Russian secret police, or *Okhrana.* If anything, Novosiltsev was even more distrustful of the Poles and their reputation for 'liberalism' than Constantine.

It was not that long since the Polish folk hero, Tadeusz Kosciusko, had led an eight-month armed uprising against Russian rule, in 1794. Not to mention the Polish cavalry employed by Napoleon to spearhead his invasion of Russia only a few years earlier. As Commissioner, Novosiltsev had more or less a free hand in every aspect of government and soon became one of the *de facto* rulers of the country, widely feared and detested.

To give an indication of how much trust there was in reality between the brothers, Novosiltsev regularly sent secret reports to Alexander (and later to Nicholas) which included surveillance updates on Constantine himself. Not to be outdone, the Secret Chancellery of Constantine's own Bureau of Internal Affairs, reported back daily and its first and most important function was not only to spy upon his brothers, Alexander (and later Nicholas) but also to maintain surveillance on government officials - including his chief adviser, Novosiltsev; the head of the military police, Rozniecki; and the Chancellor, Drucki-Lubecki.

Alexander's failure to deliver on his promises for a more liberal and democratic regime bred as much resentment in Poland, as it did in Russia. The Poles had come to expect that Alexander's commitment to establish a free and united Poland would be fulfilled but this was not what they experienced under the increasingly repressive policies of Constantine and Novosiltsev. By 1818, signs of an organised opposition had already started to emerge and in that year the first rebellion in the parliament, or *Sejm,* took place.

In 1822, the government provoked a further reaction when a law banning membership of secret societies was introduced. Predictably, this edict stimulated the formation of new opposition groups, in addition to those which already existed, particularly among students and army officers. In a joint operation conducted with the Austrian and Prussian police, members of a student organisation which had been founded at the University of Warsaw and which was known as the *Union of Free Poles* were rounded up and arrested. The other main centre of student activity was at the Polish University of Wilno (Vilnius). Novosilstev was sent to investigate the activities of an organisation called the *Society of Philomaths,* membership of which included the poet Adam Mickiewicz.[11]

Novosiltsev immediately ordered the liquidation of the organisation and sentenced ten of its leading members either to imprisonment, or exile to Russia. Mickiewicz was one of this group and soon met with Pushkin and many of the leading lights of what was to become the Russian Decembrist movement. More of a serious threat than the *Philomaths* were the secret societies which had started to flourish within the army. One of these was a radical offshoot of the masons which was at first called the *National Freemasonry* and then the *Patriotic Society.* It had been founded by a major in the Polish army, Valerian Łukasiński, a liberal who had become disillusioned with Alexander and now called for independence from Russia and the abolition of serfdom.[12]

When the activities of Łukasiński's organisation were unearthed, Constantine branded him as a traitor both to the army and to himself. Łukasiński was subjected to a two-year show trial and sentenced to hard labour. He spent nine years of a 20 year sentence in prison in Poland and, after the Polish Revolution of 1830, was taken to Russia by Constantine, where he eventually spent a further 45 years in jail.

Elsewhere in the army, one of the most active of the secret societies was based in the Lithuanian Corps, which was predominantly manned by Polish troops. However, membership of the society, called the *Comrades in Arms,* included both Russian and Polish officers. Constantine believed that, after Lukasinski's arrest, he had eliminated the threat from the *Patriotic Society* but this proved to be wishful thinking. In 1822, members of the Russian Decembrist's Southern Society made approaches to an amalgam of Polish organisations which were active in the South with proposals for an alliance, whose joint aim would be the overthrow of Tsardom. The Polish element comprised

Lukasinski's *Polish Patriotic Society* and an organisation known as the *Society of the United Slavs*.[13]

The main objective of the Russian's Southern Society was, in the event of an armed revolt, to ensure the neutrality of the Polish forces under Constantine's command. A large part of the Russian army, including the powerful Lithuanian Corps, was stationed on Polish territory. All of these troops were under Constantine's supreme command and, were they to obey orders, could be mobilised to crush any uprising.

As a result of preliminary meetings held in 1824 between leaders of the two organisations in Kiev, the Southern Society promised that it would recognise the independence of a future Poland, though where the boundary of an independent Polish state would lie remained an open question. At the same time, the Southern Society hoped that the Polish organisation would provide some practical assistance, described by the American historian, William Blackwell, as follows:

'The Poles were to prevent the Grand Duke Constantine from returning to Russia at the time of the revolution, obviously because so important a figure could be used by the enemies of the Decembrists, or indeed by the Poles themselves, for their own ends; efforts were to be made to penetrate and neutralise the Lithuanian Corps, for this powerful unit could be used to smash the revolution; the Poles were to rebel simultaneously with the Russians, an essential aspect of the coup; and, prior to this, they were to 'arrange relations between us and the political societies which function in western Europe'.[14]

The negotiations which took place between the Decembrists and the Poles were by no means straightforward. Under the leadership of Pavel Pestel, the Southern Society had developed republican objectives which were not shared by the leaders of the Polish organisation (nor, for that matter, by most of his comrades in the Northern Society).

Furthermore, most Russian officers still took for granted Catherine the Great's maxim which was to insist on the subjugation of Poland to Russian interests.

There was also the problem that, if ever a republican Poland and Russia were to be created, it would almost inevitably mean war with Austria and Prussia, nations which would not be eager to abandon their own Polish territories.

The whole question of the fate of Poland, first encountered by the Decembrists in these negotiations, was one which was to haunt relationships between Russia and Poland throughout the next two centuries. It continued through to the period when Poland became a satellite state of Soviet Russia, culminating in the *Solidarność* uprising of 1980.

The vacillation which took place during the month-long interregnum which followed Alexander's death was finally resolved by the speed with which events were unfolding beyond court circles. One of the physicians who attended to Alexander on his deathbed, Dr Robert Lee MD, observed that during his reign Alexander had performed a great service to the other sovereign heads of Europe by maintaining their authority 'while the power of their adversary was destroyed'. As he saw it, perceptively, the outlook for Russia following Alexander's death was as follows:

'The fate of this vast empire no one can certainly foretell; but that changes await it, and at no distant period, who can doubt? The army is rotten at the core. Many of the officers detest the present system of government, and desire a representative and constitutional government, and long to see the slaves educated and gradually emancipated. The soldiers cannot feel any attachment to the government which has dragged them from their homes and doomed them to a life of the severest hardship…All power being vested in the army, the changes will begin first in that quarter and will propagate themselves into all ranks of the empire. Again, I say, that no-one regrets the Emperor Alexander as a public loss, and I feel certain that out of Russia, few tears will be shed on this occasion, except by those wretched despots whom he has assisted by upholding them in their unlimited and unlawful power'.[15]

Already, in 1823, the Vasilkov branch of the Decembrists' Southern Society had proposed that the Tsar, Alexander, should be taken prisoner while on an official visit to the Bobruisk Fortress near Minsk. Their plan was that the 8th and 9th Infantry Divisions would then march on Moscow and the

Second Army would capture the chief military staff in the South; simultaneously, the Northern Society would take over the government in St Petersburg.

An alternative plan was suggested in 1824 by Sergei Muravyev-Apostol and Bestuzhev-Ryumin and supported mainly by the Kamenka branch (where Pushkin had stayed in 1820). This proposed that when Alexander came to the south to oversee the army manoeuvres at Belaya Tserkov, he would be assassinated in his bedroom at night, and the entire military staff would then be arrested. The army would then take Kiev and proceed north to Moscow. As commander of the Chernigov regiment, Bestuzhev-Ryumin would then remain in the south to maintain order and Muravyev-Apostol would organise the revolt in the capital. The third plan, proposed by Pestel, was that the revolution should begin in St Petersburg, followed by an overthrow of the government in the southern territories.

Exactly why Constantine decided against accepting the opportunity presented to him to accept the Russian throne remains something of a mystery. One explanation is that he had settled in Poland and grown to like living there, especially after his marriage to Grudzińska. He may simply have feared meeting the same fate as his father if he risked returning to St Petersburg, only to be garrotted in his bedroom. In her book about *The Princess of Siberia,* Christine Sutherland writes that: 'Another factor must undoubtedly have been the impact made on him by the assassination of his father, Tsar Paul. That memory had haunted his older brother, Alexander, all his life. Constantine, conscious of the way things happened in Russia and deeply distrustful of the guards, had no desire to end up strangled on some dark, stormy night, like his father'.[16]

His reluctance would have been even more understandable since he would have already been well aware of the plans being made by the Decembrists. His omnipresent network of spies would have informed him of the strong links between the secret societies in Poland and Russia - and that their primary aims were for the abolition of serfdom, the armed overthrow of the autocracy, and the assassination of the Tsar. These objectives were strongest in the south, where Pestel was based.

The decision to end the uncertainty created by the prolonged interregnum was finally forced soon after the Chief of the Russian General Staff, General Diebitsch, had sent a message marked 'extremely urgent' to St Petersburg, warning of 'a vast conspiracy in the army'.

Although Diebitsch's communiqué had been dispatched with the instruction 'for the Emperor's own hands' (and should, therefore, only have been seen by Constantine) it was delivered to Nicholas at six in the morning by a Colonel of the Izmailovsky Regiment, Baron Fredericks. On its arrival, Nicholas had taken it upon himself to open the package which contained a report from a government spy, the Englishman Ivan Sherwood, warning of the conspiracy and naming several officers in the St Petersburg garrison who were said to be involved.

Sherwood was a non-commissioned officer in the Russian army of the south and had been born in Kent - his father was a skilled mechanic who had been brought to Russia by Paul I. However, Sherwood was not the government's only source of information. In the south, the spy network was coordinated by the commander of all the military colonies for the region, Colonel-General Count Jan Witt, and his mistress, Karolina Sobańska.

As well as being strikingly beautiful, Sobańska also worked for him as an extremely effective Russian intelligence agent. Pushkin had met Sobańska in Kiev in 1821 and had not managed to avoid the honey trap. He had not realised that she was an accomplished *femme fatale,* specifically sent by Count Witt to develop a friendship with Pushkin in order uncover any sign of subversive activity. Remarkably, a few years later, Sobańska was delegated to carry out the same kind of surveillance on Adam Mickiewicz, shortly after his arrival in Russia.

Pushkin's friend, Philip Weigel, was so outraged when he discovered that Sobańska had 'joined the ranks of the gendarme agents' that he wrote: 'What vilenesses were concealed beneath her elegant appearance'.[17] Another of the government's agents in southern Russia, was Alexander Boshniak, a former civil servant in the Foreign Ministry known to both Count Jan Witt and Karolina Sobańska. Based on the sheer volume of intelligence received, they were both well aware that some form of revolutionary organisation existed in the south by the beginning of 1825. They were also certain that the centre of its activities were concentrated in Kamenka, the Davydov estate where Pushkin had stayed for some months in 1824.

Boshniak was instructed to infiltrate the membership of the Southern Society, was taken into the conspirators' confidence and from then on regularly reported on their activities. However, the most dangerous of the government's spies in the south was an agent called Arkady Maiboroda who had infiltrated the Southern Society to the highest levels, to the extent that he became second-in-command to Pavel Pestel. Although the reports sent by Maiborada to the government in St Petersburg, via Count Witt, were often dismissed by the Tsar, Alexander, it was his information which ultimately led to the discovery of the entire Southern Society. Alexander's final administrative act was to order the arrest of the conspirators identified by Maiboroda. The first to be detained was Pavel Pestel, on 13 December 1825, a day before the planned uprising in the North.

By this stage, the alarm bells were already ringing loud and clear in St Petersburg. On the same evening as Nicholas received the urgent dispatch from General Diebitsch, a young officer by the name of Iakov Rostovtsev also warned Nicholas of the intended rebellion, without naming names. He knew what was going on because he had been invited by several Decembrist officers to participate in the plot. Rostovstev warned Nicholas of the imminent danger if a new Tsar was installed in Constantine's absence. If this happened, he predicted a very serious revolt was likely to break out.

The impact of these reports on Nicholas and his family was profound. Among a set of papers headed '*The Interregnum of 1825 and the Decembrist Revolt according to the Memoirs of the Imperial Family*', published by the Central State Archive in 1926, is a memo written by Nicholas's wife, the Empress Alexandra Feodorovna, in which she describes this scene:

'On the night of the 13th-14th I was alone in my little study and I was crying, when I saw my husband enter. He knelt and prayed for a long time. After that he said to me: 'We do not know what awaits us. Promise me to be brave and to die honourably if we must die'. [18]

Later the same night - at five o'clock in the morning - Nicholas appeared before the officers commanding the regiments of the Guards and made a short speech, reported verbatim by the Austrian Ambassador Lebzeltern to his superior, Metternich, in which he said:

'Gentlemen, do not think that the morning will pass without trouble. It is even possible that the safety of the palace will be menaced, but I cannot guard against this effectively in advance; I know there is unrest in some regiments, but only at the decisive moment shall I be able to see on which troops to rely: until then I cannot measure the extent of the evil. However, I am calm because my conscience is clear. You know, gentlemen, that I have not sought to wear the crown; I have not the experience or the abilities needful for bearing such a heavy burden; but once God, the will of my brothers and the laws of the State have given it to me, I shall know how to defend it, and no one in the world will be able to wrest it from me. I know my duty and how to fulfil it. If misfortunes come, an Emperor of Russia must die sword in hand. However, as I cannot predict how we shall come through this crisis, it is to you, Gentlemen, that I recommend my son. As for me, should I be Emperor for only one hour, I shall prove myself worthy of the honour'.[19]

On the same day that Nicholas received the report from General Diebitsch informing him of the conspiracy afoot, Constantine's final refusal to travel to St Petersburg and be acclaimed as Tsar was also delivered. Realising that further hesitation was no longer an option, Nicholas immediately ordered the preparation of an edict announcing his succession, which appeared the very same day. He then designated 14 December 1825 to be the day on which the new oath of allegiance to himself would be taken. As soon as this decision was announced, members of the Northern Society brought forward their plans.

Notes

1   *'To Chaadayev'*, by A S Pushkin, 1818. My translation

2   See Rules of Dynastic Succession for the Imperial House of Russia: A Historical
Survey, in: http://www.imperialhouse.ru/en/imperialhouse-en/succession/385.html

3   **The Accession of Nicholas I: By Special Command of the Emperor
Alexander I**I, by His Imperial Majesty's Secretary of State, Baron Modest Adreyevich
Korff, Rare Books, 2012 (first published by John Murray in 1857), pp7-13

4   **The Imperfect Autocrat: Grand Duke Constantine Pavlovich and the Polish
Congress Kingdom**, by Angela T Pienkos, East European Monographs, Columbia
University Press, 1987, p40

5   Pienkos, ibid. p40

6   **Poland under the Dominion of Russia,** by Harro Harring, late cadet in the
Lancer Regiment of the Grand-Duke Constantine's Imperial Russian Body Guard,
James Cochrane & Co, London, 1832 (reprinted from the British Library Historical
Collection, 2015), p97

7   Harring, ibid. p6

8   Pienkos, op.cit. p42

9   Harring, op.cit. p120

10   Harring, op.cit. p105

11   Pienkos, op.cit. p56

12   Pienkos, op.cit. p57

13   Pienkos, op.cit. p59

14   **Russian Decembrist Views of Poland,** by William L Blackwell, *The Polish
Review,* Vol 3, No 4 (Autumn 1958), published by the University of Illinois Press on
behalf of the Polish Institute of Arts and Sciences of America, http://www.jstor.org/
stable/25776203 p37

15   **The Last Days of Alexander: And the First Days of Nicholas (Emperors of
Russia),** by Robert Lee, reprinted by Ulan Press in 2012, first published by Harrison
& Sons in 1854, p76

16   **The Princess of Siberia: The Story of Maria Volkonsky and the Decembrist
Exiles**, by Christine Sutherland, Quartet Books, 2001

17   **Pushkin,** by T J Binyon, Harper Collins, 2002, p163

18   **Tsar Nicholas I,** by Constantin de Grunwald, translated from the French by Brigit
Patmore, Douglas Saunders with MacGibbon & Kee, 1954, p2

19   De Grunwald, ibid. p3

'The daring of the Decembrists in the North as well as in the
South can be truly considered the prelude to the long struggle
between Autocracy and Democracy in Russia'.

Anatole Mazour, *The First Russian Revolution,* 1825[1]

11 | The Uprising of December 1825

Granted the opportunity they had been waiting for, but not on the timescale they had anticipated, leaders of the rebellion now resolved to incite the regiments of Guards to revolt, on the grounds that the proposed pledge of allegiance to Nicholas was illegal. They determined that they would march on Senate Square, where the oath to the new Tsar was due to be administered. Rather than approving the replacement of Constantine with Nicholas, they would instead proclaim the convocation of a National Assembly and the adoption of a constitution for Russia.

If necessary, they would assassinate the Tsar. Plans for the uprising on Senate Square were discussed in a feverish atmosphere at the St Petersburg apartment of Kondraty Ryleev, Pushkin's former schoolmate and fellow poet.

Ryleev was one of the few leaders of the Decembrist uprising who was not an officer of the Guards. Nevertheless, his apartment had become the focal point for the comings and goings of officers from the various regiments who intended to take part in the revolt. Other prominent participants were Pyotr Kakhovsky, a former guards officer who was also planning to go and fight for the liberation of Greece; Prince Sergey Trubetskoy, a Colonel in the Imperial Guard who was brother-in-law of the Austrian Ambassador, Lebzeltern; and two of the five Bestuzhev brothers, all of whom were active in the Northern Society.

None of the conspirators was in much doubt as to the

stakes involved. In Ryleev's view, an upheaval was essential even though there was always the possibility of failure. In one of his poems, Ryleev had written: 'A cruel fate awaits the one who first rises against the oppressor of the people. But liberty has never been gained without victims'. He now said that the tactics of revolution could be summed up in one word: 'dare'.

On the other hand, he was not overly optimistic about the likely outcome: 'I foresee that we will not succeed, and yet a crisis is inevitable. If we come to grief, our failure will serve as a lesson to those who come after us'.[2]

In the event that Nicholas, his brother the Grand Duke Michael, or any other member of the imperial family should attempt to prevent the uprising, Ryleev and his co-conspirators had resolved that they would seize the Winter Palace and bring the Imperial family to reason, by violence if necessary. Ryleev had already assigned to Pyotr Kakhovsky the responsibility of being the person who would shoot the Emperor, if they met with determined opposition.

As Ryleev and the other leaders of the Decembrists knew, the army – and, in particular, the Guards regiments – had repeatedly played the decisive role during periods of dynastic crisis throughout the 18th century in Russia. The reigns of the Empresses Anna, Elizabeth and both Catherine I and II had all relied on the backing of powerful 'favourites' like Biron, Münnich, Razumovsky, Orlov and Potemkin, men with exemplary war records and the allegiance of some of the Imperial Army's most prestigious regiments. The previous period, from the death of Peter the Great in 1725 to the murder of Paul I in 1801, was littered with palace *coups* and assassinations in what became known as '*The Age of Palace Revolutions*'.

For example, when Peter the Great died unexpectedly, in January 1725, without actually naming a successor, a *coup* was arranged by his ally, Menshikov, and a number of the other 'new men' promoted by Peter, to ensure that his wife, Catherine, be proclaimed the new ruler of Russia (Catherine I). Menshikov guessed, correctly, that the Guards regiments would make the ultimate decision on the succession, so he summoned these troops into the capital and massed them near the palace.

When an assembly of the Senate was called to confirm the

succession, any possible opposition evaporated when: '…a number of officers of the Preobrazhensky and Semyonovsky Guards who had filtered into the room shouted their agreement. At the same time, a roll of drums in the courtyard below brought the statesmen to the windows. Looking out into the darkness, they made out the thick ranks of the guard drawn up around the palace…Under the circumstances, Fyodor Apraxin's proposal that "her Majesty be proclaimed Autocrat with all the prerogatives of her late consort" was quickly accepted'.[3]

Similarly, Peter the Great's daughter, Elizabeth, came to power again thanks to her favourite, Razumovsky, and the support of the Imperial Guard. She seized her opportunity to mount a successful *coup d'etat* in the early hours of 25 November 1741. That was the fifth *coup d'état* to have taken place in 15 years, all with the support of the guard. Alexander I's grandmother, Catherine the Great, had likewise relied on her lover, Grigory Orlov, and a battalion of guards to dispense with her husband, Peter III. And Alexander had himself succeeded to throne after his father, Paul, had been killed in the most recent of these palace *coups* led by a group of Guards officers in March 1801. In Ryleev's view, the mutiny of the Semenovsky regiment in 1820 had presented a similar opportunity which could have led to Alexander being ousted. The fact that the leaders of the revolt had not seized their chance was a mistake the Decembrists should not repeat.

Nicholas was equally aware of the importance of keeping the army on his side. On the morning of 14 December, when the oath of loyalty to himself was due to be taken, his first engagement was with the generals and Regimental Commander of the Guards. Nicholas later recorded what he told the assembled gathering, which took place in Alexander's apartment: 'Having explained to them how, by the mandatory will of Constantine, to whom, but a short while ago, I had taken the oath along with them, I found myself obliged to obey this desire and accept the throne, to which I am, following his abdication, the nearest in line of succession; after which I read the will of the late emperor and the act of abdication of Constantine. Thereafter, having received from each the assurance of his loyalty and readiness to sacrifice himself, I ordered them to go to their command and administer the oath'.[4]

THE MAN WHO SHOOK HIS FIST AT THE TSAR

At first, everything seemed to be going to plan as far as Nicholas was concerned. Brigadier-General Alexey Orlov had successfully taken the oath of the regiment of Horse Guards. The Governor of St Petersburg, General Miloradovich, had reported that the city was calm and the colonel in charge of the Preobrazhensky Regiment, which was quartered next to the Winter Place, had sensibly taken the precaution of paying out 'saving funds' due to the men, which put them in pliable frame of mind.

But this apparent tranquillity was not to last. At about ten o'clock in the morning, a Captain of the Horse Guards, Baron Kaulbars, reported seeing a strong detachment of infantry, the regimental colours at their head, making their way towards Saint Isaac's Cathedral. According to Kaulbars: 'An officer, in aide-de-camp uniform, led the detachment with sword drawn and waving a paper in his left hand. He was surrounded by a crowd of excited shouting people'.[5]

As the French historian, Constantin de Grunwald, reports, this was the first evidence of rebel detachments heading towards Senate Square: '…they forced every soldier they met on the way to join them, threatening to kill them if they refused. Incited by some officers, seven hundred soldiers of the Moscow Regiment had revolted; seizing cartridges from the depot, they had severely wounded three superior officers'.[6] Having shot the commander of the regiment, Baron Fredericks, and Brigadier-General Shenshin, the regiment was now led by two captains, Prince Shchepin-Rostovsky and Bestuzhev.

Because they had arrived too late for the swearing-in ceremony on Senate Square – the Senators had taken the oath at seven in the morning – the rebels took up a defiant position on the Square, displaying what the Austrian Ambassador, Lebzeltern, described as 'that imperturbable calm and cold decision which are part of the national character'.[7] Senate Square, which till that point had remained empty, now began to fill with workers, many them involved in the construction of St Isaac's Cathedral on the south side of the Square. According to the eye-witness account of de Grunwald: 'Their sympathy seemed to be with the insurgents: however, they made way respectfully for the coaches drawn by four or six horses in which be-denizened dignitaries, accompanied by their wives in court dress, made their way to the

Winter Palace to attend the *Te Deum* being held in celebration of Nicholas's accession'.[8]

Meanwhile Pyotr Kakhovsky – who had been assigned to the role of Brutus – took to the task with gusto. Walking in front of the troops loyal to Nicholas, he brandished two pistols and a dagger and shouted cheers for the Grand Duke Constantine. When the Governor-General, Count Miloradovich, arrived standing upright on his sleigh, he first appealed for calm and then mounted the horse of an aide-de-camp and headed towards the rebels. When he began to plead with them to accept the reality that Constantine's abdication was a fait accompli, he was unceremoniously shot by Khakhovsky, at point-blank range, within yards of *The Bronze Horseman*.[9]

From about 11 o'clock onwards, news began to filter through to the Winter Palace about the events going on outside. When the Chief of Staff of the Guards, General Neidhardt came in 'utterly upset' to announce the insurrection of the Moscow Regiment and its march on Senate Square, de Grunwald reports 'there was a complete panic'.[10] In her diary, the Empress Alexandra recorded that, at midday, Nicholas had come into her room and said that he had to go: 'From his voice I could tell that the news was bad. I knew that he had not intended to leave the Palace. It gave me a shock. I went on with the business of dressing, for at two o'clock we had to be ready for the state procession of the *Te Deum*. Suddenly the door opened and the Dowager Empress appeared: her face was haggard'.[11]

'Darling', she said to me, 'things are going very badly. There is rioting'. Pale as death, unable to say a word, I threw a garment – the first to hand – over my shoulders and went with the Dowager Empress to her small study. From there we could see that the whole square in front of the Palace and as far as the Senate was full of people. We knew nothing: all we had heard was that the Moscow Regiment had rebelled'.[12]

By now, Nicholas had made his way to Senate Square, where he met with Miloradovich, moments before he was shot. The last thing he told Nicholas, in French, was: 'Things are going badly, Sire, they're surrounding the Monument (that is, *The Bronze Horseman)* but I will go and speak to them'.[13] The newly appointed Tsar's own recollections of the events on Senate Square

are worth quoting at length because they graphically convey the gravity of the situation – the revolt was not, as is often made out, a complete farce.

Nicholas reports that he first ordered General Orlov, in charge of the Horse Guards, to position his regiment in such a way as to cut off access to the insurgents on all sides, if possible, so that they would be surrounded:

'The square was then, on the cathedral side, quite blocked by fences which stretched as far as the corner of the present Synod building; the corner formed by the boulevard and the bank of the Neva served as a site for storing the stones brought for the cathedral, and between this building material and the Peter the Great monument there was no more than about 50 paces. It was in this small space, marching in rows of six, that the regiment positioned itself in two lines, with its right flank facing the monument and the left reaching almost to the fences. The insurgents were drawn up in a dense, irregular column with its back to the old Senate. Then there was still only the Moscow Regiment…Then I detailed a company of His Majesty's Preobrazhensky Regiment with Colonel Islenyev…to cross the boulevard and take the Isaakiyevsky Bridge in order to cut off access from that side to Vasilyevsky Island and cover the flank of the Horse Guards. I myself, with Adjutant-General Benckendorff, who had just arrived, went out onto the square to examine the position of the insurgents. I was met with shots…'[14]

Soon after this episode, Nicholas learned that there had been disturbances in the Izmailovsky Regiment when the oath was administered. Realising that the affair 'was now growing in significance' Nicholas sent one of his aides to speak with the Master of the Imperial Stables, Prince Dolgoruky, with instructions: 'to prepare the travelling coaches for my mother and wife'.[15] His intention was that, should the worse come to the worst, they should be taken with the children to Tsarskoe Selo under the protection of the Horse Guards:

'I myself, having sent for the artillery, went into Dvortsovaya (Palace) Square in order to secure the palace, to which both sapper battalions, the Guards and the training battalion, had been ordered to report. Before I had reached the Main Headquarters building I saw the Royal Grenadiers Regiment moving in total disorder, with their flags but without their officers. Having gone up to them, suspecting nothing, I wanted to stop them and line them up: to my 'Halt', they replied: 'We're for Constantine!'. I pointed towards Senate Square and said: 'If that's so, then that is the way you should go'.[16]

Following this advice, the entire Grenadiers Regiment, which had deserted its post at the Peter and Paul Fortress, made its way to the square, to join those Nicholas described as 'their similarly misled comrades'. 'It was fortunate it was so', he recalls, 'for otherwise there would have been bloodshed beneath the windows of the palace, and our fate would have been more than doubtful'.[17]

Soon after this close shave, a detachment of the Royal Grenadiers made a concerted assault on the Winter Palace 'with the intention of seizing the palace and, should there be any resistance, wiping out our entire family'.[18] This attack was only foiled by the intervention of a sapper battalion of the Life Guards Regiment. By now Nicholas was so pre-occupied with what was going on in Senate Square, he was completely unaware of this 'extreme danger threatening in the rear' and would have been unable to offer any resistance. With hindsight, he concludes: 'This reveals with most amazing clarity that neither I nor anyone else could have brought the affair to a satisfactory conclusion if the mercy of God had not seen fit to direct everything for the best'.[19]

On returning to his troops, Nicholas found that the artillery had arrived – but without ammunition, which was stored at a location called 'the laboratory'. When a detachment was sent to acquire the ordnance, it found that the commander of the arsenal was reluctant to grant access because he had heard that a mutiny was going on. According to Baron Modest von Korff's account, he: 'remained in considerable uncertainty to which side belonged the party which had been sent for the ammunition, and therefore could not be induced to give up the keys'.[20]

Meanwhile, the insurrection intensified: 'to the original mass of the Moscow Regiment was added the whole of the Guards Naval Crew, which joined from the Galernaya, while a crowd of Grenadiers took up position on the other side. The noise and shouts were incessant, and frequent shots flew past my head. Finally, the people also began to vacillate, and many ran across to the insurgents, in front of whom civilians could be seen'.[21]

It now became clear to Nicholas that winning the troops' allegiance to the oath was not the only reason for the rebellion: 'another extremely serious conspiracy' also became apparent: cries of 'Hurrah, the Constitution' could be heard in the crowd alongside those calling for Constantine.[22]

When Nicholas's younger brother, the Grand Duke Michael Pavlovich, proposed to act as mediator with rebels from the insurgent Brigade of Seamen, he was told that, a fortnight before 'when nobody had even heard of the illness of His Majesty the Emperor Alexander Pavlovich, they had been suddenly told that he was dead; that then they had been ordered to take the oath to his Majesty Constantine Pavlovich, which they had done, without a murmur; and that now, at last, they wanted to make them swear again, to *another* Emperor, assuring them that the first would not have their oath and refused to reign'.[23]

In his account of the conversation, Baron Korff records that the sailors asked: 'How can we, Your Highness, incur such a sin in our souls, when the person to whom we took the oath is still alive and yet we do not see him? If they begin to tamper with the oath, what will remain sacred?'. The mutinous sailors refused to budge until Constantine himself made an appearance affirming his renunciation – as things stood, they said 'we don't even know where he is'.[24]

When two of Russia's leading churchmen appeared, dressed in their full regalia for the *Te Deum* which had been due to take place at two o'clock, their attempts to influence the rebels by playing on their religious sentiments were similarly rebuffed.

As they headed towards the crowd, Kakhovsky shot his second victim, Colonel Ludwig Niklaus von Stürler, a commander in the Grenadiers.

Undaunted by the shooting of Stürler, the Metropolitan Evgeny of Kiev moved towards the crowd and called upon the rebels to abandon what Baron Korff describes as 'the criminality of treason against their lawful Tsar and the divine wrath which was awaiting the guilty'.[25]

The leaders of the revolt responded by saying that their lawful

Tsar was Constantine, and they believed that at that moment he was being held in chains near the capital. In their view, this was no business for a churchman and that, 'if the Archbishop could take two different oaths in the same week, such perjury was no example to them'.[26] They ordered the drums to beat, to drown out the sound of his voice, and threatened to shoot if he didn't leave.

When an attempt was made to clear the square with a cavalry assault it proved to be no more successful. The horses' hooves slipped on the frozen cobbles and their riders were pelted with snowballs. By three in the afternoon, the situation was becoming ever more menacing and confused and darkness was already beginning to descend on Senate Square. Some of the crowd which now packed the square hurled rocks and timber from the construction of St Isaac's in the direction of the government troops.

The sight which greeted Nicholas when he first emerged from the Admiralty Boulevard at the head of his detachment is described as follows by Baron Korff: 'Beyond the corner of the boulevard it was impossible to make way any further through the dense mass of people which thronged the whole area up to the monument of Peter the Great, the pedestal of which had been chosen by the leaders of the insurrection as a basis of operations for the accomplishment of their treason'.

Constantin de Grunwald describes the same scene as follows: 'Buffeted by the waves of the surging populace, the insurgents had formed into a square, and looked like a small island in an ocean. The soldiers were all in gala uniform – long white breeches, green tunics with gold braid – lined up as if for review. The wind ruffled the plumes of their helmets and, through the clouds, rare shafts of sunlight gleamed on their bayonets. In front of them, in the centre of the square stood the famous statue of Peter the Great. It was the creation of Falconet: an immense rock of unpolished stone served as a pedestal for a rearing horse, seemingly held on the edge of an abyss by the iron hand of the great Emperor.

'The insurgents' position was strangely symbolic – between the Temple of the Law and the monument to the Reformer, who, with outstretched arm, seemed to be showing his country the way into the future. Former Russian generations may have assisted at many a *coup d'etat* carried out under the cover of night by the Praetorian Guards in favour of this or that pretender, but the rebellion of 14th December was something quite new. Although the soldiers were naively cheering for Constantine, their leaders now revealed the real aim of the riot by greeting the heir to a line of autocrats with the cry of "Long Live the Constitution!". For the first time in the memory of man, the Russian nation seemed to rise up in the name of Law and Liberty'.[27]

As de Grunwald notes, it was later alleged (not least by Nicholas himself) that, in their ignorance, the soldiers had shouted 'Long live Constantine and Long live his wife Constitution'. An amusing enough bon mot, he suggests, since Constantine's wife was Polish, so may have had a name which was unfamiliar (though her name was Joanna. Constantine's daughter, on the other hand, *was* called Constantia). This tale has since entered into the official narrative of what happened on Senate Square, despite the fact that: 'no eye-witness states positively that they heard these shouts, which are probably an invention of the salons'.[28]

What was missing on the rebel side was any semblance of leadership. A few days before the confrontation on Senate Square, a hurried meeting of the Northern Society executive had nominated one of their most aristocratic and most moderate members, the Colonel Prince Trubetskoy, to lead the rebellion on the 14 December. As soon became clear, Trubetskoy was not a good choice. The real leader of the revolt in the north, Kondraty Ryleev, had developed such serious doubts about Trubetskoy's commitment to the cause that, on the morning of the revolt he went to see him accompanied by Pushkin's close friend Ivan Pushchin, to remind the prince that they were counting on him to be there when the troops came to take the oath.

Ryleev's suspicions were confirmed when Trubetskoy failed to appear at all on the fateful morning. He had clearly lost his nerve just when it was needed most. He later told the Investigating Commission which was set up to identify the perpetrators of the revolt that his 'tormented soul' had given him no sleep. He was arrested the day after the rebellion at the Austrian Embassy, where he had sought the sanctuary of his brother-in-law, the Austrian Ambassador, Lebzeltern. It is entirely possible that his decision had been influenced by Lebzeltern, who knew from the previous day that Nicholas had been informed about the plot and that Pestel had already been arrested.

In the absence of Trubetskoy, Ryleev took charge but he was a civilian, lacking any military expertise. He did appear for a short time in Senate Square on the morning of the revolt but soon realised that his side needed more cavalry and artillery and thereafter spent much of the rest of the day searching for reinforcements. Although Kakhovsky did shoot Miloradivich and Stürler and wounded another officer, Gastfer, he never fulfilled his promised to shoot the Tsar.

When the day came, he decided that his religion would not permit him to assassinate the emperor. Nicholas himself later remarked that it was a miracle neither he nor his younger brother, the Grand Duke Michael Pavlovich, had been shot during the day's events.

As darkness fell, Nicholas began to realise that more drastic measures would be required to clear the square. Four artillery guns were manoeuvred into position, three of them directly opposite the rebel column. Nicholas ordered that the guns be loaded with grape-shot, a vicious projectile made from a canvas bag filled with metal balls and nails. The use of such a weapon would inevitably wreak havoc when fired at close range on a tightly packed crowd of people.

After the day-long standoff, caused by a combination of indecision and confusion on both sides, a massacre was now inflicted on the rebels. Blood ran through the square and many of those who attempted to escape the carnage fled at its northern exit along the English Embankment and across the icebound River Neva. Many drowned when the ice was shattered by the combined impact of cannon fire and the weight of men and horses fleeing the square.

After the firing had ceased, the government took immediate measures to eradicate every trace of what had happened in Senate Square: 'It hastily sent workers to the scene to remove the dead and to scrub off the bloodstains. Wishing to dispose of the bodies as quickly as a possible, Alexander Shulgin, the St Petersburg Chief of Police, hit upon an ingenuous idea: he ordered them thrown into the Neva River, under the ice. It was feared that, among the many dead, there were also thrown in a number of wounded victims'.[29]

The number who vanished into the depths of the river is not known exactly. No discussion was permitted in the Russian press of what had happened to *notre amis de quatorze,* as Nicholas called them, for the next 30 years. The first historic study of the interregnum which not published until after Nicholas's death, in 1855. This was Modest von Korff's *Accession of Nicholas I,* which was commissioned years later by Nicholas I's successor, Alexander II.

Von Korff came up with a suspiciously small estimate of 80 dead. This was the number of bodies found in Senate Square and piled up against the fence surrounding St Isaac's Cathedral. A more credible figure for the total number killed in the massacre was provided by S N Korsakov of the St Petersburg police. According to the Russian historian, Melissa Nechkina, he counted a total 1,271 dead of whom 903 were civilians from the lower classes (the word he used was *chorniye*, which in Russian refers to the colour black but also can be taken to mean 'the mob' or 'common people').

Meanwhile, on the same day as the confrontation on Senate Square was unfolding, members of the Southern Society faced the serious dilemma of how to react following the arrest of their leader, Pestel, the previous day. Some thought the best policy would be to wait until 'the storm blew over' while others argued for an immediate rebellion. They did not find out about the crushing of the uprising in St Petersburg until 23 December and then realised they would need to act.

The obvious candidate to stand in for Pestel was Sergey Muravyov-Apostol but at the point when news of the events in the north came through, he had gone to regimental headquarters at Zhitomir to request a leave of absence for his friend and fellow conspirator, Mikhail Bestuzhev-Ryumin, whose mother had just died in Moscow.

Both were former officers in the Semenovsky Regiment and as such had been deprived of their rights to leave the regiment, retire or be promoted. While in Zhitomir, Muravyev-Apostol hoped to make contact with Count Moszyńsky, a leading figure in the Polish Society.

It was during his period of his absence that a communiqué arrived from St Petersburg ordering the arrest of Muravyov-Apostol and the seizure of all his papers. Bestuzhev-Ryumin was immediately instructed by his fellow conspirators to go to Zhitomir to warn Muravyev-Apostol. He first learned of the uprising in the north on Christmas Day, while at dinner with his regimental superior, Commander Rot. Muravyev-Apostol's first response was to ask his brother, Artamon, to lead a rebellion of his own Akhtyrsky Regiment but he refused, saying that such an undertaking was futile and that he feared for his family if he became involved.

Muravyev-Apostol's brother did promise that he would make contact with the United Slavs on his brother's behalf to request that they foment a revolt. However, as soon as his brother left, Artamon destroyed the message. This failure to pass on an urgent request for support from the Slavs inflicted a serious blow to the plans of the Southern Society. Muravyev-Apostol meanwhile set out to the headquarters of the Chernigovsky Regiment, intending to muster their support for a rising and then co-ordinate their rebellion with the United Slavs, who, according to the historian, Anatole Mazour, had been 'eagerly awaiting an opportunity'.

These plans reached a calamitous stage on the night of 29th December when Muravyev-Apostol and one of his brothers, Matvey, were both arrested and detained by police. Early the following morning, four members of the United Slavs appeared and successfully released the prisoners by force but this now left no option but to act at once. With the assistance of some other officers, Sergey Muravyev-Apostol roused the Chernigovsky Regiment and, on 30th December, they marched to the city of Vasilkov, not far from Kiev, where they were joined by Bestuzhev-Ryumin.

At Vasilkov, the city garrison readily joined the rebels and plans were made to take Kiev but this opportunity was not acted upon largely due to hesitation of the part of Sergey Muravyev-Apostol. His concern was that the size of the garrison at Kiev outnumbered the rebels by ten to one and might not be counted on to join their cause. The Chernigovsky instead set out on a circuitous route which, despite some success, posed no real threat. Their progress was halted entirely when a detachment of Hussars arrived, with artillery and with instructions to put down the insurrection.

When the regiment left the town of Pology on the morning of 3 January, it was met with a fusillade of grapeshot. Sergey Muravyev-Apostol was wounded in the head and his younger brother, Ippolit, seeing that their cause was hopeless and preferring death to dishonour, shot himself in the head. Afterwards, the leaders of the Chernigovsky mutiny were rounded up and sent to St Petersburg, where they joined all the members implicated in the northern revolt: 'The uprising, which had the opportunity to become a wide revolutionary movement, was destroyed in embryo. The avenging hand of the government spared no one. Every person under the least suspicion of being even remotely related to the movement was brought to the capital, where investigations were conducted on a large scale'.[30]

Unlike his counterpart in the north, Prince Trubetskoy, no one could have accused Sergey Muravyev-Apostol of lacking courage: 'He led the rebels to the scene of battle and stood with them to the last, facing the enemy without fear. Brought down with a serious wound, he still attempted to command the troops, but was crushed by a much superior force, captured, taken to St Petersburg, and hanged a few months later'.[31] Altogether, five leaders of the revolt were sent to the gallows, and hundreds more were sentenced to life sentences in Siberian labour camps.

In St Petersburg, the battle had partly been lost because none of the rebels had taken the initiative to seize the government's artillery cannon before they could be fired. The forces led by Muravyev-Apostol had no such option, faced by cannon fire in open fields. His biggest mistake had been his slowness in strategy. It is possible that swifter action could have won the support of other regiments and, had they managed to win over Kiev, may have been able to capture the arsenal and win over the artillery regiments, where the United Slavs had developed considerable influence.

Instead of this: 'Muravyev-Apostol went about cautiously, trying to secure a base, advocating ideas of liberty, composing semi-religious, semi-political leaflets, and arranging a theatrical performance led by a priest, which had no effect whatever upon the soldiers'.[32] This said, every action taken by Sergey Muravyev-Apostol had to be decided upon under desperate pressure and, in Anatole Mazour's estimation, even though they had been defeated: 'The democratic ideas of those who opened the struggle may seem feeble to later generations, the contribution of the Decembrists but small; but the shot was fired, Old Russia was challenged, and faith in future success deepened as time went on'.[33]

Following his suppression of the Decembrists, Nicholas I is reported to have told the French ambassador: 'I believe I have done a service to all governments…if the insurrection of Russian officers in December 1825 had succeeded then the whole order would have been shaken to the ground and the whole of Europe would have found itself under its debris'.

The reprisals taken by the Tsar against the Decembrists shocked contemporaries, even conservative members of the elite. Nicholas's 'victory' over 'the Five' was also celebrated by a religious service in Moscow. In his memoirs, *My Past Life and Thoughts*, the Russian revolutionary, Alexander Herzen, recalls: 'In the midst of the Kremlin, the Metropolitan Filaret thanked God for the murders. The whole of the Royal Family took part in the service…cannon thundered from the heights of the Kremlin. Never have the gallows been celebrated with such pomp; Nicholas knew the importance of the victory!'[34]

Herzen recalled: 'I was present at that service, a boy of 14 lost in the crowd, and on the spot, before that altar defiled by bloody rites, I swore to avenge the murdered men, and dedicated myself to the struggle with that throne, with that altar, with those cannon'. Herzen regarded the Decembrists as 'veritable titans, hammered out of pure steel from head to foot, comrades-in-arms who deliberately went to certain death in order to awaken the young generation to a new life and to purify the children born in an environment of tyranny and servility'.[35] Years later, in exile in London, Herzen founded the first Russian free press, a newspaper called *Polyarnaya Zvezda* (Polar Star). The front cover of the first edition featured a joint profile of the five leading Decembrists silhouetted against the night sky – Pestel, Muravyev-Apostol, Ryleev Kakovsky and Bestuzhev-Ryumin.

In an article written in April 1912, '*In Memory of Herzen*', on the 100th anniversary of his birth, the leader of the 1917 October Revolution, Lenin, described both Herzen and the Decembrists as representatives of an aristocratic revolutionary movement and revolutionary democrats 'who played a great part in paving the way for the Russian revolution'. Russia witnessed its first revolutionary movement against Tsarism in 1825, because: 'the Decembrists were the first in Russia to create a revolutionary organisation, formulate a political programme, prepare for and carry though an uprising against the feudal and absolutist system'.[36]

There was, Lenin argued, a direct line of descent from the Decembrists, through the deepening revolutionary struggles of the 19th century to the workers' revolution of 1917. The motto on the masthead of *Iskra,* the official organ of the Russian Social Democratic Party was: 'From a spark a flame will be lit'. This line – signed as 'the Decembrists reply to Pushkin' – was a long-standing slogan of the Russian revolutionary movement and was taken from a poem written by Alexander Odoevsky, a poet himself and one of the commanders of the Decembrist mutineers in Senate Square. Between 1902 and 1903, *Iskra* was edited by Lenin in an upstairs room of what is now *The Crown Taveren* on Clerkenwell Green.

The author of the 'Iskra' quote, Odoevsky, was among those who had been arrested and imprisoned in the Peter and Paul Fortress, then sentenced to hard labour and deported to Siberia. He was a close friend of Kondratei Ryleev. He was also a relative of Alexander Griboyedov, the playwright whose best-known work, *Woe from Wit,* was written as a pro-Decembrist parody of Moscow high society. The poem from which Odoevsky's famous line was taken had been written as a direct reply to Pushkin's '*Message to Siberia',* written to his Decembrist friends after they had been exiled. The poem was smuggled to them in a note Pushkin handed Alexandrine Muravyev-Apostol before she left to join her husband, Artamon, in Siberia.

Message to Siberia

Deep in the Siberian mine
Keep your patience proud
The bitter toil shall not be lost
The rebel thought unbowed.
The sister of misfortune: Hope
In the under-darkness dumb
Speaks joyful courage to your heart:
The day desired will come.
And love and friendship pour to you
Across the darkened doors
Even as round your galley-beds
My free music pours.

The heavy-hanging chains will fall
The walls will crumble at a word
And Freedom greet you in the light,
And brothers give you back the sword.
Alexander Pushkin

(*Trans. Max Eastman*) [37]

The five Decembrist leaders hanged on the ramparts at the Peter and Paul Fortress were buried secretly somewhere on Goloday Island which is situated in the Neva delta, just to the north of Vasilyevsky Island. It is named after the English word 'holiday' because English merchants would often go there for a day out on a Sunday. Low-lying and frequently flooded, Goloday Island is reminiscent of the island upon which the body of Evgeny is found in *The Bronze Horseman*. It had been used as a burial ground, known as the Smolenskaya, both by Lutherans and Catholics, since the middle of the 18th century.

On the centenary of the Decembrist Revolt, in December 1925, Goloday Island was renamed by the Bolsheviks as Decembrists' Island and Senate Square was renamed Decembrists' Square, a name which it retained until 2008. Gatherings commemorating the Decembrists are held annually in St Petersburg to this day and are traditionally attended by decendents of those who took part in the revolt.

Notes

1   **The First Russian Revolution, 1825: The Decembrist Movement: Its Origins, Development & Significance**, by Anatole G Mazour, Stanford University Press, 1937, p201

2   **K F Ryleev: A Political Biography of the Decembrist Poet**, by Patrick O'Meara, Princeton University Press, 1984, p232

3   **Peter the Great: His Life and His World**, by Robert K Massie, Abacus, 1993 (first published by Victor Gollancz in 1981), p847

4   **The First Breath of Freedom,** archive material from the Library of Russian and Soviet Literary Journalism compiled by Vladimir Fyodorov, translated by Cynthia Carlisle, Progress Publishers., 1988, p188

5   From the Memoirs of Baron Kaulbars, quoted in **Tsar Nicholas I,** By Constantin de Grunwald, Translated from the French by Brigit Patmore, Douglas Saunders with MacGibbon & Kee, 1954, p6

6   De Grunwald, ibid. p6

7   De Grunwald, p6

8   De Grunwald, p6

9   De Grunwald, p7

10   De Grunwald, p7

11   De Grunwald, p7

12   De Grunwald, pp7-8

13   **The Accession of Nicholas I** – By Special Command of the Emperor Alexander II. By His Imperial Majesty's Secretary of State, Baron Modest Andreyevich Korff. Rare Books. 2012 (first published by John Murray in 1857). p41

14   Fyodorov, pp190-91

15   Fyodorov, p191

16   Fyodorov, pp191-92

17   Fyodorov, p192

18   Fyodorov, p192

19   Fyodorov, p192

20   Korff, op.cit. p51

21   Fyodorov, pp192-93

22   Fyodorov, p193

23   Korff, op.cit. p51

24   Korff, op.cit. p52

25   Korff, op.cit. p52

26   Korff, op.cit. p52

27   De Grunwald, pp9-10

28   De Grunwald, p10

29   Mazour, op.cit. pp179-80

30   Mazour, op.cit. p196

31   Mazour, op.cit. p199

32   Mazour, op.cit. p199

33   Mazour, op.cit. p201

34   **My Past & Thoughts: The Memoirs of Alexander Herzen**, translated by Constance Garnett and with an introduction by Isaiah Berlin, University of California Press, 1991 (first translation copyright by Chatto & Windus 1968), p44

35   Herzen, ibid. p44

36   Fyodorov, op.cit. p315

37   **The Poems, Prose and Plays of Alexander Pushkin,** selected and edited, with an introduction by Avrahm Yarmolinsky. The Modern Library. New York. 1937. p62

Part 2

Arise, prophet of Russia
Don your shroud of shame
Go, the noose around your neck,
to face the execrable assassin.

Pushkin, *The Prophet*, 1826[1]

Deep in the Siberian mine
Keep your patience proud;
The bitter toil shall not be lost,
The rebel thought unbowed'.

Pushkin, *Message to Siberia,* 1827[2]

12 | Pushkin & the Decembrists

Pushkin played no direct part in the uprising on Senate Square. When it took place, he was still under house arrest at his family estate in Mikhailovskoye. However, a few days before the uprising, Pushkin received a surprise visit from one of his former schoolmates, Ivan Pushchin – who Pushkin regarded as 'my best friend, my friend beyond price'. Ivan Pushchin had been involved with the Union of Welfare since his schooldays at the Imperial Lycée. Pushchin's first instinct on becoming involved with the Union of Welfare had been to 'tell all' to Pushkin: 'His ideas always agreed with mine on *res publica,* he preached our message in his own way, both orally and in writing, in verse and prose'.[3] Subsequently, he decided that to involve Pushkin in the enterprise might be rash: 'I was already unable to decide to entrust the secret to him, for it was not my secret alone, and the least incaution could be fatal for the whole cause. The mobility of his fiery character, his association with unreliable people, made me nervous'.[4]

THE MAN WHO SHOOK HIS FIST AT THE TSAR

By 1823, Ivan Pushchin was leader of the Moscow branch of the Northern Society and had been responsible for recruiting Kondraty Ryleev into membership. Together with Ryleev, he organised the plan for the insurrection of 14 December and was among the insurgents. For his part in the uprising, the Supreme Criminal Court initially sentenced Pushchin to death, a judgement which was later commuted to penal servitude for life.

When Pushchin learned, on what turned out to be the eve of the uprising, that Pushkin had been exiled to Mikhailovskoye, he decided that he would visit him while on family leave over Christmas. His sister lived in nearby Pskov, where she was married to the commander of the local garrison. Pushchin set out for Pskov, taking with him three bottles of Veuve Clicquot. Driving through deep snow drifts, Pushchin reached Mikhailovskoye, where he first caught sight of Pushkin standing at the porch, in the snow of an unswept courtyard, barefoot and wearing only a nightshirt.

Pushkin's room was accessed directly from the courtyard and inside: 'Everywhere there was poetic disorder, everywhere there were sheets of paper covered with writing, chewed and burnt pieces of quills (he always, from his days at the Lyceum' wrote with stubs which he barely managed to hold between his fingers)'.[5] During Pushchin's visit, the conversation again touched upon Pushkin's suspicions regarding the secret society: 'When I said to him that I was not alone in entering upon this new service to the fatherland, he leapt from his chair and cried: "All this is certainly connected with Major Raevsky, who has been sitting in the fort at Tiraspol for four years and whom they cannot get anything out of"'.[6]

Raevsky had been a major in the 32nd Jäger Regiment, part of the 6th Army whose headquarters were at Tiraspol, halfway between Kishinev and Odessa. Renowned for his 'completely unrestrained freethinking', Raevsky had come under the suspicion of his superiors in 1822 and had been arrested, charged with anti-government agitation among the soldiers. A report on his activities singled out the fact that: '…in handwriting exercises, he used words such as *freedom*, *equality* and *constitution*'. He was also said to have encouraged officer cadets to believe that constitutional government was better than any other form of government, and especially better than Russian monarchic government, which, although called monarchic, 'was really despotic'.[7]

This arrest took place during the three-year period Pushkin was living in Kishinev.

In fact, Raevsky and Pushkin were both members of the same Masonic Lodge and Pushkin was the first person to tell Raevsky that he was about to be arrested when he eavesdropped on a conversation between two of Raevsky's superiors in a local hostelry.

Masons were regarded as political 'freethinkers' and, for this reason, all Masonic Lodges in Russia were abolished in 1822, beginning with the Kishinev lodge. Suspected of being part of what General Sabaneev described as the 'Kishinev gang', the investigation into Raevsky's activities dragged on for years. After his remark about Raevsky, Pushkin calmed down and told Pushchin he was not going to force him to say anything about the secret society: 'Perhaps you are right not to trust me', he said, 'Certainly I do not deserve such trust – by reason of my many follies'.[8]

During the few hours of Pushchin's visit, they soon heard the arrival of someone else at the porch. At exactly this moment, Pushkin was reading a manuscript copy of the playwright Griboyedov's Decembrist comedy, *Woe from Wit,* which Pushchin had brought him as a gift. Pushkin looked out of the window, then hastily replaced the Griboyedov with a copy of *Chetyi-Miney,* or *Monthly Readings* – a collection of the lives of the saints which is illustrated according to the months their feast days are celebrated by the Orthodox Church.

The visitor, it transpired, was a fair-haired monk, the superior at a nearby monastery who had clearly been informed of Pushchin's presence. After the monk had taken two glasses of tea (not forgetting the rum) and had gone on his way, Pushchin apologised to Pushkin for having caused this unexpected visit. Pushkin replied: 'Stop this, my dear friend! He comes to see me without that, I have been placed under his surveillance. What can I say about such rubbish! And with that he proceeded to read as if nothing had happened'. [9] When Pushchin left Mikhailovskoye, it was the last time he saw Pushkin: 12 years later, while in a Siberian prison camp, he heard the news that Pushkin had been shot in a duel.

THE MAN WHO SHOOK HIS FIST AT THE TSAR

Since arriving at Mikhailovskoye, Pushkin had already been involved in two escape plans: in the first of these his neighbour and friend, Alexey Vulf, had proposed that he would obtain a foreign passport and would take Pushkin abroad, disguised as his servant. They intended to go to Switzerland, where Pyotr Chaadaev was then living. Vulf's mother, Praskoviya Isipova,

wrote to Zhukovsky in Petersburg, warning that if Pushkin did escape abroad, she could not blame him but that it would be a dreadful loss: 'Our Pskov is worse than Siberia', she said, 'and no ardent head can remain here. He is now so concerned with his position he will jump out of the frying pan and into the fire – and then it will be too late to think of any consequences'.[10] When the scheme came to nothing, Pushkin concocted a second plan, this time claiming that he had developed an 'aneurism' in his leg and that he would need to travel to Dorpat (now Tartu, in Estonia) where it could be competently treated by the much-respected professor of surgery at Dorpat University, Ivan Moyer. Once he had reached either Dorpat or Riga, both stagingposts for travellers to Europe, he might be able to flee abroad. Or, he could possibly persuade Moyer to recommend that the condition was so complex and life-threatening that he might need to go to Paris.

When Pushkin's petition requesting permission to travel to Dorpat reached Petersburg, via his mother, in May 1825, it was read first by Field-Marshal Diebitsch, the Chief of the General Staff. Diebitsch ordered an aide to find out 'who this Pushkina, née Gannibal, is, and whether she is the mother of that Pushkin who writes verse'.[11] When Diebitsch passed on the request to Tsar Alexander, the response was: 'His Majesty the Emperor, having acquainted himself with the letter addressed to His Majesty on 6 May, has charged me, madam, to inform you that His Majesty permits your elder son to travel for treatment to Pskov, where he can find all the necessary help, without the necessity of travelling to Riga'.[12]

At the same time, Diebitsch sent an instruction to the governor at Pskov, informing him of the emperor's decision 'and requiring him to keep a close watch on Pushkin's conduct and conversation'. When this news reached Pushkin, at the beginning of July, 'it sent him into a paroxysm of rage and annoyance', feelings which simmered on within him for several months.[13]

News about the interregnum first reached Pushkin about 10 December 1825 and he first heard about the Decembrist Revolt around the 20th of December. An aspect of Alexander's sudden death which was important for Pushkin was that it raised the prospect that he might be able to secure a full pardon from whoever was to be Alexander's successor.

Convinced that his request would be a formality, he had already made plans to travel to St Petersburg *incognito* and, with Alexey Vulf's assistance, had even forged a travel permit to the capital, adopting the persona of a local *muzhik,* Alexis Kohklov, who was of a similar height, age and appearance. He abandoned this scheme when he realised the trouble it might cause. He did, eventually, set out for Petersburg on an impulse on 14 December but turned back, supposedly for superstitious reasons – three hares and a black cat had crossed his path and he had met a priest – all bad omens. Had he carried on, he planned to go directly to Kondraty Ryleev's apartment and would have arrived at the insurgents' HQ, just as the uprising was starting.

During the following weeks, Pushkin continued to agonise over what was going on: 'Why were they taking so long about proclaiming the accession of Constantine I? Why had he not been called back to his friends?'.[14] Pushkin first heard that an uprising had taken place while on a visit to the neighbouring estate of Trigorskoye. The family cook, Arseny, had just returned from St Petersburg, where he had gone to barter fruit and vegetables. Arseny burst into the drawing-room 'red-faced and breathless' and blurted out that there had been a revolt in St Petersburg, with shootings and people killed. Pushkin immediately deduced that his friends Pushchin, Küchelbecker and Ryleev must have been arrested. He fully expected to be next.

According to one of Pushkin's biographers, J Thomas Shaw, had he reached St Petersburg on 14 December: 'In that case, no doubt he would have participated. Pushkin was right in thinking there was no evidence implicating him directly in the conspiracy; however, copies of early revolutionary poems by Pushkin were found in the possession of all the Decembrists. Pushkin burned his autobiographical notes, in anticipation of search and seizure'.[15] In a letter he wrote in January 1826 to his friend and agent, Pyotr Pletneev – to whom his poem *Evgeny Onegin* was dedicated – Pushkin appealed for more information:

'What's going on where you are, in Petersburg? I don't know a thing and everybody has ceased writing to me. You probably suppose I am in Nerchinsk*. Wrongly; I have no intention of going there – but lack of information about the people with whom I have been closely connected torments me. I have been hoping that the Tsar will be gracious towards them. By the way: can't Zhukovsky find out whether I can hope for the Sovereign's condescension? I have been in disgrace for six years, and whatever you may say – I am only 26 in all. The late emperor in 1824 exiled me to my village for two irreligious lines – I don't know of any other evil deeds on my part. Won't our young Tsar permit me to remove myself to some place where it would be a little warmer – if I can't somehow be allowed to appear in Petersburg – eh?'

(*a Siberian salt-mine).[16]

Later the same month, he wrote to Vasily Zhukovsky, who was well placed in court circles:

'…it is hard for me to ask for your intercession with the Sovereign; I do not want to involve you in my mess. Probably the government has ascertained that I do not belong to the conspiracy and had no political ties with the rebels of December 14 – but in the journals it has announced disgrace for those, as well, who had any information of the conspiracy and did not announce it to the police. But just who, except the police and the government, did not know about it? There was shouting about the conspiracy in every alley, and that is one of the reasons I am guiltless. All the same, I still have not got away from the gendarmes: they can easily convict me of political conversations with some or other of the accused. And among them are enough of my friends'.[17]

Before Pushkin's rise to pre-eminence, Zhukovsky had been the foremost poet in Russia at the beginning of the 19th century. He was employed as tutor to the Tsar, Alexander I, during his childhood and then to Nicholas I's wife, the Grand Duchess Alexandra Feodorovna. He was also a family friend of the Pushkins. In his letter Pushkin teases Zhukovsky about the fact that, during the last ten years of Alexander's reign, Zhukovsky himself had barely written a line in praise of the Tsar. That said a lot and in Pushkin's view was 'the best reproach against him'. Zhukovsky's silence could even be taken as a justification for Pushkin's own approach, of 'hissing him to the very grave'. On the assumption that 'the government should even want to put an end to my disgrace', Pushkin says: 'I am ready to come to terms with it (if conditions are necessary) but I tell you positively not to answer or vouch for me. My future behaviour depends on the circumstances, on the way the government treats me'.[18]

Admitting that 'this letter is, of course, unwise' – all of his postal correspondence was routinely intercepted by the secret police – he then goes on nevertheless to spell out the extent of his association with the Decembrists:

— 'In Kishinev, I was on friendly terms with Major Raevsky, with General Pushchin and with Orlov.

— I was a Mason in the Kishinev Lodge i.e. in the one on account of which all the lodges in Russia were done away with

— Lastly, I had connections with the greater part of the present conspirators.

— The late Emperor, when he exiled me, could reproach me only with unbelief'.[19]

The General, Pavel Sergeevich Pushchin, referred to here, was a relative of Pushkin's close friend, Ivan Pushchin. He had also been the founder of the masonic lodge at Kishinev and was a member of the Union of Welfare. Raevsky and Orlov were also members of the Union of Welfare and, in 1822, had been implicated in an uprising of soldiers under their command, when – like the Semenovsky revolt a year earlier – an attempt was made to introduce stricter military discipline. Writing to his lifelong friend, Anton Delvig, at the beginning of February 1826, Pushkin again voiced his frustration at the lack of news from his friends in Petersburg: 'Get it into your heads that here in the wilds I know exactly nothing, my correspondence from everywhere has broken off...Of course, I am not implicated in anything, and if the government has leisure to think of me a little, it will be easily assured of that. But I am somehow ashamed to petition, especially now; my way of thinking is known'.[20]

Repeating that he would like to be reconciled '*fully* and

sincerely' with the government, he tells Delvig that: 'I am impatiently waiting for the determination of the fate of the unfortunate ones and the divulging of the conspiracy. I firmly rely on the magnanimity of our young Tsar. Let us not be either superstitious or one-sided – like French tragedians. But let us look at the tragedy with the eyes of Shakespeare'.[21]

At the end of February 1826, Pushkin heard that his former mentor, Karamzin, had taken ill (he died two months later). Despite their differences, this was terrible news for Pushkin – in a letter to his agent Pletneev he wrote that this was 'worse than a lot of things together – for God's sake reassure me, or else I'll be twice as afraid',[22] [in addition to worrying about the fate of the Decembrists].

In the same letter, Pushkin told Pletneev that he would not be getting a sight of his new play, *Boris Godunov,* 'until you summon me to St Petersburg'. The prolonged delay, he said, was 'a shameful business'.[23] For months, Pushkin's repeated appeals for a pardon had circulated between government departments and a pile of reports was by now building up on Nicholas's desk.

In a report he sent in June 1826, one police agent, named Locatelli, had commented that: 'Everyone is surprised to see that the famous Pushkin, long known for his subversive ideas, has not been questioned about the conspiracy'.[24] The following month, the spy Boshniak – who had been sent to infiltrate the Decembrists – was now dispatched to report on Pushkin's activities. According to Henri Troyat: 'Nicholas I's notions of literature were those of a provincial old maid: he had no conception of Pushkin's talent, but the fact that every enemy of autocracy sang his praises so unreservedly rendered his celebrity all the more suspect'.[25]

By May 1826, Pushkin's frustration at not being allowed back to St Petersburg was boiling over. Now, he heard that an obscure French poet and dramatist, Jacques-Arsène François Ancelot, had been fêted in St Peterburg by 30 'men of letters'. Writing to his friend, Vyazemsky, he raged: 'Who are these immortals? I am counting on my fingers, and I can't count that far'.

In their dealings with foreigners like Ancelot, Pushkin said the Russians neither had 'pride nor shame'. Ancelot had been let loose in the 'pigsties of the literature of our fatherland'

and subsequently published a diary in Europe ridiculing his experiences in Russia. This was all too much for Pushkin – 'I don't remember a single rhyme of his':

'It's loathsome. I, of course, despise my fatherland from head to foot – but it vexes me if a foreigner shares that feeling with me. You, who are not on a leash, how can you remain in Russia? If the Tsar gives me *liberty*, I won't remain a month. We live in a sad age, but when I imagine London, railroads, steamships, English journals, or Paris theatres and brothels, then my out-of-the-way Mikhailovskoye fills me with boredom and rage'.[26]

At the end of July, police in Moscow seized a poem entitled *December 14,* described by Troyat as 'a stream of abuse directed at the Tsar and his new chief of police, Benckendorff'. The lines were unquestionably by Pushkin and read: 'having brought down the kings, we hoist into their seats/ An assassin and a pack of executioners! Horror and shame!'.[27]

What Nicholas and his spies did not know was that these lines were part of a censored passage from a poem Pushkin had written years earlier. It was entitled *André Cheniér* and was a homage to the French poet who had been sent to the guillotine by Robespierre. Someone had simply cut and pasted Pushkin's lines and retitled them *December 14.* In August, Pushkin again wrote to Vyazemsky, asking whether it was true that their friend, the Decembrist Nicholas Turgenev, had been deported by the British government and taken by ship to St Petersburg. [This was not true. Turgenev was in England but was convicted in his absence for his Decembrism and never again returned to Russia].

Vyazemsky had just written a poem called *The Sea* and Pushkin now quipped: 'Here is what your vaunted sea is like!'. By now he had heard of the sentences passed on the Decembrists and remarked that he was still hoping Nicholas would grant clemency when his coronation took place. Otherwise, he said: 'the hanged are hanged; but penal servitude for 120 friends, brothers, comrades, is horrible'.[28]

By now, Nicholas had decided that Pushkin needed to be interrogated without further ado. An order was issued by General Diebitsch that Pushkin should be brought to Moscow, where the coronation ceremonies were about to take place. A dispatch rider, or *feldjäger,* was assigned to escort Pushkin with an instruction to bring him to Diebitsch as soon as he arrived. When a constable arrived at Mikhailovskoye to prepare Pushkin for his departure: '…he leapt up, snatched a pile of papers from his desk and stuffed them into the flames – he always kept compromising documents within arm's reach. He was surely about to be arrested because of some 'liberal' poem or absurd denunciation. He would be sentenced. Deported to Siberia'.[29]

When Pushkin and his *feldjäger* reached Moscow, on 8 September 1826, he was immediately escorted to the Chudov Monastery, inside the Kremlin, where Nicholas I had established temporary residence. In his pocket, Pushkin had a copy of his latest poem, *The Prophet.*[30] According to one observer, the Frenchman Frédéric Lacroix, in his *Les Mystères de la Russie,* there was something 'starched, strained and unnatural' about Nicholas I: 'He has the most autocratic physiognomy imaginable, he is despotism personified, a flawless illustration of absolute power…His movements have grown stiff as the result of his constant wearing of a uniform, and his gestures have acquired a peculiar artificiality'.[31] Another Frenchman, the Marquis de Custine, wrote that 'The Emperor of Russia is a military chief, for whom every day is a day of battle'.[32] Above all else, Nicholas loved two things: dress parades and mathematics.

When Pushkin was introduced into the Tsar's presence, the first words spoken by Nicholas were: 'Good morning, Pushkin. Are you glad to be back?'[33] Fully expecting to be sent to Siberia, Pushkin had thought he would simply hand a copy of his poem *The Prophet* to the Tsar and that way he would at least go out in a blaze of glory. The last lines of this poem, in its original manuscript form, were believed to have read: 'Arise, arise, prophet of Russia, clad yourself in ignominious raiment, go, and with a noose around your neck, appear before the foul murderer'.[34]

Much to Pushkin's amazement, the Tsar's first words were not as he had expected. Instead, Nicholas declared: 'My brother, the late emperor, sent you to the country in exile: I have decided to pardon you, as long as you never write anything against the government again'.[35] Pushkin replied: 'Your Majesty, I have not written anything against the government for a long time now, and in fact I have hardly written anything at all since *The Dagger*'. This statement by Pushkin, patently untrue, referred to a poem he had written four years earlier, in 1821, which was an open incitement to regicide. It included the lines:

> *The hordes of grim rebellion raise their outcry hoarse*
> *Detested, black of visage, sanguine*
> *Arose the misbegotten hangman*
> *On slaughtered Freedom's headless corpse.*[36]

Nicholas then stated: 'You were friendly with quite a few of the men I sent to Siberia?'. Pushkin replied, Yes, Majesty, I respected and liked many of those men and my feelings towards them have not altered'. 'How could anybody be a friend of that swine Küchelbecker?' asked the Tsar. Küchelbecker had shot at Nicholas's younger brother, the Grand Duke Michael, in Senate Square, but missed. Pushkin replied: 'We always took him for a fool, and what surprises us is that he was sent to Siberia along with so many men of sense and intelligence'.[37]

Pushkin did indeed regard Küchelbecker as a slightly ridiculous figure: he had once written a verse teasing him, for which Küchelbecker had taken umbrage and challenged Pushkin to a duel. When it took place, in the Volkhovo cemetery, Küchelbecker's second was Anton Delvig who stood just to his left as he was about to fire. Pushkin had shouted: 'Delvig! Stand where I am, it's safer here'.[38] Küchelbecker was so annoyed at this further insult that as he made a half-turn, his pistol fired and blew Delvig's hat off. Pushkin refused to take his shot and the quarrel was made up.

Impressed by Pushkin's *sangfroid*, Nicholas then asked: 'What are you writing these days?'. 'Hardly anything', Pushkin replied, 'the censor is very strict'. 'But why must you write things the censor cannot pass?'. 'Perfectly innocuous writings are forbidden', said Pushkin, 'The censor acts quite indiscriminately'.[39] Nicholas then held out a copy of the poem entitled *December 14* and, much relieved that he now knew why they were after him, Pushkin explained how it had actually been written years earlier. The Tsar then asked the most important question of all: 'If you had been in St Petersburg, would you have taken part in the uprising on December 14?'.[40]

Without hesitation, Pushkin replied: 'Beyond any doubt, Majesty. All my friends were in the conspiracy, it would have been impossible for me to let them down. My absence alone saved me, for which I thank God'.[41] This reply was not only extraordinarily brave, it also flattered the Tsar's sense of chivalry: 'The poet must think him very grand indeed to utter such a truth to his face. A nature as exceptional as this deserved special treatment. Why not enlist him in the service of the monarchy? He had talent, a reputation and a rather winning naïveté which might easily be exploited for the benefit of the regime – not to mention the fact that in St Petersburg it would be easier to keep an eye on the young man's behaviour'.[42]

'Have you in mind to change your ideas?' Nicholas now asked, 'Do I have your word of honour that you will mend your ways, if I give you back your freedom?'.[43] This time Pushkin did not reply: 'He felt as though he were falling off a cliff. He closed his eyes in exhaustion, shame and rapture'.[44] Pushkin then shook the Tsar's outstretched hand and Nicholas said: 'You have been foolish long enough. I hope you will be more sensible after this, and there will be no more quarrels between us. You will send everything you write to me. From now on, I shall be your censor'.[45]

As he left the imperial apartments 'with buckling knees and tear-blurred vision', Pushkin suddenly realised that his poem *The Prophet* was no longer in his pocket. Terrified that he must have dropped it inside the room, he broke into a cold sweat before spotting his wayward scrap of paper lying halfway down the staircase.[46]

Notes

1   Quoted in **Pushkin,** by Henri Troyat, translated from the French by Nancy
Amphoux, George, Allen & Unwin, 1974, p309

2   **The Poems, Prose and Plays of Alexander Pushkin,** Selected and edited, with an
Introduction by Avrahm Yarmolinsky, The Modern Library, New York, 1937, Trans.
Max Eastman, pp62-63

3   **The First Breath of Freedom.** Archive material from the Library of Russian and
Soviet Literary Journalism compiled by Vladimir Fyodorov, translated by Cynthia
Carlisle, Progress Publishers, 1988, p104

4   Fyodorov, op.cit. p105

5   Fyodorov, p109

6   Fyodorov, p109

7   **Pushkin,** by T J Binyon, Harper Collins, 2002, p144

8   Fyodorov, op.cit. p110

9   Fyodorov, p111

10   Binyon, op.cit. p200

11   Binyon, p215

12   Binyon, p215

13   Binyon, p215

14   Troyat, op.cit. p289

15   **The Letters of Alexander Pushkin.** Three Volumes in One. Translated and with
an Introduction by J Thomas Shaw, University of Wisconsin Press, 1967, Letter 172,
p316

16   Shaw, ibid. Letter 170. p301.

17   Shaw, Letter 172, p302

18   Shaw, Letter 172, p302

19   Shaw, Letter 172, p302

20   Shaw, Letter 173, p303

21   Shaw, Letter 173, p303

22   Shaw, Letter 177, p306

23   Shaw, Letter 177, p306

24   Troyat, op.cit. p302

25   Troyat, p303

26   Shaw, op.cit. Letter 184, p311

27   Troyat, op.cit. p302

28   Shaw, op.cit. Letter 188, p314

29   Troyat, op.cit. p303

30   Troyat, p309

31   Troyat, p307

32   Troyat, p307

33   Troyat, p309

34 **Pushkin: The Man and His Age**, by Robin Edmonds, Macmillan, 1994, p106

35 Troyat, op.cit. p309

36 Troyat, p310

37 Troyat, p310

38 Troyat, p310

39 Troyat, p310

40 Troyat, p310

41 Troyat, p310

42 Troyat, p310

43 Troyat, p311

44 Troyat, p311

45 Troyat, p311

46 Troyat, p311.

*I should now add that I know Pushkin and we see each other
often. Pushkin is practically my age (two months younger), very
witty and irresistible in conversation; he's read a great deal and
knows modern literature well; he has a pure and lofty conception
of poetry. He's recently written a tragedy,* Boris Godunov; *I know
a few scenes from it, it's in the historical genre, well-conceived and
beautiful in its details.*

Correspondence of Adam Mickiewicz, 1827 [1]

*Poland, bound to Russia by an insoluble tie, is like a fire-
ship attached to the side of a large vessel and obliged to sail in
company with her: in spite of every effort, and notwithstanding
a few partial explosions, the inflammable matter remains in the
incendiary vessel, and the least accident, by setting it on fire, may
occasion a terrible catastrophe.*

Secret History of the Court & Government of Russia, Schnitzler [2]

13 | Pushkin & Mickiewicz

Pushkin wrote *The Bronze Horseman,* in part, as a response
to the interpretation of the statue, and of Russia, written by
his contemporary and friend, the Polish national poet, Adam
Mickiewicz. In particular, Pushkin was reacting to passages
which appear in Mickiewicz's fiercely patriotic work, *Forefather's
Eve,* known in Poland as *Dziady.* A section of the poem, the
Digression, is scathing about Russia – the country to which he
was exiled for his political activities – and is especially disparaging
about the pretensions of its capital city, St Petersburg, and of its
most famous public statue, *The Monument to Peter the Great.*
The poem was written in four parts, the third of which was
completed immediately after the Polish Insurrection, of 1830.
Mickiewicz dedicated this part of the poem to those who had

THE MAN WHO SHOOK HIS FIST AT THE TSAR

fought for Polish freedom during the insurrection and especially for those who were then exiled to Siberia by the Russian Emperor, Nicholas I, just as the Decembrists had been.

Mickiewicz's epic is widely regarded as one of the great works of early 19th century romantic drama, on a par with Goethe's *Faust* and Byron's *Manfred,* and influenced by both. The *Dziady* was an ancient Slavic feast of ancestor worship celebrated in what is now Belarus. In the 18th century, this territory had been part of the Polish-Lithuanian Commonwealth, before it was partitioned and dismantled by the combined forces of Austria, Prussia and Russia. Part III of *Forefather's Eve* deals at length with the cruelty of the Russian Tsars and the persecution of Poland. Its main protagonist, Konrad, is a poet who has been imprisoned and exiled to Russia, like Mickiewicz himself, for conspiracy against the Tsar. The poem takes on a profoundly messianic tone in which Poland is seen to be the 'Christ of Europe', whose suffering will ultimately be rewarded by the release of all oppressed people's and nationalities.

In the '*Digression*', Mickiewicz unleashes a merciless condemnation of Russia, a country in which: 'like the desert wind the lone kibitka flies'.[3] The kibitka was a form of brisk, horse-drawn wooden sledge used by the gendarmerie (or *feldjägers)* to hunt down individuals under suspicion. They would very often arrive at night and whisk a suspect away, without informing them of where they were being taken. Every kibitka was equipped with a bell to announce its arrival. In a note to his poem, Mickiewicz explains: 'A person who has never lived in Lithuania can scarcely imagine the terror that prevails in every house at the door of which the sound of the post bell is heard'.[4]

The '*Digression*' is a lengthy poem in itself and has a number of constituent parts. It begins with an introduction entitled *The Road to Russia* in which the gendarme speeds by on his kibitka, cutting a swathe through all in his path. Mickiewicz notes: 'The common folk of Russia are fully convinced that the tsar is quite equal to carrying off any other monarch in a police kibitka'.[5] Head of the Russian Secret Police in Poland, Nikolai Novosiltsev, was renowned for the aphorism: 'There will never be peace until we so organise Europe that one of our *feldjägers* can execute identical orders in Wilno (*Vilnius*), Paris and Stamboul (*Istanbul*) with equal ease'.[6]

In a section headed *The Suburbs of the Capital*, Mickiewicz describes the palaces which line the approaches to St Petersburg. These palaces 'wherein the mighty dwell' have been adorned with Greek columns, Italian summer houses and Mandarin kiosks from Japan, but lack any 'native style or line'.[7]

These 'gorgeous brothels' have been marvellously made – 'on islands in a swamp the stones are laid', but, to build these 'monuments to our pain', he asks: 'How many false, pretended plots were foiled? How many guiltless men banished or slain? How many of our lands robbed or despoiled?'[8] Here Mickiewicz is talking about the ruthless confiscation of property, works of art and libraries appropriated by the Russian government from landed estates in the Polish provinces annexed by Russia. Mickiewicz also heaps scorn on Peter the Great's decision to build his capital in such an inclement spot, 'torn from the ocean floor and from the Finn' and where 'the cutting winds bring merely snow and sleet':[9]

> *'Men did not choose such lands; a tsar inclined*
> *To these vast swamps and bade his subjects rear*
> *A city not for their use, but for him*
> *A tribute to a tyrant's cruel whim'.*[10]

One of the most celebrated aspects of the monument to Peter the Great inside Russia was the heroic effort required to move the gigantic slab of granite from which the pedestal is made from its resting place in Finland. Rather than expressing his admiration, in his '*Digression*', Mickiewicz gently mocks the achievement:

> *'From Finland's shore, they tore this granite mound,*
> *Which, when the empress speaks and waves her hand,*
> *Floats o'er the sea and runs across the land,*
> *And falls into its place at her command.*
> *The mound is ready now, and forth he goes*
> *A Roman toga'd tsar who rules by blows:*
> *His charger gallops up the granite steep,*
> *Rearing its body for a mighty leap'.*[11]

Wandering the streets of the city, we find Mickiewicz's hero, Konrad, who is with another 'few lads…unlike others in both garb and face'. Here, he is referring to the young Polish radicals,

Mickiewicz among them, who had been imprisoned and exiled to Russia. Observing the might of the city and its granite embankments, they drop their arms, as if to say:

> '*To overturn them, man will strive in vain.*
> *Thus musing, they went on. Konrad alone*
> *Of the eleven stayed. Pale-lipped with hate*
> *He laughed, raised his clenched fist, and struck the stone,*
> *As though he summoned down a vengeful fate.*
> *Then quietly he stood, arms crossed on breast,*
> *Deep plunged in thought, and on the palace wall*
> *His sharp and knife-like glances came to rest.*
> *He seemed like Samson then, after his fall,*
> *When, captured by deceit and tightly chained*
> *He brooded how revenge might be attained*'.[12]

The similarities between this section of the '*Digression*' and their equivalent in *The Bronze Horseman*, where Evgeny shakes his fist at the Tsar, are glaringly obvious. Much the same can be said for other, similar passages in Mickiewicz's poem, right down to small descriptive detail, such as the society lady, who 'glitters in Parisian elegance, her small foot twinkling in a fur-lined shoe, her face crab-red and snowy-white of hue'. Most relevant of all, though, is that the next section of the '*Digression*' turns its attention to *The Monument of Peter the Great*. This begins:

> '*Two youths stood deep in talk one rainy night,*
> *Beneath one cloak, hand closely clasped in hand:*
> *One was that pilgrim from a western land,*
> *An unknown victim of the tsar's grim might;*
> *The other was the famous Russian bard,*
> *Beloved through all the northland for his song.*
> *Although their friendship had not flourished long,*
> *They were united by a great regard.*
> *Their souls soared over earthly trials and woe,*
> *Like twin crags jutting from an Alpine peak;*
> *Though separated by a roaring creek,*
> *They scarcely hear the tumult of their foe*
> *While each to each their towering summits lean*'.[13]

This encounter refers to an actual event, when Mickiewicz (*that pilgrim from a western land*) and Pushkin (*the famous Russian bard*) stood together at the base of the monument. According to Pushkin's closest friend, Pyotr Vyazemsky, he had witnessed just such a conversation in which Pushkin and Mickiewicz stood together in Senate Square and discussed the merits of Falconet's monument. In this section of his poem, Mickiewicz makes a direct reference to the contrasting virtues of the equestrian statue to Marcus Aurelius and Falconet's version. In a deliberate dig at the vast and all-pervasive spy network of the Russian secret police, or *okhrana*, he writes:

'In ancient Rome there shines in different guise
Marcus Aurelius, the people's pride
Who first made his name famous far and wide
By banishing the nation's crafty spies'.[14]

Mickiewicz is by no means dismissive of Falconet's more dynamic sculpture but he is very definite in his description of how he sees it and what it means:

'His charger's reins Tsar Peter has released;
He has been flying down the road, perchance,
And here the precipice checks his advance.
With hoofs aloft now stands the maddened beast,
Champing its bit unchecked, with slackened rein:
You guess it will fall and be destroyed.
Thus, it has galloped long, with tossing mane,
Like a cascade, leaping into the void,
That, fettered by the frost, hangs dizzily.
But soon will shine the sun of liberty,
And from the west a wind will warm this land –
Will the cascade of tyranny then stand?'[15]

Mickiewicz was exiled to Russia in 1824 after he had been arrested by Russia's secret police, for his involvement in radical activities at the University of Vilnius where many of the students secretly campaigned for Polish independence. Soon after his arrival in Russia, Mickiewicz became close friends with Pushkin and, even more so, with the leader of the Decembrists' Northern Society, Kondraty Ryleev.

This social circle also included one of Pushkin's closest friends, Peter Vyazemsky, and Konstantin Batyushkov, a prominent member of the Arzamas literary group and an army officer who had fought in the Napoleonic Wars. Both Vyazemsky and Batyushkov had written verses which would also provide some inspiration for *The Bronze Horseman*, especially in the introductory section where Pushkin heaps praise upon the beauty of St. Petersburg. But it is Pushkin's association with Mickiewicz and, by extension, the tortured relationship between Russia and Poland, which are more fundamental for an understanding of the rest of the *The Bronze Horseman*.

A number of strands intersect in the lives of Pushkin and Mickiewicz. Upon his arrest in Lithuania in 1823, Mickiewicz was first sent to St Petersburg where he met two of the leading Decembrists and friends of Pushkin, Kondraty Ryleev and Alexander Bestuzhev. He was then taken to Odessa where he lived in the villa owned by General Count Jan Witt, who, as well as being commander of the Russian military forces in the south – and unknown to Mickiewicz – was also in charge of the secret police. Jan Witt directed a network of government spies which included his lover, Karolina Sobańska.

Mickiewicz was transferred to Moscow towards the end of 1825 and early the following year was introduced to Pushkin by their mutual acquaintance, Sergey Sobolevsky. Mickiewicz was soon displaying a talent for improvisation which dazzled observers. In Vilnius, he had become renowned for his ability to instantly compose a verse on any given topic in Polish.

In Moscow, he would do the same thing but the improvisation would be delivered in French prose. His performances caused a sensation in Russian society. According to T J Binyon, his audiences were often so impressed that he brought them to 'a state approaching delirium'. [16] Pushkin was among those who witnessed Mickiewicz's ability to ad-lib: 'At a party given in Pushkin's honour in Zinaida Volkonskaya's salon his improvisation so impressed Pushkin, he leapt from his seat and, clutching his head in his hands, almost running around the room, exclaimed: "What genius! What sacred fire! What am I compared to him? And, throwing himself on Adam's neck, embraced him and began to kiss him like a brother'. [17]

Perhaps Mickiewicz's closest friend in Russia was Kondraty Ryleev. Mickiewicz first arrived in St Petersburg in November 1824, just before the Great Flood. Here, he met Ryleev, who gave him letters of introduction to two of the leaders of the Decembrists' Southern Society, Pestel and Muraviev-Apostol. After going to Kiev to meet them, he returned first to Moscow and then to St Petersburg where he arrived in the autumn of 1825. On his return to St Petersburg, his first call was to visit Ryleev at the apartment he shared with two other leading Decembrists, Alexander Bestuzhev and Prince Odoevsky. Ryleev, Bestuzhev, Muraviev-Apostol and Pestel all died on the scaffold for their part in the uprising – Odoevsky was exiled to Siberia.

As the Decembrist biographer, Christine Sutherland, notes: 'The poet's intimacy with the Decembrists was surprising. These men had never taken Pushkin into their confidence, yet they admitted a foreigner, a young Pole, to their most secret assemblies. The reasons, of course, were that he *was* Polish, and a close friend of Ryleev'. [18] Mickiewicz later wrote: 'I had the great privilege of knowing and enjoying the friendship of the purest and of the noblest Russian youth of the time'. [19] In his memoirs, Mickiewicz described meeting in Ryleev's apartment, 'one foggy day in October' – a few weeks before the uprising – as follows:

'There must have been more than a dozen people in the room, but at first I could not distinguish anything because of the dense blue haze of pipe and cigar smoke. They were sprawling on sofas and on the deep windowsills; young Alexander Odoevsky and Bestuzhev sat cross-legged, Turkish fashion, on a Persian carpet, on the floor. The officers had undone their tunic buttons, the civilians wore voluminous cravats à la Byron; some were dressed like Directoire dandies. Through the wide-open windows swirled great white puffs of St Petersburg fog'.[20]

As part of the proceedings, a toast was called for by 'an intense youth, pale-complexioned, with a prominent forehead, and a face like Shelley'. The toast raised was: 'Death to the Tsar!', followed by a song, also wishing death to the Tsar:

One, two knives,
One, two, three,
Long and sharp…

Comes the blacksmith,
Wields a hammer…
Big and heavy…'[21]

Mickiewicz had great admiration for Pushkin's abilities, but was less impressed by his behaviour. In one of his letters, Mickiewicz described Pushkin as being 'very witty and impetuous in conversation' and said that he also had 'a profound knowledge of contemporary literature and a pure and elevated understanding of poetry'.[22] However, Mickiewicz did not approve of Pushkin's 'often scatological or lubricious bawdiness in conversation', which he found 'distasteful'.[23] One of the poet's contemporaries, Sergey Aksakov, described what he had witnessed during a lunch attended by both Pushkin and Mickiewicz, as follows: 'The former (Pushkin) had conducted himself terribly vilely and disgustingly; the latter (Mickiewicz) beautifully. You can judge for yourself what the conversations were like: the latter was twice obliged to say "Gentlemen, decent people even when they are alone by themselves do not speak of such things"'.[24]

Mickiewicz was one of the first to have read extracts from Pushkin's play *Boris Godunov* and said that: '…the general idea is powerfully conceived; the extracts are splendid'. Mickiewicz was also one of many admirers of Pushkin's poem *The Prophet,* the one which he had kept in his pocket when he first went to meet with the new Tsar, Nicholas I. When Mickiewicz was granted permission to leave Russia, towards the end of 1828, the historian Mikhail Pogodin arranged a farewell gathering attended by many of Moscow's *literati*. Among them was Pushkin, who gave Mickiewicz a copy of his newest work, the poem *Poltava*. Mickiewicz reciprocated with an edition of Byron's works in which he wrote, in Polish: 'Byron for Pushkin, from an admirer of both'.[25]

After Mickiewicz's departure from Russia, Pushkin later wrote a tribute to him, entitled *He Lived Among Us:*

Amidst for him, a foreign tribe, no malice
In his soul did harbour he toward us, and we
We loved him. Peaceable he was, and gracious
He frequented our gathering. With him
We shared both candid thoughts

And songs (he was inspired from up above
And gazed on life from there). He'd often speak
Of ages that were yet to come
When nations, their contentions all forgotten
Would in one great family unite.
We listened to him avidly. He left
Us for the West – and with a blessing
We saw him off.[26]

In his biography of Adam Mickiewicz, the Polish-American historian, Roman Koropeckyj writes that: 'Pushkin never finished the poem, unable, as its numerous enjambments would indicate, to make sense of his conflicted feelings about the man, the poet, and the Pole'.[27]

By 1834, any notions about a united family of Slavic nations – an aspiration which both Pushkin and Mickiewicz shared, albeit from entirely different standpoints – had been completely shattered by events. In 1831, Pushkin, with the assistance of Zhukovsky, had published a collection of three poems which were widely regarded as being anti-Polish – just at the time when the Polish Revolt of 1830-31 was gradually being suppressed by superior Russian forces.

Such was the reaction to Pushkin's 'anti-Polish' trilogy – *Before the Sacred Tomb, To the Slanderers of Russia* and *Anniversary of Borodino* – that it led to accusations that he had written them to find favour with the Tsar. As the American academic, Katya Hokanson notes, the poem *To the Slanderers of Russia* provoked a particularly severe response: '…admired by monarchists and ideologists of the state, it is often despised and ignored by liberals and democrats'.[28] Mickiewicz was certainly not impressed; in his response *To My Russian Friends* he directly accuses Pushkin of 'having sold his soul forever for the favours of the Tsar' and of 'gloating at the martyrdom of friends'.[29]

There can be no doubting Pushkin's opposition to the renewed revolt in Poland: in a letter to his friend Pyotr Vyazemsky, written in June 1831, he wrote that the rebels 'must be throttled, and our slowness is tormenting',[30] but his primary aim had been to question whether liberal opinion in Europe had the right to castigate its counterparts in Russia. Much of the criticism had emanated from Paris which, ever since Napoleon's defeat, had

THE MAN WHO SHOOK HIS FIST AT THE TSAR

become a haven for Polish emigrés.

What Pushkin wanted to remind these critics was that Polish troops had been in the vanguard of Napoleon's invasion of Russia in 1812 and that they had enthusiastically taken part in the burning of Moscow, just as they had done 200 years earlier, during the Time of Troubles. In his *History of the Russian State,* Karamzin had described in detail the role played by the Liakhs (Poles) in the ransacking of Moscow, to the extent that: 'when the fires went out, they lit them anew, robbed the treasury, carried away all the plunder they found in the shops, divided into equal parts the gold, the silver and pearls, dressed themselves in velvet and drank their fill of Hungarian wine'.[31]

Furthermore, it was Russia which had mounted the opposition to Napoleon and ultimately driven him back to Paris, at a time when the rest of Europe was 'on your knees'. In one of the key passages in *To the Slanderers of Russia,* Pushkin writes:

> *'Is it for this, perchance, you hate us*
> *That Moscow's blazing shell defied decrees*
> *Of a vainglorious dictator*
> *While you were writhing on your knees?*
> *Or that we smashed that idol towering*
> *Above the realms, so Europe gained release*
> *And, saved by Russian blood, is flowering*
> *Anew in freedom, honour, peace?'*[32]

In his letter to Vyazemsky, Pushkin is not at all dismissive of the gallantry displayed by Polish troops fighting the Russians; in fact, he wonders why more had not been written about the bravery displayed by the Polish Commander-in-Chief, Jan Skrzynecki, at the battle of Ostrołeka in 1831, when the Polish forces were routed by the Russian Field Marshal, Count Ivan Diebitsch: 'Our officers saw how he galloped up on his white horse, changed his mount to another, a chestnut-coloured one, and began to command – they saw how, wounded in the shoulder, he dropped his broadsword and tumbled off his horse, how his suite hastened to him and seated him again on his horse. Then he began singing 'Poland has not Perished Yet' and his suite began to chime in, but at that very moment another bullet killed a Polish major in the crowd, and the songs were broken off'.[33]

Pushkin thought that Europeans should refrain from their condemnations of Russia because: 'For us, Poland's rebellion is a family affair, an ancient, hereditary dissension; we cannot judge it by the impressions of Europeans, no matter what their own mode of thinking may be...Of course, it is to the advantage of almost all governments to hold in such cases to the principles of *non-intervention* i.e. to avoid getting involved in others' woes. But their people just bellow and bay. The first thing you know we'll have Europe on our neck. How fortunate that we didn't get mixed up last year in the most recent French mess! Otherwise, one good turn would deserve another!'.[34]

The November uprising was one in a long series of conflicts between Poles and Russians, whose iterations had included the devastation wreaked on Moscow and the surrounding areas during the Time of Troubles, the 1794 Warsaw uprising, and in the more recent War of 1812, in which Polish cavalry were in the vanguard of Napoleon's Grande Armée. The Poles had the reputation of being particularly fierce warriors, fired up by Napoleon's pledge to grant Polish independence. After the war, and Napoleon's defeat, Europeans had increasingly transferred their feelings about the Greeks, whose uprising against the Ottomans had also been crushed, to the Poles (even though many Russians, Pushkin included, had vigorously supported the Greek uprising): 'This sympathy allowed many orators to give voice to fine sentiments about freedom and independence while casting as the villain the increasingly powerful Russian Empire, which was almost universally depicted as Oriental and barbarous, frequent use being made of imagery of rapacious Cossacks, despotism, slavery, and Russia as a mighty colossus'.[35]

Pushkin was by no means alone among Russian intellectuals in regarding these accusations as offensive, even though they would have agreed entirely with much of the underlying criticism of Tsarist Russia. One of the after-effects of the defeat of the Polish Revolt of 1830-31 was that it bred a mood of mysticism among the Polish diaspora and the emergence of a vein of 'messianism', in which the martyrdom of Poland was seen to be the route to the liberation of other peoples by its sufferings and struggles. This was a central theme of Mickiewicz's *Konrad Wallenrod*. At the same time, this messianism was often accompanied by an almost religious worship of Napoleon, even though Napoleon had always been clear that he wanted a camp in Poland, not a forum. He was not about to permit either Warsaw or Moscow to open up 'a club for demagogues'.

Alexander Herzen, who was himself exiled to Paris, later wrote a description of the time he met one of the Polish followers of Mickiewicz on the Place Vendôme, where the monument in the centre of the square is topped by a statue of Napoleon: 'When we reached the column, the Pole took off his cap. Is it possible? I thought, hardly daring to believe in such stupidity, and meekly asking what was his reason for taking off his cap. The Pole pointed to the bronze emperor…and of this man the Poles made a military incarnation of God, setting him on a level with Vishnu and Christ'.[36]

Herzen's comment on this episode, most appropriate to Pushkin's view of *The Bronze Horseman,* was as follows: 'How can we expect men to refrain from domineering or oppressing others when it wins so much devotion!'[37] Although the dispute between Pushkin and Mickiewicz over Poland unquestionably damaged their relationship, it did not eliminate the respect they held for each other. Pushkin went on to undertake translations of Mickiewicz's work and, after Pushkin's death, some reports claimed Mickiewicz had pledged that, given the chance, he would be more than willing to challenge the man that shot Pushkin, Baron d'Anthès, to a further duel.

A decade after Pushkin's death, Alexander Herzen met Mickiewicz in Paris at a gathering which had been assembled to launch a new periodical, *La Tribune des Peuples.* Mickiewicz had been lined up as one of the keynote speakers and Herzen describes how he first came across him, leaning against the marble fireplace: 'The whole impression made by this figure, by his head, by his luxuriant grey hair and weary eyes, was suggestive of unhappiness endured, of acquaintance with spiritual pain, and of the exaltation of sorrow – he was the moulded likeness of the fate of Poland…It seemed as though Mickiewicz was held back, preoccupied, distracted by something: that 'something' was the strange mysticism into which he retreated further and further'.[38] Shortly after Pushkin's death, Mickiewicz wrote an obituary of Pushkin for the French newspaper *Le Globe* in which he said:

'No country has ever managed to produce more than one person who could to such a degree combine abilities so variegated and seemingly incompatible...I knew this Russian poet rather well and for rather a long period of time; I noticed in him a nature too susceptible to first impressions and at times flighty, but always sincere, noble-minded, and capable of expressing his feelings. His shortcomings appeared to be a function of the circumstances amidst which he was raised; and what was good in him sprang from his heart'. The obituary was signed: 'A Friend of Pushkin'.[39]

Notes

1   **Adam Mickiewicz: The Life of a Romantic**, by Roman Koropeckyj, Cornell University Press, 2008, p77

2   **Secret History of the Court and Government of Russia,** Volume 2: Under the Emperors Alexander and Nicholas, by Johann Heinrich Schnitzler. Kessinger Legacy Reprints, First published 1847, p98

3   **Pushkin's Bronze Horseman: The Story of a Masterpiece**, by Waclaw Lednicki, Greenwood Press, 1978 reprint of 1955 edition, Mickiewicz's '*Digression: The Road to Russia*', p109

4   Lednicki, ibid., note 1, p109

5   Lednicki, note 2, p112

6   Lednicki, note 2, p112

7   Mickiewicz, '*The Suburbs of the Capital*', quoted in Lednicki, op.cit. p113

8   Mickiewicz, '*The Suburbs of the Capital*', quoted in Lednicki, op.cit. p113

9   Mickiewicz, '*St Petersburg*', quoted in Lednicki, op.cit. p115

10   Mickiewicz, '*St Petersburg*', quoted in Lednicki, op.cit. p115

11   Mickiewicz, '*The Monument of Peter the Great*', quoted in Lednicki, op.cit. p120

12   Mickiewicz, '*St Petersburg*', quoted in Lednicki, op.cit. p115

13   Mickiewicz, '*The Monument of Peter the Great*', quoted in Lednicki, op.cit. pp120-21

14   Mickiewicz, '*The Monument of Peter the Great*', quoted in Lednicki, op.cit. p121

15   Mickiewicz, '*The Monument of Peter the Great*', quoted in Lednicki, op.cit. p122

16   **Pushkin.** By T J Binyon. Harper Collins, 2002, p250

17   Binyon, ibid. p250

18   **The Princess of Siberia: The Story of Maria Volkonsky and the Decembrist Exiles**, by Christine Sutherland. Quartet Books. 2001, p91

19   Sutherland, ibid. p91

20   Sutherland, p91

21   Sutherland, p92

22   Binyon, op.cit. p250

23   Binyon, p250

24   Binyon, p251

25   Koropeckyj, op.cit. p113

26   Koropeckyj, p113

27   Koropeckyj, p114

28   **Taboo Pushkin: Topics, Texts, Interpretations**, edited by Alyssa Dinega Gillespie, essay by Katya Hokanson: *The 'Anti-Polish'' Poems and ' built myself a monument not made by human hands*, p284

29   Hokanson, ibid. p284

30   **The Letters of Alexander Pushkin.** Three Volumes in One. Translated and with an Introduction by J Thomas Shaw, University of Wisconsin Press, 1967, Letter 363, p489

31   Hokanson, p314

32   **Pushkin Threefold: Narrative, Lyric, Polemic & Ribald Verse,** The originals, with linear and metric translations by Walter Arndt, includes a verse translation of *The Bronze*

Horseman, Allen & Unwin, 1972, pp44-45

33   Shaw, op.cit. Letter 363, p489

34   Shaw, Letter 363, p489

35   Hokanson, op.cit. p285

36   **My Past and Thoughts.** The Memoirs of Alexander Herzen, Translated by Constance Garnett and with an introduction by Isaiah Berlin., University of California Press, 1991 (first translation copyright by Chatto & Windus 1968), p346

37   Herzen, ibid. p346

38   Herzen, p342

39   Koropeckyj, op.cit. p114

He was made Emperor, and right then
Displayed his flair and drive:
Sent to Siberia one-twenty men
And strung up five.

Pushkin on Nicholas I, 1826 [1]

Censorship had always been strict, and after the Decembrist
Revolt the government published the so-called 'cast-iron' code,
the 230 paragraphs of which were filled with dangers for even
cautious writers. Journals which succeeded with the readers were
often closed for violating the Censorship Code'.

Carl J Proffer, *The Critical Prose of Alexander Pushkin*,ß 1969[2]

14 | Despotism Personified

In less than six weeks, between 1 October and 9 November
1833, Pushkin finished his *History of Pugachev* and wrote *The
Bronze Horseman.* During this enormously productive period,
spent on the family estate at Boldino, he also completed one
of his most renowned short stories, *The Queen of Spades;* his
narrative-poem, *Angelo,* a reworking of Shakespeare's *Measure
for Measure;* plus, two contemporary versions of traditional folk-
tales; his own translations of ballads by Adam Mickiewicz; and a
handful of new short poems. This impressive batch included one
of his most beautiful poems, *Autumn* and tellingly, one of his
most troubling, *God grant that I not go mad.* Pushkin's intention
was to get these works published as soon as possible. He had
already reached an agreement with his regular publisher in St
Petersburg, the book-seller Alexander Smirdin, that *The Bronze
Horseman* would provide the centre-piece for Smirdin's new
magazine, *The Reader's Library.*

THE MAN WHO SHOOK HIS FIST AT THE TSAR

Smirdin had agreed to pay Pushkin 15,000 roubles in advance for three of the poems he brought back, including *The Bronze Horseman.* This was a substantial amount, but still not enough to alleviate Pushkin's mounting financial concerns. On 6 December, Pushkin wrote out a copy of *The Bronze Horseman* in his best handwriting and sent it to Benckendorff. Five days later it returned, peppered throughout with the Tsar's disapproving remarks. The poem, as Henri Troyat puts it, had: '…aroused all the monarch's fastidious ire'.[3]

What had most offended Nicholas was Pushkin's use of the word *kumir,* meaning tyrant, despot or idol, to describe the image of Peter the Great. Perhaps he construed – not unreasonably – that the Tsar who wreaks his revenge in the poem might not be just a metaphorical figure. As Troyat explains: 'Nicholas had guessed at another idea, more powerful and dangerous, behind the fable of the little clerk who was victim of a flood. He started when he read Eugene's words to *The Bronze Horseman*, as though they had been addressed to himself'.[4]

On the evening of 11 December, Pushkin wrote in his diary: 'I received an invitation from Benckendorff to see him the following morning. I went. *The Bronze Horseman* was handed back to me with the emperor's annotations. Question marks everywhere. I had to make a good many changes and to alter the terms of my contract with Smirdin'.[5] In the event, Pushkin's conscience would not allow him to alter the entire poem and so he decided not to publish. It remained unpublished until after his death, and only then in a watered-down version reworked by Zhukovsky. In life, as in art: 'Pushkin had suffered the same fate as Eugene. He had had to bow to the authority of the monarch. And he knew now that he would be hearing his master's ponderous gallop until he died. He would find no refuge from the pursuing idol'.[6]

The Tsar's negative response induced a state of chronic depression and 'apathetic inertia' in Pushkin. He abandoned work on his rejoinder to Alexander Radishchev, in his own *Journey from Moscow to Petersburg,* and put *The Bronze Horseman* to one side. It was only in 1836, when he needed material for his new journal, *The Contemporary,* that Pushkin returned to *The Bronze Horseman* and began to revise it in the light of the Tsar's criticisms. He never completed this task, though the prologue did appear in Smirdin's, *Library for Reading,* in December 1834.

In early April 1834, Pushkin wrote to Michael Pogodin, recently elected as Professor of History at Moscow University, to explain why he would not be able to contribute an advance copy of one of his poems to the Free Society of Lovers of Russian Literature. Pushkin had just been declared as one of four new members of the prestigious society but regarded the honour as a 'slap in the face' rather than an accolade since one of the other nominations was his arch-enemy, Fadey Bulgarin. Pushkin returned the certificate of membership because he could not contemplate having anything to do with a society which had elected them both – at exactly the same time – especially since Bulgarin had been ostracised by the English Club in Petersburg for having been, as Pushkin described him: 'a spy, a turncoat, and a slanderer'.[7]

Pushkin wrote: 'You ask me about *The Bronze Horseman,* about *Pugachev,* and about *Peter.* The first will not be published. *Pugachev* will come out by the autumn. I am approaching *Peter* with fear and trembling…why should one want to appear before the public, which does not understand one, so that four fools may berate one just short of obscenity in their journals for the next six months? The time was when literature was a noble, aristocratic field of endeavour. Now it is a flea market. So be it'.[8]

One of the means by which Pushkin was forced to find a way round the censorship regime was to write under a pseudonym: In August 1831, he sent his Moscow publisher, Peter Pletneev, the manuscript of a work 'of my friend Ivan Petrovich Belkin' with instructions that it only be submitted for 'plain censorship'.[9] These *Tales of Belkin* had, of course, been written by Pushkin himself and by this subterfuge he could avoid the dual censorship of the committee and the Tsar. The packet Pushkin sent to Pletneev was delivered by his protégé Nikolai Gogol. During the last six years of his life, the only substantial works by Pushkin that actually made it past the censors and into print, intact and under his own name, were his short story, *The Queen of Spades,* and his historical novel *The Captain's Daughter.*

A few weeks after the Tsar had so drastically expurgated *The Bronze Horseman,* he inflicted what Pushkin regarded as an even greater humiliation: on 30 December, Count Nesselrode announced that the Emperor had been 'graciously pleased' to confer Pushkin with the title of *Kammerjunker*, or Gentleman of the Bedchamber.

Pushkin took this as a calculated insult from the Tsar: not only was it the lowest possible ranking which could be bestowed under Peter the Great's Table of Ranks, it inferred an inferior status normally given to what Pushkin described as 'snot-nosed eighteen-year-olds' and certainly quite inappropriate for the nation's greatest poet. Pushkin was said to have been so furious when he heard of this appointment, at a ball given by Count Aleksey Orlov, that his friends had to drag him away to the Count's study. Pushkin's brother, Leo, later recalled: 'I do not think it proper to repeat here everything the enraged poet, foaming at the mouth, said about his appointment'.[10] Pushkin's fury was so great that, according to the memoirist, Bartenev, his friends had needed to douse him with cold water to calm him down.

Apart from the intentionally demeaning nature of the 'favour' bestowed upon him by the Tsar, Pushkin was even more infuriated because he knew fullwell it had only been granted so that Pushkin's wife, Natalya Goncharova – who was by now regarded as one of the most alluring adornments of Russian high society – would be able to attend social occasions at the Anichkov Palace, where the most exclusive receptions were held, in the presence of both the Tsar and the Empress.

The 'favour' bestowed on Pushkin came at a time when the Tsar was already known to have become a great admirer of his young wife. They had met for the first time, in the summer of 1831, when the Royal family was forced to leave the capital during the cholera outbreak and consequently had become the Pushkins' near neighbours at Tsarskoe Selo. The Tsar subsequently singled out Natalya for special attention.

Pushkin was well aware of this and had even made a joke of it to his friend, Nashchokin, describing Nicholas as 'dangling after her like some stripling officer: of a morning he purposely drives past her window several times and, in the evening, at a ball, asks why her blinds are always down'.[11]

In his novel *Death of a Poet*, Leonid Grossman has his protagonist, the Dutch attaché, d'Archaic report that: 'The

Emperor Nicholas was of extremely amorous disposition. The actresses of the French theatre told me all about the erotic secrets of the Winter Palace. Every young and beautiful woman aroused the lust of the Russian despot. Maids-of-honour, ladies-in-waiting, dancers, actresses, the pupils of the school of dramatic art, the ladies of Petersburg society all entered into the secret sphere of imperial pleasures'.[12]

Like his brothers, Alexander and Constantine, all of the Russian Tsars and heirs apparent were known to have freely exercised their *droit du seigneur*. According to the testimony of an early 19th century traveller in Russia, recorded in his *Conversation with a Lady*:

'The Tsar is an autocrat in his love affairs, as in the rest of his conduct; if he singles out a woman while taking a walk, in the theatre or in society, he says a word to the Duty Adjutant. The person who attracted the attention of the divinity comes under surveillance. If she is married, the husband is warned; if she is single, the parents are told of the honour which has befallen them. There are no examples of this distinction having ever been taken otherwise than with protestations of the most respectful gratitude. Likewise, there is no occasion when the dishonoured husband or father did not extract a profit from his dishonour'.[13]

When the author of this memoir asked the society lady who told him of this custom: 'You mean, the Tsar never encounters any resistance from the very victim of his lust?' the astonished reply was: 'Never. How could that be possible?' Asked how she would react in the same circumstance, the lady replied: 'I shall act like all the rest. Besides, my husband would never forgive me if I answered with a refusal'.[14]

Natalya Goncharova left St Petersburg in April 1834 to spend the summer months with her Goncharov family relatives in Moscow and Yaroslavets. In a letter sent to his wife while she was away, Pushkin explained why he intended to stay at home and avoid the celebrations due to take place on the occasion of the Emperor's son, Alexander, having reached his majority – a ceremony which took place on his 16th birthday: 'I have seen three Tsars, the first *[Paul I]* ordered my little cap to be taken off me, and gave my nurse a scolding on my account;

the second *[Alexander I]* was not gracious to me; although the third *[Nicholas I]* has saddled me with being a *Kammerpage* close upon my old age, I have no desire for him to be replaced with a fourth. Better let well enough alone. We shall see how our Sashka *[Pushkin's son, Alexander]* will get along with his namesake *[the future Alexander II]* born to the purple: I didn't get along with mine. God grant that he does not follow in my footsteps and write verses and quarrel with Tsars! Then he wouldn't outshine his father in verses, but neither would he fight windmills' *[my italics]*.[15]

When this letter was intercepted by the police, Benckendorff immediately made the Tsar aware of its contents. Nicholas was furious and, when he demanded an explanation, Pushkin was forced to admit that he had openly lied in order to escape court ceremonies and had displayed obvious contempt for his appointment as *Kammerjunker*. In addition, he had managed to insult three tsars including Nicholas himself, his brother Alexander and their father, Paul.

For his part, Pushkin was equally enraged that private letters to his wife had been intercepted by the *gendarmerie* and then passed on to the Tsar. In a diary entry dated 10 May 1834, he wrote:

'A few days ago, I received from Zhukovsky a note from Tsarskoe Selo. He was informing me that a certain letter of mine was circulating about the city, and that the sovereign had spoken to him about it. I imagined that the point was foul verses, full of repulsive obscenity which the public was indulgently and graciously attributing to me. But it proved otherwise…It did not please the sovereign that I referred to my becoming a *Kammerjunker*, without tender emotion and without gratitude. However, I can be a subject, even a slave, but I shall not be a flunkey and a clown, even before the Tsar of Heaven'.[16]

Pushkin concludes the same entry with the comment: 'But what profound immorality there is in the customs of our government. The police unseal a husband's letters to his wife, and take them for reading to the Tsar (a well-bred and honourable man) and the Tsar is not ashamed to admit it…no matter what you say, being an autocrat is hard'.[17]

In a follow-up letter, written two days later, he noted dryly: 'Yesterday there was a big parade, which, they say, didn't turn out well. The Tsar has placed the Heir under arrest'.[18] In his diary, Pushkin explained the reason for this harsh treatment was that the Tsar had been dissatisfied because his son had 'galloped instead of trotted' at the ceremony. In a subsequent letter, warning Natalya Nikolaevnya to be careful with their correspondence, Pushkin again expressed his abhorrence that the privacy of family relationships should be intruded upon 'in a foul and dishonourable manner'. 'Without privacy', he said, 'there is no family life. I write to you, not for the press'. It was a while, he said, 'since swinishness in anybody has astonished me'.[19]

The attentions being paid to his wife by d'Anthès and by the Tsar were not Pushkin's only problem in the years that followed his marriage to Natalya Goncharova. During his famous interview with the Tsar, when he openly admitted that he would have joined the Decembrists, Nicholas I had agreed to free Pushkin from exile if he would agree to stop publishing subversive material. What followed 'was less an outright persecution of Pushkin than a persistent niggling interference with the poet's life and work'.[20] One manifestation of this was the running battle which Pushkin was now forced to engage in with the Tsar's enforcer, Count Benckendorff. This contest was to beleaguer Pushkin throughout his few remaining years. It was through Benckendorff that Pushkin needed to submit his works to Nicholas I and from him that he would hear the Tsar's pronouncements.

Like many other high-ranking officers in the Russian army, and Nicholas himself, Benckendorff was of Baltic German origin. He had earned the Tsar's gratitude during the Decembrist Revolt because of his 'firmness' in dealing with the troops stationed on Vasilievsky Island, preventing them from reaching Senate Square. In recognition of the important role he had performed, Benckendorff was then assigned to the Investigating Commission set up to pursue and interrogate those suspected of having taken part in the rebellion.

Benckendorff was appointed head of the Third Department and Chief of Gendarmes in July 1826 and, Ronald Hingley writes, '…by virtue of the special trust reposed in Benckendorff

THE MAN WHO SHOOK HIS FIST AT THE TSAR

by the Emperor, the Third Section became, almost overnight, the senior office of the State, outranking in effect all other governmental institutions'.[21] Benckendorff became universally recognised as the second most powerful individual in the Empire, reported to Nicholas on a daily basis and travelled with him in the same carriage during their regular tours of inspection.

One of the first tasks assigned to the newly-formed Third Department was to keep Pushkin under strict surveillance, to ensure that everything he wrote was first seen both by Benckendorff and the Tsar, to intercept his mail and to closely monitor his movements. Almost as soon as the apparent armistice had been reached with the Tsar, Pushkin was in trouble. In Benckendorff's view, he had immediately infringed its assumed provisions by reading aloud sections of his new historical drama, *Boris Godunov*, which dealt with Russia's Time of Troubles [1598-1613].

When he heard of the rapturous response Pushkin's play was receiving, Benckendorff immediately wrote to rebuke Pushkin. He reiterated Nicholas's directive that he would be sole censor and the need for all of his work to go first to Benckendorff himself, or directly to the Tsar. He then wrote: 'Information has now reached me that you were pleased to read at a number of gatherings your recently composed tragedy (which Pushkin had actually described as 'a comedy'). This prompts me humbly to ask you to inform me whether this information is correct or not'.[22]

He was sure, he added, that Pushkin must be aware of 'His Majesty's magnanimous leniency towards you' and that he would be aware of the need to strive to make himself worthy of it. The obvious subtext to this was that: 'Benckendorff's elaborately formal courtesy concealed an ominous message. He was making it clear to Pushkin, firstly that he was under constant surveillance by agents of the Third Department; secondly, that he had misunderstood the Tsar's censorship conditions; all works had to be submitted, before being either read or published; thirdly, and most sinisterly, that his release from exile was not absolute, but that he was on parole'.[23] For a supposedly unbiased view of the literary merit of *Boris Godunov,* Benckendorff turned to Pushkin's arch-enemy, the journalist and police informer, Fadey Bulgarin. This was a reward for the paper Bulgarin had just written for the Third Department entitled *'Something on the*

Tsarskoe Selo Lycée and its spirit'.

According to Bulgarin, the 'Lycée spirit': 'is when a young man does not respect his elders, treats his superiors familiarly, his equals haughtily, and his inferiors contemptuously, with the exception of those occasions when it is necessary, as a *fanfaronade,* to show oneself a lover of equality'.[24] Bulgarin was Pushkin's fiercest enemy:

'He was no ordinary journalist: He was the director of the *Northern Bee* and had purely and simply sold himself to the Third Section. He published articles dictated by Benckendorff, set the authorities on to his literary foes, wrote secret reports and took commissions for recommending shops, restaurants and other commercial enterprises to his readers. This official blackmailer and paid police informer turned into a raging tiger if anyone dared to interfere with his pecuniary or artistic interests'.[25]

In his report to Benckendorff, on his assessment of Pushkin's play, Bulgarin wrote that its 'literary merit was considerably lower than expected', that it was not an 'imitation of Shakespeare, Goethe, Schiller' but that it seemed like 'a collection of pages torn out of a novel by Scott'.[26] Acting on Bulgarin's report, Nicholas stated: 'I consider that Mr Pushkin's aim would be fulfilled, were he to turn his Comedy, *after purging it as necessary,* into a historical tale or novel in the manner of *Walter Scott'.* According to T J Binyon, Pushkin replied: 'I regret I am incapable of refashioning that which I have once written'.[27] Following Pushkin's refusal to amend his original text, it took another five years before *Boris Godunov* cleared the censors.

In 1829, Fadey Bulgarin published his own version of the False Dmitry story, *Dmitry Samozvanyets* (Dmitry, the Pretender). Bulgarin's attempt: 'shamelessly plagiarised Pushkin's unpublished play, while simultaneously espousing a safer, more officially acceptable interpretation of the Time of Troubles, Boris Godunov and Tsar Dmitry than was found in Pushkin's play. Benckendorff (who despised Pushkin) and the censors, actively helped Bulgarin by making certain that his novel was published long before Pushkin's play ever saw the light of day. Bulgarin gloated over his success at Pushkin's expense; in fact, he made a small fortune from his very popular novel and was even awarded a gold ring for it by the Tsar'.[28]

Bulgarin's novel was heavily annotated, with notes written by a young protégé of Bulgarin and St Petersburg University professor, Nikolai Ustrialyov. Part of the intention of these notes was to discredit Pushkin's portrayal of the False Dmitry as a heroic figure, popular with the Russian people. Before writing *Boris Godunov*, Pushkin had conducted serious historical research for the first time and had been guided by the pioneer work of his childhood guru, Karamzin. One of the genuine innovations to historiography introduced by Karamzin had been to study West European sources as well those from the Russian chronicles. From eyewitness accounts written during the Time of Troubles, Pushkin soon discovered that foreign reports – unlike the censored Russian sources – often showed 'that the Russian people welcomed the pretender Dmitry with joy and helped put him on the throne'.

One of these accounts had been written in 1607 by a French mercenary, Captain Jacques Margeret, who had managed to act both as co-commander of foreign troops under Tsar Boris and as captain of Tsar Dmitry's bodyguard. Karamzin was the first Russian historian to draw attention to Margeret's description of events, from his book *The Russian Empire and Grand Duchy of Muscovy: A Seventeenth-Century French Account*. In Karamzin's case, this was mainly because he approved of Margeret's belief that absolute monarchy was the best form of government for Russia.

When Pushkin came to study exactly the same sources, he was more fascinated to discover that, during the Time of Troubles, 'the Russian people had dared to rebel against sitting Tsars' (just as they had done, yet again, in December 1825 – and as Evgeny would do in *The Bronze Horseman*). Ustrialyov's role, on behalf of Bulgarin, had been to cast doubt on the veracity of Margeret's eyewitness account and, in some instances, to do so by dishonest translations.

Karamzin died suddenly, in June 1826, just as the 11th volume of his *History of Russia* was being published. By this time, his established interpretation of developments in Russia and support for an autocratic regime had become the incontestable official orthodoxy. One consequence of this was that: 'As Nicholas I's regime became increasingly conservative, sharp criticism and official displeasure awaited writers who dared to challenge Karamzin's work'.[29] Pushkin soon found that not only was publication of *Boris Godunov* being blocked, but Benckendorff was actively promoting Bulgarin to don the mantle of Karamzin as court historiographer. At the same time, Bulgarin's business partner, Nikolay Gretsch, was awarded the privilege of publishing the second edition of Karamzin's *History.*

In the months leading up to his marriage, Pushkin was deep in debt and still unable to get *Boris Godunov* published. By now, he realised that anything which contradicted the official view of the Time of Troubles would never reach the press. Both Benckendorff and the Tsar were still acutely aware of the potential for an uprising against serfdom in Russia and as a result: 'Realistically, that meant the provocative 1825 version of Pushkin's play was a complete non-starter'.[30]

Against all his better judgement, Pushkin finally agreed to publish a more palatable version of the play. The revised version of *Boris Godunov* finally made it into print in December 1830 (with a publication date of January 1831) just as Russian troops were poised to invade Poland. Two of Pushkin's closest friends – the poet Zhukovsky and his literary agent, Pletneev – had agreed to carry out the necessary revisions and guide it through the final stages of censorship and publication. The main objective was to bring the story into line with Karamzin's official view of events.

In later years, both Zhukovsky and Pletneev made clear that the changes they made to the 1831 edition of *Boris Godunov* were the direct result of pressure from the Tsar and the censors. Zhukovsky still owned a manuscript copy in which much of the material deleted from the play had been personally marked up by the Tsar. One of the first people to receive a copy of the published play was Pyotr Chaadaev, later to be described as a 'madman' by Nicholas I. On 2 January 1831, the day after publication, Pushkin sent a copy to Chaadaev, in Moscow, with the note: 'Here my friend, is one of the works which I love the most. You will read it, since it is by me – and you will tell me your opinion of it. Meanwhile, I embrace you, and I wish you a Happy New Year'.[31]

Whereas Pushkin's first readings of the play had been greeted with a rapturous response, in 1826, the published version of 1831 was mauled by the critics. As Chester Dunning writes, they 'accused Pushkin of slavishly following Karamzin's official interpretation of history, of producing a poor version of Shakespearean drama, and of writing a disjointed and incoherent play devoid of any real meaning'.[32] Nevertheless, the play did make money and Pushkin was granted a stipend of 10,000 roubles from the Tsar. Furthermore, much to Bulgarin's fury, Pushkin was appointed successor to Karamzin as court historiographer and was granted access to the imperial archives – ostensibly to work on his planned *History of Peter the Great.*

For a short period, Pushkin's *volte-face* over *Boris Godunov* and his hugely unexpected advancement by the Tsar alleviated his financial worries. However, it also intensified the bitter rivalry with Bulgarin. Backed by Benckendorff, Bulgarin and his partner, Nikolay Gretsch, had been co-publishers of the first privately owned newspaper in Russia, the *Northern Bee (Severnaya Pchela).* The paper had sole rights to the publication of political views and, according to the historian Nurit Schleifman, Bulgarin and Gretsch 'had acquired this monopoly in return for the latter's services to the Third Section and as a reward for converting their paper into a mouthpiece for the regime'.[33]

The educated elite of Russia, including Pushkin, were scathing in their criticism of the *Northern Bee,* whose editorial line was a cross between the *Daily Mail* and *The Sun:* 'Its publishers, Gretsch and Bulgarin, came to epitomise opportunism, reaction and journalistic corruption, and Bulgarin in particular acquired notoriety as a police spy, a master of intrigue and the progenitor of the Russian sensational press'.[34] The paper was, nevertheless, extremely popular – but it was despised by the new generation of writers 'without exception' because of the way it encouraged 'the constant interference of the police in every aspect of literary life'.[35]

In 1829, Pushkin infuriated Benckendorff when he absconded to the Caucasus, without first gaining official permission. He returned having written what ranks as some of his finest prose, in the combined travelogue and war journalism of his ground-breaking *Journey to Arzerum.* Benckendorff and the Tsar were both livid that Pushkin's account of the war did not sufficiently glorify the Russian army and that he had treated both sides in the conflict with equal respect.

Responding to Pushkin's public denunciation of his own

plagiarism, in purloining entire sections of *Boris Godunov* and passing it off as his own work, Bulgarin even had the effrontery to counter-attack, claiming that Pushkin had liberally helped himself to passages from his own work and from Griboyedov's play *Woe from Wit.* The *Literary Gazette's* ironic comment on this was that:

'There is a still more serious charge of plagiarism to be levelled at Pushkin: that he borrowed from *Dmitry the Imposter,* and with the help of his plunder was able, with his (albeit not mentioned by name) habitual cunning, to produce the historical tragedy of *Boris Godunov* – even though, by some strange concourse of circumstance, it was written five years before the inception of Mr Bulgarin's historical novel'.

The feud between Pushkin and Bulgarin, and between Pushkin and Benckendorff, continued unremittingly throughout the last few years of his life. In an article clearly aimed at Pushkin at the climax of the 'plagiarism' row (but not naming him) Bulgarin wrote that Pushkin was:

'…by nature a Frenchman, serving Bacchus and Pluto more faithfully than the Muses, who has expressed no useful truth, no lofty ideas, or elevated sentiments in his work, whose heart is cold and lifeless as an oyster, and whose head is like a child's rattle, filled with resounding rhymes but empty of ideas…He hurls his rhymes at everything holy, boasts of his liberal views to the people and slyly grovels at the feet of the mighty…'.[36]

Pushkin responded with his own vitriolic attack on Bulgarin, published in the *Literary Gazette,* in which he likens him (again anonymously) to the notorious police official Vidocq. Like Bulgarin, Vidocq: 'writes reports against his enemies, accuses them of debauchery and liberalism, and carries on about honourable feelings and independence of convictions'. And all this even though he is married to 'one of those poor creatures whose functions necessitate her constant surveillance' – a reference to the fact that Bulgarin was married to a former prostitute.[37]

All of this culminated in an outrageous slur on Pushkin's ancestry, in which Bulgarin used the *Northern Bee* as a platform from which to write:

'It is public knowledge that a Spanish-American poet and fervent emulator of Byron, who is the offspring of a mulatto or mulatress, I forget which, began to claim that one of his ancestors was a Negro prince. City Hall archives subsequently established that there had indeed been a lawsuit between a captain and his lieutenant over the disputed possession of a Negro. The captain proved that he had bought the man for a bottle of rum. Little did he think that day, that a certain maker of verse would later boast of his descent from a Negro. *Vanitas Vanitatum...' (Vanity of Vanities).*[38]

Pushkin's reply to this insult was not only to defend his black ancestry but also to castigate the 'slaves and flatterers' surrounding the throne. He vigorously defended his ancestor Abraham Hannibal in his poem *My Genealogy* and this time his crossfire did not stop there.

As the Soviet historian, Dmitry Blagoy, puts it, he now gave them 'a precise socio-historical description': 'This was a court and society clique of upstarts (no historical traditions, contempt for the ordinary people, a superficial European gloss, but without the advanced European culture). These were the high-ups who had achieved wealth and power as the result of favouritism and palace coups in the 18th century'.[39]

One of the individuals Pushkin targets here is Sergey Uvarov, a former liberal and member of the Arzamas literary sociey, who, like both Bulgarin and Gretsch, had seamlessly switched to the side of reaction after the crushing of the Decembrist Revolt. Uvarov was one of those who had become a member of the new aristocracy by virtue of his marriage to the daughter of the wealthy magnate, Count Razumovsky – nephew of the Empress Elizabeth's rags-to-riches lover, Razumovsky 'the Night Emperor'.

In 1832, Uvarov was appointed Minister of National Education, in succession to his father-in-law. One of the measures Nicholas was eager to introduce in the wake of the Decembrist Revolt was a reform of the education system which would protect the *status quo* and neutralise the threat of 'foreign ideas' and 'pseudo-knowledge'. In this role, Uvarov did have some success in improving educational standards. But he also worked hard to ensure that there would be 'No University Pugachevs'. As Minister of Education, he was also the person in overall command of the official censorship.

According to the eminent Russian historian, Solovyev, Uvarov was brilliantly endowed mentally and widely cultured but he was also 'a manservant at heart; he did not spare any means or any flattery to please his master' – who was, of course, Nicholas I. Uvarov was the person who coined the maxim 'Orthodoxy, Autocracy & Nationality' – known as *narodnost* – which was to provide the official ideology for the regime of Nicholas I. Uvarov was also noted for his excessive self-esteem and vanity. Even his friends admitted there was 'no baseness to which he would not stoop' and that he was 'implicated up to the eyeballs in shady business'.[40]

Another former member of the Arzamas Society, the Decembrist Alexander Turgenev, accused Uvarov of having 'incriminated everybody' after the uprising of 1825. Uvarov was also suspected by many of his contemporaries of having been one of the culprits responsible for the death of Pushkin. After he had published his lampoon mocking Pushkin's black ancestry, Bulgarin admitted to his colleague, Nikolay Gretsch, that he got the idea from Uvarov.

Pushkin was the first to attempt to contradict the official orthodoxy of *narodnost* – whose primary aim was to bolster the centuries-old folk traditions of subservience to the Tsar. As had happened with *Boris Godunov,* Pushkin's interpretation of Russian history now brought him into direct conflict with Uvarov, with the publication of his *The History of Pugachev*: '… the subject of which not only did not fit into the framework of Uvarov's formula but directly refuted it, since it was one of the most important and popular uprisings against the autocratic system'.[41] As Pushkin had written at the end of the book, it shook the nation 'from Siberia to Moscow and from the Kuban to the forests of Murom'.[42]

Uvarov regarded even the choice of topic as an affront and tried to have it banned (he was later to do the same with Pushkin's article on Radishchev). Pushkin again hit back with a satirical poem, ridiculing Uvarov's notorious greed and the stupidity of his 'imbecile' subordinate Dundukov, who was Chairman of the

Board of Censors and had been a former homosexual lover of Uvarov. Pushkin called him Dunduk – the blockhead and wrote of him:

In the Academy of Sciences, sits Prince Dunduk.
It's said that such an honour is unbefitting to Dunduk;
Why then does he sit? Because he is an arse-hole'.[43]

At the time, Uvarov was impatiently awaiting the death of his father-in-law, who was ill with scarlet fever. Through his wife, Uvarov was the direct heir to the Sheremetev fortune but, much to Uvarov's consternation, the Count unexpectedly made a full recovery and Uvarov, the precipitous heir, became a public laughing stock. Pushkin's epigram *On the Recovery of Lucullus,* purporting to come from the original Latin, was a direct parody of Uvarov's plight which somehow escaped the censors and not surprisingly threw Uvarov into a rage when it was published.

A few days after publication of Pushkin's broadside, Uvarov was reported to have launched into a tirade in the presence of his subordinates in the Department of Education. He approached one of the official censors, P I Gaevsky, and said: 'You, Pavel Ivanovich, have doubtless read what this ruffian and scoundrel has written about me?'. He then instructed Gaevsky to proceed at once to the Chairman of the Censorship Committee, Dunduk: '…and tell him from me that he should immediately instruct the Censor Committee that not one, but two, three, four censors are to be appointed over the writings of this ruffian'.[44]

There was more to what Alexander Turgenev described as Pushkin's 'immortal derision' than simply personal animosity: 'Pushkin had exposed Uvarov to public obloquy as a dishonest and 'low miser', a trickster, lick-spittle, money-grubber and embezzler, the main ideologist of reaction, who was in charge of public education and the country's sciences'.[45] The downside of the widespread hilarity produced by Pushkin's epigrams was that they earned him even more enemies – Uvarov and Dundukov now joined the ranks of the Nesselrodes and Bulgarins he had offended.

During this period, Pushkin had more pressing matters to deal with. On 29 March 1836, an Easter Sunday, his mother, Nadezhda Pushkin, died after a prolonged illness. Pushkin left St Petersburg early in April and accompanied his mother's body on its journey to the Svyatogorsk Monastery, near the family estate at Mikhailovskoye. She was buried at Mikhailovskoye, at the Church of the Assumption, on 13 April, near the graves of her parents, Mariya and Osip Hannibal. While he was there, Pushkin presciently reserved a plot for himself, next to his mother's grave.

For the weeks leading up to his mother's death, Pushkin had been working tirelessly on the launch of his new journal, *The Contemporary*. The first edition, which was published on 11 April, included his foray into war journalism, *A Journey to Arzerum*. Articles were also contributed by Zhukovsky, Gogol, Yazykov and Vyazemsky. Pushkin's commitment to launching the publication was such that:

'Pushkin gave up his own royalties; he worked for nothing, collected contributions, corrected proofs, supervised sales – although page layout, printing, distribution and book-keeping were all minor matters, in his view'.

The censor, meanwhile:

'took pains to make sure that nothing would be done to smooth the path for the diabolical Pushkin. Underlings, terrified by the poet's reputation, picked over every paragraph with fastidious malice, sat on the galleys for weeks, imperturbably delayed the publication of every issue'.[46]

The Minister of the Interior, Uvarov, sent out instructions to his minions that they be doubly vigilant with *The Contemporary:*

'Story after story was rejected on the most spurious grounds. Benckendorff upbraided Pushkin for publishing an article by a cornet of the guards without first obtaining permission from the chief of police, his commanding officer. Uvarov wrote to the chairman of the board of censors: "It is not fitting for officials attached to my ministry to have anything to do with persons of such pernicious mentality as Pushkin"'.[47]

Pushkin was also reprimanded by the Third Section when they discovered that he had received a letter sent by his former Lycée schoolmate, exiled Decembrist and would-be regicide, Küchelbecker. Pushkin was soon sorry ever to have become involved with journalism. The first edition of *The Contemporary* was not a critical success and in a letter to Natalya, Pushkin wearily wrote: 'Cleaning out Russian literature is like cleaning out the latrines; it is the job of the police…the devil take them! My very blood is turning to bile!' [48]

Even though she was in advanced stage of pregnancy, Natalya too was much involved in the journals affairs but soon travelled to the villa they had rented on Kamenny Island to complete her confinement. The couple's second daughter, another Natalya, was born on 24 May and christened three days later at the Church of the Birth of John the Baptist on the island.

By now, the odds were stacking up against Pushkin but he did his best to mount a fightback. On 31 December 1835, he sent Benckendorff a copy of his own translation of a memoir written by the French career soldier, the Brigadier Moreau de Brasey, who had accompanied Peter the Great at the historic Battle of the Pruth. At the same time, he added the following: 'I make bold to disturb Your Excellency with a most humble request. I should like during next year, 1836, to publish four volumes of items of a purely literary (e.g. of tales, poems etc) historical, scholarly nature, and critical analyses of Russian and foreign literature; something on the order of the English quarterly *Reviews*.'[49]

This request was a watered-down version of one which Pushkin had made earlier the same year, when he had first thought to produce a newspaper which would be a direct challenger to Bulgarin's *Northern Bee*. He also planned to publish a quarterly literary journal. Pushkin had hoped to solve his financial problems this way but the application was refused by the Tsar. Pushkin's collaborator on the revised proposal was his friend, Prince Odoevsky, who had suggested the less-than-snappy title of the new periodical should be: *The Contemporary Chronicler of Politics, Sciences and Literature, containing a survey of the most noteworthy events in Russia and other European states, in all branches of political, scientific and aesthetic activity from the beginning of the third (the last) decade of the 19th century*.'[50]

Permission for the quarterly, whose title was wisely shortened to *The Contemporary*, was finally granted, with the proviso that it would be devoid of any explicitly political content. The first edition came out in April 1836 and included an article by Nikolai Gogol, entitled *Morning of a Man of Business: Petersburg Scenes*.

Three more editions appeared the same year and one more was ready for publication just before Pushkin's death. From the outset, every edition of the journal was dogged by wrangling with the censors. The person who was overall in charge of censorship for *The Contemporary* was Pushkin's adversary, Dondukov-Kursakov. As chairman of the censorship committee, he had appointed the strictest of the censors, Krylov, to monitor the content of Pushkin's journal. Because individual censors were always too timid to take decisions themselves, the result was that they continually referred decisions back to the full censorship committee and then up to its chairman, Dondukov-Kursakov.

In a letter to the chairman, on 6 April 1836, Pushkin made clear his frustration at the damaging effect all this to-ing and fro-ing was having on his journal. Noting that Krylov seemed incapable 'in and of himself' to make up his mind to pass articles Pushkin had submitted for publication, Pushkin complained that:

'...such a double censorship takes an excessive amount of time for me, so that my journal cannot come out on schedule. I do not complain of superfluous mistrustfulness on the part of my censor, I know that on him lies a responsibility which is perhaps not delimited by the Censorship Regulations. But I make bold to request Your Highness for the authorisation to choose myself an additional censor, in order that thus the examining of my journal can be made twice as rapid. Without this, it will come to a halt and fail'.[51]

By the time the second issue of *The Contemporary* appeared, after constant interference from the censors, Pushkin was already thundering: 'I do not know what offense has been committed by Russian writers, who are not only submissive, but also of themselves in agreement with the spirit of the government. But I do know that they have never been so oppressed as now'. [52]

To illustrate his annoyance, he submitted an article entitled '*Castrated by military censorship*' for the fourth edition of *The Contemporary*, which was published in November 1836. Prevented from publishing his own newspaper, which might have been a money-spinner, Pushkin's subscriber-base for the journal was too small and its publication too infrequent for it to be profitable. The result was that Pushkin's financial troubles multiplied.

In June 1836, he was forced to borrow 8,000 roubles from his friend, Prince Nikolay Obolensky, and the following month, Pushkin's wife became so concerned about their money problems that she wrote a desperate letter to her brother, divulging that: '…now my situation is such that I consider it even my duty to assist my husband in that difficult situation in which he finds himself'. In this letter, Natalya voices her concern that 'it is not fair that the whole burden of keeping my large family should fall on him alone'.[53]

Since their marriage, Natalya had given birth to four children – two boys and two girls – and at the same time Pushkin was effectively paying for the upkeep of the rest of his family which was overburdened with penniless relatives.

'I openly confess to you', Natalya wrote, 'that we are in such a calamitous situation that there are days when I do not know how to carry on the household, my head spins. I very much do not want to disturb my husband with all my little domestic troubles, I already know how sad and depressed he is, cannot sleep at night, and, consequently, is in such a state he is not able to work to provide us with the means for existence: in order to compose, his head must be free'.[54] In his biography of Pushkin, T J Binyon writes: 'This hardly seems the letter of a woman interested in nothing but her fashionable toilette and her social success; nor of one who would have been seduced by the attractions of a d'Anthès'.[55]

In addition to the salacious gossip on the extent to which Natalya had welcomed the attentions of both d'Anthès and the Tsar, Pushkin was confronted by a new political controversy. In October 1836, his old friend and former mentor, Pyotr Chaadaev, sent him, from abroad, a copy of the latest edition of the Russian literary journal *Telescope* which – much to Pushkin's amazement – contained a Russian translation of the first of Chaadaev's *Philosophical Letters*.

Chaadaev's polemic had already caused a furore when it was first published, in French, nearly a decade earlier because it had been so scathing about Russia's backwardness and what he regarded as the poverty of its contribution to world history. The immediate result of the publication of this letter in Russian for the first time was that the editor of the journal, Nadezhdin, was arrested and exiled to Siberia; the censor, Alexey Boldyrev, who had misguidedly allowed Chaadaev's work to be published was sacked; Chaadaev himself was declared 'clinically insane' and put under the daily observation of a physician.

On 19 October 1836, Pushkin drafted an extended response to Chaadaev, thanking him for sending what he refers to as 'the booklet' and expressing astonishment at having seen it translated and published. He then launched into a prolonged discourse on those aspects of Russian history where he finds himself in disagreement with Chaadaev, but nevertheless concludes:

'After having taken issue with you, I must tell you that many things in your letter are profoundly true. One must admit that our social life is a sad thing. The absence of public opinion, the indifference towards all duty, justice and truth, the cynical disdain for human thought and dignity are truly distressing. You have done well to say it out loud'.[56]

In the event, this letter was never sent. Pushkin wrote a number of different drafts but before he posted any of them he was warned, by Alexandra Rosset's brother Klementy, of the actions which were about to be taken against Chaadaev, Nadezhdin and Boldyrev. Klementy strongly recommended that Pushkin think twice about what he had written and to 'defer' sending it in the post. Fearing that some of the doubts he had expressed on Russian history might be misinterpreted as disapproval of Chaadaev, Pushkin kept the letter, noting on it: 'A falcon does not peck out another falcon's eye'.[57]

Notes

1   **Pushkin Threefold: Narrative, Lyric, Polemic & Ribald Verse**, The originals, with linear and metric translations by Walter Arndt, includes a verse translation of *The Bronze Horseman,* Allen & Unwin, 1972, p27

2   **The Critical Prose of Alexander Pushkin,** with critical essays by four Russian romantic poets, edited and translated by Carl R Proffer, Indiana University Press, 1969, p6

3   **Pushkin,** by Henri Troyat. Translated from the French by Nancy Amphoux. George, Allen & Unwin. 1974, p466

4   Troyat, ibid. p467

5   Troyat, p467

6   Troyat, p467

7   **The Letters of Alexander Pushkin,** Three Volumes in One, Translated and with an introduction by J Thomas Shaw, University of Wisconsin Press, 1967, Letter 482, p638

8   Shaw, op.cit. Letter 482, p638

9   Shaw, Letter 391, p524

10   **Pushkin**, By T J Binyon, Harper Collins, 2002, p437

11   Binyon, ibid. pp566

12   **Death of a Poet,** A novel of the last years of Alexander Pushkin, by Leonid Grossman, Translated from the Russian by Edith Bone, Hutchinson International Authors, 1951, p176

13   Quoted in **The Sacred Lyre**, Essays on the Life and work of Alexander Pushkin, by Dmitry Blagoy, Raduga Publishers, English translation published in 1982, first published in Russian 1979, p383

14   Blagoy, ibid. p383

15   Troyat, p482

16   Shaw, op.cit. Letter 496, p650

17   Shaw, Letter 499, p652

18   Grossman, op.cit. p176

19   Grossman, p178

20   **The Russian Secret Police,** Muscovite, Imperial Russian and Soviet Political Security Operations, by Ronald Hingley, Simon and Schuster, 1970, p39

21   Hingley, ibid. p32

22   **Pushkin,** by T J Binyon, Harper Collins, 2002, p253

23   Binyon, ibid. p.53

24   Binyon, p253

25   **Pushkin,** by Henri Troyat, Translated from the French by Nancy Amphoux, George, Allen & Unwin, 1974, p381

26   Binyon, op.cit. p254

27   Binyon, op.cit. p255

28   **Rethinking the Canonical Text of Pushkin's Boris Godunov,** by Chester

Dunning, *The Russian Review*, Vol 60, No. 4,. October 2001, *http://www.jstor.org/ stable/2679368* p584

29 Dunning, ibid. p585

30 Dunning, p586

31 **The Letters of Alexander Pushkin.** Three Volumes in One, Translated and with an Introduction by J Thomas Shaw, University of Wisconsin Press, 1967, Letter 336, p449

32 Dunning, op.cit. p587

33 **A Russian Daily Newspaper and Its New Readership: 'Severnaya Pchela', 1825-1840,** by Nurit Schleifman, *Cahiers du Monde Russe et Soviétique*, Vol. 28, No. 2. April-June 1987, *http://www.jstor.org/stable/20170573* p128

34 Schleifman, ibid. p127

35 Schleifman, p127

36 Troyat, op.cit. p383

37 Shaw, op.cit. Letter 171 '*Of Vidocq's memoirs'*, p242

38 Troyat, op.cit. p385

39 **The Sacred Lyre: Essays on the Life and work of Alexander Pushkin**, by Dmitry Blagoy, Raduga Publishers, English translation published in 1982, First published in Russian 1979, p368

40 Blagoy, ibid. p369

41 Blagoy, p371

42 **The History of Pugachev,** by Alexander Pushkin, Translated by Earl Sampson, Introduction by Orlando Figes, Phoenix Press, 2001 (Russian edition first published in 1833), p109

43 Binyon, op.cit. p484

44 Blagoy, op.cit. p372

45 Blagoy, op.cit. p372

46 Troyat, op.cit. p508

47 Troyat, op.cit. p508

48 Troyat, p508

49 Shaw, op.cit. Letter 588, p747

50 Binyon, op.cit. p.491

51 Shaw, op.cit. Letter 606, p758

52 Shaw, op.cit. Letter 632, p777

53 Binyon, op.cit. p538

54 Binyon, op.cit. p539

55 Binyon, op.cit. p539

56 Shaw, op.cit. Letter 637, p779

57 Shaw, footnote to Letter 637, p797.

*The Grand Crosses, Commanders and Chevaliers of the Most
Serene Order of Cuckolds, gathered in Grand Chapter under
the presidency of the venerable Grand Master of the order, His
Excellency D L Naryshkin, have unanimously nominated Mr
Alexander Pushkin coadjutor to the Grand Master of the Order
of Cuckolds and historiographer of the Order.
Signed: Permanent Secretary Count I Borkh*

Anonymous 'Diploma' sent to Pushkin, 4 November 1836[1]

15 | Pushkin's Fatal Gamble

By 1836, Pushkin had become an isolated figure in Petersburg
high society. He had ridiculed nearly every prominent figure
in the city with his epigrams and lampoons: ministers and
generals, censors, journalists and policemen. He had pilloried his
adversaries such as Uvarov, the Nesselrodes, Dundukov-Korsakov
and Bulgarin, not to mention Nicholas and Benckendorff: 'All
this joined the poet's enemies together in a single phalanx and
formed a united front of hate and vengeance against him'.[2] At the
tip of this formation was the Tsar himself, who detested Pushkin
but coveted his wife: 'In Petersburg, where there are no secrets,
it had been known to everyone for some time that the Emperor
had fallen in love with Pushkin's wife. Society was all agog. What
would be the outcome of this amorous duel? Meanwhile people
whispered, sniggered, and expressed their amazement: Pushkin was
not allowed to leave the capital. Why? The Emperor was showing
d'Anthès special favour: could it be that he was encouraging, for
personal reasons, the attentions the Chevalier-Guard was paying
the poet's wife?'[3]

While on a trip to Moscow, in May 1836, Pushkin mentioned
this gossip in a letter to Natalya: 'And about you, my darling,

some talk is going about which isn't reaching me in its entirety, because husbands are always the last in the city to discover about their wives. However, it seems that you have driven a certain person to such despair with your coquetry and cruelty that he has acquired himself in solace a harem of theatrical trainees. That is not good, my angel. Modesty is the best adornment of your sex'.[4]

The 'certain person' Pushkin is referring to here was the Tsar.

By the autumn of 1835, Natalya had another new admirer, the emigré monarchist, George d'Anthès. George d'Anthès was a career soldier who had completed his military training at the premier French military academy of Saint-Cyr. During his time at the academy he was recognised as one of his company's crack shots. He was also a dedicated royalist, or 'legitimist', loyal to the House of Bourbon. Precisely how or why he had arrived in Russia is a matter of some confusion.

According to one version, d'Anthès made his way overland from the Alsace and it was on this hazardous journey that he took ill. As the story went, he was then only rescued from certain death by the timely arrival of the Baron van Heeckeren, the Dutch Ambassador, who happened to be making his return journey from Holland to his post in St Petersburg at the same time.

A contemporary report in *St Petersburg News,* however, records that the Dutch Ambassador had actually arrived by steamship from Lübeck weeks earlier. It said that van Heeckeren was among the 42 passengers who arrived at Kronstadt on the steamer *Nicholas I* after a 78-hour sea journey on 8 October 1833. The first definite record of d'Anthès' arrival, made by the French embassy in St Petersburg, has him signing in a month later, on 2 November 1833, when his address was given as the English Hotel, on Galernaya Street.

What we do know for certain is that d'Anthès came to St Petersburg armed with a recommendation from the heir to the Prussian throne, Prince Wilhelm, the Prince of Orange. The prince was married to the Tsar's sister, Anna Pavlovna. As brother-in-law to the Tsar, Wilhelm knew that Nicholas I 'would certainly welcome a French *legitimist* with open arms'. Nicholas regarded himself as the supreme leader of the European counter-revolution – such was his pride in his obduracy, it earned him the soubriquet 'Gendarme of Europe'.

The uprising which had taken place in Senate Square on the same day as his investiture reinforced his hatred of the slightest hint of revolution. When there were renewed outbreaks across Europe in 1830, Nicholas stood in the vanguard with other European powers, which now: 'declared war to the knife on all those presumptuous enough to challenge their absolute, complete and unlimited superiority'.[5]

In this political climate, Pushkin typified everything that Nicholas detested: 'The Russian Tsar has in general a great aversion to writers of any kind, but in the case of Pushkin this general antipathy has turned into a personal enmity. The Emperor saw in Pushkin a political opponent, an enemy of his cause, a dangerous free-thinker, deserving persecution and prosecution'.[6]

Georges d'Anthès had other powerful family connections in St Petersburg, apart from the Tsar. He was related, on his mother's side, to two of the most prominent figures in the imperial court, the Count and Countess Nesselrode. Karl Nesselrode was Russia's foreign minister for forty years, from 1816 to 1856. He was a leading figure in the Holy Alliance of European monarchical powers and had led the Russian delegation at the Congress of Vienna. His wife was one of the *grande dames* of Russian high society. She held deeply conservative views and detested Pushkin, a feeling which was mutual.

Thanks to his connections, d'Anthès was fast-tracked for the entrance exam to join the prestigious Chevalier Guard Regiment, a position normally held exclusively by sons of the oldest and wealthiest families of the Russian nobility. The substantial expenses involved were taken care of by van Heeckeren, who had already been stationed in St Petersburg for more than a decade and was notorious for his 'bilious tongue and widely scheming nature'.[7] The society hostess, Dolly Ficquelmont, wrote of von Heeckeren that: 'Here, he is considered a spy for Nesselrode, a conjecture that gives the clearest idea of his personality and character'.[8]

The precise nature of the relationship between d'Anthès and van Heeckeren is one of the more byzantine aspects of the goings-on which preceded Pushkin's death. Almost from the moment they both arrived in St Petersburg, van Heeckeren had treated d'Anthès as though he was his own son. He had exerted all his influence to ensure that d'Anthès would be given a commission in the Guards and there was more than a suspicion that their relationship was homosexual.

This theory appeared to be confirmed by the fact that: 'By the beginning of 1835 van Heeckeren had become passionately attached to the younger man – a feeling reciprocated by d'Anthès – and urgently sought a means by which they might live together without provoking prurient gossip'.[9] Eyebrows were further raised when van Heeckeren began to investigate legally adopting d'Anthès as his son.

Under the articles of the French civil code – which remained in force in the Netherlands until 1838 – no evidence was available proving a relationship which could be justify an adoption: 'Both in Holland and in St Petersburg, this pseudo-adoption was considered most peculiar and aroused much speculation'.[10] In the event, van Heeckeren managed to circumvent the stipulations of the French civil code by appealing directly to the King of the Netherlands, William I 'to grant d'Anthès Dutch nationality, to admit him to the Dutch nobility and to allow him to change his name to Heeckeren'.[11] One of Pushkin's closest friends, Alexander Karamzin, told his brother that d'Anthès was adopted by Heeckeren for reasons which even now are still entirely unknown to the public, 'which avenges itself with conjectures'.[12]

Among several possible explanations was the story which emerged from a social gathering held at the grand residence of the Russian Foreign Minister, Nesselrode, in November 1836. According to one of those who attended this society 'rout' – Pavel Dmitrievich Durnovo, the son-in-law of the Minister of Court, Prince Volkonsky – the general opinion of the company was that d'Anthès was an illegitimate son of the Dutch King, Wilhelm I. A variant put forward by the respected Russian writer and medical doctor, Vikenty Veresayev, was that d'Anthès was indeed the illegitimate son of the Dutch King: the missing link in the story was that his mother was van Heeckeren's sister and that is why Heeckeren was so keen to have d'Anthès adopted.[13]

By the autumn of 1835, d'Anthés had become a regular companion of Natalya Pushkina, née Goncharova, and her sisters. During the peak period for society balls and receptions, which traditionally took place at the time of the late winter carnival, d'Anthès met and danced with Natalya most days in the first few months of 1836. But, despite this constant attention, Pushkin's wife would not fully succumb to his advances.

Part of the officer class's code of seduction in those days was that unmarried girls should be left alone; married women were desirable and legitimate prizes. Despite d'Anthès repeated affirmations of his 'love' for Natalya, it was not long before he was also seen to be in hot pursuit of Mariya Baryatinskaya, 17-year old daughter of the Princess Baryatinskaya. The Baryatinskys were one of the foremost and wealthiest families in Petersburg. d'Anthès was a close friend of Mariya's brother, Alexander, who was a lieutenant in his own regiment, the Life Guards. By the end of March 1836, d'Anthès had become a regular caller at the Baryatinsky household.

Two months later, at the end of July, a grand fête with fireworks marked the end of the Chevalier Guards' manoeuvres at Krasnoye Selo. The company then moved to their next bivouac, on the northern, Vyborg bank of the Neva. This shifted the centre of gravity of social life back to 'the islands' and at the same time allowed d'Anthès to instantly ditch his interest in Mariya Baryatinskaya and renew his pursuit of Natalya Pushkina. This time, d'Anthès made no attempt to disguise his attentions. As well as seeking her out at society gatherings, he began to send Natalya books and theatre tickets, often accompanied with short notes and inappropriate comments: 'He was becoming daily more obsessed with her, and daily more outrageous in his behaviour towards her'. D'Anthès' conduct became so reprehensible that, as a gesture to social proprieties, he began to publicly court Natalya's sister, Ekaterina:

'But this charade deceived neither society nor Pushkin. Together with his ever more pressing financial worries, his difficulties with the censorship, and the ill-success of *The Contemporary*, the realisation that d'Anthès had renewed his addresses to Natalya produced in him that state of heightened irritability he had known earlier in the year; this time, however, it was combined with an unconcealed hostility towards the young Frenchman'.[14]

At a party held to celebrate the 'name day' of Sofiya Karamzina,

THE MAN WHO SHOOK HIS FIST AT THE TSAR

on 17 September, Pushkin was described by the hostess as appearing 'melancholy, abstracted and worried'. In a letter to her brother, Sofiya wrote: 'His depression makes me depressed. His wandering, wild, distraught gaze rests only, with disquieting attention, on his wife and on d'Anthès, who continues exactly the same farce as before... it was pitiful to see Pushkin's face opposite, framed in the door, silent, pale and menacing. My God, how stupid it is!' [15]

By this stage, the whole of fashionable society in St Petersburg was talking about d'Anthès' attentions to Pushkin's wife. They regularly saw one another at the houses of mutual friends and at society balls: 'The dreadful word 'cuckold' began to buzz around Pushkin's ears like a pestilent autumn fly'.[16] At one of the balls an oafish young noble, the villainous Prince Dolgorukov, put up his fingers in the shape of a horn behind Pushkin's head, at the same time winking in d'Anthès direction and grinning to his friends'.[17]

Less than a month after Chaadaev had been declared 'insane', Pushkin himself came under renewed attack and this time his patience finally snapped. The blue touchpaper was kindled on the morning of 4 November 1836, when, at his apartment on the Moika embankment, Pushkin received several copies of a fake 'certificate' which had been sent via the newly established city post. The anonymous document, handwritten in French, ridiculed him as a cuckold. Identical copies were delivered the same morning to a number of Pushkin's closest friends.

The obvious aim of this mock award was to place Pushkin in the same bracket as Dmitry Naryshkin, the Chief Master of the Hunt, who had earned the reputation as the most notorious cuckold of the age: it was common knowledge that Naryshkin had knowingly turned a blind eye to the fact that, over many years, his wife Maria Naryshkina was mistress to the Tsar, Alexander I. There was little doubt that this prolonged affair had taken place, since she had borne him three children.

It was rumoured that Naryshkin had been handsomely rewarded for his easy acceptance of the royal prerogative – in the form of an annual salary of 40,000 assignation roubles from the Emperor. The fake diploma clearly insinuated that, since Pushkin drew a state salary of 5,000 roubles a year, much the same was going on between Pushkin, his wife and Alexander's successor, Nicholas I. The signatory to the 'award', Count I Borkh, had been mentioned for two reasons. The first was that both he and his wife were renowned for their licentious behaviour: Pushkin himself had once remarked to a friend, when the Borkh's carriage went by: 'There go two exemplary couples. The wife, you know, sleeps with the coachman, and the husband with the postillion'.[18] The second possible reason for including Borkh's name was that his wife, Emma, was a distant cousin of Pushkins' wife.

One of the other recipients of the certificate was Count Vladimir Sollogub. As soon as he received his copy, Sollogub took it round to Pushkin's flat. Pushkin's immediate response was: 'It's like getting shit on one's hands. It's unpleasant but one washes one's hands, and that's an end to it'. Then, he added: 'My wife is an angel. No suspicion can touch her'.[19] Pushkin initially acted as though the anonymous message was a vile slander and feigned indifference. In reality, he was furious:

'Although he greeted this nugget of filth with an affectation of serene contempt, Pushkin was in reality no longer able to control himself. He was shaking with impotent fury, reeling and shuddering as though he had been publicly whipped.
Half the town had received copies of the 'diploma'. His wife was flouted, his name dragged through the mud. What face could he wear in public? How could he ever dare to write another poem? He wanted to smite the slanderer, denounce him, brand him, kill him'.[20]

Long before the scurrilous 'diploma' arrived through the mail, Pushkin knew of the nasty rumours circulating in high society. He had already received several anonymous letters, all defamatory and handwritten in an elaborate script. One was handed to him while at dinner at the home of his publishing adversary, Nikolai Gretsch. Pushkin had immediately left the house without saying a word. Other letters appeared under his napkin at a restaurant and inside his coat at the theatre. What Pushkin did not know yet was the extent of the involvement in this developing intrigue of van Heeckeren.

When the Dutch Ambassador returned to Russia, in September 1836, following a period of diplomatic activity, he began to take on a more active role in d'Anthès' renewed pursuit of Natalya and their combined effort to humiliate Pushkin. As Henri Troyat notes:

'Had the husband been anyone other than Pushkin, the ambassador would assuredly have counselled d'Anthès to hold back. But Pushkin was the sworn enemy of the Nesselrodes and thereby of Heeckeren himself, who was a close friend of the Foreign Minister. By dishonouring Pushkin, d'Anthès would not only be obliging the mandarins. He would earn the respect of all the people in power. He would move a step up the ladder. It was a question of his career'.[21]

Heeckeren was an important figure in the Nesselrode *coterie*, the social hub of the most conservative elements in St Petersburg. Count Nesselrode, of Baltic German descent, was Russian Foreign Minister for over 40 years. According to Troyat, he liked Heeckeren for his wit, elegance and violently monarchist sympathies: 'He sensed in him a man of his own rank, of his breed, and accepted him as a member of that far-flung fraternity which, from the Faubourg Saint-Germain to Vienna and from Vienna to St Petersburg, ran Europe, according to Metternich'.[22]

As they saw things, the danger facing the crowned heads of Europe was that: 'If we do not unite and pit our iron determination to remain masters against these new illiterate plebs, they will sweep us away like chaff. We shall again witness all the horrors of the notorious French rebellion, when bloodthirsty lawyers and pamphleteers threw the best heads of the old aristocracy into the sawdust basket of the guillotine. We must organise and prepare for a merciless struggle'.[23]

Nesselrode's association with the Austrian diplomat and Foreign Minister, Metternich, was such that contemporaries were said to have called him 'Austrian Minister of Russian Foreign Affairs'. For her part, the Countess Nesselrode was venomous in her opposition to Pushkin, an antagonism which appears to have developed at an early stage: her husband was in charge at the Foreign Ministry when Pushkin was exiled to the south in 1820. He was also involved in the Tsar's refusal to allow Pushkin to return to the capital from Kishinev in 1823 and in his subsequent transfer from the south to his second period of exile at Mikhailovskoye.

When the Pushkins moved to St Petersburg in 1831 after their marriage, Pushkin had aroused the Countess Nesselrode's displeasure when he took exception to her having invited Natalya to an evening party at the Anichkov Palace without his knowledge. In an account of this episode given by Henri Troyat: 'Countess Nesselrode snorted at the vulgarity of this upstart Negroid pen-pusher. By insulting her, he had made himself another enemy – and a powerful one, for the Nesselrode clique was enormous'.[24] In his novel *Death of a Poet,* Leonid Grossman describes the countenance of the Countess as follows:

'This is a matron of fifty, with the build of a grenadier and a puffy face on which is imprinted an expression of inveterate arrogance. Her sagging cheeks draw the corners of her lips downwards, and this, coupled with her bulging eyes, lend her face an unmistakable resemblance to a frog. She enjoys unbounded authority in St Petersburg society, at court and even in the imperial family. This is to a considerable extent due to her implacable hatred of anything smacking of liberalism. Her personal connections and her husband's position make her the life-centre of Russian reaction and a kind of representative in St Petersburg of European counter-revolution'.[25]

When d'Anthès took ill in October 1836 and was confined to his room (quite possibly to deal with a bout of syphilis) van Heeckeren stepped in to continue the pursuit of Natalya on behalf of his adopted son. He followed Natalya around, telling her the insane passion she had inspired, and insisting that George was capable of killing himself if she persisted in refusing him. At a ball given by the assembly of the nobility, he is even alleged to have suggested that she leave Pushkin and run away to live with d'Anthès abroad – a proposition which Natalya indignantly rejected'.[26]

Just how manipulative the activities of Van Heeckeren and d'Anthès had become is clear from the Machiavellian scheming expressed in a letter written by d'Anthès from the Chevalier Guards barracks, on 16 October. The previous day, d'Anthès had spent an evening at the salon of Vera Vyazemskaya, where Natalya was among the other guests, unaccompanied by Pushkin. D'Anthès claimed that Natalya's mere presence nearly drove him 'mad with mental suffering'. But he then went on

THE MAN WHO SHOOK HIS FIST AT THE TSAR

to implore van Heeckeren to attend a further reception being given by the Bavarian ambassador the following evening, where he knew Natalya would be present and where he proposed that van Heeckeren should take the opportunity to engage her in a private conversation. d'Anthès then suggests the following approach:

'I think you ought to go up to her openly and say to her, so that her sister can't hear, that you absolutely must talk to her seriously. Then ask her whether she happened to be at the Vyazemskys yesterday; when she answers yes, you say that you thought so and that she can do you a great favour; you tell her what happened when I came home yesterday as though you had seen it yourself, that my servant became frightened and woke you at two in the morning, that you questioned me a lot, but could get nothing out of me, and that you're convinced that I had a quarrel with her husband and that you're turning to her to avoid a calamity...'.[27]

In the margin, d'Anthès adds: 'But you didn't need my words, you yourself had guessed that I'd lost my head because of her and observing the change in my behaviour and character had convinced you of it, and therefore it was impossible that her husband hadn't noticed it too'. [28] As T J Binyon remarks: 'This is an extraordinary letter to write about a woman with whom one is ostensibly in love. To take the least heinous offence first, it is hardly the act of a gentleman to ask one's father (if only by adoption) to act as pander to further one's attempts at adultery'.[29]

Two weeks later, on 2 November 1836, the final episode in the plot to implicate Natalya in an adulterous involvement with d'Anthès took place at the apartment belonging to Idaliya Poletika. This was located in the officers' quarters on Zhakarevskaya Street. Poletika was married to Alexander Mikhailovich, an officer in the same regiment as d'Anthès. Poletika had invited Natalya to visit her apartment, without divulging who else would be present.

Natalya later described to Vera Vyazemskaya what happened when she arrived at the Poletika's: 'She had been shown into the drawing room to find there not Idaliya, who had gone out, but d'Anthès'. Natalya recalled that, in a melodramatic scene which borders on the farcical, d'Anthès had behaved in an extraordinary fashion: 'He had taken out a pistol and threatened to shoot himself, if she did not give herself to him'. Not knowing how to escape d'Anthès attentions, Natalya responded by wringing her hands and speaking as loudly as she could. She was only saved further mortification when Idaliya Poletika's four-year-old daughter wandered into to the room and, using the youngster as a shield, Natalya managed to escape.[30]

Natalya was not the only person to be shocked by this incident. The head of the chancellery at the Ministry of War, Count Adlerberg – a close associate of the Tsar and the person who had smoothed d'Anthès path of entry into the Chevalier Guards – now advised that d'Anthès be sent to the Caucasus in order to separate him from Natalya. This recommendation was rejected by the Tsar's younger brother, the Grand Duke Michael Pavlovich, who was commander-in-chief of d'Anthès' regiment.

Grand Duke Michael – who had narrowly escaped being shot by Pushkin's friend, Küchelbecker, during the uprising on Senate Square – much admired d'Anthès for his 'puns, his fine moustache and his dancing', even though d'Anthès' record as a guardsman was abysmal: 'He amassed a heap of disciplinary warnings with perfect aplomb, left the ranks ahead of his superiors, lit cigars when his company stood at ease after a review, missed his fixed periods of duty, arrived late for roll call. The regiment's historiographer calculated that Baron d'Anthès received forty-four official reprimands during his brief sojourn in the army'.[31]

The manifest leniency displayed towards d'Anthès was highly suspect. The Tsar's younger brother was regarded in society as a 'pretty wit', but he was also reviled by all the other troops for his merciless cruelty. Known by the ridiculous, Prussian title, of *Generalfeldzeugmeister:* 'The soldiers of St Petersburg trembled at the mere mention of his name. From his father, the mad Emperor Paul, he had inherited a passion for a drill so merciless as to amount to methodical torture'.[32] Evidently, d'Anthès was exempt from this stringent regime.

The histrionic scene which took place at Idaliya Poletika's apartment happened just two days before Pushkin received his unwelcome 'diploma' in the mail. After Sollogub had come round with his copy and his visit had ended, Pushkin sat down with Natalya to discuss the contents of the envelope. By all accounts, Natalya confessed to Pushkin the whole history of her relationship with d'Anthès and during the course of the conversation showed Pushkin some of the notes d'Anthès had sent. Pushkin; '…never doubted for a moment Natalya; nor, in light of the events of the preceding weeks, should we. D'Anthès behaviour is not that of a successful lover whose liaison has come to an end, but that of a rejected, desperate, and psychologically unbalanced suitor'.[33]

That is clearly one interpretation, but it might equally be argued that everything d'Anthès did was a pretence and that his aim all along, in cahoots with van Heeckeren, was to humiliate Pushkin by deliberately fuelling scandalous rumours about his much younger wife. More to the point, neither van Heeckeren nor d'Anthès would have had the audacity to behave in this way, not because of any psychological imbalance, but because they knew there would be no comeback from the imperial court: 'Pushkin's destruction was not the work of any single individual, be it d'Anthés, Heeckeren or Nesselrode, taken separately; it was achieved by the whole of Petersburg high society, profoundly hostile to the poet who had relentlessly opposed their political and social doctrines and fearless flung his poisoned and deathless sarcasms in their teeth'.[34]

Pushkin's response to the poison-pen message he received on 4 November 1836 was twofold. First, convinced that the scurrilous hoax had been written by van Heeckeren, on Dutch embassy paper and using the embassy seal, Pushkin issued a challenge to a duel. This was addressed directly to van Heeckeren but meant for both the father and his adopted son, d'Anthès – as Pushkin saw it, these were the twin collaborators in his persecution. Pushkin's friend Vyazemsky later wrote: 'From the instant he received the anonymous letters, Pushkin suspected Heeckeren senior of having written them, and he died with that idea'. Vyazemsky adds that: 'We were never able to ascertain the basis for his supposition…until after Pushkin's death, when a fortuitous discovery gave it a degree of probability'.[35] What this discovery was is still not known.

Pushkin's next reaction was to make an urgent effort to settle his financial accounts with the government of Nicholas I. Two days after he received the 'diploma', he wrote to the Tsar's

Finance Minister, Count Igor Kankrin, requesting that he be allowed to repay all the debts he owed to the Treasury, which amounted to 45,000 roubles in total. Pushkin proposed to pay this amount in full and immediately. The only way he could afford to do this was to raise the necessary finance through the sale of the family estates at Boldino, which had been bestowed to Pushkin by his father. The major obstacle to this proposition was that Pushkin had no right to sell it while his father was still alive. However, he was entitled to mortgage the estate and the 220 'souls' who worked on it, either to the Treasury or to another private individual.

Pushkin's primary aim with this letter was to counter any suggestion that his own position in relation to Nicholas I might be the same as that between the cuckold, Dmitry Naryshkin, and his wife's lover, Alexander I. There was no proof that Naryshkin had ever received money from Alexander but Pushkin had received a loan of 20,000 roubles to enable the publication of his *The History of Pugachev* in March 1834 and had also been granted a further advance of 30,000 roubles in September 1835 to pay off some earlier debts: 'The mention of Naryshkin in the certificate and the designation of Pushkin as 'historiographer' was a scarcely concealed hint at his own position: he already received a salary from the government for doing historical research and holding the court rank of *Kammerjunker*, and attending court functions, where 'the popularity of Mme. Pushkina extended… to the Tsar himself'.[36]

Pushkin's secondary objective in his letter to Kankrin was to seek an assurance 'which is important for me' that he should not bring Pushkin's request to have his debts settled to the attention of the Tsar. Probably, Pushkin wrote, the Tsar would not want such a repayment anyway 'even though it is not at all burdensome to me'. Moreover, he feared that Nicholas: '… might even order that my debt be forgiven me, which would place me in an extremely painful and embarrassing situation: for in such a case I would be compelled to refuse the Tsar's favour, and that could seem an impropriety, pointless braggadocio or even ingratitude'.[37] More to the point, such an outcome could be seen to confirm the most damning accusation of the 'certificate', that there was a more incriminating explanation for the Tsar's generosity.

THE MAN WHO SHOOK HIS FIST AT THE TSAR

It is a measure of Pushkin's desperation that he even imagined Kankrin would comply with either of these requests without first seeking a response from the Tsar: 'The gross illogicality and ludicrous impracticality of the proposals reveal, more than anything else, how psychologically confused and disturbed Pushkin was at the time. While, over the next few months, when dealing with subjects which did not touch on his own personal position, he was able to act normally and bring his intellect sensible and incisively to bear, at other times he could fall into a state bordering on lunacy'.[38]

A fortnight later – on 21 November – Kankrin replied that, for the government, the acquisition by the Treasury of landowners' estates was 'in general inconvenient' and that 'in any such case, imperial permission must be sought'.[39] In other words, there was not the slightest chance that either Kankrin or the Tsar would do anything to extricate Pushkin from his predicament.

According to the Russian Pushkinologist, Vadim V Kozhinov: 'From 5 November on Pushkin was working not on preparations for a duel, but on his investigation to determine who had written the 'diploma'. In particular, he asked his former Lycée classmate, M L Yakovlev, for an expert analysis of the 'diploma'.[40] Since leaving the Lycée, Yakovlev had become one of the country's foremost handwriting experts and had been employed as Director of the Imperial Typography since 1833.

Soon afterwards, no later than mid-November, Pushkin became convinced that Heeckeren had produced the 'diploma', although he also believed, and told Sollogub, that the initiator was Countess Nesselrode, the wife of the Minister of Foreign Affairs'.[41] Sollogub did not mention Countess Nesselrode's name in his memoirs, which he wrote in 1854, because at that stage her husband was still alive and would have been a formidable foe. Instead, Sollogub confined himself to his recollection that Pushkin: '…suspected a certain lady, whom he named to me, of having composed…the diploma'. According to Kozhinov: 'Many researchers have concluded that this meant Countess Nesselrode, beyond any doubt'.[42]

Another of Pushkin's contemporaries, the ambassador for Württemburg in St Petersburg, with the onomatopoeic title Prince Hohenlohe-Langenberg-Kirchberg, wrote in a memoir that there were two strands of opinion in the city about the anonymous letters. One was that the person behind them was Pushkin's old adversary, Uvarov. This was the view which enjoyed the public's greater confidence. The other opinion, he said, was: '...the government's opinion, based on the identity of the placement of the punctuation, on the peculiarities of the handwriting and the similarity of the paper, accuses Heeckeren'.[43]

Another prime suspect, regarded as 'by far the most likely perpetrator' by T J Binyon, was the 'malicious prankster', Prince Pyotr Dolgorukov, a civil servant at the Ministry of Education who was known to delight in stirring up mischief. Dolgorukov was the joker who had been seen mocking Pushkin at an evening soiree, displaying the two-fingered symbol for cuckoldry behind his back. No matter how compelling the arguments implicating Dolgorukov may be, as Binyon admits: 'Comparisons of his handwriting with that of the anonymous letters have, however, proved inconclusive, and as yet no conclusive proof of his guilt – or innocence – has been discovered'.[44]

Despite Pushkin's own unshakeable conviction that the van Heeckerens were responsible for having sent the 'diploma', this view is not shared by some more modern historians. For example, Binyon states that: 'Whoever the sender of the anonymous letters was, it seems highly unlikely, to say the least, that he (or she) was acting in concert with Heeckeren as has been maintained'.[45]

This opinion is also shared by Kozhinov, who wrote that: 'Like many other people, I doubt that Heeckeren was party to producing the 'diploma' – if only because it would have been extremely risky for him to undertake such a forgery'.[46] It would also have been unlikely that van Heeckeren, despite being well-informed about Petersburg society, would have known that much about the philandering duo, the Borkhs, and the fact that the wife was Natalya Pushkina's second cousin once removed.

The fact that the Tsar believed in Heeckeren's guilt 'might speak in favour of his involvement' not least because Nicholas 'had great possibilities for obtaining information'.[47] On the other hand, years after the event, Nicholas's son, Tsar Alexander II, was said to have loudly proclaimed at a private gathering: 'Well, now they know the author of the anonymous letters which were the cause of Pushkin's death; it was Nesselrode'.[48]

In his article *The Mystery of Pushkin's Death,* Kozhinov makes out a compelling case for the involvement of the Nesselrodes. To begin with, he notes that it was well known:

'that the Nesselrodes really hated Pushkin, who had been assigned to Ministry of Foreign Affairs service in his early years, beginning June 1817. On 8 July 1824, it was under pressure from Nesselrode that Alexander I dismissed the poet from service and exiled him to the village of Mikhailovskoye'.

When Nicholas I lifted Pushkin's exile, on 27 August 1826, and ordered Pushkin's return to the Ministry of Foreign Affairs, Nesselrode refused to pay Pushkin his allotted back salary of 5,000 roubles. There was known to be acute animosity between Pushkin and the Countess Nesselrode. The Nesselrodes and their circle represented the 'submarine monsters' Pushkin had risen up against: they were: 'the denizens of the high society morass, the ultra-reactionary, anti-popular, anti-national elite of courtiers…who had long harboured malice against the Russian national genius who opposed them and had now decided, by the most foul means, to get rid of him'.[49]

The conceivable involvement of the Nesselrodes does not, however, preclude the participation of van Heeckeren and d'Anthès: 'It should also be mentioned that the Nesselrodes were very well disposed towards Heeckeren and, for a special reason: d'Anthès was a relative or, more precisely, an in-law of Count Nesselrode'.[50] The Countess Nesselrode, in the words of well-informed observer, Pavel Vyazemsky, was: '…a powerful representative of the international *areopagus*, which held its sessions in the Paris suburb of St Germain, at the salon of Prince Metternich in Vienna, and at Countess Nesselrode's salon in Petersburg'. A former classmate of Pushkin's, M A Korff, who had observed Countess Nesselrode at close quarters, once remarked that: 'Her enmity was terrible and dangerous'.[51] Furthermore: 'The clash between Pushkin and the Nesselrode couple was other than 'personal' in nature…it was the most profound sort of confrontation – political, ideological and moral'.[52]

Just as the Countess Nesselrode hated Pushkin, he in turn: 'missed no opportunity to lampoon his stubborn antagonist, who could scarcely speak Russian, with epigrams and anecdotes'.[53] According to Pushkin's friend, Peter Vyazemsky, Pushkin detested the Countess Nesselrode even more than he did Fadey Bulgarin. There is no conclusive evidence linking the Nesselrode salon to the appearance of the 'diploma'. However, several well-known Pushkin scholars, from diverse viewpoints, have pointed up the likelihood of their participation.

One of these was the Pushkin archivist, Shchegolev, who wrote, in the 1928 edition of his research, that: '…the involvement of the wife of the Minister of Foreign Affairs was a bit too close'.[54] In 1938, the symbolist poet, Georgy Chulkov, concluded that: 'In M D Nesselrode's salon…the idea of the Russian people's right to an independent political role was excluded…they hated Pushkin because they discerned in him a national force, which was entirely alien to them in spirit'.[55] And, in 1956, the Soviet scholar, I L Andronnikov, asserted that: 'Countess Nesselrode's hatred for Pushkin was boundless…contemporaries suspected her of having composed the anonymous 'diploma'…there is almost no doubt she inspired that base document'.[56]

Kozhinov acknowledges that the views expressed in post-revolutionary Soviet scholarship might not always be totally reliable. But it is also the case that the poet, Vladislav Khodasevich, who was to become leader of the Berlin circle of Russian émigrés at the time of the Bolshevik revolution, had written an article in the émigré newspaper, entitled *Countess Nesselrode and Pushkin,* in which he wrote 'with great conviction' that the Countess had commissioned the 'diploma'.[57]

It is also the case that the People's Commissar of Foreign Affairs in the Bolshevik government, between 1918 and 1930, Georgy Chicherin – who worked closely with both Lenin and Trotsky – belonged to a family of prominent diplomats well-informed about what was going on in the Ministry of Foreign Affairs under Nesselrode. Chicherin's grandfather knew Pushkin personally and took it for granted that Countess Nesselrode was the initiator of the 'diploma'. However, in Chicherin's view, the person who carried out the malevolent endeavour was not van Heeckeren but an employee of the Ministry of Foreign Affairs known as F I Brunnov, who had served alongside Pushkin in Odessa in 1823-24. According to Vadim Kozhinov, Brunnov had 'annoyed the poet with his subservience to superiors'. In 1830, Brunnov became a 'special assignments officer' for Nesselrode.[58]

Regardless of which of these theories is correct, there is no doubt that Pushkin, instinct following his *tête à tête* with Natalya was to settle matters once and for all with those he regarded as his most immediate tormentors, the van Heeckerens, *père et fils*. The day after he received the anonymous letters, Pushkin issued his challenge to a duel. When it arrived at the Dutch Embassy, on the morning of Thursday, 5 November, d'Anthès was on duty with his regiment.

Van Heeckeren, the elder, received the letter in his absence and at midday called on Pushkin where he accepted the challenge on d'Anthès's behalf but requested a delay of 24 hours, to which Pushkin agreed. The following day, van Heeckeren paid a second visit to Pushkin. This time, he pleaded for a further week's grace and claimed that, although the challenge was accepted, he had not yet had the opportunity to speak to his adopted son. This statement is commonly thought to be a lie because d'Anthès' time on guard duty had ended at noon the previous day, allowing him plenty of time to convey the message.[59]

Equally, it might be argued that d'Anthès did not yet know, and that if he discovered van Heeckeren had been playing for time, could well have interpreted that as an act of cowardice. Either way, Pushkin acceded to van Heeckeren's request and agreed to postpone the duel for 15 days. At this point, we enter the realms of the bizarre: Van Heeckeren used the time available to make every possible effort to convince Pushkin to withdraw his challenge. Pushkin's wife and his closest friends also did all they could to avert the confrontation.

On Saturday, 7 November, Zhukovsky went to the Dutch Embassy to see van Heeckeren. D'Anthès was again on guard duty: at a regimental inspection on 4 November he had carried out his duties as troop commander so inefficiently that his Major-General, Grünewaldt, had issued him with five extra 24-hour guard duties – on 6, 8, 10, 12 and 14 November – each of which lasted from noon till noon the following day. Granted an audience with van Heeckeren, Zhukovsky was about to explain why he had taken on the role of intermediary, without Pushkin's knowledge, when van Heeckeren dropped the bombshell that d'Anthès was not in love with Natalya but rather with her older sister, Ekaterina.

According to Shchegolev's research, van Heeckeren even went

so far as to claim that d'Anthès had been: '...begging his father to consent to their marriage, but he, finding the marriage unsuitable, had not given his consent. Now, however, seeing that further obstinacy on his part led to a misunderstanding which threatened to have grievous consequences, he had finally given his consent'.[60] Though Zhukovsky did not realise, this was all a complete tissue of lies: d'Anthès had never considered marrying Natalya's sister, the whole scheme had been concocted by van Heeckeren in the hope that it might prevent the duel.

The reason for this was that he knew the ignominy which would follow if his activities over the previous months were exposed: 'It was only after he had painted, in the blackest terms, the consequences, both for his and for d'Anthès' career, of fighting a duel with so well-known a figure as Pushkin, that his protégé had consented to the stratagem'.[61] Thinking this astonishing *volte-face* allowed a way out, Zhukovsky hurried to tell Pushkin and was amazed at his reaction: instead of being pleased, he flew into a violent rage. He saw right through the deception and, as well as being irritated by Zhukovsky's interference: '...his rage was directed at d'Anthès and van Heeckeren, who, he believed, had taken the coward's way out by inventing the proposal of marriage'.[62]

Over the coming weeks, Pushkin's fury at this latest twist in what had now become an absurd charade remained unabated. Pushkin refused repeated attempts made both by Zhukovsky and Natalya's aunt, Ekaterina Zagryazhskaya – a former lady-in-waiting to the Empress – to broker an honourable settlement. It was only when Zhukovsky informed Pushkin of the revelation, fed to him by van Heeckeren, that d'Anthès had already seduced Ekaterina that Pushkin finally agreed to withdraw his challenge.

If this story was true (and with van Heeckeren that was always open to doubt) and Pushkin had refused to back down it would have left his sister-in-law in an invidious position: 'Other than the loss of Ekaterina's virginity, it is difficult to imagine 'a matter', which, if disclosed, would simultaneously avert the duel and do as much harm to d'Anthès honour as the anonymous letter had to Pushkin's'.[63]

Pushkin interpreted the official announcement that d'Anthès eventually made – that he was seeking the hand of Natalya Goncharova's sister, Ekaterina, in marriage – as a total capitulation by d'Anthès, even though he doubted it would ever happen. The announcement of the engagement caused a sensation in society and provoked: 'a flood of gossip…amazement was universal'.[64] Ekaterina Karamzina was reported to have said: 'It is unbelievable, this marriage…I mean!'. Her brother, Andrey, was equally astonished, saying: 'I wonder if I'm not dreaming, or at least whether d'Anthès wasn't in a dream when he made his move'. For Sofiya Bobrinskaya: 'It is some kind of mystery of love, of heroic self-sacrifice, it is Jules Janin, it is Victor Hugo. It is the literature of our day. It is exalted and ludicrous'.[65]

The big question in everyone's mind was what possible rationale could there be for d'Anthès' bewildering decision. The initial explanation offered up by van Heeckeren, that it was the logical outcome of d'Anthès devotion to Ekaterina, fooled nobody – his pursuit of Pushkin's wife, Natalya, had been talk of the town for months. His fall-back position, which gradually came to be accepted among van Heeckeren's social clique, was that d'Anthès had sacrificed himself in order to preserve Natalya's honour. In a letter he sent to Count Nesselrode, in March 1837 (a few weeks after Pushkin's death) van Heeckeren wrote, with what Binyon describes as: 'a barefaced unscrupulousness which is almost endearing', explaining that it was his 'high sense of morality which induced my son to put his future in chains in order the save the reputation of the woman he loved'.[66]

During the coming weeks leading up to what, if van Heeckeren was to be believed, amounted to a shotgun wedding – Pushkin's attention now turned to van Heeckeren himself. The duel with d'Anthès had initially been set to take place on 21 November but now that he had succeeded in making d'Anthès look ridiculous, Pushkin decided that, as Henri Troyat puts it:

'He had finished with d'Anthès, 'the puppet' all right; but Heeckeren, the man who pulled the strings needed separate treatment. The cancelled duel and last-minute marriage must not be allowed to give people the idea that Pushkin had been mistaken when he named the Netherlands Ambassador as the cause of the whole affair. By training his sights on van Heeckeren, Pushkin was trying to get at the Nesselrodes, Uvarovs, Gagarins and Dolgorukovs, the whole 'power elite' of the capital'.[67]

Notes

1   **Pushkin,** by T J Binyon, Harper Collins, 2002, p559

2   Shaw, op.cit. Letter 612, p763

2   **Pushkin's Button,** The Story of the Fatal Duel which killed Russia's Greatest Poet, By Serena Vitale, Translated from the Italian by Ann Goldstein and Jon Rothschild, Fourth Estate, 1999, p10

4   Vitale, ibid. p14

5   Grossman, op.cit. p173

6   Grossman, p174

7   Vitale, p15

8   Binyon, op.cit. p518

9   Binyon, p518

10   Binyon, p518

11   Binyon, p519

12   Binyon, p519

13   Binyon, p519

14   Binyon, p546

15   Binyon, p547

16   **A S Pushkin: A Biographical Sketch**, by V V Veresayev, Co-Operative Publishing Society of Foreign Workers in the USSR, Moscow, 1937, p51

17   Binyon, p564

18   Binyon, p560

19   Binyon, p560

20   Troyat, op.cit. p539

21   Troyat, p537

22   Troyat, p524

23   Grossman, op.cit. p112

24   Troyat, op.cit. p440

25   Grossman, op.cit. p70

26   Binyon, op.cit. p548

27   Binyon, op.cit. p555

28   Binyon, p555

29   Binyon, p556

30   Binyon, p558

31   Binyon, p516

32   Grossman, op.cit. p134

33   Binyon, op.cit. p561

34   Grossman, op.cit. p176

35   **About Pushkin** (from *My Half Century* - Selected Prose), By Anna Akhmatova, edited by Ronald Meyer, Ardis Publishers, New York, 2013, p222

36   **The Letters of Alexander Pushkin,** Three Volumes in One, translated and with an introduction by J Thomas Shaw, University of Wisconsin Press, 1967, p821

37 **Pushkin** by T J Binyon. Harper Collins. 2002. p568

38 Binyon, ibid., p568

39 Binyon, p568-89

40 **The Mystery of Pushkin's Death,** by Vadim V Kozhinov, Translated from the Russian by Rachel Douglas, Published in *Fidelio,* Journal of the Schiller Institute, Vol. 8 No. 3, Fall 1999; Special Edition *Alexander Pushkin: Russia's Poet of Universal Genius* on 200th anniversary of Pushkin's birth, p78

41 Kozhinov, ibid. p78

42 Kozhinov, p78

43 **About Pushkin** (from *My Half Century* - Selected Prose). By Anna Akhmatova, Edited by Ronald Meyer, Ardis Publishers, New York. 2013, footnote 38, p403

44 Binyon, op.cit. p565

45 Binyon, p565

46 Kozhinov, op.cit. p81

47 Kozhinov, p81

48 Kozhinov, p81

49 **The Sacred Lyre: Essays on the Life and work of Alexander Pushkin**, by Dmitry Blagoy, Raduga Publishers, English translation published in 1982, first published in Russian 1979, p402

50 Kozhinov, op.cit. p82

51 Kozhinov, p83

52 Kozhinov, p83

53 Kozhinov, p82

54 Kozhinov, p83

55 Kozhinov, p83

56 Kozhinov, p83

57 Kozhinov, p83

58 Kozhinov, p83

59 Binyon, op.cit. footnote, p566

60 Binyon, p569

61 Binyon, p570

62 Binyon, p570

63 Binyon, footnote, p575

64 Binyon, p584

65 Binyon, p585

66 Binyon, p585

67 **Pushkin,** by Henri Troyat, translated from the French by Nancy Amphoux, George, Allen & Unwin, 1974, p554.

Grinding his teeth and clenching his fists
Seemingly seized by some mysterious force
He at first starts to tremble, then splutters with hate
'So be it, miracle worker - just you wait!'

Pushkin, *The Bronze Horseman,* 1833[1]

'His hand upon his breast he presses
Softly, and falls, as, misty-eyed
His gaze not pain, but death expresses'.

Pushkin, *Eugene Onegin,* 1825-1832[2]

16 | Duel at Black River

The practise of duelling had become so popular in Russia by the beginning of the 18th century, and the number of casualties so high, that Peter the Great introduced a law in 1715 banning participation in duels and threatening death by hanging for those who took part (and survived). The whole point of a duel was not so much to kill the opponent - the aim was to restore one's perceived honour over some real or imagined insult by showing a willingness to risk a duel. As a result, most duels were in reality fought as a formality: of the 322 recorded to have taken place in Russia between at the end of the 19th century, for example, only 15 had a fatal outcome. Pushkin himself is thought to have taken part in 29 duels during his lifetime before his fatal encounter with d'Anthès. Pushkin wrote several drafts of his challenge to van Heeckeren. When he showed his friends Zhukovsky and Sollogub what he had written, they were both horrified. After Pushkin had called him in to his study, he closed the door behind him and said: 'I am going to read you my letter to Heeckeren senior. With the son, everything has been settled.

Now for the old boy'.[3]

As Pushkin read the letter aloud, Sollogub recalled: 'His lips were trembling, his eyes were bloodshot, he was terrifying to behold, and it was then I understood the reality of his African ancestry. What could I say to such an impassioned fury?' With the aid of Zhukovksy, Pushkin was eventually persuaded not to send his letter but he intimated that he would keep a copy, 'with the intention of using it later, if the occasion arose'.[4] The letter to van Heeckeren, written in French, is worth quoting verbatim, not least for its sheer venom:

Baron

First of all, permit me to summarise everything that has just taken place. The behaviour of your son had been known to me for a long time and could not be a matter of indifference to me, but since it was kept within the bounds of propriety and since, moreover, I knew how much on that score my wife deserved my trust and my respect, I contented myself with the role of an observer free to intervene when I might think proper. I well know that a handsome face, an unlucky passion, two years' perseverance always may end by producing some effect on a young woman's heart, and that then the husband, at least if he is not a fool, becomes quite naturally the confidant of his wife and the master of her conduct. I shall admit to you that I was not without misgivings. An incident, which at any other moment would have been very disagreeable, came quite fortunately to rescue me from the difficulty: I received anonymous letters. I saw that the moment had come, and I availed myself of it. You know the rest: I made your son play a role so ludicrous and pitiful that my wife, astonished at so much truckling, could not refrain from laughing, and that the emotion which she had perhaps come to feel in response to this great and sublime passion, faded into the coolest and most deserved disgust.

But you, Baron, will permit me to observe that your role in all this affair is not the most seemly. You, the representative of a crowned head, have paternally acted as the pander of your bastard, or the one so called; all the behaviour of this young man has been directed by you. You dictated the sorry jokes which he has just been reciting and the various things which he has taken a hand in writing. Like an obscene old woman, you would go and lie in wait for my wife on every corner, in order to speak to her of your son and when, ill with syphilis, he was kept home for treatments, you would say, vile man that you are, that he was dying of love for her. You would murmur to her: 'Give me back my son'. That is not all.

You see that I know all about it. But wait, that is not all: I have told you that the affair was getting complicated. Let us return to the anonymous letters. You well surmise that they may be of interest to you.

On November 2, you received a piece of news from your son which gave you much pleasure. He told you that I was angry, that my wife was afraid...that she was losing her head. You decided to strike a blow that you thought would be decisive. An anonymous letter was composed by you.

I received three copies of the half score which were delivered. This letter had been fabricated with so little caution that at first glance I was on the trail of the author. I did not trouble myself about it any further; I was sure of finding my knave. Sure enough, in less than three days of searching, I knew positively what to believe.

If diplomacy is the art of knowing what is done at others' houses and of making game of their plans, you will do me the justice to admit that you have been vanquished on all points. Now I am arriving at the object of my letter. Perhaps you desire to know what prevented me up to the present from dishonouring you in the eyes of our court and of yours. I shall tell you.

I am, you see, a good, unsophisticated person, but my heart is sensitive. A duel is no longer enough for me, and whatever may be its outcome, I shall not consider myself sufficiently avenged either by the death of your son, or by his marriage, which would seem to be a good joke (which, it must be added, troubles me very little), or finally by the letter which I have the honour to be writing you, and a copy of which I am keeping for my personal use. I want you yourself to take the trouble to find reasons which would suffice to make me pledge not to spit in your face, and to annihilate the last traces of this miserable affair, from which it will be easy for me to make an

THE MAN WHO SHOOK HIS FIST AT THE TSAR

excellent chapter in my history of cuckoldry.
I have the honour to be, Baron
Your most humble and most obedient servant
A Pushkin[5]

This letter to van Heeckeren did not survive intact and, in its original version, was never sent. However, Pushkin kept the letter and used it as the basis for the one which he did send to van Heeckeren in January 1837, which precipitated the duel. Some Pushkin scholars believe that the second letter Pushkin wrote on 21 November, also in French, was addressed to Count Benckendorff, knowing full well that it would immediately be passed on to the Tsar. However, the letter was addressed only 'Count' and some other historians believe it was addressed to Count Nesselrode, not Benckendorff. For example, Vadim Koshinov argues that: '… a letter accusing a citizen of a foreign country, never mind an ambassador, of composing the 'diploma' would have been addressed precisely to the Minister of Foreign Affairs'.[6] Either way, Pushkin thought better of sending it. Whether it was meant for Benckendorff or Nesselrode, Pushkin's second letter read:

Count!

I have just cause and believe myself obliged to inform Your Excellency of what has just taken place in my family. On the morning of 4 November, I received three copies of an anonymous letter, injurious to my honour and that of my wife. From the appearance of the paper, from the style of the letter, from the manner in which it was worded, I recognised from the first moment that it was written by a foreigner, by a man of high society, by a diplomat.

I started making enquiries. I learned that seven or eight persons had received, on the same day, a copy of the same letter, in a double envelope, the inner of which was sealed and addressed to me. The majority of the persons who received them, suspecting a vile deed, did not send them to me. People in general were indignant at such a despicable, such an unprovoked insult. But while repeating that the conduct of my wife has been irreproachable, they said that the pretext of this infamy was the assiduous court which M d'Anthès has been paying her.

It did not suit me to see the name of my wife linked on this occasion with the name of anyone whatever. I had M d'Anthès so informed. The Baron de Heeckeren came to my house and accepted a duel for M d'Anthès, asking for a delay of fifteen days.

It turns out that in the interval granted, M d'Anthès fell in love with my sister-in-law, Mlle. Goncharova, and that he made her a marriage proposal. Public report having informed me of this, I had the request made to M d'Archaic (M d'Anthès's second) that my challenge should be regarded as not having taken place. Meanwhile I made sure that the anonymous letter was from M Heeckeren, which I believe it my duty to call to the attention of the government and of society.

Being the sole judge and defender of my honour and that of my wife, and consequently asking for neither justice nor vengeance, I neither can nor will provide anyone whatever with the proofs for what I assert.

In any case, I hope, Count, that this letter is a proof of the respect and of the trust which I bear toward you.

With these feelings, I have the honour to be, Count, your most humble and obedient servant.[7]

Two days after Pushkin had written these letters – neither of which were actually sent – a conversation took place between Pushkin and the Tsar. This was arranged for Pushkin by Zhukovsky and took place on 23 November, with the Chief of Police Benckendorff in attendance. As Vadim Koshinov writes: 'Unfortunately, the content of this conversation of theirs, as well as the next one, which took place three days before the duel, can only be guessed'.[8]

The Tsar was already aware of d'Anthès pursuit of Natalya and the fact that he had suddenly become engaged to her sister, Ekaterina. It may be that the Tsar did not know about Pushkin's challenge and the reason for its withdrawal, since duelling was meant to be a capital offense. On the other hand, both Zhukovsky and Benckendorff did know. Some reports suggest that, at Pushkin's audience with the Tsar, he promised the Emperor that he would not allow matters to reach the point of a duel with d'Anthès - though what was said about the content of his letters to van Heeckeren and the 'Count' is not known.

Nor do we know anything about how the Tsar responded to the insinuation in the anonymous 'diploma' that the Tsar himself was as infatuated with Pushkin's wife as d'Anthès. What we do know is that for the next two months, until 23 January 1837, Pushkin held to his promise not to take any further form of precipitate action. But this did not stop d'Anthès from continuing to press his attentions on Natalya. At one society reception held at the Vyazemsky's, on the day before New Year's Eve - attended by Pushkin, Natalya, d'Anthès and Ekaterina - d'Anthès went out of his way to provoke Pushkin by moving deliberately to Natalya's side and staying there the whole evening. Another guest at the reception, Sofiya Karamzina, described the scene as follows: 'Pushkin is continuing to behave in the most foolish and absurd manner possible; he snarls like a wildcat and gnashes his teeth every time he mentions the subject of the marriage'.[9]

D'Anthès' marriage to Ekaterina Goncharova eventually took place on 10 January in a dual Roman Catholic and Russian Orthodox ceremony. Standing in as 'father' and 'mother' to d'Anthès at the wedding were van Heeckeren and the Countess Nesselrode. Among the witnesses were Count Stroganov, chair of the Moscow censorship committee which had condemned Chaadayev; the French attaché, d'Archaic, who was a cousin of d'Anthès and soon to act as second in the duel with Pushkin; and two of d'Anthès' fellow officers, Captain Betancourt and Colonel Poletika, the husband of Pushkin's bitter enemy, Idlaya Poletika. Idalya was also an illegitimate daughter of Count Stroganov.

Pushkin refused to attend and delegated his wife to represent him at the ceremony. Natalya left immediately after the service and d'Anthès was no longer permitted to enter the Pushkin household. The newlyweds moved into van Heeckeren's extremely well-appointed private residence on Nevsky Prospect. Immediately after the wedding, van Heeckeren made a series of attempts to smooth relations with Pushkin - not for altruistic reasons but because he suspected that an ongoing rift between the two households would stimulate rumours.

According to T J Binyon: 'He got the newly married couple to call at the Moika apartment; they were not received. He made d'Anthès write to Pushkin, expressing the hope that the past might be forgotten ...Pushkin did not bother to answer. He made d'Anthès write again. Pushkin took the letter unopened to Ekaterina Ivanovna, intending to ask her to return it to d'Anthès, but, meeting Heeckeren, attempted to give it to him. Heeckeren refused, because it was not addressed to him. Furious, Pushkin threw it in his face, saying, 'You shall take it, you scoundrel'.[10]

Because of the intensity of the ongoing antagonism between Pushkin, van Heeckeren and d'Anthès, it is understandable that, as Vadim Kozhinov describes it: 'It cannot be denied that this historical tragedy had the *superficial* appearance of a family one, and so it was seen, and continues to be, by the great majority of people'.[11] D'Anthès' provocative behaviour and Pushkin's indignant response were witnessed at a series of high profile social gatherings over the entire Christmas and New Year period. And this convinced many onlookers, among them some of his closest friends, that Pushkin's anger was entirely motivated by excessive and unfounded jealousy of d'Anthès.

There is even a hint of this in Sofiya Vyazemskaya's description of what was happening with Pushkin as being 'very strange' because it could not be explained solely by the facts as she knew them. What most of these observers were entirely unaware of was that looming beyond the domestic tragedy of the Pushkin-Natalya-d'Anthès entanglement, a much more serious collision was imminent on the nexus involving Pushkin, the Nesselrode salon - and the Tsar himself.

As Vadim Koshinov explains: 'The partisans of the *family* version of the duel maintain that d'Anthès and Heeckeren, supposedly having learned of Pushkin's promise to the Tsar not to resort to a duel (and this is, it must be said, a lightweight supposition), acted ever more blatantly because they thought they could do so with impunity, thus driving the poet into a state of extreme agitation…', the consequence of which was that he finally sent his insulting letter to Heeckeren.[12]

But the actual trigger for this improvident gesture - just as it was to be for Evgeny in *The Bronze Horseman* - was not d'Anthès' insufferable conduct. The major transformation in Pushkin's attitude was an encounter with the Tsar which came about on the night of 23-24 January when he attended one of the highlights of the winter season - the annual ball which took place at the house of Count Ivan Vorontsov-Dashkov and the

Countess Alexandra Kirilovna, favoured both by the cream of St Petersburg society and the imperial court.

The Tsar was present at the ball and at some stage in the evening met Natalya. During a brief conversation, he counselled her to have a care for her reputation, a comment which she repeated to Pushkin. Nicholas also talked with Pushkin and is again thought to have touched upon the rumours circulating about Natalya. Disguising his actual feelings, Pushkin thanked the Tsar for expressing such an interest, but '…gratitude was the last thing on his mind'.[13]

The Tsar had made similar remarks when they last met in November and then Pushkin had been furious that, in his view, 'the emperor should have usurped a right which he felt to be his alone'.[14] When Nicholas repeated his suggestion that Natalya should perhaps be more careful about her public conduct with d'Anthès, Pushkin's anger returned 'in darker, more dangerous form, exacerbated by the conviction that his marital problems were the sole topic of conversation in St Petersburg'.[15]

When the Tsar responded to Pushkin's half-hearted response with: 'But could you have expected anything else from me?', Pushkin reportedly replied: 'Not only could, Sire, but, to speak frankly, I suspected you too of paying court to my wife'.[16] At the same event, d'Anthès' behaviour became ever more outrageous: 'he followed Natalya around the ball, danced several times with her, partnering her in a quadrille; and going in after to supper with his wife, said loudly and sarcastically to Ekaterina, within Pushkin's earshot 'Come my lawful one'.[17]

Spoken in French, the wording '*Allons, ma légitime*' meaning lawfully-wedded wife, obviously hinted that d'Anthès also had another, illegitimate wife or mistress. Later, d'Anthès was said to have leaned over to Natalya and, with what sounds like a suspiciously well-rehearsed aside, sleazily remarked that he'd heard his wife and sister-in-law both had the same chiropodist. But now he knew: '*…que votre cor est plus beau que celui de ma femme*', playing on the fact that the French words for corn, *cor*, and body, *corps*, both have the same pronunciation.

During a more agreeable interlude, Pushkin met one of the highest-ranking officers in the Russian army. This was General Karl Toll, who had taken part in the suppression of the Pugachev

Revolt. Two days later, Pushkin sent a copy of his *The History of Pugachev* to General Toll, together with a letter thanking him for 'the attention with which you have honoured my first historical effort' and noting that his interest 'fully rewards me for the indifference of the public and the critics'.[18]

Pushkin finished the letter with a statement uncannily pertinent to his own situation: 'No matter how strong the prejudice of ignorance may be, no matter how avidly slander may be accepted, one word spoken by a person such as you destroys them forever'. He then goes on to add: 'Genius discloses the truth at first glance and "the truth is mightier than the Tsar" says the Holy Writ'.[19]

In the view of Vadim Koshinov, it seems more than likely that this reference to the Tsar is connected to the conversation Pushkin had with Nicholas the previous night: 'But that, of course, is only a surmise. What is indisputable, is that it was precisely the conversation with the Emperor (whatever its nature may have been) that *determined* the shift in the poet's mind and conduct'.[20]

On Monday, 25 January, the day immediately after Pushkin had spoken with the Tsar, Pushkin went back to the letters he had written to van Heeckeren and to the 'Count' - either Benckendorff or Nesselrode - two months earlier. The one he addressed directly to van Heeckeren was now subjected to some revision. It was shorter and more concise but he had already decided that it would now be sent, regardless of the promise he had made to the Tsar.

Much of the tone and content of the new letter is the same as he had written in his earlier drafts but it now includes direct references to the incidents of the previous evening, including the sentence: 'You probably dictated the sorry jokes he has just been reciting and the vacuous things which he has taken a hand in writing'. The main change is in the final paragraph, where Pushkin now wrote:

'You well realize, Baron, that after all this I cannot have my family to have anything to do with yours. On this condition, I consented not to follow up this filthy business and not to dishonour you in the eyes of our court and of yours, as I had the power and intention of doing. I do not care for my wife to hear any more of your paternal exhortations. I cannot permit your son, after the despicable conduct he has demonstrated, to dare to speak a word to my wife, nor still less to recite guardhouse puns to her and play at devotion and unlucky passion, for he is only a coward and only a scoundrel. I am therefore obliged to address myself to you, in order to pray you to put an end to this little game, if you desire to avoid a new scandal, from which most certainly I shall not shrink'.[21]

The whole tenor of the letter was so deliberately offensive that, when it arrived the following morning, van Heeckeren was horrified by what he read and, just as he had done in November, struggled to work out an adequate response. In a letter he later wrote to his superior, the Dutch Foreign Minister, Verstolk van Stolen, van Heeckeren explained the lengthy delay he took in replying to Pushkin as being due to the late arrival of his challenge. This was untrue. The real reason was that Pushkin's letter put him in a predicament which was only resolved when he went to dine with his close ally in the Nesselrode clique, recognised arbiter of disputes within the aristocracy, and one of the richest men in Russia, Count Grigory Stroganov.

Not wishing to be governed solely by his own opinion, he wrote: 'I at once consulted my friend, Count Stroganov - his view being in accordance with mine, I communicated the letter to my son and a cartel was addressed to M Pushkin'. In an almost identical latter sent to Nesselrode two days later, he adds the detail that d'Anthès was taking up Pushkin's challenge rather than himself because he had asked for it 'as a proof of my affection, to give him the preference'.[22]

On the afternoon of 26 January, d'Anthès appointed d'Archaic as his second for the duel. d'Archaic called on Pushkin and handed him a letter from van Heeckeren in which he said that the contents of Pushkin's letter had been 'so far beyond the limits of what is acceptable' that he refused to reply to all its details. 'It only remains for me to inform you' he said, 'that Vicomte d'Archaic will call on you to arrange with you the place where you will meet with Baron Georges Heeckeren and that this *rencontre* will not admit of any delay'.[23]

Pushkin waved the letter aside but accepted the verbal challenge delivered by d'Archaic on d'Anthès' behalf. Having dragged on for months, when there seemed to be no way out of the quagmire into which Pushkin's life had descended, matters now moved to a rapid conclusion. The morning after Pushkin had accepted d'Anthès's challenge, he rose early, drank tea and sat down to write. A letter came from d'Archaic, requesting that Pushkin send his second to discuss arrangements. This was a problem for Pushkin because the person he had asked to act as his own second, Vladimir Sollogub, was no longer available: he had been posted to Kharkov to join the staff of the new Governor General, Count Alexander Stroganov.

To an extent, Sollogub's absence was to Pushkin's advantage: he doubted Sollogub's resolve and: '…did not want anyone who would insist on reconciliation or run to Zhukovsky with news of the deal'.[24] It was also important that he chose a person who would either not be overly concerned about being arrested - acting as second in a duel was regarded as a criminal act - or who would be immune to prosecution by virtue of their diplomatic status. This clearly was the case both for d'Anthès's second, d'Archaic - the French attaché - and, of course, van Heeckeren - the Dutch ambassador. According to one account, there was a reason Pushkin had deliberately chosen not to enlist the services of a second right away and that was so that he could more easily outmanoeuvre the authorities.[25]

If so, the ploy did not work as he had hoped: the previous evening he had attended a ball at the Razumovskys', where he appeared calm and was seen to be laughing, chatting and cracking jokes. At this reception, he recognised one of the diplomats from the English embassy, Arthur Magenis, who, like Pushkin, was a regular at the salon of Dolly Ficquelmont. Because of his diplomatic status, Magenis would have been immune from prosecution if he had agreed to act as second in the duel. Unfortunately for Pushkin, Magenis was not at all enthusiastic about taking on this role and, according to DuVernet: 'Magenis went directly to the government's Third Section and the highest government representative he knew, advising them of what Pushkin was asking for'.[26]

In the DuVernet account, when this information was communicated to the Tsar, he advised Benckendorff to send a regiment right away to arrest the offenders and stop the challenge. What the Tsar did not know was that Benckendorff already knew what was going on, from van Heeckeren himself. According to DuVernet: '…together they conspired with Count Nesselrode, Count Stroganov, Count Uvarov, and several others who agreed that having one less enemy of the aristocracy, to the autocracy, and to God would not be such a bad thing for Russia'.[27]

This coterie then weighed up the consequences and came to the conclusion that: '…if Pushkin came out of it without a scratch, then he would go to prison; and, after all, d'Anthès was a trained soldier and had a decent aim. If d'Anthès survived, that would suit their plans just fine. Benckendorff feigned his compliance before leaving the Tsar's quarters, but then did nothing'.[28]

Pressed by d'Archaic to comply with the duelling code, which required that he officially name his second, Pushkin set off to call on his close friend, Klementy Rosset, who had already agreed in November to act as second, so long as no attempt was made at reconciliation. In the event, the Rossets were not at home, so Pushkin ordered the coachman to drive on to Panteleymonskaya Street nearby, where another of his friends from the Lycée, Konstantin Danzas, lived: 'Like Rosset, Danzas was an unmarried military man - a lieutenant-colonel in the engineers - qualities which made him suitable for a second's role. But, unlike Rosset, he was not part of any of the sets, social or literary, which Pushkin frequented'.[29] This was an added advantage, because it meant that he was less likely to spread news of what was going on and set the alarm bells ringing.

In some accounts, Pushkin met Danzas on Panteleymonskaya Street by accident and merely asked him to be the witness to a conversation he was about to have with d'Archaic at the French Embassy, without any mention of a duel. Others discount the chance nature of this meeting, or that it ever took place: they believe that Pushkin had already enlisted Danzas as his second and that the story of the chance encounter was a fiction, intended to minimise Danzas's involvement should the duel result in a court-martial. Either way, Pushkin and Danzas then set off to visit d'Archaic and finalise the conditions of the duel.

According to Vikenty Veresayev: 'When Danzas brought Pushkin these conditions in written form, Pushkin did not bother to read them but agreed to everything and sent Danzas off to buy pistols'.[30] Pushkin then sat down to work on his magazine,

The Contemporary and opened a book he had just bought by Alexandra Ishimova *The History of Russia in Tales for Children*. Ishimova was a translator who had agreed to provide translations for the next issue of his journal of writings by an English poet who Pushkin admired. The poet was Barry Cornwall, the pseudonym of Bryan Waller Procter, and the translations Pushkin had asked for were from the edition of Cornwall's work, *Dramatic Scenes*.

At 2.30 in the afternoon the two seconds, Danzas and d'Archaic, signed the protocol they had drawn up, setting out the conditions for the duel. It read:

— The two adversaries will be placed twenty paces apart, each five paces from the two barriers which will be ten paces apart.

— Each armed with a pistol, at a given signal they may, while advancing on one another, but without ever passing the barrier, make use of their arms.

— It is further agreed that once a shot has been fired, neither of the two adversaries will be allowed to change position, so that the one who has fired shall in every case be exposed to the fire of his adversary at the same distance.

— After the two parties have fired, if there is no result, the affair will begin again as before, the adversaries being placed at the same distance of twenty paces, and the same barriers and same conditions being maintained.

— The seconds will be the intermediaries responsible for any communication between the adversaries on the ground.[31]

At the appointed hour, Pushkin met Danzas at Wolff's pastry shop on Nevsky Prospect and they both set off by sleigh. They drove through the snow to the agreed venue for the duel - the Kommendantskaya Dacha at Chernaya Rechka. Both parties arrived at about half-past-four, where: '...the skies were clear, but the wind had got up, and there were fifteen degrees of frost'.[32]

In Pushkin's day, seven different types of pistol duel were recognised in Europe and the rules for each were set down in a recognised text, the canonical *Essay on the Duel*, by Count Châteauvillard. The two seconds appointed for the duel between Pushkin and d'Anthès, Danzas and d'Archaic, had chosen the third option, known as *advancing*, where the adversaries are placed 35 to 40 paces apart.

At the command, they advance towards the barrier which is

10 paces in front of them and they may fire at any time after the command has been given. On the day of Pushkin's final duel, however, they had ignored one of the cardinal rules: that the adversaries should never be fewer than 15 paces apart. If Pushkin and d'Anthès had both advanced fully to the barriers before firing, there would only have been 10 paces between them. When d'Anthès fired his shot, there were eleven.

Describing the scene, Veresayev writes: 'The two seconds and d'Anthès began stamping a broad path in the snow along which the two opponents were to advance. Pushkin, wrapped in a bearskin coat, remained sitting on a snowdrift, waiting impatiently. The seconds paced out the required distance on the path, laid their fur coats in the snow to mark the barriers, and began loading their pistols'.[33]

D'Anthès had a pair of pistols made by Karl Ulbricht of Dresden, which d'Archaic had borrowed from Ernest de Brabante, the son of the French ambassador. Pushkin's successor as Russia's most-loved poet, Mikhail Lermontov, was killed in a duel by the same set of pistols three years later, on 18 February 1840. The guns were loaded with 20 grams of gunpowder and paper wads which, in this case, were made from lottery tickets. The bullets were made of lead balls packed down on top of this charge. Danzas gave the signal to start the duel with a wave of his hat. Like so much else about the story of Pushkin's life, and indeed his own writings, what happened next is open to a number of different interpretations.

According to Veresayev: 'Pushkin quickly advanced to his barrier, halted and began to take aim. But, at the same time, d'Anthès, who was still one pace away from his barrier, fired. Pushkin fell on the greatcoat that marked his barrier. He lay motionless, face downwards. D'Anthès and the seconds came running to him. Pushkin came to, raised his head, and said: 'Wait, I feel I have enough strength to shoot'.[34]

D'Anthès then returned to his place and, as was permissible under the rules, took his stand sideways to minimise the target. Veresayev again: 'Pushkin rose to his knees in a crouching posture and began to aim. He was a long time taking aim. At length a shot rang out. D'Anthès fell. Pushkin dropped his pistol and shouted: 'Bravo!'. Then he again fell senseless in the snow. However, it was only the violent shock that had knocked d'Anthès off his feet. The bullet had pierced the fleshy part of his arm and struck a button on his trousers. The button had saved him'.[35]

In his fictionalised account of the duel, *Death of a Poet,* Leonid Grossman explains what happened, through the eyes of d'Archaic, as follows:

'The poet obviously expected d'Anthès to advance to the barrier, intending to discharge his weapon at that moment. D'Anthès had to frustrate this design. His military training and the experience gained in active service gave him an indubitable strategic superiority over the swashbuckling poet. His victory in the duel was not due only to his marksmanship, as Pushkin probably imagined, but also to his correct manoeuvring after the signal, a matter which apparently never occurred to the poet, and which was the cause of his death and defeat. D'Anthès followed a correct tactical procedure: by deliberately dawdling on his way to the barrier and shooting suddenly, he forestalled his enemy's fire. Aware of the fact that a fatal outcome was inevitable, he aimed ruthlessly at the body, a shot that might cause instant death'.[36]

When d'Anthès was obliged to return to the barrier to allow Pushkin to take his shot, d'Anthès' superior training again counted: he took up the classic 'second position'. This meant that he: '…turned his right side towards his opponent, thus offering a smaller target, and covering his breast with his right arm, he laid the barrel of his discharged pistol to the side of his face, forming a natural and permissible shield in this position. He was not omitting a single detail permitted by the rules, and to this he owed his life'.[37]

Pushkin had been wounded in the stomach and the bullet had shattered his sacrum, the triangular pelvic bone at the base of the spine: 'In the abdominal cavity, fragments of bone were pressing against the intestines. In such cases, the first requirement of medicine is to afford the bowels complete rest, to stop their action by means of opium'.[38] But that is not what happened. After being stretchered back to his apartment on the Moika Embankment and taken into his study, he was attended to by a team of physicians. One of these was Nikolay Arendt, the Tsar's surgeon, who '…for some utterly incomprehensible reason…

THE MAN WHO SHOOK HIS FIST AT THE TSAR

prescribed a clyster for the patient' (whereby a fluid is injected into the lower bowel by way of the rectum).[39]

The result of this treatment, Veresayev notes: '…was horrifying. Pushkin's eyes rolled wildly and seemed ready to start out of their sockets; his face was bathed in cold sweat; his hands grew cold. Despite all efforts of will, he uttered such cries that everyone was horror-stricken'.[40] At one point, he asked his valet to bring him a pistol from the drawer so that he could shoot himself, because the suffering had become so unbearable. He died after two days of excruciating pain. Meantime, news of the duel had spread very rapidly throughout the city. A large crowd began to gather on the pavement outside Pushkin's apartment. The size of the crowd became so great that Danzas called upon the Preobrazhensky Guards to place sentries by the entrance, to allow visitors to come and go without hindrance. By this stage: 'A throng of worshippers, friends and inquisitive strangers filled the antechamber, the stairway, the street outside. One old man told his neighbours: 'Lord, I can remember the death of Field Marshal Kutusov! They didn't make such a fuss over him!'.[41]

The dimensions of the crowd outside grew so large, that:
'The Moika Embankment, in front of the house where Pushkin had died, presented a spectacle absolutely unique for those times. Crowds of people in ever growing numbers came pouring like a tide to pay the last salute to Pushkin. According to the testimony of eye-witnesses, from thirty to fifty thousand people came to see Pushkin in his coffin. Coaches came driving to the Moika from all ends of the city. Those taking cabs simply said "To Pushkin's" to indicate the address'.[42]
What was noticeable about this crowd, however, was that:
'the high nobility were conspicuous by their absence. Those who thronged to Pushkin's coffin were students, professional men, government officials of lower rank, traders, the "commoners" - in short, the radical middle class, then only just arising in Russian society. It was at Pushkin's funeral that the radical middle class first appeared in the public arena and made itself felt as a social force'.[43]
By contrast, the doyens of St Petersburg high society completely shunned Pushkin. Instead, they headed to the Dutch Embassy, to congratulate van Heeckeren: 'The Netherlands Embassy was

thronged with distinguished visitors. A long line of carriages stretched before the residence. Count and Countess Nesselrode, and Count and Countess Stroganov were permanent fixtures in the Heeckeren dining-room. There were expressions of compassion for poor, sweet Ekaterina, so sorely tried in the first days of her marriage, and of felicitation for d'Anthès, who had freed Russia of a notorious liberal'.[44]

The outburst of public indignation at Pushkin's death both amazed and frightened the Tsar. At first, he had shown little concern at the death of Russia's greatest ever poet but had completely exonerated d'Anthès. His younger brother, the Grand Duke Michael had said 'Good riddance!' when he heard the news. Nicholas was very soon forced to revise this attitude by the force of public opinion and to make out that he too was deeply distressed by what had happened and to acknowledge that Pushkin's death was a great loss to the nation. D'Anthès was cashiered and expelled from Russia, Heeckeren was forced to vacate his apartment on the Nevsky Prospect, auction his belongings and return to Holland in disgrace.

However, at the same time as these relatively meek punishments were meted out to d'Anthès and van Heeckeren, the Tsar acted with the utmost haste to prevent the manifestation of public grief and anger which had accompanied Pushkin's death from boiling over into something more dangerous. For example, the newspapers were strictly instructed to observe what was described as 'a suitable discretion and tone of propriety'. Benckendorff ordered the censors to suppress all obituary notices.

When the literary supplement to the obscure journal, *The Russian Veteran,* slipped through the net and published a short obituary notice, framed in black - the only publication which managed to escape the censors - it was reprimanded for saying that 'The sun of our poetry has set' and that 'Pushkin has perished in the midst of a great career'. Its author, Krayevsky, was summoned by the chair of the Board of Censors, Pushkin's old adversary, Prince Dundukov, and told:

'I must inform you that the Minister [Uvarov] is very, very displeased with you. What is the meaning of this article about Pushkin? What is this black border around the obituary of a man who had no official rank and no administrative position? The sun of our poetry! Pray, why this honour? 'Pushkin died in the prime of his magnificent career!' What career? Sergey Semyonovich (Uvarov) very rightly said, 'Was Pushkin a general, a military chief, a minister, a statesman?' He died before he was forty...writing does not constitute a magnificent career'.[45]

In St Petersburg, Uvarov issued instructions that university professors and their students should not be allowed to leave their classes for the funeral. Benckendorff banned the first performance of Pushkin's play, *The Covetous Knight,* and the police were ordered to confiscate and destroy all copies of a new portrait of Pushkin, framed in black and captioned: '*The Fire has gone out on the Altar*'.[46]

Despite these drastic measures, Pushkin's works began to sell like hotcakes in Alexander Smirdin's bookshop: 'The latest edition of *Eugene Onegin* became impossible to find. The shop took an incredible sum of forty thousand roubles in two days. Benckendorff did not like it. Hitherto, the Russian people had never wept or rejoiced except on order from the Tsar. And here they were taking an initiative. Weeping without having been told to do so. Venturing to express their own opinion. It smelled of revolt. What would it be like on the day of the funeral?'. Troyat Benckendorff's exact views on the subject, were published the following year in his *Report on Police Activities in 1837.* It reads:

'At the beginning of the year, our celebrated poet Pushkin died of an injury received in a duel. Pushkin had a double personality: He was a great poet and a great liberal, the enemy of all authority...These two sides of Pushkin's character determined the identity of his advocates. They formed a circle, composed of all the literary figures and liberals in society. Both groups reacted keenly, energetically, to Pushkin's death; there was a remarkable congregation of mourners around his body; there was a move to give him a state burial...It was difficult to know whether these gestures were intended to honour Pushkin the liberal or Pushkin the poet. In this uncertainty, and taking into consideration the view of right-minded people, i.e. that there was a danger that this so-called 'popular' expression of the grief of the crowd upon the poet's death might develop into a deplorable spectacle of triumph for the liberals, the executive office considered itself bound to adopt secret measures to suppress all honours. This was done'.[47]

In the official announcement of the details for Pushkin's funeral, mourners were requested to go to the Cathedral of St Isaac (inside the Admiralty) at 11am on 1 February. Pushkin's body was due to be conveyed from the house to the cathedral in the afternoon of 31 January, but because of police fears about the size of the crowd which might gather, the authorities ordered that the coffin be removed, not to St Isaac's but to the Church of the Holy Face, which forms the centre-piece of the cresent-shaped riding school and stables of the Horse Guards Regiment.

On the evening of 31 January, under instruction from Benckendorff (and, more than likely, the Tsar) police arrived in numbers and occupied the apartment on the Moika, where they removed Pushkin's body and took it to the Konyushennaya [Horse Stable] Church. Military patrols were posted in the houses adjoining Pushkin's apartment, while groups of Benckendorff's spies hung around the entrance. On the day of the funeral service the church was cordoned off by police and only those having special invitation cards were admitted. Mourners who had received invitations to attend a service at St Isaac's, arrived to find the doors closed. The service held in the church adjoining the stables was witnessed only by people in uniform or holding specially issued tickets:

'The little church was overflowing with an apathetic crowd of epaulets, decorations, spurs, lorgnettes, high headdresses and white gloves, Courtiers, generals, ambassadors, princesses. Count Ficquelmont was there, and de Brabante, the French ambassador - the only one who had seen fit to pay respects to Pushkin in his coffin - and the hideous, livid Uvarov, squirming from the pricks of indigestion or conscience...
Among those absent were the ambassadors of England and Greece - diplomatically ill, perhaps; Baron Heeckeren, who was not invited, and Liebermann, the Prussian ambassador, who would have considered it degrading to attend the funeral of a "liberal".'[48]

The arrangements which Benckendorff made to ensure that Pushkin's coffin was transferred to its final resting place, next to his mother at the family estate in Pskov, were every bit as meticulous: 'Benckendorff had stage-managed the proceedings with maniacal attention to detail. Everything was to take place at night. In secret. With police guards. A revolution can be ignited so quickly'.[49]

At midnight on 3 February, three troikas drew up in front of the church in Konyushennaya Square: 'A police officer climbed into the first. The coffin, tied with stout rope and stout straps and covered with tarpaulin went into the second, along with Nikita Kozlov - Pushkin's old servant, who had been with him since childhood and who had followed him into exile. The third troika was occupied by Pushkin's old friend, Alexander Turgenev, who then accompanied Pushkin on his final journey. When the cortège arrived at Pskov, on the evening of 4 February, the local governor was presented with a message, from the Tsar:

> 'It is the will of His Majesty the Emperor that you forbid all special events, all receptions, in short, all ceremonies other than those normally performed in connection with the funeral of a gentleman, as dictated by the rites and customs of our religion. I should add that the funeral has already taken place here'.[50]

The letter had been signed by the Tsar on 2 February and sent from St Petersburg. The governor showed the letter to Turgenev in confidence. In March 1837, a month or so after Pushkin's funeral, d'Archaic received a report from his superior, the Baron de Brabante, detailing the outcome of the proceedings which had taken place in St Petersburg, on 3 February, against the participants in the duel. Its verdict was handed down on the 19 February:

> 'Your friend George de Heeckeren (d'Anthès)', Brabante wrote: '… had to hear some stern strictures passed on him before he was given his freedom, bought at the price of banishment'.

Initially, the court martial's sentence was based on the ancient military articles and condemned him to death by hanging. But the commanders of the Guards regiments, Brabante continued:

> '…taking into account the youth of the condemned man, recommended that reduction to the ranks and transfer to a distant garrison should be substituted for the gallows'.[51]

D'Archaic was escorted out of Russia on 2 February, in order to avoid any possible diplomatic embarrassment. Pushkin's second,

Danzas, who was charged with having failed to prevent the duel, was handed a sentence of two months' guardhouse arrest. When d'Anthès left St Petersburg for the last time as Private Heeckeren, on 19 March 1837, with a police escort to take him to the border, he happened to be seen by Pushkin's friend, Turgenev, who reported that he was sitting in a sleigh 'wearing a cap embroidered with silk or gold thread and looking in very high spirits'.[52]

Count Stroganov, who had encouraged van Heeckeren to issue a challenge following receipt of Pushkin's letter - and who also paid the costs of Pushkin's funeral - later wrote to van Heeckeren: 'When your son Georges learns that I have the jar (a crystal vase given as a present to Stroganov from Heeckeren) tell him, too, that his Uncle Stroganov is keeping it as a monument, to remind him of the outstanding noble and loyal conduct he displayed during his last month in Russia'.[53]

On 14 March 1837, the Dutch Foreign Minister, Verstolk van Soelen, gave van Heeckeren permission to leave St Petersburg as soon as his replacement had reached Russia. There had been threats from the public to smash the embassy windows. Although the *beau monde* of Russian society continued to take van Heeckeren's side, the Tsar's opinion had hardened against him: the extent of the ambassador's involvement in the whole sordid affair was becoming more widely known and this could reflect badly on the Tsar.

In a letter to his brother, the Grand Duke Michael, written on 3 February, Nicholas acknowledged that: 'This incident has given rise to a host of speculations, extraordinarily stupid for the most part, of which the censure of Heeckeren's behaviour is alone justified and deserved; he did indeed behave like a vile blackguard'. However, when Zhukovsky requested that Nicholas issue a special imperial receipt immediately after Pushkin's death, in order that Pushkin's substantial debts could be paid off and to provide for his family - as he had done after Karamzins' death - the Tsar refused.[54]

He did grant that the debts be paid, that a pension be paid to Natalya, and that Pushkin's works be published at government expense but when Zhukovsky asked that Pushkin's achievement be celebrated in the same manner as Karamzin's, Nicholas said: 'My dear fellow, listen, I will do everything that I can for

Pushkin, but I will not write as I did for Karamzin; we forced Pushkin to die like a Christian, but Karamzin lived and died like an angel'.[55]

Later Nicholas remarked to Dmitry Dashkov, the Deputy Minister of Justice: 'What a crackbrain Zhukovsky is! He pesters me to appoint the same pension for Pushkin's family as for Karamzin's. He will not understand Karamzin was a man who was almost a saint, but what was Pushkin's life like?'.[56] Zhukovsky was to get another shock when he imagined that he alone would be in charge of examining Pushkin's papers, in line with principles which he thought had been agreed with the Tsar: 'He was therefore disconcerted, and indeed somewhat insulted to learn that he would be assisted by one of Benckendorff's subordinates, General Leonty Dubelt, the chief of staff of the gendarme corps'.[57] On 7 February, the seals which Zhukovsky had placed on Pushkin's study were removed and all the written material was packed into two chests which were then taken to Zhukovsky's rooms in Shepelvsky House.

Here, Zhukovsky and Dubelt combed through all of Pushkin's manuscripts, letters and notebooks. Zhukovsky was required to submit every single document and letter he found in Pushkin's study to Benckendorff before destroying it or returning it to its author. Zhukovsky was horrified at being forced to examine Pushkin's private papers in front of the police and to minutely examine the letters of friends which might include incriminating remarks. If nothing else, this experience was an eye-opener for Zhukovsky, who had never understood the reasons for the depths of Pushkin's anger: 'It allowed Zhukovsky to understand at last the fatal role played by the government in the poet's undoing'.[58]

Two months after Pushkin's death, the court which had investigated the duel and which passed sentence on d'Anthès recorded that 'the criminal conduct of Pushkin himself merited the same penalty as the accused, Heeckeren - the gallows'.[59] Writing to d'Archaic, the French Ambassador, Baron de Brabante, commented: 'Is it not strange that the life story of this great man should end with an official death sentence pronounced in the name of the monarch and aristocracy who were in reality his slayers?'.[60]

Notes

1   **The Bronze Horseman,** by Alexander Pushkin Main text in Russian edited with introduction, notes and vocabulary by T E Little, Bristol Classical Press, 1974, my translation

2   **Eugene Onegin: A Novel in Verse,** by A S Pushkin, translated with an introduction and notes by Stanley Mitchell, Penguin Books, 2008, Chapter IV, Canto 31, p135

3   **Pushkin,** by Henri Troyat, translated from the French by Nancy Amphoux, George, Allen & Unwin, 1974, p554

4   Troyat, ibid. p554

5   **The Letters of Alexander Pushkin.** Three Volumes in One. Translated and with an Introduction by J Thomas Shaw, University of Wisconsin Press, 1967, Letter 651, p805

6   **The Mystery of Pushkin's Death,** by Vadim V Kozhinov, translated from the Russian by Rachel Douglas, Published in *Fidelio,* Journal of the Schiller Institute, Vol. 8 No. 3, Fall 1999, special edition *Alexander Pushkin: Russia's Poet of Universal Genius* on 200th anniversary of Pushkin's birth, p79

7   Shaw, op.cit. Letter 652, p807

8   Kozhinov, op.cit. p79

9   Binyon, op.cit. p588

10   Binyon, op.cit. p604

11   Kozhinov, op.cit. p84

12   Kozhinov, op.cit. p80

13   Binyon, op.cit. p610

14   Binyon, op.cit. p610

15   Binyon, op.cit. p610

16   Binyon, op.cit. p610

17   Binyon, op.cit. p610

18   Binyon, op.cit. p611

19   Shaw, op.cit. Letter 672, p819

20   Kozhinov, op.cit. p80

21   Shaw, op.cit. Letter 670, p817

22   Binyon, op.cit. p614

23   Binyon, op.cit. p614-15

24   Binyon, op.cit. p615

25   **Pushkin's Ode to Liberty: The Lives and Loves of Alexander Pushkin**, by M A DuVernet, XLibris, 2014, p475

26   DuVernet, ibid. p475

27   DuVernet, p475

28   DuVernet, p475

29   Binyon, op.cit. p619

30   **A S Pushkin: A Biographical Sketch**, by V V Veresayev, Co-Operative Publishing

Society of Foreign Workers in the USSR, Moscow, 1937, p54

31 Binyon, op.cit. p620

32 Veresayev, op.cit. p55

33 Veresayev, op.cit. p55

34 Veresayev, op.cit. p55

35 Veresayev, op.cit. p55

36 **Death of a Poet,** A novel of the last years of Alexander Pushkin, by Leonid Grossman, translated from the Russian by Edith Bone, Hutchinson International Authors, 1951, p231

37 Grossman, ibid. p231

38 Veresayev, op.cit. p58

39 Veresayev, p58

40 Veresayev, p58

41 Troyat, op.cit. p585

42 Veresayev, op.cit. p60

43 Veresayev, p60

44 Troyat, p590

45 Troyat, p591

46 Troyat, p591

47 Troyat, p592

48 Troyat, p593

49 Troyat, p595

50 Troyat, p595

51 Grossman, op.cit. p250

52 Binyon, op.cit. p63

53 Troyat, op.cit. p610

54 Binyon, op.cit. p642

55 Binyon, op.cit. p642

56 Binyon, op.cit. p642

57 Binyon, op.cit. p643

58 Troyat, op.cit. p603

59 Grossman, op.cit. p.251

60 Grossman, op.cit. p.251

The monument I've created is not touched by human hands
The path that leads the nation to it shall never be o'ergrown
Its summit will soar much higher than
Even the mighty Alexandrovsky Colonne.

Pushkin, *Exegii Monumentum,* 1836 [1]

Evgeny… will be crushed, and his protest will never be heard
– or, rather, it would never have been heard if it had not been
transmitted by Pushkin, whose poet's vocation it was to hear and
give voice to the voiceless.

Edmund Wilson, *Pushkin,* 1926 [2]

17 | Pushkin's Everlasting Monument

In his original draft for *The Bronze Horseman,* Pushkin includes a lengthy excursus – entirely lost in the final version – in which he defends his right to choose such a lowly character as Evgeny to be the hero of his new narrative poem. Evgeny's social status has become a simulacrum of Pushkin's own. A descendant of ancient boyar stock, he now found himself a socially insignificant person among a social elite where neither his ancestry, nor his genius as a poet, seemed to count for much. In the poem, Evgeny has sunk so low that he no longer mingles with the nobility at all; he has become one of the common people and it is the ordinariness of his status which makes his collision with the power of the city and of the Tsar even more compelling. The underlying theme of the poem is what the Russian literary critic, D S Mirsky, describes as the opposition between the irreconcilable rights of the state and those of the individual: 'The Bronze Emperor is the incarnation of the ambitions and aspirations of the Empire, to which are sacrificed individual lives, in order that the great and unnatural city might stand and thrive. There is no attempt to veil the incompatibility of the two points of view: they stand in bold and tragic contrast'.[3]

In his reworking of the original story, Pushkin had abandoned what Mirsky describes as the 'rambling and digressive style of the older novel'. Instead of the stanza format used for *Onegin,* the poem now consists of a Prologue and two Cantos of about 550 lines. It is written in what Mirsky describes as: 'unstanzaed octosyllabics, with frequent overflow, a form more akin to Pushkin's later blank verse than is the stanzaed and end-stopped metre of *Onegin*'.[4]

One of the more remarkable features of *The Bronze Horseman* is that it has more than one central character: Pushkin's anti-hero 'poor Evgeny', is only one of several *dramatis personae* ,which include the monument to Peter the Great, the city itself and the Great Flood of 1824. In an Appendix to his 1963 biography of Pushkin, D S Mirsky includes Edmund Wilson's prose translation of *The Bronze Horseman,* together with an introductory essay, in which Wilson says that: 'The poem deals with the tragic contradiction between the right to peace and happiness of the ordinary man and the right to constructive domination of the state'.[5]

Although Evgeny's protest appears futile in the poem, the Emperor does not win a moral victory, which is why: 'Nicholas I was well-advised in forbidding the publication of the poem'. The only triumph that the bronze tyrant does achieve is: 'terrible, demoniac, and inhuman'. In his essay, Edmund Wilson wonders aloud how *The Bronze Horseman* might be received in Stalin's Russia: '…after all, Peter the Great is the figure to whom the laureates of Stalin most willingly compare him and to whom he is said to be most willing to be compared. The dissident and the irreverent, like Evgeny, hear behind them a horseman, not of bronze but of steel, and no matter where they go, they cannot escape him…'.[6]

There is of course a universal aspect to this antagonistic and paradoxical relationship between the interests of the state and those of the individual. In Pushkin's day, it would have been all too easy to regard it as a metaphor for the crushing of the Decembrist Revolt in 1825 or for the suppression of the Polish Revolt of 1830. But it also could have had an equal resonance with the massacre inflicted on peaceful demonstrators by mounted cavalry at Peterloo Fields in Manchester in 1819. In present-day Russia, it might even be recognised in events such as the persecution and eventual murder of the Russian journalist Anna Politkovskaya, or the state's antipathy to any semblance of a free press.

In another of his books, *A Window on Russia,* Edmund Wilson comments that: 'One often finds reactionary Russians writing about *The Bronze Horseman* as if it were simply a glorification of the ruthless authority of Peter the Great, to which the lives of Evgeny and his sweetheart are quite properly sacrificed'. This interpretation, he remarks, is about as imperceptive or obtuse as it would be for an English person to see only patriotism in Henry V and not realise that Falstaff is of more interest to Shakespeare than the King. Wilson recalls hearing a speaker at a conference, held in celebration of the defence of Leningrad against the Nazis, quote the famous lines from Pushkin's poem – 'Where dost though gallop, haughty steed? And where wilt thou plant thy foot?' – as though they were a battle cry. It had apparently never occurred to this person, he recalls, that: '…the whole point of Pushkin's poem is that the hoof of Peter's charger has crushed the Russians as well as their enemies'.[7]

The ambiguity which is an essential component of *The Bronze Horseman,* and which is epitomised in the poetic image of a man-made statue which then comes to life, has its distant origins in the story of Pygmalion, the Cypriot sculptor who falls in love with one of the statues he has created. Although this legend appears in many guises in Greek mythology, it is probably best known from one of the passages in Orpheus's Song from Ovid's *Metamorphoses* in which Pygmalion's creation 'is concealed by art' to such a rare degree that:

'In the course of time, he successfully carved an amazingly skilful statue in ivory white as snow, an image of perfect feminine beauty – and fell in love with his own creation. This heavenly woman appeared to be real: you'd surely suppose her alive and ready to move, if modesty didn't preclude it'.

(Metamorphoses. Book 10. 248-251)[8]

At the time of the annual Venus (Aphrodite) festival in Cyprus, Pygmalion makes his offering to the gods and then whispers his

THE MAN WHO SHOOK HIS FIST AT THE TSAR

wish that he might one day wed 'a woman resembling my ivory maiden'. When he next returns home and kisses the statue, he finds that his wish has been granted and that the statue comes to life:

The ivory gradually lost its hardness, softening, sinking, yielding beneath his sensitive fingers. Imagine beeswax from Mount Hymettus, softening under the rays of the sun; Imagine it moulded by human thumbs into a hundred of different shapes…
(*Metamorphoses.* Book 10. 281-288)[9]

The idea of a statue coming to life or, conversely, of an animate object being turned to stone is a recurring theme in art and literature. In his book *The Dream of the Moving Statue,* the author Kenneth Gross writes: 'The idea of the animated statue appears everywhere. One finds it in fairy tales and philosophy, in ancient magic and romantic novellas, in classical ballet and modern television commercials (for wine, perfume, coffee, soap, game shows and body-building, to name just a few)'.[10] A modern British audience is more likely to know of the Pygmalion story through its more recent incarnations, such as the Broadway musical *My Fair Lady,* based on George Bernard Shaw's stage play, *Pygmalion,* or Willy Russell's *Educating Rita.*

From the point of view of a writer or artist, like Pushkin, the importance of fantasies about animated statues Gross writes, is that they can: '…suggest how the reciprocal ambitions of writing and sculpture animate each other, and the paradoxical figures of life and voice their conflict can generate; they also point to the ambivalent crossings of fear and desire that continue to bind our fantasies and memories to the realm of unliving images and objects'.[11] Gross's book opens with a chapter on Charlie Chaplin's 'artful clowning' with statues which come to life in his film *City Lights.*

In Pushkin's day, classical references were still very much in vogue: before he was commissioned by Catherine the Great to build a monument to Peter the Great, its sculptor, Etienne Falconet, had already made his mark with a marble statue which depicts Pygmalion kneeling 'at the feet of the statue which he brings to life': *Pygmalion aux pieds de sa statue qui s'anime.* Another example appears in the bas-relief which adorns Carlo

Rastrelli's bronze bust of Peter the Great, showing Peter himself in the role of the sculptor carving the perfect image of a woman, Galatea – who, in this instance, represents New Russia.

In 1922, the Russian poet Vladislav Khodasevich published a volume called *Articles on Russian Poetry* in which he suggests a possible source for the 'original nightmare fantasy' from which three of Pushkin's stories later emerged. These were *The Little House in Kolomna*, *The Queen of Spades* and *The Bronze Horseman*, sometimes collectively referred to as Pushkin's *Petersburg Tales*.[12]

This source was a story called *The Lonely Little House on Vasilievsky Island,* which had first been published in the almanac *Northern Flowers* in 1829. The significance of this story to Pushkin's *oeuvre* was first noted by the Pushkin scholar Shchegolev in a Russian newspaper called *The Day,* in December 1912. It was then published in full in the January 1913 edition of the magazine, *Northern Notes.* The published version of *The Lonely Little House on Vasilievsky Island* was attributed to Vladimir Titov, who wrote under the pseudonym, Titus Kosmokratov – but we know that he had first heard the tale from Pushkin, who told the story one evening in 1829 during a soirée at the Karamzins. One of the people who witnessed this recital – Pushkin's friend Delvig – later reported that his recitation had: '…made such an impression on a young writer named V P Titov, who was there, that he was unable to sleep that night and later wrote the story down from memory'.[13]

The 'Kosmokratov' story was subsequently included in Volume IX of the 1956-58 edition of Pushkin's collected works, compiled by Boris Tomashevsky. A convoluted and sinister tale of a love triangle, a mysterious gambling countess and dark, satanic forces, the dramatic turning point of *The Lonely Little House on Vasilievsky Island* finds the hero, Pavel, outside the entrance to the countess's mansion, up to his knees in snow and being beckoned to by a tall figure in a cloak, who then vanishes into an alley. Pavel signals a cab and orders the driver to take him home but soon comes to realise he has been driven far beyond the city limits.

Remembering the stories of cab drivers who have cut their customers' throats: 'He sees that, in large figures, strangely formed, the cab is labelled '666' – which is, as he afterwards remembers, the number of the Beast of the Apocalypse. He strikes the driver with his stick and feels that he is beating not flesh but bones. The driver turns his head and reveals a grinning skull which repeats the words of his rival in love, Varfolomey: 'Be quiet, young man: you're not dealing with one of your own kind'.[14]

After this alarming encounter: 'Pavel crosses himself, the sleigh overturns in the snow and he hears a wild laugh, there is a terrible whirling gust of wind: and he finds himself alone outside the city gates'.[15] As Edmund Wilson notes: 'One recognises in the statue of Peter the Great that turns its head and terrifies Evgeny by asserting its despotic authority, the cabby of the Vasilievsky story who turns his head with more or less the same effect'.[16]

In all three of the *Petersburg Tales,* the central characters – Pavel, Herman and Evgeny – are driven insane, the victim of apparently diabolical and supernatural powers. It may be no coincidence says Wilson, that already, at the time these stories were written, 'the forces of evil were closing in on Pushkin'.[17] Another important source of inspiration for *The Bronze Horseman* was the influential 19th century American novelist, Washington Irving, best known for his short stories *Rip Van Winkle* and *The Legend of Sleepy Hollow* in which a headless horseback rider terrorises a previously peaceful rural community.

In the spring of 1829, Washington Irving was already a literary celebrity. That year he travelled to Spain and went on an expedition from Seville to Granada in the company of a member of the Russian Embassy in Madrid. Irving's account of this journey, and the legends of Spain that he collected on his way, were later published in a book called *Tales of the Alhambra.* Pushkin had seven books by Washington Irving in his library, including a French edition of this book, *Les Contes de l'Alhambra,* published in Paris in 1832.

One of the stories in Irving's book is *The House of the Weathercock,* or *La Casa del Gallo de Viento,* which stands directly opposite the Alhambra, on the highest peak in Granada and above the River Darro. By then in ruins, the building was once a royal palace of the Moors and had been so named because of the weathervane which was placed on one of its turrets.

Intriguingly, this wind gauge takes the shape of a bronze horseman. The face of the horseman normally pointed towards the city as if keeping guard over it but, if any foe appeared, the figure would turn in that direction and level his lance as if ready for action. In ancient times, Irving writes: 'This weathercock was regarded by the Moslems of Granada as a portentous talisman. According to some traditions it bore the following Arabic inscription: '*Calet el Bedici Aben Habuz, Quidat ehahet Lindabuz*', which, translated into English means:

> '*In this way, says Aben Habuz the Wise,*
> *Andaluz guards against surprise*'.[18]

Aben Habuz was a Moorish sultan of Granada who regarded the weathercock as 'a perpetual admonition of the instability of Moslem power'. [19] It was also said to bear the prediction that: 'Andaluz shall one day vanish and pass away'. One Moslem historian, who had been present when the weathervane was removed and taken down for repair, said that he had seen the inscription with his own eyes and it actually read, in verse:

> '*The horseman, though a solid body, turns with every wind*
> *This to a wise man reveals a mystery*
> *In a little while comes a calamity*
> *To ruin both the palace and its owner*'.[20]

Shortly after meddling with the weathervane, Washington Irving recounts, the following extraordinary event occurred: 'As old Muley Abul Hassan, the Sultan of Granada, was seated under a sumptuous pavilion reviewing his troops, who paraded before him in armour of polished steel and gorgeous silken robes, mounted on fleet steeds, and equipped with swords, spears and shields embossed with gold and silver – suddenly a tempest was seen hurrying from the south-west'.[21]

This passage has an obvious parallel with Pushkin's description of the troop manoeuvres held on the Field of Mars in St Petersburg at the beginning of *The Bronze Horseman* and the subsequent deluge brought about by the Great Flood of 1824.

Washington Irving's account of the calamity which engulfs Granada continues, like Pushkin's description of the flood in St Petersburg, as follows:

> 'In a little while black clouds overshadowed the heavens and
> burst forth with a deluge of rain. Torrents came roaring down

from the mountains, bringing with them rocks and trees, the Darro overflowed its banks; mills were swept away, bridges destroyed, gardens laid waste; the inundation rushed into the city, undermining houses, drowning their inhabitants, and overflowing the square of the Great Mosque. The people rushed in affright to the mosques to implore the mercy of Allah, regarding this uproar of the elements as the harbinger of dreadful calamities; and, indeed, according to the Arabian historian Al Makkari, it was but a type and prelude of the direful war which ended in the downfall of the Moslem kingdom of Granada'.[22]

In one of her numerous essays on Pushkin, written in the early 1930s, the great Russian poetess, Anna Akhmatova, was the first to point out that Pushkin's verse tale, *The Golden Cockerel*, composed in 1834, was not, as had long been thought, based on Russian folklore but was in fact inspired by Washington Irving's story *Legend of the Arabian Astrologer*. This story, which also comes from his *Tales of the Alhambra*, explains how and why the weathercock was built for the fortress of the Moorish king, Aben Habuz, on the advice of his Arabian astrologer and magician, Ibrahim.

In Pushkin's retelling of this story, a Russian Tsar, Dadon, takes the place of Aben Habuz. The difference is that, as Akhmatova notes: 'In Irving's tale the central characters, the king and the astrologer, who is also threatening, are parodied, whereas Pushkin is ironic only about the Tsar, who is a completely grotesque figure'.[23] The reason for this, she writes, is that: 'The trappings of a folk tale here serve to mask the political meaning'.[24]

In the 18th century, the genre of 'Arabian' tale in Russian literature had often provided cover for a political lampoon or satire. In Derzhavin, for example, the senate had been referred to as the Divan. Likewise, Radishchev had refashioned the Russian folktale *Bova* to attack the autocracy, a fact which Pushkin had himself noted in his 1834 essay on Radishchev.[25] The elements of 'personal satire', Akhmatova writes, 'are disguised with especial care. This is explained by the fact that Nicholas I was the object of the satire'.[26]

Just as the bronze horseman on the weathervane of the Moorish sentinel in Alhambra was seen as a protector of the city, so the *Bronze Horseman* came to be regarded as a guardian of St Petersburg. This conviction dates to the time of Napoleon's invasion of Russia, when it was feared that, if St Petersburg was over-run by the Grand Armée, the monument to Peter the Great might suffer the same fate as the four bronze horses of San Marco in Venice – which had been requisitioned by Napoleon's troops. The city authorities seriously considered dismantling Falconet's monument and removing it to safekeeping until one of the local commanders, Major Baturlin, reported having had a dream during which the statue had jumped off its pedestal and galloped to the summer residence of the Tsar, Alexander I.

On arrival, the bronze statue of Peter supposedly spoke to the reigning monarch, Alexander, saying: 'Young man, what have you done to my country? But don't worry, so long as I remain in my place, the city has nothing to fear'.[27] Baturlin recounted his dream to the influential Prince Golitsyn, a man renowned for his mysticism, and so the statue stayed. Even during the 900 days of the German blockade of the city, then called Leningrad in WWII, The *Bronze Horseman* remained in place, under a protective mound of wooden planks and earth.

Like the *Bronze Horseman,* there is another famous monument in St Petersburg which is dedicated by one Tsar to another, in this case by Nicholas I to his elder brother Alexander I. This takes the form of a freestanding granite column, the Alexander Column (or *Alexandrovskaya Kolonna*) which stands in the centre of Palace Square, between the Winter Palace and the headquarters of the General Staff. This monument was unveiled on 30 August 1834 (St Alexander of Constantinople's Day) in the aftermath of the crushing of the Polish uprising of 1830.

The Alexander column is made from a single, free-standing piece of red granite, 25 metres long, which was transported from Virolahti in Finland. The four sides of the pedestal on which the column stands are decorated with bronze bas-reliefs depicting glorious episodes in Russia's military history. On the side of the pedestal facing the Winter Palace is a bas-relief depicting winged figures holding a plaque which bears the words: *'To Alexander from a grateful Russia',* in memory of his victory over Napoleon.

The same panel includes figures representing the Nieman and Vistula – the two longest rivers in Poland, which had been traversed by Napoleon in both directions during the Great

Patriotic War and by Russian troops during the Polish Revolt.

The bronze reliefs are also embossed with more ancient representations such as the shield of Prince Oleg of Novgorod and the helmet of Alexander Nevsky. The column is topped with a statue of an angel trampling a serpent and holding aloft a cross. The face of the angel is said to be a likeness of Alexander I. The total height of the monument, with pedestal and statue, is 47.5 metres.

At the time it was built, the Alexander Column was the highest structure in St Petersburg. Indeed, one of the stipulations for the architect was that it must be higher than the Vendôme Column in Paris, which had earlier been built by Napoleon to commemorate his own victory over the Russians at the Battle of Austerlitz in 1807. Apart from the perennial issue of whose column was the biggest, there was another, more serious, reason for the competition with the Vendôme Column: it is wrapped in a façade of spiralling bronze plates, modelled on Trajan's Column in Rome. The bronze carapace was recovered from melted-down cannon captured from the Russians, including 180 taken at Austerlitz.

In his study of the Russian monarchy, *Scenarios of Power,* the American Historian, Richard S Wortman, describes the ceremonial surrounding the unveiling of the Alexander Column as representing 'the first and most widely publicized glorification of dynasty and nation ever to have taken place in Russia: 'The serried ranks of an estimated 120,000 troops were lined up in Palace Square…for a ceremony that marked the Alexandrine column as a votive object in the cult of dynasty'.[28]

Accounts published at the time, one of them by Pushkin's close friend, Zhukovsky, described the spectacle as 'the epitome of the political order that had lifted Russia to heights of power and international prestige'.[29] Designed by the same French architect who built St Isaac's Cathedral in Senate Square, Auguste de Montferrand, the Alexander Column was intended to be: 'a blunt statement of Russia's exemplification of Western conceptions of Empire'.[30]

One person who did not attend the ceremony was Pushkin, who intentionally absented himself from the capital to avoid having to witness the unveiling. Among Pushkin's very last poems, dated 21 August 1836, is a reworking of an ode by the Roman poet, Horace – *Exegii monumentum aere perennius* (I have raised a monument more permanent than bronze). In the original version of this ode, Horace confidently predicts his enduring fame as the first and greatest of the lyric poets of Rome.

In his version, Pushkin similarly forecasts the immortality of his work, and makes the specific prediction that: 'Its summit will rise even higher than the Alexander Column'. Pushkin's reworking of *Exegii Monumentum* reads:

'The monument I've created is not touched by human hands
The path that leads the nation to it shall never be o'ergrown
Its summit will soar much higher than
Even the mighty Alexandrovsky Colonne

No, I shall not perish – my art shall be my requiem
Conquer death, and from my dust ascend
So long as on this mortal earth
There be but one poet to comprehend

Through all of great Russia, they'll heed my name
And hear my voice in every native tongue
By descendants of the proud Slav and the Finn
Wild Tungus and Steppe Kalmuck it shall be sung.

I'll always be a friend to the people
My gift brings comfort to the downfallen
For in this dread time, I too have craved freedom
And urged compassion for our ill-fated kinsmen

Take heed then, good muse, by the word of God
Treat praise and slander alike; that's the rule
Neither take offense, nor expect reward…
And never argue with a fool'. [31]

There can be no doubt that Pushkin was accurate with his prediction. In the 1960's, Anna Akhmatova wrote that: 'Whereas, the first decades of the 19th century are now referred to as 'the Pushkin era', Pushkin's opponents in the imperial court are almost entirely forgotten: 'All the beauties, ladies-in-waiting, mistresses of the salons, Dames of the Order of St Catherine, members of the Imperial Court, ministers, aides-de-camp and non-aides-de-camp, gradually came to be called Pushkin's contemporaries and were later laid simply to rest in card catalogues and name indices (with garbled birth and death dates) as appendices to Pushkin's works'.[32]

Pushkin's revenge on his adversaries was that: 'He conquered time and space...In the palace halls where they danced and gossiped about the poet, his portraits now hang and his books are on view, while their pale shadows have been banished from there forever. And their magnificent palaces and residences are described by whether Pushkin was ever there or not. Nobody is interested in anything else'.[33] More recently, Evgeny Dubrenko writes:

> 'Pushkin's unique place in the Russian national consciousness owes less to his greatness as a poet than to the fact that a myth of Pushkin lies at the heart of the Russian national identity which is defined by a conflict between a lofty image of Russia's majesty, and the bleakness of her past, and uncertainty of the present. It can be defined as a cross between an inferiority complex and a superiority complex. Russianness is realised in a dichotomy that was engendered by Pushkin'.[34]

Pushkin's contribution has been so great, says Dubrenko, that: 'It was he who created that Russia which, in the words of the 19th century poet, Tyutchev, 'the mind cannot grasp' by creating an enchanting fairy tale about this huge, cold, bleak and cruel land. Pushkin made possible Turgenev's young noblewomen, Tolstoy's noble heroes, Chekhov's good-natured protagonists, Bunin's dark alleys and Blok's beautiful stranger, the captivating music of Tchaikovsky and Rachmaninov, the painter Isaac Levitan's melancholy canvases and Diaghilev's exquisite ballets. That is why Pushkin is of such vital importance to Russians, and why his status in Russia is so hard for foreigners to fathom'.[35]

This adulation of Pushkin in Russia did not come about overnight. During the entire century which elapsed between the publication of his first poems to the outbreak of the October Revolution in 1917, only a few of his works had been translated into the various languages of the Russian empire. By contrast, between 1918 and 1936, an estimated 335 editions of Pushkin were published, with 18.6 million copies of his works printed in total. The special editions printed for the 1937 anniversary of his death ran to 13.7 million copies. In the entire period up to 1954 it is estimated that more than 84.5 million copies of Pushkin's works appeared in 1,932 editions, in 82 languages. For the 150th anniversary of his birth, in 1949, 252 editions and 10 million copies of Pushkin's works were published in Russian as well as 1.5 million copies in translation in 76 minority languages.[36]

During the Soviet era, idolisation of Pushkin became so entrenched in Russia that, as the writer Lydia Libedinskaya recalls, as a schoolgirl in the 1960s: 'To Pushkin we dedicated poetry, essays and dreams. We dreamed about Pushkin. We talked to him as though he were alive...Pushkin, Pushkin, Pushkin'.[37] In the words of Evgeny Dobrenko: 'Pushkin became a veritable fetish'.

Responding to this state-sponsored cult of Pushkin, in 1982 the Soviet-era artist, Boris Orlov, draped a bronze of Pushkin in outlandish regalia as the General Secretary of the Communist Party, Leonid Brezhnev. Nevertheless, adulation of Pushkin during the Stalin era did have its limits. In the mid-1930s, the Russian playwright, Mikhail Bulgakov (best known in the West for his St Petersburg novel *The Master and Margarita),* produced a four-act play about the events leading up to Pushkin's death, entitled *Last Days.*

In an introduction to an English translation of six of Bulgakov's plays, published in 1991, Lesley Milne writes that: 'The name of Pushkin was always important to Bulgakov as a benchmark for the 'Russian writer'. Like Molière, Pushkin is both an ethical model and an affirmation of the triumph of art. Pushkin's relationship to Tsar Nicholas I offers a paradigm of the artist's path, and his example protects the author from straying into the swamps of servility to an autocrat'.[38]

Like Pushkin, Bulgakov had first-hand experience of dealing with an autocrat: in March 1930, he had received notification from the censors that his new play, *Molière,* had not been passed for public performance. In acute financial distress, and as a publicly declared pariah, Bulgakov wrote to the Soviet government pleading for permission either to be given work in the theatre or to be allowed to emigrate with his wife. The letter was sent to seven different addresses but only Stalin replied.

On 18 April 1930, Stalin phoned Bulgakov, four days after the suicide of the poet Mayakovsky, and granted him a post as assistant director at the Moscow Arts Theatre, probably because the death of two such renowned artists at the same time would not have been good publicity. Just as Pushkin had rejoiced when his known association with the Decembrists was overlooked by Nicholas I, Bulgakov was initially euphoric but, as Lesley Milne writes: '…gradually came to understand that he had been saved from 'destitution, the street and death' only to be locked up inside a Soviet Union which offered no outlet for his creativity'.[39]

Several theatres had indicated their interest in performing Bulgakov's play about Pushkin, to coincide with the centenary of his death in 1937. Both Shostakovich and Prokofiev had held discussions with him about the possibility of turning it into an opera. But all such discussions were dropped 'when Shostakovich came under attack for writing 'muddle instead of music'.

When Bulgakov's play *Molière* was finally produced by the Moscow Arts Theatre in 1936, it was removed from the repertoire after only seven performances and denounced in *Pravda*. In Bulgakov's play *Last Days* Pushkin does not appear at all, but his death is presented as a court conspiracy, which was an acceptable viewpoint in 1937. The real problem was that the climax of the play makes explicit the real political motive for his murder: 'The burial scene is reminiscent of the demonstrations of 1905 and 1917: a student climbs a lamppost to declaim to the crowd Lermontov's forbidden poem *Death of the Poet;* a noble officer addresses those assembled with the words: 'Fellow citizens! Pushkin was the victim of premeditated murder. And this despicable crime is an offense against our people…a great citizen has died because unlimited power has been placed in the hands of unworthy men who treat the people like slaves. Even if they related to events a century old, such speeches were much too dangerous for 1937. Performance of the play was banned'.[40]

In the period after WWII, Pushkin became one of the Soviet Union's ideological weapons in the Cold War. He was portrayed as an ardent fighter for the national dignity of the Russian people in the face of the contemporary 'slanderers of Russia'. In an article published on Pushkin's birthday, in a 1949 edition of the party newspaper, *Pravda,* Pushkin's writings on America were cited as confirmation of the cultural superiority of Soviet Russia.

This claim was based on a coruscating article Pushkin had written, in the third edition of his journal *The Contemporary* (towards the end of 1836). This referred to *The Narrative of John Tanner,* the recollections of an America explorer who had spent 30 years in the wilds, living among the country's native inhabitants. Tanner's 'narrative' had first been published in New York in 1830. Pushkin had a copy of the French edition in his library – published in two volumes, in Paris, in 1835.

In his article, Pushkin set out to question some of the widespread assumptions made by 'more thoughtful Europeans' about American customs and decrees and had concluded that, because of John Tanner's writings:

'The respect felt for this new nation and for its code, the fruit of most advanced enlightenment, was very much shaken. People saw with astonishment, democracy in all its disgusting cynicism, with all its cruel prejudices, in its unbearable tyranny. Everything noble and disinterested, everything that raises man's spirits, crushed by implacable egoism and the passion for comfort; the majority, an insolently persecuting society; negro slavery in the midst of education and freedom; class persecution among a people who have no nobility; cupidity and envy on the part of the electorate; timidity and flattery on the part of the legislators; talent forced into voluntary ostracism out of regard for equality; the rich man putting on a ragged coat so as not to offend in the street the proud penury he secretly despises; such is the picture of the American States recently put before us'.[41]

Alongside the Pushkin who had been transformed into a tool of the Soviet authorities and a useful weapon in the ideological war with the West, was an entirely different Pushkin myth nurtured by the Russian intelligentsia, most of whom had been forced out of the public discourse. Within these circles, Evgeny Dobrenko writes: 'the Pushkin myth reaches maturity'.[42] The undisputed high priestess of this circle was Anna Akhmatova, who had survived Stalin's terror and for whom, in the words of Sergey Gandlevsky, Pushkin was the 'diety' in her temple. As far as she was concerned: 'The leading poet is Pushkin; that holds for the 20th century, too. All the rest trail in second and third place'.[43] As things turned out, the 200th anniversary of Pushkin's birth, celebrated in 1999, happened to coincide with the collapse of the Soviet Union.

One of the first writers to gain a reputation for satirising the official Soviet myth was Daniil Kharms, whose *Anecdotes from the Life of Pushkin* were a parody of the many sycophantic tributes which had been written about him during the 1937 celebrations. But Kharms paid a heavy price for his levity. The avant-garde literary societies he was associated with were banned by Stalin and he was arrested in 1941 'for spreading defeatist propaganda' just before the Siege of Leningrad started. He starved to death in prison the following year while Leningrad was ravaged by famine. In an article written for the *Literaturnaya Gazeta,* in September 2001, Vladimir Smirnov wrote that Pushkin was a 'supra-literary phenomenon'. Some authorities argue that he is first and foremost a poet of Russian orthodoxy, others – such as the Archimandrite Michael Ardov that his poetry is 'blasphemous'.

What this means, says Evgeny Dobrenko, is that: '…his tremendous susceptibility to manipulation for ideological purposes remained unchanged'. To some he can be represented as a Soviet non-believer and militant atheist, for others, he is a holier-than-thou believer. During the Soviet era, Pushkin was portrayed as an ardent revolutionary who would have welcomed the Great October which had given the people their long-awaited 'liberty' and which had shattered the accursed 'despotism' into 'fragments' on which 'were written the names of Pushkin, the Decembrists, the Revolutionary democrats'. Others make out that he was a respectable monarchist and staunch conservative.

As an example of the enduring potency of Pushkin's image, *The Moscow Times* reported, in September 2014, that a renowned Dutch translator of Russian literature, Hans Boland, had refused to accept the Medal of Pushkin which was established by the Russian government in 1999 to commemorate extraordinary individual achievements in arts and culture.

In the strongly worded rejection letter which was sent to the Russian Embassy in The Hague, Hans Boland explained that the reason for his rejection was that: 'I would with great gratitude accept this honour if it wasn't for President Vladimir Putin whose behaviour and way of thinking I despise. He represents a big threat to freedom and peace on our planet'.

Hans Boland went on to say that: 'Every connection between him (Putin) and me, his name and the name of Alexander Pushkin is disgusting and intolerable for me'.[44] As the *Moscow Times* noted, Boland would have been the first Dutch national to receive the medal of Pushkin. He is Holland's foremost translator of Russian literature, having brought Dutch readers the works of such literary greats as Pushkin and Lermontov, as well as contemporary authors.

On 12 November, 2010, the international foreign correspondent of *The Herald Tribune*, Serge Schmemann, filed the following report for *The New York Times*, from La Fère in Northern France:

'On a grey, chilly autumn day, an unusual cluster gathered by the stern red-brick barracks of a former artillery academy here … to attend the unveiling of a curious plaque. Alongside the luminaries of the town and province were high representatives of Russia and Estonia, as well as the ambassadors of Cameroon and the Sultan of Logone-Birni (now in Cameroon) resplendent in the colourful garments of their African homeland. The requisite speeches were delivered and all shivered at attention as the local marching band wrestled with the European Anthem (more familiar as Beethoven's *Ode to Joy*). Then the Sultan, Mahamat Bahat Marouf, was ushered forward to pull the veil off a modest plaque affixed to the wall'.

The report goes on to say that the legend inscribed on the base of the memorial, in French and Russian, declared that: 'Abraham Petrovich Gannibal, born in Logone-Birni in 1696 and deceased in Russia in 1781, chief military engineer and general-in-chief of the Imperial Russian Army was a graduate of the royal artillery academy of La Fère. It also noted that he was the great-grand-father of Russia's greatest poet, Alexander Pushkin'.[45]

On 6 June 2016, on the final day of the annual, open-air book fair which has been established outside the Kremlin in Moscow's Red Square, the anniversary of Pushkin's birthday was celebrated with a performance by the virtuoso Russian-born violinist, Vadim Repin, and the Novaya Rossiya (New Russia) Symphony Orchestra. Repin played a violin version of Lensky's aria from Tchaikovsky's opera, *Eugene Onegin*. On the same day, in St Petersburg, the 217th anniversary of Pushkin's birth was celebrated at the Pushkin Museum which is housed in the apartment on the embankment of the Moika Canal, where he lived at the end of his life and where he was taken after being shot in the duel with d'Anthès.

According to a report filed for the St Petersburg TV Channel, entrance to the museum was made free of charge for the day; readings of Pushkin's comic stories, *The Little House in Kolomna* and *Count Nulin,* were given by noted Russian actors and actresses in the courtyard; and an orchestra played extracts from Rimsky-Korsakov's opera *Mozart and Salieri,* which is based on a drama by Pushkin. Crowds stretched for several hundred metres from the entrance of the apartment, just as they had done on the day – 10 February 1837 – that inhabitants of the city heard the news of Pushkin's tragic death.

Notes

1   Pushkin, *Exegii Monumentum,* 1836, my translation

2   **Pushkin,** by D S Mirsky, introduction by George Siegel, includes a prose translation of *The Bronze Horseman* by Edmund Wilson, Dutton, 1963, Appendix, p259

3   Mirsky, ibid. p210

4   Mirsky, p210

5   Mirsky, p254

6   Mirsky, p260

7   **A Window on Russia: For the Use of Foreign Readers**, by Edmund Wilson, Macmillan, 1972 (first published 1943), p24

8   **Metamorphoses by Ovid: a New Verse Translation**, translated by David Raeburn, with and introduction by Denis Feeney, Penguin Books, 2004, Book 10, *Orpheus' Song: Pygmalion,* p394 lines 248-251

9   Ovid, ibid. Book 10, lines 281-288

10 **The Dream of the Moving Statue,** by Kenneth Gross, The Pennsylvania State University Press, 2006, Preface, pxv

11 Gross, ibid. ppxv-xvi

12 **A Window on Russia: For the Use of Foreign Readers**, by Edmund Wilson. Macmillan, 1972 (first published 1943), *Notes on Pushkin,* p188

13 Wilson, ibid. p189

14 Wilson, p190

15 Wilson, p191

16 Wilson, p192

17 Wilson, p193

18 **Tales of the Alhambra,** by Washington Irving.

19 Irving, ibid. p tbc

20 Irving, p tbc

21 Irving, p tbc

22 Irving, p tbc

23 **About Pushkin** (from *My Half Century: Selected Prose)*, by Anna Akhmatova, edited by Ronald Meyer, Ardis Publishers, New York, 2013, p159

24 Akhmatova, ibid. p160

25 Akhmatova, p160

26 Akhmatova, p160

27 **The Bronze Horseman: Falconet's Monument to Peter the Great**, by Alexander M Schenker, Yale University Press, 2003, p296

28 **Scenarios of Power: Myth and Ceremony in Russian Monarchy from Peter the Great to the Abdication of Nicholas II**, by Richard S Wortman, Princeton University Press, 2006, p149

29 Wortman, ibid. p149

30 Wortman, p149

31 Pushkin, *Exegii Monumentum,* 1836, my translation

32 Akhmatova, op.cit. p148

33 Akhmatova, p148

34 Essay on *'Pushkin in Soviet and post-Soviet Culture'* by Evgeny Dobrenko, in **The**

Cambridge Companion to Pushkin, edited by Andrew Kahn, Cambridge University Press, 2006, p202

35   Dobrenko, ibid. p202

36   Dobrenko, p209

37   Dobrenko, p207

38   **Six Plays**, by Mikhail Bulgakov, translated by Michael Glenny, William Powell and Michael Earley, introduced by Lesley Milne, Methuen Drama, 1998 (first published in 1991), pxxi

39   Milne, ibid. pxiv

40   Dobrenko, op.cit. p213

41   **Pushkin on Literature,** selected, translated and edited by Tatiana Wolff, The Athlone Press, 1986, article No. 303, p410, *John Tanner.* First published, unsigned, in the third issue of *The Contemporary* (1836)

42   Dobrenko, op.cit. p213

43   Dobrenko, p213

44   *Moscow Times*, 7 September 2104, https://themoscowtimes.com/news/dutch-translator-refuses-pushkin-medal-blaming-putin-39114

45   *New York Times*, 12 November 2010, 'Of African Princes and Russian Poets', by Serge Schmemann.

Appendix 01

Pushkin and his English Translators

Most of the great works of 19th century Russian literature were first introduced to an English-speaking audience thanks to the translations undertaken by a remarkable English woman, Constance Garnett. She was brought up in a household where both her Scottish father, David Black, and her mother, Clara Patten, had an aptitude for languages; each had dabbled in translations of novels, from German and Italian respectively. Constance went to university at Newnham College, Cambridge, where she opted to study Latin and Greek. When she subsequently moved to the East End of London in the 1880's she became an enthusiastic socialist, attending political meetings and moving in the same social circles as Annie Besant, Eleanor Marx, Bernard Shaw and William Morris. Constance was one of the first female librarians ever employed in the UK, at the newly established People's Palace on the Mile End Road – now part of the Queen Mary & Westfield College of London University. The man who would become her father-in-law, Richard Garnett, was Superintendent of the Reading Room at the British Museum between 1875 and 1884.

Constance Garnett's interest in the Russian language did not really begin until her husband, Edward, made the acquaintance of a Russian exile, Felix Volkhovsky, who had recently escaped from Siberia. Volkhovsky was an active member of the revolutionary group known as *Narodnaya Volya* (People's Will) which carried out the assassination of Tsar Alexander II of Russia in 1881. Because of his activities, Volkhovsky had been imprisoned for six-and-a-half years in solitary confinement in the Peter and Paul Fortress in St Petersburg before spending the next 11 years exiled to Siberia. During his detention, the youngest of his three daughters died and his wife committed suicide.

When he came to London, Volkhovsky worked on the émigré journal, *Free Russia,* and ran an émigré bookshop in Hammersmith. He encouraged Constance Garnett to learn Russian and supplied her with her first Russian dictionary and grammar book. Soon after, she translated her first novel, Goncharov's *A Common Story.* Her typical routine was to do four or five pages a day, with the aid of a dictionary. Constance Garnett's vocation to translate Russian literature blossomed further when a friendship developed with two more Russian émigrés – the founder of *Free Russia,* Sergey Stepniak, and his wife, Fanny.

Stepniak had fled Russia after taking part in the assassination of the much-hated Chief of Police in St Petersburg, General Nikolai V Mezentsev. When he was informed of the hunger strike taking place during the trial of 193 'nihilists' – an event which was witnessed by Dostoevsky and later incorporated into his novel, *The Brothers Karamazov* – Mezentsev had been quoted as saying 'Let them starve. I have ordered their coffins'.[1]

Constance Garnett's grasp of Russian gradually improved to the extent that she was asked if she would act as interpreter at a fund-raising effort for the Russian Social Democrats when they held their Fifth (and, as it turned out, final) Congress, in 1907. This took place at the Brotherhood Tabernacle Church – off Southgate Road, in Islington. It meant meeting with a delegation of seven Russians, at a fund-raising dinner party', which included Maxim Gorky, George Plekhanov and Lenin. Because her spoken Russian was shaky and she claimed she would not understand the Marxist political terminology, Constance proposed that Fanny Stepniak stand in for her. In the event, they both went along. Surrounded by the impeccably-dressed English, Lenin made a short, blunt and embarrassed speech 'as though his presence patently belied his convictions'.[2]

Constance Garnett's determination to pursue her career as a translator developed fully under the influence of the Stepniaks. For the next 30 years, beginning in the early 1890s, Garnett translated more than 70 novels from the Russian. Her earliest efforts dealt with the works of Ivan Turgenev: she translated most of his best-known novels in a two-year period, starting with *Rudin* in 1894 and then completing *A Nest of Gentlefolk, On the Eve, Smoke, Sportsman's Sketches* and *Fathers and Sons* in 1895. In the following decade, Constance Garnett completed translations of Leo Tolstoy's *Anna Karenina* in 1901 and *War and Peace* in 1904.

She translated virtually all of Feodor Dostoevsky's novels and short stories during the next decade, including *The Brothers Karamazov* (1912), *The Idiot* and *The Possessed* (1913), *Crime and Punishment* (1914) and *The Gambler* (1917). She was also among the first to recognise the genius of Anton Chekhov and produced translations of many of his short stories and of his plays *The Cherry Orchard, Three Sisters, Uncle Vanya* and *The Seagull* in the early 1920s. These were then followed by Nikolay Gogol's *Dead Souls* (1922), *The Overcoat* (1923) and *The Government Inspector* (1926). At the same time, she completed her translation of Alexander Herzen's political memoir, *My Past and Thoughts* (1924).[3]

Anton Chekhov was a year older than Constance Garnett and considered to be the leading writer of the younger generation in Russia. This reputation was almost entirely founded on the success of his short stories. He had been awarded the prestigious Pushkin Prize for Literature in 1888.

When she heard about the critical reception of Chekhov's first play *The Seagull* (it had bombed on its first night at the Alexandrinsky Theatre in October 1896, but subsequently received much more favourable reviews) she wrote to Chekhov, in English, offering to translate the play. She said she had admired Chekhov's short stories and had already translated two of them. Now, she said: 'I hear that your play, *The Seagull,* has made a great sensation in Petersburg. If you would care to entrust me with the translation of it, I would make every effort to bring it before the English public'.[4]

She told Chekhov she had some influence with the independent theatre in London, with several drama critics and publishers and that her translations of Turgenev had been well received. In addition, she added: 'My father-in-law, Dr Garnett (Keeper of Printed Books of the British Museum) wishes me to ask you for a complete list of your writings, that we may add them to the Library of the Museum'.[5] Virtually all of the translations published by Constant Garnett are works of prose, either short stories or novels. Her only published translation of a poem appeared in the *Nation,* in 1908, and this was a sonnet by Pushkin entitled *To the Poet.*

This translation also appears in one of the first comprehensive collections of Pushkin's writings to become available in English. This is *The Poems, Prose and Plays of Alexander Pushkin,* which was published by the Modern Library of New York in 1937 to coincide with the centenary of Pushkin's death. Compiled by the head of the Slavonic Division at the New York Public Library, Avrahm Yarmolinsky, this collection comprises an edited selection of translations of Pushkin's lyrics and ballads, narrative poems, folk tales, dramatic writings and prose. Among the translations in this book is one made by one of Pushkin's former tutors at the Lycée, Thomas B Shaw. This is *The Lay of the Wise Oleg,* Pushkin's take on one of the Russian primary chronicles.[6]

Most of the other translations of Pushkin's work contained in this book were undertaken by contemporaries of Yarmolinsky, a majority of them by his wife, Babette Deutsch. Oliver Elton's version of *The Bronze Horseman* and Constance Garnett's translation of Pushkin's address *To the Poet* are also included, as is Max Eastman's translation of Pushkin's dedication to the Decembrists, *Message to Siberia.*

Eastman was an early champion of Pushkin in New York radical circles at the time of the WWI and the Russian Revolution. He was co-founder of a radical journal of politics and the arts called *The Liberator* (later to become *The Workers' Monthly),* which published such writers as e e cummings, John Dos Passos, Ernest Hemingway and Edmund Wilson.

Eastman also raised the money to send the journalist John Reed to Russia in 1917 and published Reed's accounts of the Bolshevik Revolution in *The Liberator.* These reports were later published collectively as *Ten Days that Shook the World.* In 1922, Eastman went to Russia on a fact-finding tour for a year and nine months. He was in Russia during the period when Lenin died and witnessed the emerging clash between Leon Trotsky and the gravedigger of the revolution, Joseph Stalin.

Eastman sided with Trotsky and began a friendship with him

which lasted through to his exile in Mexico, where Trotsky was murdered by one of Stalin's henchmen in 1940. Eastman translated several of Trotsky's works into English, including his monumental three-volume *History of the Russian Revolution.*[7]

He also edited and published an American edition of Marx's *Das Kapital* and wrote several volumes of memoirs recording friendships and encounters he had with leading figures of his day, among them Charlie Chaplin, Albert Einstein, Sigmund Freud, Paul Robeson and Mark Twain (who was a friend of his parents). Eastman also translated several of Pushkin's poems, including his lewd, anti-clerical romp *The Gavriliad,* in which the Virgin Mary is seduced in turn by God, Satan and the Archangel Gabriel.

Despite the accusation that Constance Garnett's translations from the Russian often use outdated terms, that she occasionally omits difficult passages and that she does not always reflect the style of the author she is translating, Constance Garnett's work has nevertheless stood the test of time. When one of the current authorities on Chekhov, Donald Rayfield, came to revise his selected stories in *The Chekhov Omnibus* of 1994, he opted for Constance Garnett's translations to provide the basis for the new edition. Explaining his decision, Professor Rayfield wrote: '…a translator has to have a writer's gift as well as a linguist's skills, and we are often forced to choose between a talented writer who is an amateur linguist and a professional linguist who is an amateur writer. In the case of this selection of Chekhov stories, the deciding factor has been that the errors of an amateur linguist can be corrected, while the style, the subtle flow of a talented writer is inimitable'.[8]

Constance Garnett, Rayfield emphasises, suffered from many disadvantages: '…she had a patchy knowledge of Russian mores and religion, and had little acquaintance with the seamy side of life anywhere; she had been taught Russian imperfectly by the anarchist refugee Stepniak Kravchinsky…spent only two seasons in Russia and was never a confident speaker; she had no good dictionaries and few experts to consult; she worked under enormous pressure, attempting to provide the entire corpus of Russian prose for the English-speaking reader…'. Nevertheless: 'While she makes elementary blunders, her care in unravelling difficult syntactical knots and her research on the right terms for Chekhov's many plants, birds and fish are impressive. Above all, she was a natural writer…Constance Garnett's fidelity to Russian word order and to Chekhov's convoluted punctuation is a strength, not a weakness: she keeps nuances and continuity which more orthodox English style loses'.[9]

Two of Garnett's sternest critics were the Russian-born authors, Joseph Brodsky and Vladimir Nabokov. Brodsky criticised Garnett for blurring the distinctive authorial voices of different Russian writers, to the extent that: 'The reason English-speaking readers can barely tell the difference between Tolstoy and Dostoevsky is that they aren't reading the prose of either one. They're reading Constance Garnett'. For his part, Nabokov reckoned that Garnett's translations were typically 'dry and flat, and always unbearably demure'. When he was working on a study of Gogol's *The Inspector General,* using her translation, he complained: 'I can do nothing with Constance Garnett's dry shit'.[10]

Vladimir Nabokov was not a great admirer of any attempts to translate literary works from Russian into English, other than his own. When he came to undertake his translation of Pushkin's 'novel in verse' *Evgeny Onegin,* Nabokov proclaimed that it was a work which had already been 'mistranslated into many languages'.

The worst offenders, in his view – 'unfortunately available to college students' – were: '*Eugene Onéguine,* translated by Lieutenant-Colonel Spalding; *Eugene Onegin,* translated by Babette Deutsch in *The Works of Alexander Pushkin,* selected and edited by Avrahm Yarmolinsky; *Evgeny Onegin,* translated by Oliver Elton); *Eugene Onegin,* translated by Dorothea Prall Radin and George Z Patrick'.[11]

Nabokov's assessment of these attempts was as follows: 'All four are in meter and rhyme; all are the result of earnest effort and of an incredible amount of mental labour; all contain here and there little gems of ingenuity; and all are grotesque travesties of their model, rendered in dreadful verse, teeming with mistranslations. The least offender is the bluff, matter-of-fact Colonel; the worst is Professor Elton, who combines a kind of irresponsible verbal felicity with the most exuberant vulgarity and the funniest howlers'. In his view, the three German versions he had seen were 'the worst of the lot': one was 'beneath contempt', another 'bristles with incredible blunders and ridiculous interpolations'.[12] According to Nabokov, Russians themselves were responsible for 'the two greatest insults which have been hurled at Pushkin's masterpiece – the vile Tchaikovsky opera and the equally vile illustrations by Repin which decorate most editions of the novel'.[13]

One of the main troubles with would-be translators, Nabokov concluded: 'is their ignorance'. In his opinion, anyone who sets out to attempt a translation of *Onegin,* needed first: '… to acquire exact information in regard to a number of relevant subjects, such as the Russian Fables of Ivan Krylov, Byron's works, French poets of the 18th century, Rousseau's *La Nouvelle Heloïse,* Pushkin's biography, banking games, Russian songs relating to divination, Russian military ranks at the time as compared to Western European and American ones, the difference between cranberry and lingonberry, the rules of the English pistol duel as used in Russia, and the Russian language'.[14]

In what was to become his own theory on translation, Nabokov identified three definite conclusions he had arrived at, while working on *Onegin.* These were as follows:

— It is impossible to translate *Onegin* in rhyme.
— It is possible to describe in a series of footnotes the modulations and rhymes of the text as well as all its associations and other special features.
— It is possible to translate *Onegin* with reasonable accuracy by substituting for the 14 rhymed tetrameter lines of each stanza 14 unrhymed lines of varying length, from iambic dimeter to iambic pentameter.[15]

In an article he published in *Partisan Review (Vol. 22)* in 1955, entitled *Problems of Translation: Onegin in English,* Nabokov said his ideal would be to produce translations 'with copious footnotes, footnotes reaching up like skyscrapers to the top of this or that page so as to leave only the gleam of one textual line between commentary and eternity…when my *Onegin* is ready, it will either conform exactly to my vision or not appear at all'.[16] In the event, Nabokov's non-rhyming version of Pushkin's 'novel-in-verse' did appear, about a decade later, and conformed exactly to his vision. It was first published in a four-volume hardcover edition in 1964. This comprises a translator's introduction in Volume 1 together with a 'linear' translation of the poem; Volumes 2 and 3 provide an extensive, line-by-line and virtually word-by-word commentary on each chapter of the poem; and Volume 4 provides an Index to the whole, monumental enterprise.

The index alone runs to 109 pages and Nabokov's commentary is more than a thousand pages long. But there are no rhymes, except in the Appendix which includes a facsimile of Pushkin's original, barely decipherable but nevertheless in Russian and in verse. In the foreword to Volume 1, Nabokov explains his thinking thus: 'In transporting *Eugene Onegin* from Pushkin's Russian into my English I have sacrificed to completeness of meaning every formal element including the iambic rhythm, whenever its retention hindered fidelity. To my idea of literalism I sacrificed everything (elegance, euphony, clarity, good taste, modern usage, and even grammar) that the dainty mimic prizes higher than truth. Pushkin has likened translators to horses changed at the posthouses of civilisation. The greatest reward I can think of is that students may use my work as a pony'.[17]

When Nabokov's translation of *Eugene Onegin* finally appeared, it led to an extraordinary and acrimonious public feud between Nabokov and his former close friend and associate, Edmund Wilson. By the 1960s, both men were leading lights in the New York literary firmament. Nabokov had first established his reputation as a Russian author before arriving in New York but became famous in the West due to the huge commercial success of his novel *Lolita,* which was first published in 1955. Long before Nabokov's arrival in New York, Wilson was already a fixture on the literary scene. He had gone to school with Scott Fitzgerald and knew just about every important name in American public life since the 1920s. Wilson was the first to find work for Nabokov when he came to New York. In his role as literary editor of *The New Republic* Wilson commissioned book reviews from Nabokov within a few months of his arrival as an émigré in May 1940.

The pair, who maintained a friendship over the next 25 years, addressed each other in an extensive and endearing correspondence, later published by the American scholar, Simon Karlinsky, in a volume entitled *Dear Bunny, Dear Volodya*. Their friendship was predominantly based on a shared interest in literature and, oddly enough, in lepidoptery. Nabokov's first full-time job in New York was as an entomologist at the American Museum of Natural History and he later became curator of Lepidoptera at Harvard University's Museum of Comparative Zoology.

Just as Nabokov's approach to the translation of Pushkin was ideosyncratic, so was his approach to lepidoptery. The renowned palaeontologist Stephen Jay Gould once noted that Nabokov could be something of a stick-in-the-mud and had never accepted that the counting of chromosomes could be a valid way to distinguish species of insects. Instead, he preferred the older method which relied on the microscopic comparison of their genitalia. The Harvard Museum of Natural History still keeps Nabokov's genitalia cabinet, in which he stored his collection of male butterfly genitalia. Though not, presumably, those of his male literary rivals.

Although Nabokov and Wilson held literary, scientific and personal interests in common, their political attitudes were entirely different. Nabokov had been born into a prominent family of the Russian nobility. His grandfather was Justice Minister under Tsar Alexander II; his father was a leading liberal and secretary to the Provisional Government of Kerensky after the February revolution of 1917; his mother was grand-daughter to the millionaire owner of a gold-mine. Nabokov was 18 when the Bolsheviks took power in October 1917 and his family was then forced into exile, first to England, then Berlin, before finally leaving for New York. Meantime, Nabokov's father was shot dead in Berlin, not by a Bolshevik, but by a Russian monarchist. He was killed attempting to protect the intended target, Pavel Milyukov, leader of the Constitutional Democratic (Kadet) Party in exile.

Wilson had a comfortable enough background, too, growing up in New Jersey and New York Upstate. His father was a jurist who had been considered for a position on the US Supreme Court. But, unlike Nabokov, Wilson developed a deep antipathy to any manifestation of entrenched privilege and, like many of the generation which lived through the depression years of

1930's America, became an admirer of Soviet Russia, exactly at the time when the hopes and aspirations which had inspired the October Revolution were being systematically crushed by Joseph Stalin: 'Wilson, like the majority of American writers of the time, was swept up by a wave of doubts about the validity of his society's traditional structure and institutions. The Sacco and Vanzetti case, the Harlan County miners, the unemployment and the breadlines convinced many that a newer and better social model was needed'. [18]

In the spring of 1935, Wilson travelled to Russia on a Guggenheim Fellowship, hoping to do research on the Russian Revolution at the Marx-Engels Institute in Moscow. During this visit, he met D S Mirsky – author of *A History of Russian Literature* – and it was Mirsky who stimulated Wilson's interest in Pushkin.

According to the author of *The Nabokov-Wilson Letters,* Simon Karlinsky, Wilson specifically undertook to learn Russian at the end of his trip so that he would be able to read Pushkin in the original. [19]

In 1937, to coincide with the Pushkin centenary, Wilson wrote an essay *In Honour of Pushkin* and, two years later, he published an essay on *The Bronze Horseman,* together with his own prose translation of Pushkin's narrative poem. Both essays appear in Wilson's book *The Triple Thinkers,* which also analyses the works of A E Housman, Flaubert, Henry James and Bernard Shaw and discusses Marxism and Literature. [20] The feud which erupted between Wilson and Nabokov in 1965 caused an absolute sensation. It began when *The New York Review of Books* published a review, by Wilson, highly critical of Nabokov's translation of *Eugene Onegin.*[21]

Nabokov then wrote a reply, which was published in the same journal later that year and this was followed by a more detailed rebuttal in the February 1966 edition of another literary journal, *Encounter.* According to Simon Karlinsky: '…the exchange generated the kind of excitement that an evenly matched, no-holds barred fight usually does and many literary and scholarly figures jumped into the fray, taking sides, egging on the two opponents and administering a few indiscriminate kicks of their own in this or that direction'.[22]

Edmund Wilson's opening salvo, in a review which was headed *The Strange Case of Pushkin and Nabokov*, pulled no punches. He briefly acknowledges that he was a personal friend of Nabokov – 'for whom he feels a warm affection sometimes chilled by exasperation' – but immediately goes on to say: 'Since Mr Nabokov is in the habit of introducing any job of this kind which he undertakes by an announcement that he is unique and incomparable and that everybody else who has attempted it is an oaf and an ignoramus, incompetent as a linguist and a scholar, usually with the implication that he is also a low-class person and a ridiculous personality, Nabokov ought not to complain if the reviewer, though trying not to imitate his bad literary manners, does not hesitate to underline his weaknesses'.[23]

Shortly before Nabokov's own translation of *Eugene Onegin* appeared, another version had been published by the German-born Pushkin scholar and translator, Walter Arndt. In the April 1964 edition of *The New York Review of Books,* Nabokov subjected Arndt's translation to his characteristic brand of withering contempt. The author of a soon-to-be-published translation might find it 'awkward' to criticize a just-published translation of the same work, Nabokov said, but:

'…in the present case I can, and should, master my embarrassment: for something must be done, some lone, hoarse voice must be raised, to defend both the helpless dead poet and the credulous college student from the kind of pitiless and irresponsible paraphrast whose product I am about to discuss'.[24]

Nabokov declared that he was ready to admit to a 'certain morbid fascination' for Walter Arndt's perseverance in the 'monstrous undertaking' of 'twisting some five thousand Russian iambic tetrameters, with a rigid pattern of masculine and feminine rhymes, into an equal number of similarly rhymed English tetrameters'.[25]

By contrast, Nabokov limited his effort 'to a plain, prosy and rhymeless translation'. But that did not prevent him from then launching in to a systematic hatchet job on the Arndt translation. The entire review was taken up with itemising what he regarded as a combination of shoddy mistranslations, the use of comic scansion, burlesque rhymes, crippled clichés, vulgarisms,

Germanisms and stale style, howlers, inadequate knowledge of Russian, wobbly English and padding.[26]

In a reply, published in the same issue of the *NYRB*, and entitled *Goading the Pony,* Walter Arndt expressed no surprise that Nabokov found it possible to 'master his embarrassment': 'All prior invaders of the precinct of *Onegin* translation have found him coiled at the exit and have been dosed, jointly and severally, alive or posthumously, with much the same mixture of arrogance, cuteness and occasional distortion'.[27] 'The living among them', says Arndt: 'may again relish with a certain fascination the fine sparkle of pure venom behind the sacerdotal (albeit genuine and admirable) solicitude for textual integrity'.[28]

Arndt noted that he obviously differs from Mr Nabokov: '... on the manner, or even the possibility, of conveying a poetic message across cultural and linguistic boundaries, and even on where and how to make the inevitable sacrifices'. His own idea of the translation's purpose is not to seat the would-be reader of Pushkin 'on the kind of prose pony he provides...and then goading him...up a pyramid of footnotes every bumpy line or two, throughout a multi-volume trek'.[29]

Arndt did not doubt 'the scholarly yield and value' of Nabokov's undertaking: 'I have no doubt it will be outstanding and many besides myself have been eagerly looking forward to it for a decade'. But what it will supply is copious and accurate *information* 'and not an inkling of the poetic impact which a verse translation, diluted and flawed as it must be, can at least intermittently convey'.[30]

The way Edmund Wilson saw it, Walter Arndt was to be congratulated for having attempted the *tour de force* of translating the whole of *Onegin* into the original iambic tetrameter and rather intricate stanza form. By contrast, by sticking to a 'literal' translation, which quite often 'simply jolts into prose', Nabokov had managed to produce: 'a bald and awkward language which has nothing in common with Pushkin, or with the usual writing of Nabokov'.

With what Wilson describes as Nabokov's 'sado-masochistic Dostoyevskian tendencies so acutely noted by Sartre', his sole achievement had been to: 'torture both the reader and himself by flattening Pushkin out and denying to his own powers the scope for their full play'.[31]

The single, characteristic Nabokovian trait that Edmund Wilson recognised in 'this uneven and sometimes banal translation' is 'the addiction to rare and unfamiliar words, which, in view of his declared intention to stick so close to the text… are entirely inappropriate here'. What was the point of having to resort to the Oxford English Dictionary (OED) to seek out an English word the reader has never seen and would never have any occasion to use? 'To inflict on the reader such words is not really to translate at all, for it is not to write idiomatic and recognisable English'.[32]

Nabokov's 'aberrations' in this line, Wilson said: '…are a good deal more objectionable than anything I have found in Arndt': 'He gives us, for example, *remomorating, predicament, curveted, habitude, drummers, formalistic, gleam, diet, shipped* and *scrab*. All these can be found in the OED, but they are all entirely dictionary words, usually labelled 'dialect', 'archaic' or 'obsolete'. The upshot is clear:

'I am sorry to say that, although Arndt is no great poet and that his effort to stick to the rhyme scheme sometimes leads him to a certain farfetchedness, his version is, in general, much closer to *Onegin* than any of the others I have sampled and is likely to give the reader a better idea of what the poem sounds like in Russian than Nabokov's so tortured version'.[33]

Edmund Wilson is especially critical of what he refers to as Nabakov's *obiter dicta,* or incidental remarks, which are: '… partly the result of Nabokov's compulsion to give unnecessary information: he cannot mention a book, however obscure, which has influenced or been mentioned by Pushkin or which contains something similar to something in *Onegin* without inserting his opinion of it; and partly the result of his instinct to take digs at great reputations'.[34]

The list of poets, novelists, playwrights and critics from throughout the ages who fall below Nabokov's exacting standards spares few blushes. So, Virgil, the Roman poet who wrote two of the greatest epics in world history, *The Iliad* and *The Aeneid,* is dismissed as 'insipid' and a 'pale pederast' and Voltaire is chastised for having written 'abominably pedestrian verses'.[35]

In a similar vein, Rousseau is dismissed for his 'morbid,

intricate and at the same time rather naïve mind'; Sheridan for his 'singularly inept comedy'; Goethe for his 'queer strain of triviality'; Stendhal for his 'paltry literary style'; Balzac for his 'much overrated vulgar novelette'; and Belinsky for being 'famous, but talentless'. Dostoyevsky, is said to have been 'a much overrated, sentimental and Gothic novelist of the time' and *Pyotr Ilyich*, Tchaikovsky's operatic version of Pushkin's *Eugene Onegin*, is both 'silly' and 'slapdash'.[36]

As the Harvard professor and another fellow Russian émigré, Alexander Gerschenkron, commented in his contribution to the Nabokov-Wilson battle royal, all of this stuff might have impressed the undergraduates at Cornell University where Nabokov lectured. However, he says: 'most of this remarkably foolish abuse is heaped quite gratuitously in that it has no bearing at all on *Eugene Onegin* or Pushkin in general'. [37]Gerschenkron conceded that Nabokov's commentary was a 'monumental handiwork' which contained 'real intuitions, numerous flashes of brilliance and a mass of solid learning'. It was a 'seminal contribution' and 'the fruit of enormous industry, skill and erudition'.[38]

Nevertheless, Gerschenkron concluded: 'It is indeed deplorable that so much of Nabokov's great effort is so sadly distorted by the desire to be original at all cost, by confused theorising, by promises that never could be redeemed, by spiteful pedantry, unbridled emotions and, last but not least, by unrestrained egoism'. All of this, he said, might annoy some readers: 'It will revolt others'. All told, Gerschenkron summed up Nabokov's work as one which: 'can and should be studied, but despite all the cleverness and occasional brilliance, it cannot be read'.[39]

Wilson also concedes that Nabokov's extensive 'commentary' to the poem – 'if one skips the *longueurs*', '...does make very pleasant reading, and it represents an immense amount of labour – labour which the author, in a letter, once described to me as *achovy*, a delightful Russian adjective which means that something makes you say "*ach!*". This I can well believe'. [40] Nabokov's 'commentary' is, indeed, quite extraordinary, detailing, as it does, every possible influence on Pushkin's construction of the poem, the meaning of references to individuals, events in Russian history, literary influences or nuances of language.

All told, Edmund Wilson doubts whether anyone could have explored Pushkin's sources so thoroughly: 'Mr Nabokov seems really to have done his best to read everything that Pushkin could possibly have read and has shown that he took over from poetry and fiction a good many current phrases'. However, he also thought that Nabokov underrated Pushkin's knowledge of English and that, on this, he 'quite disregards the evidence'.[41]

Pushkin's competence in languages, according to Wilson, was in fact considerable.

Going by the volumes of Pushkin's notes and miscellaneous papers which had been published, many extracts were from English writers which Pushkin had copied out in English. These included passages, or whole poems, by Byron, Wordsworth, Coleridge and Barry Cornwall and a quotation from Francis Bacon.

They also contained passages, poems and documents in French, German, Italian, Spanish and Polish and 'show that with Hebrew and Arabic he had at least got as far as the alphabets'. Pushkin was also capable of composing Latin epigrams and at the time of his death had not only been studying Greek but had translated and transcribed two odes by the Greek poet, Sappho.[42]

One of the aspects of Vladimir Nabokov's commentary for *Onegin* that Edmund Wilson did find 'particularly satisfactory' was his discussion of Pushkin's relations with the Decembrist conspirators. As he explains, Pushkin had planned a Tenth Canto, or Chapter Ten, for the poem in which he intended that the central character, *Evgeny Onegin,* would try to bring a purpose to his otherwise futile life and join the Decembrist conspirators in their quest for a constitutional government in Russia.

Only fragments of this chapter remained because Pushkin was only too aware that its contents were politically explosive – so much so that he intentionally mixed the verses, writing consecutive lines in different corners of the page and some of it in a form of code, or cryptogram. Pushkin worked on *Eugene Onegin* between 1825 and 1830. This was at a time when he was under constant police surveillance. After Nicholas I had spent the first six months of his reign investigating the causes of the Decembrist uprising and punishing its perpetrators, he had set about having the censorship code redrafted and, in July 1826, the Third Department of His Imperial Majesty's Own Chancery was established. From then on, Pushkin's mail was intercepted and he had to submit anything he wrote for inspection, first to its chief, Count Alexander Benckendorff, then, through him, directly to the Tsar.

Eventually, fearing that he would be in serious trouble should his Chapter Ten ever be detected by the censorship or the police, Pushkin burned the manuscript in 1830, and never rewrote it. Nevertheless, a few fragments survived and, as the Russian-born American historian George Vernadsky had shown, even special students of Pushkin paid no attention to these drafts until 1910, when P O Morozov, a Pushkin scholar, succeeded in deciphering the fragments. Nabokov devotes an entire chapter to the missing fragments of the Tenth Canto in his commentary and in this he not only minutely examines every known aspect of their content and meaning, he also picks the code used by Pushkin – albeit, as Wilson notes, without 'telling us, as we should like to know, exactly what this cryptogram was'.[43]

In fact, as he acknowledges, Nabokov had based his own analysis on research which by then had already been carried out by eminent Soviet academicians, beginning with Morozov and then followed by Lerner, Gofman and Tomashevsky. To give an idea of the lengths Pushkin had gone to disguise his intentions in Chapter Ten, the section of the manuscript which is written in cryptogram comprises a half-sheet of paper, folded in two. As Nabokov explains, the cryptogram is written: '…with columns of lines decipherable as sixty-three discrete verses, on the inner side of both quarters, the right-hand page containing thirty-two verses, and the left-hand page, thirty-one verses. The paper has an 1829 watermark, and the pages have been numbered in red ink by the police'.[44]

According to Nabokov, it wasn't difficult for Morozov to break Pushkin's 'clumsy' code but the task of deciphering the cryptogram was not made any easier by the method used by Pushkin to mix up the order of his lines and stanzas: 'Pushkin's plan in scrambling the fifth line was, I think, to make things more difficult by starting with stanza five, then going to the next, then leaving one out, then leaving two out, and so on'.[45]

The significant flaw in this plan proved to be that Pushkin was a 'wretched cryptographer' and that implementation of his plan turned out to be disastrous. As a result: 'When he consulted his set of fourth lines, he failed to notice that he had left out stanzas V (five) and X (ten), so that when he wrote down the fifth lines of what he thought were IV (four), VI (six), VIII (eight) and X (ten), these proved to be actually IV (four), VI (six), VIII (eight) and XI (eleven)'. Nabokov concludes that Pushkin soon noticed there was something wrong with his cipher 'and in utter disgust gave up the whole matter'.[46]

Apart from the surviving fragments, we know from a memoir written by a Captain Yuzefovich, what Pushkin intended would happen next to *Onegin*. Yuzefovich served in the Russian Imperial Army stationed in the Caucasus at the same time as Pushkin – an experience which Pushkin describes vividly in his own memoir *Journey to Arzrum (or Erzerum)*. Yuzefovich recalled that Pushkin told him one day, in June 1829, that: 'Onegin will either perish in the Caucasus or join the Decembrist movement'.[47]

We also know about the existence of Chapter Ten from diary entries, letters and notes written in the margins of two of Pushkin's drafts: one of these appears in manuscript of his story *The Blizzard,* written on 20 October 1830, where Pushkin has scribbled: 'Oct. 19 was burned X Canto'; the second is a note which simply says: 'In X Canto'. This appears in the margin of *Onegin's Journey,* another chapter of the poem which was never completed (it would have been Chapter Eight).[48]

Pyotr Vyazemsky later recorded in his diary that, in December 1830 – two months after the burning of Chapter Ten – Pushkin had recited from memory a set of stanzas which, according to Vyazemsky, dealt with: 'the events of 1812 and later ones. A splendid chronicle'. Vyazemsky then quotes lines from Pushkin's recitation which correspond with those in the remaining fragments of Chapter 10.

Most convincing of all is the recollection made by Alexander Turgenev, a lifelong friend of Pushkin. A letter written to his brother Nikolay, who had been a prominent member of the Decembrist's Union of Welfare and who was by then then living permanently in Paris (in 1832) contains the following passage: 'Here are some immortal lines about you: Alexander Pushkin could not publish a certain part of his *Onegin* in which he describes the latter's travels across Russia and the insurrection of

1825: he mentions you among others...' [49] Alexander Turgenev had figured prominently during various episodes in Pushkin's life. He had helped to enrol Pushkin at the Tsarskoe Selo Lycée in 1811; interceded to ensure that Pushkin's exile in 1820 took him to the warm South, not the frozen North; arranged his transfer to Odessa in 1823; and, after Pushkin's funeral service at the Konyushennaya (Royal Stables) Church, in St Petersburg, Turgenev accompanied Pushkin's coffin to the Svyatogorsky Monastery in the Province of Pskov, where he was buried on 6 February 1837.

As Simon Karlinsky notes in his introduction to his own book, *The Nabokov-Wilson Letters*, there had always been two opposing magnetic poles in their intellectual relationship. The one, drawing them together, was Pushkin. The other, forcing them apart, was Lenin. Shortly after he returned from Russia, in 1937 – at the time of the Pushkin Centennial – Wilson had published an essay on *Eugene Onegin* and then an essay on *The Bronze Horseman*, together with his own prose translation of the poem. As Karlinsky stresses: 'The inclusion of these two essays in Wilson's book, *The Triple Thinkers (1938)* '...was a pioneering event in American criticism, since for most American critics and readers of that time Russian literature started with Turgenev (and probably ended with Gorky)'.[50]

The beginning of Wilson's contact with Nabokov had coincided with Wilson's renewed interest in Pushkin. The two collaborated on a translation of Pushkin's verse play, *Mozart and Salieri* (the text of which later provided the screenplay for the highly successful movie, *Amadeus*). A further series of essays on Pushkin written by Wilson for *The Atlantic Monthly*, were then included in his book *A Window on Russia*.

Again, these were the direct result of discussions and exchanges on the subject with Nabokov. But, as Simon Karlinsky notes, it becomes clear from the correspondence that Nabokov and Wilson's involvement with Pushkin's writings and biography began to give rise to something like a 'proprietary attitude' on each side, to the extent that: 'The initially amicable disagreements about Pushkin's metrical variety or lack of it and the extent of his proficiency in Latin or English, gradually acquire an impatient edge, pointing towards the later explosive disagreement over the

Onegin translation and commentary'.[51]

Nabokov's strictures on his preference for literal translations of Pushkin established an orthodoxy that Pushkin's poetry was, to all intents and purposes, 'untranslatable'. This dominant view bedevilled the approach to Pushkin for decades to come and it is only really in the last few years that the smoke has started to clear from this particular battlefield. To begin with, as many commentators have pointed out, Nabokov was not entirely consistent in his approach to translations. Nabokov had been born into what he himself described as 'a perfectly normal trilingual childhood'. This meant that he read and wrote Russian, English and French by the time he was seven years old.

By the time he was 14, he had read everything written by Tolstoy, Shakespeare and Flaubert in their original languages. As well as then becoming a scientist at Harvard and a professor at Stanford, Cornell and Harvard, Nabokov had also been a life-long translator, from English, French and German into Russian and from Russian into English and French. As a boy, Nabokov had been besotted with stories of the Wild West and, at the age of 11, translated one of these tales – *The Headless Horseman* – by the 19th century Scots-Irish American novelist, Mayne Reid, into French. His translation of Lewis Carroll's *Alice in Wonderland* into Russian, which he undertook at the age of 22, is widely regarded as one of the best translations ever done and, in the early 1930s, he translated the prologue to Goethe's *Faust*. He also sought permission from James Joyce to translate *Ulysses* into Russian and signed a contract to translate Tolstoy's *Anna Karenina* but neither of these projects came to fruition.

When Nabokov arrived in New York in 1940, he had intended to force himself to write in English but discovered that best way for him to make money was to translate from Russian. This he did, translating works by Pushkin, Lermontov and Tyutchev which were published under the title *Three Russian Poets,* in 1944. Nabokov also translated works by the Russian poets, Fet and Khodasevich and, during his time teaching Russian at American universities he translated more Russian poetry for his students. In each of these instances, Nabokov 'consistently violated the literal approach' he had insisted was essential in both Russian and English translations of poetry, retaining the form, rhyme and metre of the original texts.[52]

That said, it is also the case that Edmund Wilson is not entirely consistent in his insistence that Pushkin's poetry could be effectively translated into English. When he came to work on Pushkin's *The Bronze Horseman* for his book *The Triple Thinkers,* Wilson translated the entire poem in prose, making no attempt whatever to reproduce the rhyme and meter of the original. In the introduction to his translation, Wilson says: 'It would be impossible to reproduce in English the peculiar poetic merits of *The Bronze Horseman.* The terseness and compactness of Pushkin's style, which constitutes one of the chief difficulties of translating him, reach a point in this poem where, as Mirsky says, the 'words and their combinations' are 'charged to breaking point with all the weight of meaning they can bear'.[53]

Nevertheless, Wilson says he still believes 'it is worth the while to attempt to present *The Bronze Horseman* in English'. At the time he was writing, in 1948, he was aware of only one English translation of the poem and that had that been done by Professor Oliver Elton. This version was published by Avrahm Yarmolinsky in his *The Poems, Prose and Plays of Alexander Pushkin* (1936). Wilson rates Oliver Elton's effort as 'a very respectable performance: it has certain merits which mine cannot pretend to. Professor Elton, following Pushkin's rhymed verse, has been able to succeed far better than I in catching the tumult and movement of the poem, and he has occasionally struck off a fine Pushkinian line: but he has blurred the effect of the whole by diluting it with a kind of stock romantic verbiage'.[54]

In recent years, the growing popularity of translation theory as an academic field of interest has introduced a new generation of students to Nabokov's 'thundering assault on the folly of trying to translate rhyme by rhyme'. According to David Bellos, Director of the Program in Translation and Intercultural Communication at Princeton University, Nabokov's views on poetry translation have coloured many arguments in the translation studies field with a 'peculiarly vituperative tone'.[55]

In his book *Is that a Fish in Your Ear – The Amazing Adventure of Translation,* Bellos asks why it was that Nabokov took such an uncompromising stance: 'There's a profound reason for his frankly uncharacteristic modesty in this case. Who can rival

Pushkin? No Russian writer can dream of doing such a thing – yet every Russian writer also dreams of unseating Pushkin from his throne'. Because of this, the stakes for Nabokov, more than they might have been for just about anyone else, were exceptionally high.[56]

Bellos assumes that, had he tried to recast Pushkin in English verse, he probably 'could have done so like no other had he let himself dare'. In fact, Nabokov had translated some stanzas of *Onegin* into English verse in the 1950s already but then, according to Bellos, what happened was that he 'turned around in fright. He could see he was not Pushkin. Later on, he adopted his servile-path of pseudo-literal translation not because it was relevant to the study or practice of literary translation, but because it helped hide that embarrassing fact'.[57]

It is worth quoting in full David Bellos's overall assessment of Nabokov's 'public lesson in poetry translation'. In his view, it is 'threadbare and misleading': 'There are far more ways than three of translating fixed form. A 'paraphrase' is not the only alternative to 'lexical' translation and the latter can in no way even now be done by a machine. The 'literal' style Nabokov proposes and claims to use is just what anyone else would call plain prose. Nabokov's introduction to his exhaustive exploration of all the allusions and referential meanings of the words of Pushkin's novel tells us many interesting things (about Nabokov, about Russia, about language and style) but nothing about the translation of form'.[58]

To emphasise the point, David Bellos notes that several verse translations of *Eugene Onegin* into English are now available. When an Indian postgraduate came across a second-hand copy of the version published by Charles Johnston in 1972, he composed a story of his own life using the same regular form. His name was Vikram Seth and his book, *The Golden Gate* was later described by Gore Vidal as 'The Great Californian Novel', just as the Russian critic, Belinsky had described Pushkin's *Eugene Onegin* one hundred years earlier as presenting 'an encyclopaedia of Russian life'.[59]

Even more remarkably, Seth's *Golden Gate* subsequently fell into the hands of an Israeli scholar, Maya Arad, who then read *Onegin* in the original Russian and went on to write her own 'novel in verse' *Another Place, a Foreign City*, in 2003. If the formal constraints of *Eugene Onegin* can be used to tell stories of America and Israel, asks Bellos, why can't they be used to equal poetic effect to tell the very story that Pushkin told. Nabokov, he says, 'claims this is 'mathematically impossible'. Mathematics has nothing to do with it. What he meant was he wasn't going to try'.[60]

One translator who did produce an exceptional verse translation of Pushkin's *Eugene Onegin* is the English translator and Russian scholar, Stanley Mitchell. Like Constance Garnett before him, Mitchell was an inhabitant of London's East End. The difference being that he was born there, in Clapton, in 1932. Both of his parents were Jewish immigrants, his mother from Belarus and his father from the Ukraine. They spoke Yiddish at home.

During his stint of National Service, Mitchell learnt both German and Russian and after the war went to Oxford, where his specialist subjects were Russian literature and art and comparative literature. Like Constance Garnett, Mitchell was a committed socialist. He joined the Communist Party at Oxford but then left after the Hungarian Uprising of 1956. In 1963, he wrote an influential article for the *New Left Review*, entitled *Romanticism and Socialism*, and introduced two important works of Marxist theory to an English-speaking audience. These were *The Historical Novel* by the Hungarian Marxist, Georg Lukács (1962) and *Understanding Brecht* by Walter Benjamin (2003).

Lukács's views on Pushkin had an important influence on Mitchell and are outlined in *Pushkin's Place in World Literature*, from his book of essays, *Writer and Critic* (1978).[61] Mitchell's triumphant verse translation of *Eugene Onegin* was published by Penguin Books in 2008, three years before he died.[62] As Mitchell explains in his introduction to *Eugene Onegin*, the idea for the translation originated in a series of seminars held in 1966 in the Literature Department of the newly founded University of Essex, where he was the first ever lecturer in Russian literature.

At the time, he notes: 'Pushkin was much less known in Britain than he is now and considered untranslatable'. This was because of the tablets of stone passed down by Nabokov. 'A group of us, questioning this and the notion of untranslatability as such, undertook a collective translation of *Eugene Onegin*. Our poet-professor, Donald Davie, was to provide the verse. The project failed, and Davie died, but without his initiative, I should never have embarked, many years later, on the present version'.[63]

Stanley Mitchell's translation of *Eugene Onegin* follows on from the Charles Johnston 1977 version, which 'was the first to put Pushkin's poem on the map in English-speaking countries', inspiring Vikram Seth and others. Johnston was a diplomat, married into the Russian aristocracy and his translation had about it, Mitchell thought, an aura which was a bit: 'old-fashioned like those autumnal productions of Chekhov that once flourished on the English stage'.[64]

Commenting on the earliest of the *Onegin* verse translations into English, by Oliver Elton, Mitchell says that: 'there is little lightness about his translation, which is full of 18th or early-19th century phraseology – 'thou', 'thee', 'tis', 'twas', 'fain', 'nay' and many inversions and contortions…Pushkin's language is modern by comparison with Elton's and is felt to be modern in Russia today'.[65] Oliver Elton was the King Alfred Professor of English at Liverpool University. He had family roots in the landed gentry and had taught himself Russian.

As for Nabokov's version of *Onegin,* Stanley Mitchell says that, in his opinion, it is a hybrid of 'period' and artifice, which prefigures the post-modernism of another translator of Pushkin, the American Douglas Hofstadter. Hofstadter, a cognitive scientist at Indiana University, regarded the variability of translations as 'incontrovertible evidence of the limitless flexibility of human minds'. Whereas Nabokov still holds the text sacrosanct 'apart from his bizarre archaisms', Hofstadter turns it into 'a quarry of personal interpolations and alterations, retaining only stanza, rhyme and metre, all, he assures us, in a Pushkinian sense of fun'.[66]

Mitchell was, clearly, not entirely convinced: 'I have attempted in my translation to write it in a contemporary idiom that avoids the antiquarian or the modern/postmodern'.[67] Mitchell preferred the approach taken by another American, James Falen, Professor Emeritus of Russian at Tennessee University. His translation of *Onegin*, published in 1980, managed to synthesize influences from the Nabokov translation while retaining Pushkin's stanzas. Mitchell says: 'I am at one here with the American, James Falen, who remarked of his admirable 1990 version of *Onegin* that he aimed 'to adapt the rhythms of the poem to the rhythms of English speech today and to avoid 'the sorts of inversions and verbal contortions that in his view marred earlier translations'. There is no need for dated words, Mitchell thought, other than for metrical reasons: 'The rhyming and metrical format of *Onegin* declares that it is a historical work. It is not a form that is common today'.[68]

Another contemporary translator of Russian poetry and literature, Robert Chandler, writing about Stanley Mitchell's life for *The Independent,* said that his translation of *Eugene Onegin* is one of the finest of all verse translations from Russian into English.[69]

When he wrote about his experience *On Finishing My Translation of Eugene Onegin,* for the literary journal *Cardinal Points,* Mitchell recalled that: 'When I was translating *Onegin* my shrink asked me, as they always do, what I 'felt' about it, how I responded to this or that character. I pondered and replied that I felt nothing, that I only had one concern – to get the translation as 'right' as possible in terms of style, vocabulary, rhyme and meter. In other words, my task was purely technical. 'Feeling' was confined to the intensity of the task. I was retired but had never worked so hard at anything before. The translation took between seven and ten years. Every stanza was a struggle'.[70]

Before he started on the translation, he said that he had regarded his life as a failure 'because of the bipolar disorder which nearly ruined me'. There had been several periods during the translation when he had either been depressed or manic. But, after he had finished, he knew: 'I shall never have to feel a failure again. Repeating Pushkin's self-congratulation on finishing another piece of work, I said of mine: 'Well done, you son of a bitch!'.[71]

Stanley Mitchell was 75 when he finished his translation of *Eugene Onegin.* In his final years, he had already started work on a verse translation of Pushkin's *The Bronze Horseman.* This remained unfinished when Stanley Mitchell died in 2011 but the manuscript was completed in exemplary fashion by Anthony Wood and published in 2015 in *The Penguin Book of Russian Poetry.*[72]

In Pushkin's day, poetry was regularly translated from one language to another, mostly into French. In an unfinished article he wrote for his own magazine *The Contemporary*, shortly before his death, Pushkin noted that: 'For a long time the French disregarded their neighbours' literatures – being exclusively faithful to the models of the seventeenth century they did not recognise any foreign writer as being equal to those who had immortalised their shores'. This is the opening quote in the article which Pushkin wrote in defence of John Milton who 'of all great foreign authors… was most unfortunate as far as France was concerned'.[73] Pushkin took particular issue with Victor Hugo's 'dull and monstrous' play *Cromwell* for the way in which it represents Milton: 'as a pathetic madman and insignificant windbag'.

But the main purpose of the article was to say something about the translation of Milton's *Paradise Lost* which had been published by the doyenne of French romanticism, the vicomte de Chateaubriand. Pushkin was relieved to discover that Chateaubriand's attempt 'to a certain extent smooths over some of the sins of the young French writers, who had so innocently yet so cruelly insulted that mighty shade'. However, there is one aspect of the translation to which Pushkin drew particular attention: this was the fact that Chateaubriand has translated Milton 'almost word for word, as close a rendering as French syntax allowed'. For Pushkin, this appears: 'an arduous and thankless task, passed over unnoticed by the majority of readers and one which can be appreciated by one or two specialists!' The question which then arises is: 'But is the new translation a success?'. Pushkin's answer to this question is especially interesting in the light of the Nabokov-Wilson controversy:

'There is no doubt that in attempting to render Milton *word for word* Chateaubriand could not in his version preserve accurately both the meaning and the idiomatic turns of phrase. A literal translation can never be true to its original. Every language has its own locutions, its accepted rhetorical figures, its assimilated expressions which cannot be translated into another language simply by using the corresponding words. Take a basic phrase: *Comment vous portez-vous?* How do you do? Try and translate these word for word into Russian. If even the Russian language, which is so flexible and rich in idioms and locutions, so derivative and adaptable in its relations with foreign languages, is not suitable for line-by-line or word-for-word translations, how can French, so cautious in its habits, so jealous of its traditions, so unfriendly even to those languages which belong to the same family, endure such a test? This is rapidly true in a tussle with Milton's language – a poet at once refined and naïve, sombre, obscure, expressive, independent and audacious to the point of absurdity'.[74]

The monumental fallout between Vladimir Nabokov and Edmund Wilson was not confined to their views on literary translation, it also had an intensely political aspect. In December 1940, Wilson published his book *To the Finland Station*, which documents the intellectual origins of the Russian revolution in the ideas of Western thinkers such as Hegel, Saint-Simon, Marx and Engels as well as those of the Russians revolutionaries Herzen, Chernyshevsky, Trotsky and Lenin.

Nabokov thought highly of the extensive research Wilson had undertaken but he was not so impressed by his portrayal of Lenin as 'the only true spokesman for Russian socialism and Marxism' and for what he regarded as Wilson's unfair dismissal of Lenin's other socialist and liberal opponents as 'representatives of the bourgeoisie'.[75]

In *To the Finland Station* and in his book of 'twelve essays on literary subjects', *The Triple Thinkers,* Wilson depicted Lenin as 'a warm-hearted humanitarian, a freedom-loving democrat and a sensitive critic of literature and the arts'. In an essay entitled *Marxism and Literature,* which is included in *The Triple Thinkers,* Wilson recounts that, 'like most Russians', Lenin was sensitive to music. Maxim Gorky had once famously described how Lenin loved Beethoven's *Appassionata* sonata so much he had said he would like to listen to it every day.[76]

For Nabokov, whose family had fled the revolution, this was all too much. His own novel, *The Gift* had also explored the origins of the Russian Revolution through the biography of Nikolai Chernyshevsky, one of the early adherents of utopian socialism and founder of the Narodniks. Nabokov's central theme in *The Gift* was that the roots of totalitarianism in Russia could all be discerned in 'the ostensibly libertarian but actually dogmatic and fanatical ideologies of an earlier generation'.

And the main representative of this tendency, in Nabokov's view, was Lenin, who made no secret of his admiration for Chernyshevsky's devotion to the overthrow of Tsarism. He consciously chose the title of Chernyshevsky's immensely popular work *What is to be done?* for his own pamphlet on the 'burning questions of the day', which he wrote in 1902. Lenin was said to have pored over Chernyshevsky's book for weeks, at the age of 18, and later kept returning to it.[77]

When it was published in 1863, Chernyshevsky's *What is to be done?* sold more books than any other since the start of printing in Russia. According to Avrahm Yarmolinsky it became the Bible of the radical youth: 'For all its glaring defects as a work of fiction it made effective propaganda for women's emancipation, for Socialism, and, indirectly, for revolution'. It was first published in the pages of *The Contemporary,* the journal founded by Pushkin.

Nabokov thought it inconceivable that anyone could regard Lenin as a kindly humanitarian. In a poem he wrote as a teenager, in 1917, he described Lenin's Bolsheviks as 'grey, rag-tag people'. In his later novel *Bend Sinister,* a fantasy about the coming to power of a despotic dictator, Nabokov interspersed quotes from Lenin's speeches and from the Soviet Constitution with what he called 'gobs of Nazi pseudo-efficiency'. Edmund Wilson, in turn, took a dim view of Nabokov's attitude towards Lenin and the Bolsheviks. In one of his letters to Volodya (his pet name for Nabokov), he said: 'You are not good at this kind of subject which involves questions of politics and social change, because you are totally uninterested in these matters and have never taken the trouble to understand them'.[78]

In a postscript to his essay *Pushkin and Nabokov*, Wilson wrote that, even as a Russian, Nabokov had a 'rather peculiar status'. Nabokov's parents were immensely rich and, in his own account of his boyhood, he described how his father, wanting to be true to his democratic principles, had decided to send his son to the kind of school where the other pupils would not be well-off but this had only 'aroused a certain amount of ridicule, inspired by class discrimination, by having him brought in a limousine – which seems to show a strange lack of tact'.[79]

One wonders', says Wilson, 'how much Nabokov is aware

of his double snobbery: on the one hand, to social inferiors; on the other, to the stupid old-liners (*conservatives)* whom he has never ceased to dread. With the ordinary, vulgar Russian, among whom he includes the makers of the Russian Revolution, he feels no solidarity at all'. In Wilson's view, Nabokov: 'despises the Communist regime and, it seems to me, does not even understand how it works or how it came to be'.[80]

This was not the first time Nabokov had been involved in a controversy over his politics and translation theory. A few years earlier, he had crossed swords with another Russian expat, and pre-eminent translation theorist of his day, Roman Jakobson. In an article on *Translation Theory and Cold War Politics,* Brian Baer of Kent State University argues that 'the relationship between these two enormously talented individuals raises important questions regarding translation and politics, translation and exile, the agency of the translator, the connection of theory to history, and the very identity of the literary text which are still relevant today'.[81]

Although the argument between Nabokov and Jakobson was less acrimonious than the one with Wilson, their respective theoretical positions were to become extremely influential in the subsequent development of translation theory. Jakobson had been born in Moscow, studied Slavic languages at the Philological Faculty of Moscow University, learned Sanskrit in St Petersburg and, in 1915, established the Moscow Linguistic Circle, dedicated to the study of poetic language. He also co-founded the St Petersburg group OPOIAZ (Organisation for the Study of Poetic Language) and later the Prague Linguistic Circle. Jakobson developed contacts with avant-garde literary and artistic circles everywhere he went and was a close friend of many of the radical artists and poets known as the Futurists, whose manifesto 'A Slap in the Face of Public Taste' (1912) demanded that the classical literary canon be 'thrown from the steamship of modernity'.

In his essays on Pushkin, Nabokov had advocated literal translation, which meant requiring 'absolute accuracy even at the expense of formal properties – such as the subtle harmonies of Pushkin's verse – in order to convey a range of denotive, connotative and expressive meanings through a combination of explication and footnotes'. Jakobson, by contrast, declared the possibility of translating virtually anything. He said that languages only differed 'in what they must say, not in what they can say', denounced word-for-word translation, thought the concept of complete semantic equivalence was impossible and maintained that Nabokov's *bête noire* – paraphrase – was a legitimate translation strategy.

At a poetry reading held at the Café of Poets in Moscow in 1918, Jacobson came up with the idea of translating one of Mayakovsky's, poems *They Don't Understand Anything* into Old Church Slavonic, the language of Russian Orthodox Church services. The aim being to: 'add to the poem another level of estrangement, a quality considered by the Russian formalists to be a fundamental feature of any literary work and certainly a central theme of the poem', which recounts a fantastic and bizarre visit to a barbershop.[82]

As Brian Baer comments, this pointed to the paradox in the positions adopted by Jakobson and Nabokov in that the scholar, Jakobson, advocated 'creative' solutions to translation problems, whereas the writer, Nabokov, demanded 'sacrifice' on the part of the translator. The row between Jakobson and Nabokov crystallised around a proposed joint translation of a medieval Russian chronicle, *The Lay of Igor's Campaign.* The only manuscript copy of this text had first been discovered in 1795 in the library of the Spaso-Yaroslavsky monastery in Yaroslavl. It had then been sold as part of a collection to a local landowner, and distant relative of Pushkin, Count Alexey Musin-Pushkin.[83]

Musin-Pushkin made a copy for Catherine the Great the following year and had it published in 1800. The original manuscript was destroyed, along with the rest of Musin-Pushkin's library, during the Great Fire of Moscow in 1812. Almost from the moment it was published, the tale of Igor's campaign caused much debate in literary circles, mainly due to doubts over its authenticity. The poem told the tale of an unsuccessful early 13th century campaign by the Rurik Prince of Novgorod, Igor Svyatoslavich, against nomadic warriors of the steppe known as the Polovtsians. The text appeared to have been written much later, in the 15th century, but, if genuine, it would be the sole surviving example of an early Slavonic text in which there was no trace of Church Slavonic.

Pushkin himself had taken a keen interest in this discovery. In 1836, he began an unfinished article on *The Lay of Igor's Campaign* in which he notes that: 'Some writers expressed doubts as to the genuineness of this ancient monument to our poetry and aroused heated protests'. Pushkin's own view was that: 'A happy imitation can deceive the ignorant but it cannot escape the scrutiny of the real expert…neither Karamzin, nor Yermolaev, nor A K Vostokov, nor Khodakovsky, ever doubted the genuineness of *The Lay of Igor's Campaign*'. Even the great German historian and sceptic, Schlözer, who doubted its authenticity before he had seen it, soon changed his mind: '… having read it, he admitted it to be a genuinely ancient work and did not even consider it necessary to bring forward proofs of this, so obvious did the truth appear to him!'[84]

The most obvious proof, as far as Pushkin was concerned, was the text itself. He could not believe that any of the recognised Russian writers of the 18th century were capable of imitating its 'spirit of antiquity'.

Karamzin might know enough about the history, but he was no poet. Derzhavin barely knew the Russian language of his day, let alone that of the medieval period, while the other possible candidates 'all combined had not as much poetry in them as is contained in Yaroslavna's lament, and in the description of the battle and flight'.[85]

Even more convincing, Pushkin thought, was the poem's subject matter: 'To whom could it have occurred to take as a subject for a poem an obscure expedition by an unknown prince? Who could have obscured with such skill certain places in his poem by using words since discovered in ancient chronicles or traced in other Slavonic dialects, where they yet remain in all the freshness of common usage? That would be to assume a knowledge of *all* Slavonic dialects. Supposing someone were to possess this knowledge, would such a jumble be natural?'[86]

According to Pushkin biographer, Tatiana Wolff, Pushkin knew *The Lay of Igor's Campaign* by heart and had planned to publish an annotated edition. He spoke about the poem a great deal in the last years of his life and left among his papers two heavily annotated modern versions of the poem. On a visit to Moscow University in

1832 he had met one of the academics who questioned the text, M T Kachenovsky, and was reported to have hotly disputed with him the question of its authenticity.

Roman Jakobson had studied *The Lay of Igor's Campaign* in his first year at Moscow University and continued to vouch for its authenticity right through to the 1960s. In the late 1940s, Jakobson prepared a translation of the poem into French along with Marc Szeftel, a Russian specialist who worked in the history department at Cornell University in New York. It was published, in French, in 1948, as *La Geste du Prince Igor*, with an English translation by Samuel Cross.[87]

Independently of this, and during the time he too was working at Cornell, Nabokov had undertaken his own translation of the poem into English for his students and, when he came to write a review of the Jakobson-Szeftel edition, marked it down as 'stilted' and then set about preparing his own, line-by-line translation of the text.

In a footnote to the foreword of his second translation, Nabokov wrote: 'I made a first attempt to translate *The Song of Igor's Campaign* in 1952. My object was utilitarian – to provide my students with an English text. In that first version I followed uncritically Jakobson's recension as published in *La Geste du Prince Igor*. Later, however, I grew dissatisfied not only with my own – much too readable – translation but also with Jakobson's views. Mimeographed copies of that obsolete version which are still in circulation at Cornell and Harvard should now be destroyed'.[88]

Despite Nabokov's swipe at his efforts, Jakobson proposed to include Nabokov's translation of *Igor* in a volume of Russian classics for students that he was editing, but by the time Nabokov's translation was finished, in 1959, they had broken off relations. When Jakobson went on a visit to Moscow, in 1956 – and reportedly wept on his arrival in his home town – Nabokov withdrew from the project and chastised Jakobson for his 'little trips to totalitarian countries'.[89]

This being at the height of the Cold War, and in the same year as the Soviet suppression of the Hungarian Uprising took place, Nabokov had become convinced that Jakobson's emotional homecoming was less than genuine and that he was more likely working as a foreign agent for the Russians. In the aftermath of this dispute, Jakobson effectively scuppered Nabokov's attempt to land a job at Harvard. Pressured by colleagues to offer an academic appointment to Nabokov on the grounds that he was 'big' after the success of *Lolita,* Jakobson reportedly replied: 'an elephant is also big, but no one would suggest that an elephant chair the department of zoology'.[90]

The question marks over the authenticity of *The Lay of Igor's Campaign* – which Jakobson had defended on philological grounds – became completely politicised in Russian émigré circles, particularly in the 1930s and 1940s, against a background of international hostilities and war. Edmund Wilson recalled attending a debate which took place at the École Libre de Hautes Études in New York in 1942, where he observed that the question had evidently become 'a patriotic issue'.

He had witnessed the famous émigré Russian historian, George Vernadsky, read a paper, in which he remarked that the French, not content with having destroyed the original copy of *The Lay of Igor's Campaign* at the time of Napoleon's invasion, seemed now to want to deprive Russia of the honour of having produced the poem: 'Every time he demonstrated, writing words upon a blackboard, that some detail of ancient warfare or dress had been confirmed by subsequent discovery, the Russians present broke into applause'. Roman Jakobson was also in the audience and he 'could not contain himself and made tumultuous interruptions'.[91]

Nabokov disliked the patriotic tone of Vernadsky's contribution and increasingly, Jakobson became associated in Nabokov's mind with: 'the crude politicisation of literature and art that marked Cold War culture both in the USSR and the United States'. This pretence of lofty detachment was convenient for Nabokov. He himself said that he was quite content to be labelled 'an old-fashioned liberal' and to deny that his novels had any political dimension at all but, at the same time, he could be regularly counted upon: 'to denounce or belittle all Soviet and Communist initiatives and institutions'.

In a recent article on the Nabokov-Wilson vendetta in the journal *Studies in 20th and 21st Century Literature,* the author Tim Conley notes that: 'Nabokov's rise to fame and prestige in the United States was never blocked or hampered by his (from the point of view of patriotic publishers and editors) very opportune condemnations of Communist oppression. His 'liberal' preference to remain silent, to offer no public comment on any other political question, likewise does not seem to have hurt his reputation'.[92]

His independent stance did not stop him taking sides over the Vietnam War either: 'It is also worth remembering that the Nabokov-Wilson controversy was played out at the same period of time in which Ho Chi Minh was breaking off peace talks with Lyndon Johnson…not only did Wilson and Nabokov differ in their interpretations of Russian history, literature and language, they also found themselves on opposite sides concerning the Vietnam conflict. Wilson, against, had pointedly snubbed a White House invitation to dinner in June 1965 (when he was probably very hard at work on his review of *Onegin*); later in the same year Nabokov wrote a telegram of support to President Johnson for his 'admirable work' – which, at the time, involved carpet-bombing the Vietnamese countryside.[93]

When Nabokov's multi-volume translation of *Eugene Onegin* went to press, in 1964, the publisher was an organisation called the Bollingen Foundation. The founder of the Bollingen Foundation, Paul Mellon, was one of the wealthiest men in America. When *Fortune* magazine published the first of its 'rich lists', in 1957, it estimated that Mellon, his sister and his two cousins were among the richest eight people in the USA, with fortunes, from the family's Mellon Bank, each worth between 400 and 700 million dollars (or, from 3.4 to 5.9 billion dollars in today's money). Paul Mellon is a recognised patron of contemporary arts and also of his *alma mater,* Yale University, but he had also worked as an overseas agent for the wartime intelligence agency, the Office of Strategic Services (OSS), forerunner of the CIA.

The primary objective of the OSS was to conduct espionage, propaganda work and subversion behind enemy lines – that is, against the Nazis. But, after the war, the focus of the US government's concerns returned to the perceived Soviet threat. As the American playwright, Arthur Miller, later explained, the reason for the switch that took place at the end of the war was as follows: 'To be sure, the four years of our military alliance

THE MAN WHO SHOOK HIS FIST AT THE TSAR

against the axis powers were only a reprieve from a long-term hostility that had begun in 1917 with the Revolution itself and merely resumed when Hitler's armies were destroyed. But there was simply no question that without Soviet resistance Nazism would have conquered all of Europe as well as Britain…or so I thought. Thus, the sharp post-war turn against the Soviets and in favour of a Germany unpurged of Nazis not only seemed ignoble but threatened another war that might indeed destroy Russia but bring down our own democracy as well'.[94]

The primary aim of the Bollingen Foundation was to promote a conservative viewpoint, out of concern that too many American writers of the day were regarded as leftists and revolutionaries. The foundation's first ever poetry prize was awarded to Ezra Pound, in 1949, at a time when he was an inmate at the St Elizabeth's Hospital for the Insane. Pound had been a major figure in the early modernist movement, and as foreign editor of several American literary magazines was among the first to champion the works of such writers as T S Eliot and James Joyce. But, after the WWI, Pound moved to Italy and throughout the 1930s and 1940s became a vocal apologist for Mussolini, expressed support for Hitler, and wrote for *Action,* a propaganda sheet produced by the British Fascist, Oswald Mosley.

In one article, Pound argued that the English were a slave race, governed since Waterloo by the Rothschilds. During WWII, Pound was paid by Mussolini's fascist government to make radio broadcasts criticising the US, its President, Franklin D Roosevelt and the Jews. These had included virulently anti-semitic tirades addressed to: 'Mr Jewsevelt', 'Franklin Finkelstein Roosevelt', 'Stinkie Roosenstein', and 'kikes, sheenies, and the oily people'. Pound argued that *Mein Kampf* was 'keenly analysed history', signed one letter to his publisher with a 'Heil Hitler' and argued that the Third Reich was the 'natural civilizer' of Russia.[95]

In this, it must be said, Ezra Pound's views were not vastly out of line with those still being widely held throughout the West at the end of the war, where different varieties of fascism and dictatorship were eagerly supported by some sections of the upper classes, in order to create a barrier against the spread of revolution. At the end of WW1 much the same had happened when the Western powers provided enthusiastic backing for the

White Armies fighting the Bolsheviks, even though their anti-semitism was notorious.

Pound was arrested by American forces in Italy in 1945 on charges of treason and taken to the Army Disciplinary Training Centre, north of Pisa, where he was kept in one of the 'death cells', a series of six-by-six outdoor steel cages lit up at night by floodlights. It was this, his lawyers claimed, which had triggered his mental breakdown. Deemed unfit to stand trial, he was incarcerated in the psychiatric hospital for the next 12 years. During this period, he completed work on his *The Cantos,* published in 1948 as *The Pisan Cantos,* and it was for these that he was awarded the Bollingen Prize in 1949, by the Library of Congress.

The award triggered enormous controversy. According to one report, the outrage over his collaboration with Mussolini was so great that, up to that point, the main topic of conversation had been the best way he might be executed. Arthur Miller described him as 'worse than Hitler'. He was quoted as saying: 'In his wildest moments of human vilification Hitler never approached our Ezra…he knew all America's weaknesses and played them as expertly as Goebbels ever did'. The President of the Poetry Society of America, Robert Hillyer, attacked the committee which had voted for Pound and told journalists he 'never saw anything to admire in Pound, not one line'. For the Bollingen Foundation, though, Pound was an ideal figurehead because he represented 'the ultimate in mandarin culture they were trying to preserve and promote'. His reputation had initially been built on his contribution to poetry and the movement known as Imagism, much of which was derivative of classical Chinese and Japanese poetry which valued clarity, precision and economy of language. Many of these poems had been translated from the Chinese and Japanese originals by Pound who then championed the development of a style which was admired by many of his contemporaries, including T S Eliot, e e cummings, Auden and, later, Ginsberg.

Nonetheless, the decision to award Pound the prize re-inflamed all the art-versus-politics disputes that had been raging since the 1930s and seemed to confirm what many on the left feared: that there was a disposition amongst those who called themselves liberals to forgive, or at least ignore, the historic compromises which had led many artists – many of whom were now comfortably relocated in America – to use their creative talent in flattery of Fascism'.[96]

The Bollingen Foundation was only one of a number of institutions established in the post-war period with the specific aim of counteracting a perceived left-wing bias among the cultural elite. At the height of the Cold War, the US government committed vast resources to a secret programme of cultural propaganda. This was managed by the CIA and its centrepiece was an umbrella organisation, the Congress for Cultural Freedom. Its mission was: '…to nudge the intelligentsia of western Europe away from its lingering fascination with Marxism and Communism towards a view more accommodating of 'the American Way".[97] The secretary of the Congress for Cultural Freedom was Vladimir Nabokov's cousin, the composer, Nicholas Nabokov. During the course of the Cold War, as part of its struggle to disseminate anti-communist ideals, the Congress came to value any literary works or writers from Russia who could be identified as either standing apart from, if not in direct opposition to Soviet politics and ideology.

Hundreds of books of Russian literature were published under CIA sponsorship, including Boris Pasternak's *Doctor Zhivago* and the works of Chekhov. In this climate, Pushkin represented a 'highly contested commodity' and Nabokov's *Onegin* translation 'fits the pattern'. Such an ideological impetus might even 'help explain the publishing risk of producing four volumes filled largely by pedantic and occasionally digressive notes'. Moreover, it would not be difficult to imagine why an organisation which aimed to promote a 'mandarin culture' would look to Nabokov. Not only did the original publishers of Nabokov's *Onegin* have a collateral agenda, much the same can be said for the journals which published the Nabokov-Wilson polemic.

The dispute began with the publication of Edmund Wilson's article *The Strange Case of Pushkin and Nabokov* in the July 15, 1965, edition of *The New York Review of Books*, or *NYRB*. It was no accident that Wilson had chosen this journal. It had been set up, in 1963, in direct competition with another literary magazine called *Encounter* which provided a platform for some of the best minds of the day but which, by 1962, had been exposed as one of the CIA's secretly funded cultural assets.

The organisational genius behind the CIA's Congress for Cultural Freedom, Michael Josselson, referred to *Encounter* as 'our greatest asset'.

The central purpose of the *NYRB* from the outset had been to clearly signal: '…that not all American intellectuals were happy to act as Cold War legitimists orbiting around the national security state …Far from being apologists for American power, the *NYRB* writers were thinkers who rallied to the review's readiness to denounce imperialism just as it denounced Communism'.

When Nabokov replied to Wilson's opening salvo, he did so not in the pages of the *NYRB* but instead in an edition of *Encounter* (Volume 26. No.2. 1966). In a follow-up letter responding to *Nabokov's Reply,* Edmund Wilson wondered aloud why he had chosen to change the forum from the *NYRB* to *Encounter,* not least because: 'It is unfortunate – though not perhaps for Mr Nabokov – that the readers of *Encounter* may not have seen my original article or the correspondence which followed it'.[98]

As Wilson saw it, the obvious explanation was that: 'Nabokov's abrupt relocation of the debate worked in his favour in the same way as a complete change of jury midway through a trial, after the prosecution's case has been made, is bound to see the defence's prospects brighten'. More specifically, Nabokov was 'now playing to an audience more attuned to his own views and 'mandarin' style'.[99]

At its peak, the Congress for Cultural Freedom had offices in 35 countries. It employed: '…dozens of personnel, published over 20 prestige magazines, held art exhibitions, owned a news and features service, organised high-profile international conferences and rewarded musicians and artists with prizes and public performances'.[100]

The equivalent to the Congress for Cultural Freedom in Britain was its affiliate, the British Society for Cultural Freedom, and its offshoot, the Information Research Department (IRD), set up by Clement Attlee's Labour government to combat Communism. Headed by Ernest Bevin, the entire operation was effectively a secret Ministry of Cold War. The British Society for Cultural Freedom was formed in January 1951 at a meeting of The Author's Society, in Whitehall Court. When Nicolas Nabokov travelled to London to rally support for the new organisation, among those he met were T S Eliot, Isaiah Berlin, the head of the Third Programme of the BBC and Richard Crossman, General Secretary of the Labour Party.

Faced with the problem that Stalin's Russia, latterly at least, had been an ally of Britain and America during the war, the role of the IRD became how to dispel the myth of 'good old Uncle Joe', which they themselves had created. Frances Stonor Saunders again: 'Many British intellectuals and writers had worked for the government in its propaganda departments during the war: now they were being called upon to disabuse the British public of those lies they had worked so inventively to protect'.

To achieve this aim, the IRD was tasked with feeding nuggets of 'factual' information to journalists and other members of the intelligentsia, who were then expected to recycle those facts in their own work. This was a delicate operation.

As the IRD's first boss, Ralph Murray, explained: 'It is important that in the UK, as abroad, there should not be created a public impression that the Foreign Office is organising an anti-communist campaign. It would embarrass a number of persons who are prepared to lend us valuable support if they were open to the charge of receiving anti-communist briefs from some sinister body in the Foreign Office engaged in the fabrication of propaganda directed at the Soviet Union'.[101]

One of the agents who worked for the IRD was Robert Conquest, later to become one of the most highly praised, albeit virulently anti-communist, of the Western historians of Russian history. After studying Soviet History at Oxford – where he had briefly been a member of the Communist Party at the same time as Labour leader, Dennis Healey, and the novelist, Kingsley Amis – Conquest was posted to the School of Slavonic and East European Studies (SSEES) in 1943 to study Bulgarian. From there, he had been posted as a liaison offer to the Bulgarian forces, under Soviet command, attached to the Third Ukrainian Front. At the end of the war he remained as a press officer at the British legation in Sofia before joining the IRD in 1948.[102]

The way the IRD set about collating its 'facts' for its propaganda counter-offensive was: 'to collect and summarise reliable information about Soviet misdoings, to disseminate it to friendly journalists, politicians, and trade unionists, and to support, financially and otherwise, anti-communist publications'.[103]

Conquest had a team of 10 assistants reporting to him at the IRD and one of these, Celia Kirwan, was the person who approached George Orwell to ask if he would provide information on other journalists who might have Soviet sympathies.[104] Her 'Orwell List', discovered after her death in 2002, included a number of journalists on *The Guardian* and *The Observer,* as well as the Marxist historian, E H Carr, and Charlie Chaplin. In an article written for *The Guardian* in 1978, headlined *Death of the Department That Never Was* – the journalist David Leigh wrote that by the time the IRD had been abolished – by Labour's Foreign Secretary, David Owen, in 1977 – its list of suspected Soviet sympathisers included a cross-section of the General Council of the TUC and about 100 journalists.[105]

Notes

1   **Constance Garnett: A Heroic Life**, by Richard Garnett, Sinclair-Stevenson, 1991, p85

2   Garnett, ibid. p234

3   Glossary of translations by Constance Garnett, Garnett, ibid. pp.361-362

4   Garnett, p161

5   Garnett, p162

6   **The Poems, Prose and Plays of Alexander Pushkin,** Selected and edited, with an introduction by Avrahm Yarmolinsky, The Modern Library, New York, 1937

7   **History of the Russian Revolution,** by Leon Trotsky, Translated by Max Eastman, Pathfinder, 2014 (first published 1932)

8   **The Chekhov Omnibus: Selected Stories**, translated by Constance Garnett, revised with additional material, introduction and notes by Donald Rayfield, Everyman, 1994, pxxi

9   Rayfield, ibid. pxxi

10   'The Translation Wars – How the race to translate Tolstoy and Dostoevsky continues to spark feuds, end friendships, and create small fortunes', by David Remnick, *The New Yorker*, 7 November 2005

11   **Eugene Onegin: A Novel in Verse**, by A S Pushkin, translated by Vladimir Nabokov, with a Commentary and Index, two-volume paperback edition, Bollingen Foundation (1964), Princeton University Press, 1990. Volume II, Commentary and Index, pp3-4.

12   Problems of Translation: 'Onegin' in English, by Vladimir Nabokov, *Partisan Review,* Vol. 22. 1955

13   Nabokov, ibid. p505

14   Nabokov, ibid. p506

15   Nabokov, ibid. p512

16   Nabokov, ibid. p512

17   **Eugene Onegin: A Novel in Verse**, by A S Pushkin, translated by Vladimir Nabokov, with a Commentary and Index, two-volume paperback edition, Bollingen Foundation (1964), Princeton University Press, 1990, Volume I, Foreword, px

18   **The Nabokov-Wilson Letters, 1940-1971,** edited, annotated and with an introduction essay by Simon Karlinsky, Weidenfeld and Nicolson, 1979, p3

19   Karlinsky, ibid. p5

20   **The Triple Thinkers: Twelve Essays on Literary Subjects**, by Edmund Wilson, includes the author's translation of Pushkin's *The Bronze Horseman,* Farrar, Straus and Giroux, 1976 (first published 1938)

21   The Strange Case of Pushkin and Nabokov, review of Vladimir Nabokov's translation of Eugene Onegin, by Edmund Wilson, *The New York Review of Books*, 15 July 1965

22   Karlinsky, op.cit. p5

23   Wilson, op.cit. p1

24   On Translating Pushkin: Pounding the Clavichord, article by Vladimir Nabokov

in *The New York Review of Books,* Volume 2, Number 6, 30 April 1964, p14

25   Nabokov, ibid. p14

26   Nabokov, ibid. p14

27   Goading the Pony, article by Walter Arndt, replying to Vladimir Nabokov, in *The New York Review of Books,* Volume 2, Number 6, 30 April 1964, p16

28   Arndt, ibid. p16

29   Arndt, ibid. p16

30   Arndt, ibid. p16

31   Wilson, op.cit. p2

32   Wilson, op.cit. p2

33   Wilson, op.cit. p6

34   Wilson, op.cit p13

35   Wilson, op.cit p13

36   Wilson, op.cit p13

37   A Manufactured Monument?, article by Alexander Gerschenkeron in *Modern Philology,* Volume 63, Number 4, 1966, pp336-347 and p342

38   Gerschenkeron, ibid. p347

39   Gerschenkeron, ibid. p347

40   Wilson, op.cit. p12

41   Wilson, op.cit. p12

42   Wilson, op.cit. p13

43   Wilson, op.cit. p17

44   Nabokov, *Eugene Onegin,* vol II. op.cit. p365

45   Nabokov, *Eugene Onegin,* vol II, op.cit. p374

46   Nabokov, *Eugene Onegin,* vol II, op.cit. p374

47   Nabokov, *Eugene Onegin,* vol II, op.cit. p312

48   Nabokov, *Eugene Onegin,* vol II, op.cit. p313

49   Nabokov, *Eugene Onegin,* vol II, op.cit. p313-314

50   Karlinsky, op.cit. p11

51   Karlinsky, op.cit. p11

52   **Nabakov Translated: A Comparison of Nabakov's Russian and English Prose,** Oxford University Press, 1977

53   Wilson, *The Triple Thinkers,* op.cit. p49

54   Wilson, *The Triple Thinkers,* op.cit. p50

55   **Is That a Fish in Your Ear?** The Amazing Adventure of Translation, by David Bellos, Penguin Books, 2011, p142

56   Bellos, ibid. pp143-144

57   Bellos, ibid. p144

58   Bellos, ibid. p144

59   Bellos, ibid. p145

60   Bellos, ibid. p146

61   **Writer and Critic: And other essays** by Georg Lukács, edited and

translated by Professor Arthur Kahn, Merlin Press, 1978

62 **Eugene Onegin: A Novel in Verse,** by A S Pushkin, translated with an introduction and notes by Stanley Mitchell, Penguin Books, 2008

63 Mitchell, ibid. pxlv

64 Mitchell, ibid. pxlii

65 Mitchell, ibid. pxlii

66 Mitchell, ibid. pxliv

67 Mitchell, ibid. pxliv

68 Mitchell, ibid. pxliv

69 Obituary of Stanley Mitchell, by Robert Chandler, *The Independent,*
7 November 2011

70 'On Finishing My Translation of *Eugene Onegin',* *Cardinal Points* Literary Journal,
http://www.stosvet.net/12/mitchell/

71 Mitchell, ibid. p5

72 **The Penguin Book of Russian Poetry,** includes a verse translation of *The Bronze Horseman* by Stanley Mitchell and Anthony Wood, edited by Robert Chandler, Boris Dralyuk & Irina Mashinsky, Penguin Books, 2015

73 'On Milton and Chateaubriand's Translation of *Paradise Lost'.* **The Critical Prose of Alexander Pushkin.** With critical essays by four Russian romantic poets, edited and translated by Carl R Proffer, Indiana University Press, 1969, pp213-224

74 Proffer, ibid. pp.220

75 Karlinsky, op.cit. p12

76 Marxism and Literature, by Edmund Wilson, *The Triple Thinkers*, op.cit. p200

77 'Lenin and Chernyshevsky' by Nadezhda Krupskaya in **On Literature and Art,** by V I Lenin, Lawrence & Wishart, 1978

78 Karlinsky, op.cit. p22

79 **A Window on Russia: For the Use of Foreign Readers,** by Edmund Wilson, Macmillan, 1972 (first published 1943), p235

80 Wilson, ibid. p235

81 'Translation Theory and Cold War Politics: Roman Jakobson and Vladimir Nabokov in 1950s America', by Brian James Baer, Chapter in **Context, Subtexts and Pretexts,** Benjamin's Translation Library 2011, p1

82 Baer, ibid. p178

83 Baer, ibid. p181

84 **Pushkin on Literature,** selected, translated and edited by Tatiana Wolff, The Athlone Press, 1986. Unfinished article, *The Lay of Igor's Campaign,* written in 1836 but not published until 1855, Entry 306, p451

85 Pushkin, ibid. p451

86 Pushkin, ibid. p452

87 Baer, op.cit. p181

88 Baer, op.cit. p182

89 Baer, op.cit. p182

90 Baer, op.cit. p171

91   Baer, op.cit. p183

92   *Eugene Onegin* and the Cold War Monument: How Edmund Wilson Quarrelled with Vladimir Nabokov, article by Tim Conley of Brock University, published in: *Studies in 20ᵗʰ and 21ˢᵗ Century Literature*', volume 38, Issue 1, Article 4, *http://dx.doi. org/10.4148/2334-4415.1002* p9

93   Conley, ibid. p10

94   Quoted in **Who Paid the Piper? The CIA and the Cultural Cold War,** by Frances Stonor Saunders, Granta Books, 1999, p48

95   Saunders, ibid. p250

96   Saunders, ibid. p250

97   Saunders, ibid. p1

98   Conley, op.cit. p9

99   Conley, op.cit. p9

100 Saunders, op.cit. p2

101 Saunders, op.cit. p59

102 Robert Conquest Obituary, *The Telegraph,* 4 August 2015

103 'Orwells' List', review in the *New York Review of Books,* by Timothy Garton Ash, 23 September 2003

104 Robert Conquest Obituary, *The Guardian,* 5 August 2015

105 'Death of the Department That Never Was', by David Leigh. *The Guardian,* 27 January 1978

Works consulted

The Bronze Horseman

The Bronze Horseman. Falconet's Monument to Peter the Great, by Alexander M Schenker. Yale University Press. 2003

Pushkin's Bronze Horseman: The Story of a Masterpiece, by Waclaw Lednicki. Greenwood Press. 1978 reprint of 1955 edition

Pushkin, by D S Mirsky. Introduction by George Siegel. Includes a prose translation of *The Bronze Horseman* by Edmund Wilson. Dutton. 1963

Pushkin Threefold: Narrative, Lyric, Polemic & Ribald Verse. The originals, with linear and metric translations by Walter Arndt. Includes a verse translation of *The Bronze Horseman.* Allen & Unwin. 1972

The Penguin Book of Russian Poetry. Includes a verse translation of *The Bronze Horseman* by Stanley Mitchell and Anthony Wood. Edited by Robert Chandler, Boris Dralyuk & Irina Mashinsky. Penguin Books. 2015

The Queen of Spades and Selected Works by Alexander Pushkin. Translated from the Russian by Anthony Briggs. Includes a verse translation of *The Bronze Horseman.* Pushkin Press. 2012

The Triple Thinkers. Twelve Essays on Literary Subjects, by Edmund Wilson. Includes the author's translation of Pushkin's *The Bronze Horseman.* Farrar, Straus and Giroux. 1976 (first published 1938)

Verse from Pushkin & others. Selected poems of Pushkin, Nekrasov, Tyuchev, Blok and Akhmatova. Translated by Oliver Elton. Edward Arnold & Co. 1935

The Bronze Horseman, by Alexander Pushkin. Main text in Russian. Edited with Introduction, Notes and Vocabulary by T E Little. Bristol Classical Press. 1974

The Bronze Horseman, by Alexander Pushkin. Main text in Russian. Edited with Introduction, Notes, Bibliography and Vocabulary by Michael Basker. Bristol Classical Press. 2003

The Bronze Horseman. Selected poems of Alexander Pushkin. Includes complete translation of *The Bronze Horseman,* in blank verse. Translated and introduced by D M Thomas. Secker & Warburg. 1982

Alexander Pushkin. Selected verse by Pushkin, edited by ADP Briggs. Includes verse translation of *The Bronze Horseman.* J M Dent. 1997

Pushkin's 'The Bronze Horseman', by Andrew Kahn. A critical study of *The Bronze Horseman* and its poetic form. Bristol Classical Press. 2006

Russian Poems. Translated with Notes by Charles Fillingham Coxwell. Introduction by Prince Mirsky. Includes verse translation of *The Bronze Horseman.* C W Daniel. 1929.

Pushkin: The Bronze Horseman. Includes Lyric Poems and The Shot: A Novella. Introduced and Translated by Robert Powell-Jones. With a Foreword by John Bayley. Stone Trough Books. 1999

Talk about the Last Poet. A Novella in Verse and other Poems including Potted Memoirs, with new Verse Translations of *The Bronze Horseman* by Alexander Pushkin and *The Novice* by Michael Lermontov, by Charles Johnston. The Bodley Head. 1981

Poems by Pushkin and Lermontov. Translated by Charles Johnston. The Bodley Head. 1984

The Bronze Horseman. Selected poems of Alexander Pushkin. Translated and introduced by D M Thomas. Secker & Warburg. 1982

The Bronze Horseman: A St Petersburg Story. Verse translation by John Dewey. Published in *Translation and Literature,* Vol.7, No.1 (1998). Edinburgh University Press. *http://jstor.org/stable/40339775*

The Bronze Horseman: A Petersburg Tale. Blank verse translation by Alistair Noon. Longbarrow Press. 2010

The Bronze Horseman. Verse translation by Yevgeny Bonver. Poetry Lover's Page. March 2005. *http://www.poetryloverspage.com/poets/pushkin/bronze_horseman.html*

My Talisman: The Poetry & Life of Alexander Pushkin, by Julian Henry Lowenfeld. In English and Russian. Published by Green Lamp Press. 2010

Pushkin's 'The Bronze Horseman': An Agonistic Vision, by Maria Banerjee. *Modern Language Studies*. Vol. 8, No. 2. Spring 1978. *http://www.jstor.org/stable/3194520*

Pushkin. Selected verse with an introduction and prose translations by John Fennell. The Penguin Poets. Penguin Books. 1964

The Bronze Horseman, by A S Pushkin. The Library of Russian Classics. Edited with an introduction, notes and a vocabulary by Elizabeth Hill. Bradda Books. 1961

How *The Bronze Horseman* Was Made, by Priscilla Meyer. Wesleyan University. *www.academia.edu/5446624*

Pushkin's *The Bronze Horseman* and the Epic Tradition, by John Kevin Newman. Comparative Literature Studies. Penn State University Press. Vol. 9, No. 2. June 1972. *www.jstor.org/stable/40245993*

Pushkin's *The Bronze Horseman* and Irving's *The Legend of Sleepy Hollow:* A curious case of Cultural Cross-Fertilisation? By Catherine Nepomnyashchy. *Slavic Review.* Vol. 58, No. 2. Special Issue: Alexsandr Pushkin 1799-1999 (Summer 1999). *www.jstor.org/stable/2673075*

Erecting Monuments, Real and Imagined: Brodsky's Monuments to Pushkin within the Context of Soviet Culture, by Rebecca Pyatkevich. *Ulbandus Review.* Vol 12 Pushkin (2009/10). Columbia University Slavic Department. *http://jstor.org/stable/25748204*

The Statue in Puškin's Poetic Mythology. Essay by Roman Jakobson in his book *Language in Literature*.
Harvard University Press. 1987

Ovid's Poetry of Exile. Translated into verse by David R Sharitt. The John Hopkins University Press. 1990

Equestrian Statue of Peter I by Carlo Rastrelli and V Petrov. Aurora Art Publishers. Leningrad. 1972

Note: A full list of all the versions of *The Bronze Horseman* available in English to date is published online by York University, at: *http://www-users.york.ac.uk/~pml1/bronze_horseman/* Included in this list are a combination of complete translations in verse, in blank verse and in prose and a number of partial translations.

Biographies of Pushkin

Pushkin, by Ernest J Simmons. Harvard University Press. 1937

Alexander Pushkin 1799-1837. His Life and Literary Heritage, with an English Bibliography, by Samuel H Cross and Ernest J Simmons. The American Russian Institute for Cultural Relations with the Soviet Union. 1937 (special publication, on the centenary of Pushkin's death)

Pushkin, by Henri Troyat. Translated from the French by Nancy Amphoux. George, Allen & Unwin. 1974

Pushkin. The Man and His Age, by Robin Edmonds. Macmillan. 1994

Pushkin, by Elaine Feinstein. Weidenfeld and Nicolson. 1998

Pushkin, by T J Binyon. Harper Collins. 2002

Young Pushkin - A Novel, by Yury Tynyanov. Translated from the Russian by Anna Kurkina Rush and Christopher Rush. Angel Books. 2007

A S Pushkin - A Biographical Sketch, by V V Veresayev. Co-Operative Publishing Society of Foreign Workers in the USSR. Moscow. 1937

Pushkin's Button. The Story of the Fatal Duel which killed Russia's Greatest Poet, by Serena Vitale. Translated from the Italian by Ann Goldstein and Jon Rothschild. Fourth Estate. 1999

Alexander Pushkin, by Robert Chandler. With translations of his poetry by Robert Chandler, Stanley Mitchell and Antony Wood. Brief Lives. Hesperus Press. 2009

Death of a Poet. A novel of the last years of Alexander Pushkin, by Leonid Grossman. Translated from the Russian by Edith Bone. Hutchinson International Authors. 1951

Pushkin: Death of a Poet, by Walter N Vickery. Indiana University Press. 1968

Writing the Story of Pushkin's Death, by Leslie O'Bell. *Slavic Review*. Vol. 58, No. 2. Special Issue: Aleksandr Pushkin 1799-1999. Summer 1999. *http://www.jstor.org/stable/2673078*

A Duel with the Tsar, by Igor Trefimov. *The Russian Review*. Vol. 58, No. 4. October 1999. *http://www.jstor.org/stable/2679229*

The Mystery of Pushkin's Death, by Vadim V Kozhinov. Translated from the Russian by Rachel Douglas. Published in *Fidelio*, Journal of the Schiller Institute. Vol. 8 No. 3, Fall 1999. Special Edition: *Alexander Pushkin: Russia's Poet of Universal Genius* on 200th anniversary of Pushkin's birth.

Pushkin's Ode to Liberty. The Lives and Loves of Alexander Pushkin, by M A DuVernet. XLibris. 2014

National Pushkin Museum. The Pushkin Apartment Museum. 12 Moika Embankment. St Petersburg. Nearest Metro: Nevsky Prospect. Open daily except Tuesday and the last Friday of each month 10.30am to 6pm: *http://www.museumpushkin.ru/eng/apartment-museum-pushkin.html*

Works by Pushkin

The Poems, Prose and Plays of Alexander Pushkin. Selected and edited, with an Introduction by Avrahm Yarmolinsky. The Modern Library. New York. 1937

Eugene Onegin - A Novel in Verse, by A S Pushkin. Translated with an introduction and notes by Stanley Mitchell. Penguin Books. 2008

Eugene Onegin - A Novel in Verse, by A S Pushkin. Translated by Vladimir Nabokov, with a Commentary and Index. Two-volume paperback edition. Bollingen Foundation (1964). Princeton University Press. 1990

Eugene Onegin - A Novel in Verse. By A S Pushkin. In Russian, with an introduction by Ronald Hingley, vocabulary compiled by Frances F Sobotka and bibliography by A D P Briggs. Bristol Classical Press. 1991 (first published in 1960 by Bradda Books)

Eugene Onegin - A Novel in Verse, by A S Pushkin. A Novel Versification, by Douglas Hofstadter. With sketches by Achille Varzi and chapter heads by the translator. Basic Books. 1999

Yevgeny Onegin - A Novel in Verse, by A S Pushkin. Translated from the Russian with an introduction and a note on the translation by Anthony Briggs. Pushkin Press. 2016

Boris Godunov, by Alexander Pushkin. Adapted for the Royal Shakespeare Company by Adrian Mitchell from a literal translation by Alisa M Voznaya. Oberon Books. 2012

Boris Godunov and other Dramatic Works. Translated with notes by James E Falen. Introduction by Caryl Emerson. Oxford World Classics. Oxford University Press. 2009

Rethinking the Canonical Text of Pushkin's Boris Godunov. By Chester Dunning. *The Russian Review*. Vol 60, No. 4. October 2001. *http://www.jstor.org/stable/2679368*

The Uncensored Boris Godunov: The Case for Pushkin's Original Comedy, by Chester Dunning, Caryl Emerson, Sergei Fomichev & Lidia Lotman. University of Wisconsin Press. 2006

The History of Pugachev, by Alexander Pushkin, Translated by Earl Sampson. Introduction by Orlando Figes. Phoenix Press.2001 (Russian edition published in 1833)

The Captain's Daughter, by Alexander Pushkin. Translated by Robert Chandler and Elizabeth Chandler. NYRB Classics. 2014

The Captain's Daughter: A Poetics of Violence, by Alexander Groce. *Ulbandus Review*. Vol.13, Violence. 2010. *http://www.jstor.org/stable/25748214*

The Letters of Alexander Pushkin. Three Volumes in One. Translated and with an Introduction by J Thomas Shaw. University of Wisconsin Press. 1967

The Stone Guest. A Play in four scenes by A S Pushkin. Translated and published by Ricky Vernio

The Critical Prose of Alexander Pushkin. With critical essays by four Russian romantic poets. Edited and translated by Carl R Proffer. Indiana University Press. 1969

Pushkin on Literature. Selected, translated and edited by Tatiana Wolff. The Athlone Press. 1986

Alexander Pushkin. Selected poems, edited by A D P Briggs. Everyman. 1997

Dubrovsky - A novel, by A S Pushkin. Translated from the Russian by Tatyana and Ivy Litvinov. Raduga Publishers. Moscow. 1987

The Penguin Book of Russian Verse. Introduced and edited by Dmitri Obolensky, with plain prose translations of each poem. Penguin Books. 1965

Verses and Versions - Three centuries of Russian Poetry. Selected and translated by Vladimir Nabokov. Edited by Brian Boyd and Stanislav Shvabrin. Introduction by Brian Boyd. Harcourt Inc.2008

The Golden Cockerel and other Fairy Tales, by Alexander Pushkin. Translated from the French by Jessie Wood. Illustrated by Boris Zvorykin. Introduction by Rudolf Nureyev. Doubleday. 1990

A Commentary to Pushkin's Lyric Poetry, 1826-1836, by Michael Wachtel. The University of Wisconsin Press. 2011

The Pushkin Centenary: Preparations in the USSR. *The Slavonic and East European Review.* Vol. 15, No 44. January 1937. *http://www.jstor.org/stable/4203235*

Drawings of the Poet. Compilation of Pushkin's sketches by Abram Markovich Efros. Academia. Moscow. 1933. *www.digitalcollections.nypl.org*

Pushkin: Exegi Monumentum. Translation by A Z Foreman. *http://poemsintranslation. blogspot.co.uk/2013/pushkin-exegi-monumentum-from-russian.html*

Note: *A List of Works by and about Pushkin,* compiled by the Slavonic Division of the New York Public Library in 1937, is available online, at: *http://feb-web.ru/feb/pushkin/ biblio/pie/pie-001-.htm* .

Critical appreciations of Pushkin

The Pushkin Handbook. Edited by David M Bethea. The University of Wisconsin Press. 2005

The Cambridge Companion to Pushkin. Edited by Andrew Kahn. Cambridge University Press. 2006

Alexander Pushkin. Critical essays selected and edited by Harold Bloom. Chelsea House Publishers. 1987

Alexander Pushkin. A Critical Study, by A D P Briggs. Croom Helm. 1983

Taboo Pushkin. Topics, Texts, Interpretations. Edited by Alyssa Dinega Gillespie.

Russian views of Pushkin. Edited and translated by D J Richards and C R S Cockrell. William A Meeuws. 1976

Two Hundred Years of Pushkin (Volume 2). Alexander Pushkin: Myth and Monument. Edited by Robert Reid and Joe Andrew. Rodopi. 2003

Pushkin. A collection of Articles and Essays on the Great Russian Poet A S Pushkin selected by the USSR Society for Cultural Relations with Foreign Countries. University Press of the Pacific. 2002 (reprinted from the 1939 edition)

Alexander Pushkin - A Celebration of Russia's best-loved writer. Edited by A D P Briggs. Foreword by John Bayley. Afterword by Isaiah Berlin. Hazar Publishing. London. 1999

Pushkin's Historical Imagination, by Svetlana Evdokimova. Yale University Press. 1999

The Poetics of Impudence and Intimacy in the Age of Pushkin, by Joe Peschio. Universiy of Wisconsin Press. 2012

The Sacred Lyre. Essays on the Life and work of Alexander Pushkin, by Dmitry Blagoy. Raduga Publishers. English translation published in 1982. First published, in Russian, in 1979

Centennial Essays for Pushkin. Edited by Samuel H Cross and Ernest J Simmons. Russell & Russell. 1937

Metapoesis - The Russian Tradition from Pushkin to Chekhov, by Michael C Finke. Duke University Press. 1995

Writer and Critic. And other essays by Georg Lukács. Edited and translated by Professor Arthur Kahn. Merlin Press. 1978 (essays first published in Hungary in the 1930s and 1940s)

Strolls with Pushkin, by Abram Tertz (aka Andrei Sinyavsky). Translated by Catharine Nepomnyashchy and Slava Yastremski. Yale University press. 1993

Pushkin and the Genres of Madness: The Masterpieces of 1833, by Gary Rosenshield. The University of Wisconsin Press. 2003

Onegin's Morals: The etiquette of duelling in 19ᵗʰ century Russia, by Donal Rayfield, Emeritus Professor of Russian at Queen Mary & Westfield College, University of London. *www.roh.org.uk/news/onegins-morals-the-etiquette-of-duelling-in-19th-century-russia*

Pushkin - A Comparative Commentary, by John Bayley. Cambridge at the University Press. 1971

Pushkin - Homage by Marxist Critics. With essays by Gorky, Lunacharsky, Zeitlin and Vinogradov. Translated from the Russian by Bernard Guilbert Guerney. Edited by D W Talmadge. Critics Group. 1937

Anna Akhmatova - Poet & Prophet, by Roberta Reeder. Allison & Busby. 1995

Distant Pleasures – Alexander Pushkin and the Writing of Exile, by Stephanie Sandler. Stanford University Press. California. 1989

Commemorating Pushkin - Russia's Myth of a National Poet, by Stephanie Sandler. Stanford University Press. California. 2004

Bits of Table Talk on Pushkin, Mickiewicz, Goethe, Turgenev and Sienkiewicz, by Waclaw Lednicki. International Scholars Forum. University of California. Martinus Nijhoff - The Hague. 1956

Language in Literature, by Roman Jakobson. Edited by Krystyna Pomorska and Stephen Rudy. The Belknap Press of Harvard University Press. 1987

About Pushkin (from **My Half Century** - Selected Prose), by Anna Akhmatova. Edited by Ronald Meyer. Ardis Publishers. New York. 2013

History of Russia

Karamzin's Memoir on Ancient & Modern Russia. A Translation & Analysis, by Richard Pipes. The University of Michigan Press. 2008 (first published 1959)

A History of Russia, by George Vernadsky. New Haven, Yale University Press. 1969 (first published 1929)

Brief History of Russia (Two Volumes), by M N Pokrovsky. Martin Lawrence. 1933

A Short History of Russia. With Seven Maps, by R D Charques. Pheonix House. 1956

Russia under the Old Regime, by Richard Pipes. Weidenfeld & Nicolson. 1974

A History of Russia, by Nicholas V Riasanovsky. Oxford University Press. Fifth edition 1993

A Short History of Russia, by R D Charques. Pheonix House. London. 1956

The Crisis of Medieval Russia, 1200-1304, by John Fennell. Longman History of Russia Series. 1983

Medieval Russia. A Source Book, 850-1700. Edited by Basil Dmitryshyn. Holt, Rinehart & Winston.1990 (first published in 1967)

Lord and Peasant in Russia – From the Ninth to the Nineteenth Century, by Jerome Blum. Princeton University Press. 1961

Russia and the Golden Horde – The Mongol Impact on Medieval Russian History, by Charles J Halperin. Indiana University Press. 1987

The Formation of Muscovy, 1304-1613. Robert O Crummey. Longman. 1987

The Time of Troubles. A Historical Study of the Internal Crisis and Social Struggle in Sixteenth and Seventeenth-Century Muscovy, by S F Platonov. Translated by John T Alexander. University Press of Kansas. 1985

The Early History of the Russia Company, 1553-1603, by T S Willan. Manchester University Press. 1956

Ivan the Terrible, by Henri Troyat. Translated from the French by John Pinkham. Phoenix Press. 1984

Ivan the Terrible. First Tsar of Russia, by Isabel de Madariaga. Yale University Press. 2005

The Origins of Autocracy: Ivan the Terrible in Russian History, by Alexander Yanov. Translated by Stephen Dunn. University of California Press. 1981

The Making of Russian Absolutism, 1613-1801, by Paul Dukes. Longman. 1990 (first published 1982)

Reinterpreting Russian History. Readings, 860 -1860s. Compiled & Edited by Daniel H Kaiser and Gary Marker. Oxford University Press. 1994

Russian Rebels, 1600-1800, by Paul Avrich. Allen Lane. The Penguin Press. 1972

The Great Cossack. The Rebellion of Stenka Razin against Alexis Mikhailovich, Tsar of All the Russias, by Cecil Field. Herbert Jenkins Limited. 1940

Russia Against Napoleon. The Battle for Europe, 1807-1814, by Dominic Lieven. Penguin Books. 2010

Rites of Peace. The Fall of Napoleon & the Congress of Vienna, by Adam Zamoyski. Harper Perennial. 2007

In the Vanguard of Reform. Russia's Enlightened Bureaucrats 1825-1861, by W Bruce Lincoln. De Kalb. Northern Illinois University Press. 1982

Russia in the Age of Reaction and Reform, 1801-1881, by David Saunders. Longman. 1992

Road to Revolution - A Century of Russian Radicalism, by Avrahm Yarmolinsky. Collier Books. New York. 1962.

Road to Revolution - A Century of Russian Radicalism, by Avrahm Yarmolinsky. Princeton University Press. 1986

Roots of Revolution. The History of the Populist and Socialist Movements in 19th Century Russia, by Franco Venturi. Translated from the Italian by Francis Haskell. Introduction by Isaiah Berlin. Phoenix Press. 1988 (first published in Great Britain by Weidenfeld & Nicolson in 1960)

From Napoleon to Stalin and other Essays, by E H Carr. Macmillan Press. 1980

Russia's Empires - Their Rise and Fall: From Prehistory to Putin, by Philip Longworth. John Murray. 2005

The Twilight of Imperial Russia, by Richard Charques. Oxford University Press.1958

The Development of Capitalism in Russia, by V I Lenin. Progress Publishers. 1977 (first published in 1899)

The Shadow of the Winter Palace - Russia's Drift to Revolution 1825-1917, by Edward Crankshaw. Da Capo Press. 2000 (first published 1976)

History of the Russian Revolution, by Leon Trotsky. Translated by Max Eastman. Pathfinder. 2014 (first published 1932)

To the Finland Station. A Study in the Writing and Acting of History, by Edmund Wilson. Macmillan. 1972 (first published 1940)

Pushkin and the Tsars

The Romanovs - Ruling Russia 1613-1917, by Lindsey Hughes. Continuum Books. 2008

The Romanovs - Autocrats of All the Russias, by W Bruce Lincoln. Anchor Books. 1981

Scenarios of Power. Myth and Ceremony in Russian Monarchy from Peter the Great to the Abdication of Nicholas II, by Richard S Wortman. Princeton University Press. 2006

Peter the Great. The Struggle for Power, 1671-1725, by Paul Bushkovitch. Cambridge University Press. 2001

Peter the Great Transforms Russia. Edited and with an introduction by James Cracraft. Problems in European Civilization Series. D C Heath & Company. 1963

Peter the Great and the Emergence of Russia, by B H Sumner. Edited by A L Rowse. English Universities Press. 1950

The Reforms of Peter the Great - Progress Through Coercion in Russia, by Evgenii V Anisimov. Translated with an introduction by John T Alexander. M E Sharpe. 1993

Russia in the Age of Peter the Great, by Lindsey Hughes. Yale University Press. 1998

Peter the Great - His Life and His World, by Robert K Massie. Abacus. 1993 (first published by Victor Gollancz in 1981)

Russia under Peter the Great, by Voltaire. Translated by M F O Jenkins. Fairleigh Dickinson University Press. 1983 (first published in two parts, as The History of the Russian Empire under Peter the Great. Part One in 1759 and Part Two in 1763)

On the Corruption of Morals in Russia, by Prince M M Shcherbatov. Edited and Translated, with an Introduction and Notes, by A Lentin. Cambridge at the University Press. 1969

Catherine the Great. Love, Sex and Power, by Virginia Rounding. Arrow Books. 2007

The Romance of an Empress: Catherine II of Russia. By Kazimierz Waliszewski. First published, from the French, by William Heinemann. London. 1895. Classic Reprint Series by Forgotten Books. 2015

Catherine the Great & Potemkin - The Imperial Love Affair, by Simon Sebag Montefiore. Weidenfeld & Nicolson. 2016 (first published 2000).

Memoirs of Louis Philippe Comte De Segur. Edited with an Introduction by Eveline Cruickshanks. The Folio Society. London. 1960

Nikolay Novikov: Enlightener of Russia, by W Gareth Jones. Cambridge University Press. 1984

Russian Overseas Commerce with Great Britain During the Reign of Catherine

II, by Herbert H Kaplan. American Philosophical Society. Independence Square. Philadelphia. 1995.

The First Russian Radical: Alexander Radishchev 1749-1802, by David Marshall Lang. George Allen & Unwin. 1959

The Philosophical Ideas of Alexander N Radishchev, by Jesse V Clardy. Vision Press. 1964

The Empress and her Protégé: Catherine II and Radishchev, by Allen McConnell. *The Journal of Modern History.* Vol. 36, No.1. *http://www.jstor.org/stable/1874423*

A Journey from St Petersburg to Moscow, by Aleksandr Nikolayevich Radishchev. Translation by Leo Wiener. Edited with and Introduction and Notes by Roderick Page Thaler. Harvard University Press. 1958.

The Empress Catherine II's Notes on the *Journey*. Published in Wiener/Thaler. These notes were first published by Osip Bodyansky in 1865 and reprinted in Radishchev's *Complete Works,* as edited by Borozdin, Lapshin and Shchegolev.

Pushkin's Literary Gamble, by Allen McConnell. *The American Slavic and East European Review.* Vol. 19, No. 4. December 1960. *http://www.jstor.org/stable/3001281*

Terrible Tsarinas. Five Russian Women in Power, by Henri Troyat. Translated by Andrea Lyn Secara. Algora Publishing. 2001

Constantine Pavlovich: An Appraisal, by Franklin A Walker. *Slavic Review.* Vol. 26, No. 3. September 1967. *http://www.jstor.org/stable/2492727*

Memoirs of Prince Adam Czartoryski and His Correspondence with Alexander I (Volume 1), by Adam Jerzy Czartoryski. With Documents Relative to the Prince's Negotiation with Pitt Fox and Brougham and an Account of his Conversations with Lord Palmerston and other English Statesmen in London in 1832. First published 1888. Reprinted by Gyan Books (Facsimile Publisher), 2015

Memoirs of Prince Adam Czartoryski and His Correspondence with Alexander I (Volume 2), by Adam Jerzy Czartoryski. With Documents Relative to the Prince's Negotiation with Pitt, Fox and Brougham and an Account of his Conversations with Lord Palmerston and other English Statesmen in London in 1832. . First published 1888. Reprinted by Forgotten Books: www.ForgottenBooks.com. 2015

Alexander I, by Janet M Hartley. Longman. 1994

Vienna 1814 - How the Conquerors of Napoleon made Love, War, and Peace at the Congress of Vienna, by David King. Broadway Paperbacks. New York. 2008

The Last Days of Alexander: And the First Days of Nicholas (Emperors of Russia), by Robert Lee. Reprinted by Ulan Press in 2012. First published by Harrison & Sons in 1854.

Alexander of Russia - Napoleon's Conqueror, by Henri Troyat. Translated by Joan Pinkham. New English Library. 1982 (first published in 1980 as Alexandre I: Le Sphinx du Nord)

The Emperor Alexander I, by E M Almedingen. The Bodley Head. London. 1964

Imperial Legend - The Mysterious Disappearance of Tsar Alexander I, by Alexis S Trubetskoy. Arcade Publishing. 2002

The Accession of Nicholas I – By Special Command of the Emperor Alexander II, by His Imperial Majesty's Secretary of State, Baron Modest Adreyevich Korff. Rare Books. 2012 (first published by John Murray in 1857)

Tsar Nicholas I, by Constantin de Grunwald. Translated from the French by Brigit Patmore. Douglas Saunders with MacGibbon & Kee. 1954

Nicholas I and Official Nationality in Russia, by Nicholas V Riasanovsky. University of California Press. 1974 (first published 1959)

Nicholas I - Emperor and Autocrat of All the Russias, by W Bruce Lincoln. Northern Illinois University Press. 1989

Secret History of the Court and Government of Russia. Volume 2: Under the Emperors Alexander and Nicholas , by Johann Heinrich Schnitzler. Kessinger Legacy Reprints. First published 1847.

The Marquis de Custine and his Russia in 1839, by George F Kennan. Princeton University Press. 1971

Letters from Russia, by Astolphe Louis Leonor, Marquis de Custine. First published, 1844. Penguin Classics 2014.

Fighting Words: Imperial Censorship and the Russian Press, 1804-1906, by Charles A Ruud. University of Toronto Press. 1982

The Russian Secret Police. Muscovite, Imperial Russian and Soviet Political Security Operations, by Ronald Hingley. Simon and Shuster. 1970

The Third Department - The establishment and practices of the political police in the Russia of Nicholas I, by P S Squire. Cambridge at the University Press. 1968

A Russian Daily Newspaper and Its New Readership: 'Severnaya Pchela', 1825-1840, by Nurit Schleifman. *Cahiers du Monde Russe et Soviétique*. Vol. 28, No. 2. April-June 1987. *http://www.jstor.org/stable/20170573*

Some Comments on the Role of the Intelligentsia in the Reign of Nicholas I of Russia, 1822-1855, by Nicholas V Riasanovsky. *The Slavic and East European Journal,* Vol. I, No. 3. Autumn 1957. *www.jstor.org/stable/304154*

Atlas of Russia and the Soviet Union, by Robin Milner-Gulland, with Nikolai Dejevsky. Phaidon. 1989

The Dent Atlas of Russian History - From 800bc to the Present Day, by Martin Gilbert. J M Dent. Second edition 1993 (first edition 1972)

Red Fortress - The Secret Heart of Russia's History, by Catherine Merridale. Penguin Books. 2014

A History of the Modern World, 1815-1910, by Oscar Browning. Popular Edition. Cassell and Company. 1916

Secret Diplomatic History of the 18th Century, by Karl Marx. Edited by his daughter, Eleanor Marx Aveling. Swan Sonnenschein & Co. London. 1899. Reprinted by Forgotten Books. 2015. P.79

Metternich, by Constantin de Grunwald. Translated from the French by Dorothy Todd. The Falcon Press. London. 1953

The Moor of Peter the Great

The Moor of Peter the Great, by Alexander Pushkin. Included in the Complete Prose Tales of Alexander Sergeyevitch Pushkin. Translated from the Russian by Gillon R Aitken. Vintage. 1993 (first published 1966)

Pushkin and Gannibal. Article by Vladimir Nabokov. *Encounter*. Volume 19. Number

1. July 1962, pp.11-26

Gannibal - The Moor of Petersburg, by Hugh Barnes. Profile Books. 2005

Abraham Hanibal, Prince of Logone - Pushkin's African Ancestor, by Dieudonne Gnammankou. Translated from the French by Edyth Watt. Books of Africa. 2015 (first published in French in 1999)

Under the Sky of My Africa. Alexander Pushkin and Blackness. Edited by Catherine Nepomnyashchy, Nicole Svobodny and Ludmilla A Trigos. North-western University Press. 2006

Russia and the Negro - Blacks in Russian History and Thought, by Allison Blakely. Howard University Press. 1986

A Black Woman's Odyssey through Russia and Jamaica. The Narrative of Nancy Prince. Markus Wiener Publishers. Princeton. 1990 (first published 1850)

My Genealogy. By A S Pushkin. Translated by Ivan Eubanks, with a Commentary and Annotations by Ivan Eubanks and Sonia I Ketchian. The Pushkin Review. Vol 12-13 Symposium. 2009-10.

http://www.pushkiniana.org/index.php?option=com_content&view=article&id=193:euban ks-translation1213&catid=135&Itemid=258

Pushkin's Aestheticized Defence of his African Heritage in his poem 'My Genealogy', by Sonia I Ketchian. *The Pushkin Review.* Vol 12-13 Symposium. 2009-10. *http://www. pushkiniana.org/index.php?option=com_content&view=article&id=194:ketchian-symposium 1213&catid=134&Itemid=257*

Pushkin and the Decembrists

Chaadaev and His Friends - An Intellectual History of Peter Chaadaev and His Russian Contemporaries, by Raymond T McNally. The Diplomatic Press.1971

Chaadaev's Evaluation of Peter the Great, by Raymond T McNally. *Slavic Review.* Vol. 23, No.1. March 1964. *http://www.jstor.org/stable/2492374*

Filling the Gap between Radischchev and the Decembrists, by Marc Raeff. *Slavic Review.* Vol. 26, No.3. September 1967. *http://www.jstor.org/stable/2492724*

The Mutiny of the Semenovsky Regiment in 1820, by Joseph L Wieczynski. *The Russian Review.* Vol. 29, No. 2 (April 1970). *http://www.jstor.org/stable/127361*

The First Russian Revolution, 1825. The Decembrist Movement: Its Origins, Development & Significance, by Anatole G Mazour. Stanford University Press. 1937

The First Breath of Freedom. Archive material from the Library of Russian and Soviet Literary Journalism compiled by Vladimir Fyodorov, translated by Cynthia Carlisle. Progress Publishers. 1988

K.F.Ryleev. A Political Biography of the Decembrist Poet, by Patrick O'Meara. Princeton University Press. 1984

The Princess of Siberia. The Story of Maria Volkonsky and the Decembrist Exiles, by Christine Sutherland. Quartet Books. 2001

The Decembrist Myth in Russian Culture, by Ludmilla A Trigos. Palgrave MacMillan. 2009

Conspiracy against the Tsar - A Portrait of the Decembrists, by Natan Eidelman. Translated from the Russian by Cynthia Carlisle. Progress Publishers. 1985

Pushkin and the Decembrists, by George V Vernadsky. From Centennial Essays for Pushkin. Edited by Samuel H Cross and Ernest J Simmons. Russell & Russell. 1937

The Four Horsemen - Riding to Liberty in Post-Napoleonic Europe, by Richard Stites. Oxford University Press. 2014

The Decembrists, by Leo Tolstoy. The Perfect Library. 1868. On demand print 2016.

Pushkin and Mickiewicz

Adam Mickiewicz - The Life of a Romantic, by Roman Koropeckyj. Cornell University Press. 2008

Russia, Poland and the West - Essays on Literary and Cultural History, by Wacław Lednicki. Kennikat Press. 1966 (first published 1954)

The Cambridge History of Poland: From Augustus to Pilsudski (1697-1935). Edited by W F Reddaway, J H Penson, O Halecki & R Dyboski. Cambridge at the University Press. 1941

Polish Politics and the Revolution of November 1830, by R F Leslie. University of London. The Athlone Press. 1956

The Polish Way. A Thousand Year History of the Poles and their Culture, by Adam Zamoyski. John Murray. 1987

Poland under the Dominion of Russia, by Harro Harring, Late cadet in the Lancer Regiment of the Grand-Duke Constantine's Imperial Russian Body Guard. James Cochrane & Co. London. 1832 (reprinted from the British Library Historical Collection. 2015)

Konrad Wallenrod: An Historical Poem, by Adam Mickiewicz. Translated from the Polish into English verse by Miss Maude Ashurt Biggs. Ballantyne, Hanson & Co. 2011 (first published 1828)

Forefathers' Eve, by Adam Mickiewicz. Translated by Charles S Kraszewski. Glagoslav Publications. 2016

Mickiewicz in Russia, by Gleb Struve. The Slavonic and East European Review. Vol. 26, No. 66. November 1947. *http://www.jstor.org/stable/4203918*

Mickiewicz and Pushkin, *by J Krzyzanowski. The Slavonic and East European Review. Vol. 6, No. 18. March 1928. http://www.jstor.org/stable/4202214*

Pushkin, Mickiewicz and 'The Horse of Stone' , by Christopher Cairney. *The Conradian.* Vol. 29, No. 2. 'Nostromo' Centennial Essays. Autumn 2004. *http://www.jstor.org/stable/20873531*

Pushkin, Tyutchev, Mickiewicz and the Decembrists: Legend and Facts, by Waclaw Lednicki. The Slavonic and East European Review. Vol. 29, No. 73. June 1951. *http://www.jstor.org/stable/4204246*

The Imperfect Autocrat - Grand Duke Constantine Pavlovich and the Polish Congress Kingdom, by Angela T Pienkos. East European Monographs. Columbia University Press. 1987

Polish Scholarship and Pushkin, by Roman Jakobson. The American Slavic and East European Review. Vol. 5, No. 1-2 . May 1946. *http://www.jstor.org/stable/2491582*

Russian Decembrist Views of Poland, by William L Blackwell. The Polish Review. Vol 3, No 4 (Autumn 1958). Published by the University of Illinois Press on behalf of the

Polish Institute of Arts and Sciences of America. *http://www.jstor.org/stable/25776203*

Poland in the Decembrists' Strategy for Revolution, by Franklin A Walker. The Polish Review. Vol 15, No 2 (Spring 1970). Published by the University of Illinois Press on behalf of the Polish Institute of Arts and Sciences of America. *http://www.jstor.org/stable/25776902*

Constantine Pavlovich: An Appraisal, by Franklin A Walker. Slavic Review. Vol 26, No 3 (September 1967). Association for Slavic, East European and Eurasian Studies. *http://www.jstor.org/stable/2492727*

N N Novosil'tsov, the Polish Years, by Frank W Thackeray. The Polish Review. Vol 28, No 1 (1983). Published by the University of Illinois Press on behalf of the Polish Institute of Arts and Sciences of America. *http://www.jstor.org/stable/25777931*

In Defense of Empire: 'The Bronze Horseman' and 'To the Slanderers of Russia', by Katya Hokanson. Published in *Beyond the Empire: Images of Russia in the Eurasian Cultural Context* ed. Tetsuo Mochizuki, 21st Century COE Program Slavic Eurasian Studies. Hokkaido University Slavic Research Center. April 2008.

Repositioning Pushkin and Poems of the Polish Uprising, by Megan Dixon. Published in *Polish Encounters, Russian Identity* eds. David L Ransel and Bozena Shallcross. Bloomington. Indiana University Press. 2005.

St Petersburg

St Petersburg - Three Centuries of Murderous Desire, by Jonathan Miles. Hutchinson. Penguin Random House. 2017

The Architectural Planning of St. Petersburg, by Iurii Alekseevich Egorov. Translated by Eric Dluhosch. Ohio University Press. 1969

The Companion Guide to St Petersburg, by Kyril Zinovieff and Jenny Hughes. Companion Guides. Boydell & Brewer. 2003

Nevsky Prospect, by Nikolai Vasilyevich Gogol. Edited with introduction, bibliography, notes and vocabulary by Michael Pursglove. Bristol Classical Press. 2002 (first published in 1835)

Petersburg, by Andrei Bely. Translated and introduced by Robert A Maguire and John E Malmstad. Indiana University Press. 1978

Petersburg Tales/Marriage/The Government Inspector, by Nikolai Vasilyevich Gogol. Translated and edited by Christopher English. Oxford World Classics. Oxford University Press.2008

The Double: A Petersburg Poem, by Fyodor Dostoevsky. Dover Publications.1997

The Nose, by Nikolai V Gogol. Aegypan Press. 2011 (first published in Pushkin's journal, The Contemporary, in 1836)

Plays and Petersburg Tales, by Nikolai Vasilyevich Gogol. Translated and edited by Christopher English, with an Introduction by Richard Peace. Oxford, 1995

Sunlight at Midnight - St. Petersburg and the Rise of Modern Russia, by W Bruce Lincoln. Perseus Books. 2002

St Petersburg - A Cultural History, by Solomon Volkov. Translated by Antonina W Bouis. The Free Press. 1995

The Great Flood of 1824

A Detailed Historical Account of all the floods that Occurred in St. Petersburg. Published on the instruction of the State Admiralty Department, by V.N.Berkh. St. Petersburg. 1826.

The Flood of Thessaly, the Girl of Provence and other Poems, by Barry Cornwall (pseudonym of Bryan Waller Procter). Henry Colburn & Co. London. 1823. Reprinted from the British Library Historical Collection 2015

Leviathan, by Thomas Hobbes. Edited with and Introduction and Notes by J C A Gaskin. Oxford World's Classics. Oxford University Press. First published 1651. This edition published 1996, reissued 2008.

Enquiry Concerning Political Justice: And Its Influence on Morals and Happiness, by William Godwin. Edited and with an Introduction and Notes by Isaac Kramnick. Penguin Classics. 2015

Lives of the Necromancers, or An Account of the Most Eminent Persons in Successive Ages Who Have Claimed for Themselves or to Whom has been Imputed by Others, the Exercise of Magical Power, by William Godwin. Echo Library. 2006 (first published 1834).

Things as They Are; *or* **The Adventures of Caleb Williams.** In Three Volumes, by William Godwin. First printed for E Crosby, Stationers Court, Ludgate Street, London 1794. Edited, with an Introduction by Maurice Hindle. Penguin Books. 1988.

Frankenstein, or **The Modern Prometheus.** In Three Volumes, by Mary Wollstonecraft Shelley. First published 1818 by Lackington, Hughes, Harding, Mavor & Jones. This edition: Penguin Classics. 2003

Caleb Williams and *Frankenstein:* **First-person Narratives and 'Things as They Are',** by Gay Clifford. From the Pennsylvania inline edition of *Frankenstein – The Modern Prometheus. http://knarf.english.upenn.edu/*

Satan and Prometheus, by Peter L Thorslev. From *The Byronic Hero.* University of Minnesota Press. 1962. *http://www.jstor.org/stable/10.5749/j.ctttsh8q.11*

A Study of Shelley's *'Prometheus Unbound',* by Lillian Steichen. *The Sewanee Review,* Vol. 12, No. 1. January 1904. The John Hopkins University Press. *www.jstor.org/stable/27530603*

The Dating of Shelley's *'On the Devil, and Devils',* by Stuart Curran and Joseph Anthony Wittreich Jnr. *Ketas-Shelley Journal.* Vol. 21/22 (1972/1973). Keats-Shelley Association of America. *www.jstor.org/stable/30212742*

Prometheus and the Caucasus, by Frederic D Allen. *The American Journal of Philology.* Vol. 13, No. 1. 1892. The John Hopkins University Press. *www.jstor.org/stable/288028*

The Theme of Paradise Lost, by Elbert N S Thompson. *PMLA.*Vol. 28, No.1. 1913. Modern Language Association. *www.jstor.org/stable/456677*

The Marriage of Heaven and Hell, by William Blake. Dover Publications. 1994

Blake's *Job* - A Message for Our Time, by Andrew Solomon. Palambron Press. 1999 (first published 1993)

Metamorphoses. By Ovid. A New Verse Translation. Translated by David Raeburn, with and Introduction by Denis Feeney. Penguin Books. 2004

Horace - The Complete Odes and Epodes. A new translation by David West. Oxford World's Classics. Oxford University Press. 2008 (first published 1997).

Paradise Lost - A Poem Written in Ten Books, by John Milton. Edited and with an introduction by John Leonard. Penguin Classics. 2003. First published and folded by Peter Parker under Creed Church, near Aldgate; and by Robert Boulter at the Turks Head in Bishopsgate; and Matthias Walker under St Dunstan's Church in Fleet Street. 1667

Prometheus Unbound. A Lyrical Drama in Four Acts, by Percy Bysshe Shelley. Edited by Thomas Hutchinson MA. First published 1820.

Tales of the Alhambra, by Washington Irving. Editorial Everest. 2008 (first published 1832). p.115

'Pussy Riot hit back at Church Criticism'. RIA Novosti. March 27, 2012. Archived from the original on October 27, 2012. *http://pussy-riot.livejournal.com*

Theoi Greek Mythology: Exploring Mythology in Classical Literature and Art.

Revolutionary ideas in early 19th century Russia

From the Other Shore & the Russian People and Socialism, by Alexander Herzen. Translated, from the Russian, by Moura Budberg, and from the German, by Richard Wollheim. Introduction by Isaiah Berlin. Oxford University Press. 1979

Origins of the Russian Intelligentsia. The Eighteenth-Century Nobility, by Marc Raeff. A Harvest Book. 1966

Russian Subjects. Empire, Nation and the Culture of the Golden Age. Edited by Monika Greenleaf and Stephen Moeller-Sally. North-western University Press. 1998

Madman or Criminal: Government Attitudes to Petr Chaadaev in 1836, by Richard Tempest. *Slavic Review.* Vol. 43, No. 2. Summer 1984. *http://www.jstor.org/stable/2497843*

My Past & Thoughts. The Memoirs of Alexander Herzen. Translated by Constance Garnett and with an introduction by Isaiah Berlin. University of California Press. 1991 (first translation copyright by Chatto & Windus 1968)

The Herzen Reader. Collected essays of Alexander Herzen. Edited and translated from the Russian with an introduction by Kathleen Parthé. With a critical essay by Robert Harris. North-western University Press. Evanston, Illinois. 2012

The Romantic Exiles. A Nineteenth-Century Portrait Gallery, by E H Carr. A Peregrine Book. 1968 (first published 1933)

Europe in the 18th Century - Aristocracy and the Bourgeois Challenge, by George Rude. Phoenix Press. 1972

Dostoevsky: The Seeds of Revolt 1821-1849, by Joseph Frank. Robson Books. 1977

The French Revolution in Russian Intellectual Life, by Dmitry Shlapentokh. Transaction Publishers. 2009

Voltaire in Exile. The Last Years, 1753-78, by Ian Davidson. Atlantic Books. 2005

Falconet: His Writings and His Friend Diderot. By Anne Betty Weinshenker. Librairie Droz. 1966

Lermontov: Tragedy in the Caucasus, by Laurence Kelly. Robin Clark. 1983 (first published 1977)

Diplomacy and Murder in Tehran - Alexander Griboyedov and Imperial Russia's Mission to the Shah of Persia. Tauris Parke Paperbacks. 2002

The Age of Revolution - Europe 1789-1848, by Eric Hobsbawm. Abacus. 2014 (first published 1962)

Radical voices of the Age

Rights of Man, Common Sense and Other Political Writings, by Thomas Paine. Edited with an Introduction and Notes by Mark Philp. Oxford World's Classics. Oxford University Press. 2008

The Roots of Romanticism – The A W Mellon Lectures in the Fine Arts, 1965. The National Gallery of Art, Washington DC, by Isaiah Berlin. Edited by Henry Hardy. Pimlico. 2000

Selected Writings, by William Hazlitt. Oxford World's Classics. Oxford University Press. 2009

The Spirit of the Age, or, Contemporary Portraits, by William Hazlitt. First published 1825. This edition: Oxford World's Classics. Oxford University Press.

Rights of Man: Being an Answer to Mr. Burke's Attack on the French Revolution, by Thomas Paine, Secretary for Foreign Affairs to Congress in the American War. Frist published for J S Jordan, 166 Fleet Street, London. 1791. This edition, includes Common Sense and Other Political Writings: Oxford World's Classics. Oxford University Press. 2008

Burns the Radical. Poetry and Politics in Late Eighteenth-Century Scotland, by Liam McIlvanney. Tuckwell Press. 2002.

The Legend of Sleepy Hollow and Other Stories - The Sketch Book of Geoffrey Crayon, Gent, by Washington Irving. Penguin Books. 1988 (first published 1819).

Ned Ludd & Queen Mab. Machine-Breaking, Romanticism and the Several Commons of 1811-12, by Peter Linebaugh. Retort Pamphlet Series. PM Press. 2012

Poetry and Popular Protest - Peterloo, Cato Street and the Queen Caroline Controversy, by John Gardner. Palgrave Macmillan. 2011

Red Shelley, by Paul Foot. Bookmarks. 1984

The Reception of P B Shelley in Europe. Edited by Susanne Schmidt and Michael Rossington. Continuum.2008

Shelley's Socialism. Two Lectures by Edward Aveling and Eleanor Marx Aveling. Leslie Preger Oxford Bookshop. 1947 (25 copies were first printed for private circulation only in 1888)

The Necessity of Atheism: together with excerpts of revolutionary verse. By Percy Bysshe Shelley. National Secular Society. 1968

A Defence of Poetry and Other Essays, by Percy Bysshe Shelley. First published in 1840. Reprinted by Amazon 2016.

Young Romantics. The Shelleys, Byron and Other Tangled Lives, by Daisy Hay. Bloomsbury. 2010

Dramatic Scenes, with Other Poems, by Barry Cornwall. First published in 1820. Reprinted Boston: Ticknor and Fields (1857) and by Forgotten Books (2015).

Paradise Lost, by John Milton. Edited with an introduction and notes by John Leonard. Penguin Books. 2000 (first published in 1667)

Literary criticism

A History of Russian Literature, by D S Mirsky. Edited and abridged by Francis J Whitfield. Routledge & Kegan Paul. 1949

Handbook of Russian Literature. Edited by Victor Terras. Yale University Press. 1985

The Dream of the Moving Statue, by Kenneth Gross. The Pennsylvania State University Press. 2006

Cultural Mythologies of Russian Modernism: From the Golden Age to the Silver Age. Edited by Boris Gasparov, Robert P Hughes and Irina Paperno. University of California Press. 1992

The Historical Novel, by Georg Lukács. Translated from the German by Hannah and Stanley Mitchell. Pelican Books. 1981 (first published 1962)

Art and Revolution. Ernst Neizvestny and the Role of the Artist in the USSR. Granta Books. 1993 (first published 1969)

Marxism and Literary Criticism, by Terry Eagleton. Methuen & Co. 1976

Mikhail Bakhtin, by Katerina Clark and Michael Holquist. The Bellnap Press. 1984

Semantics, Culture and Cognition. Universal Human Concepts in Culture-Specific Configurations, by Anna Wierbicka. Oxford University Press. 1992

Literature and Revolution. By Leon Trotsky. Redwords. 1991 (translation by Rose Strunsky first published in 1925)

On Literature and Art. Selected writings by V I Lenin. Progress Publishers. 1967

The Hedgehog and the Fox. An Essay on Tolstoy's View of History, by Isiah Berlin. Second Edition. Edited by Henry Hardy. Foreword by Michael Ignatieff. Weidenfeld & Nicolson. First published. 1953. Paperback edition 2104.

The Gathering Storm. Shakespeare's English and Roman history plays: A Marxist analysis, by Paul N Siegel. Redwords. 1992

With Shakespeare's Eyes. Pushkin's Creative Appropriation of Shakespeare, by Catherine O'Neill. University of Delaware Press. 2003

Creating Literature Out of Life. The Making of Four Masterpieces - *Death in Venice, Treasure Island, The Rubáiyát of Omar Khayyám, War & Peace*, by Doris Alexander. The Pennsylvania State University Press. 1996

Fyodor Dostoevsky - A Writer's Life, by Geir Kjetsaa. Translated from the Norwegian by Siri Hustvedt and David McDuff. MacMillan. 1987

Six Plays, by Mikhail Bulgakov. Translated by Michael Glenny, William Powell and Michael Earley. Introduced by Lesley Milne. Methuen Drama. 1998.

Russian Language

Universe of the Mind – A Semiotic Theory of Culture, by Yuri M Lotman. Translated by Anna Shukman. Introduction by Umberto Eco. Indiana University Press. 2000 (first published 1990).

The Development of Russian Verse - Meter and its Meanings. By Michael Wachtel. Cambridge University Press. 1998

Myths and Folk-Tales of the Russians, Western Slavs and Magyars, by Jeremiah Curtin. First published in 1890. Reprint by General Books.

Russian Fairy Tales. From the collections of Alexander Asanafyev. Translated by Norbert

Guterman. Commentary by Ramon Jakobson. Pantheon Books. 1973 (first published 1945)

The History of the Russian Language from the 17th Century to the 19th, by V V Vinogradov. University of Wisconsin Press. 1969

The Russian Language - A Brief History, by G O Vinokur. Translated by Mary A Forsyth. Edited by James Forsyth. Cambridge at the University Press. 1971

The Russian Word's Worth. A humorous and informative guide to Russian language, culture and translation, by Michele A Berdy. Glas Publishers. 2012

The Oxford Russian-English Dictionary, by Marcus Wheeler. General editor G O Unbegaun. Second Edition. Oxford at the Clarendon Press. 1992

The Oxford English-Russian Dictionary. Edited by P S Falla. Clarendon Press. Oxford. 1992

Dictionary of Literary Biography. Volume 150: Early Modern Russian Writers, Late Seventeenth and Eighteenth Centuries. Edited by Marcus C Levitt. A Bruccoli Clark Layman Book. Gale Research. 1995

Pushkin and his English Translators

Pushkin and his English Translators, by Max Eastman. New Republic. 9 December 1936. *www.newrepublic.com*

Pushkin, the Russian Poet. Sketch of Pushkin's Life and Works by Thomas B Shaw, Adjunct Professor of English Literature at the Imperial Alexander Lyceum. The Project Gutenberg EBook of Blackwood's Edinburgh magazine. No. 1: Volume 57, No. 356. June 1845. *www.gutenberg.org*

Pushkin the Russian Poet. Specimens of his lyrics. Translated from the Russian original by Thomas B Shaw, Adjunct Professor of English Literature at the Imperial Alexander Lyceum. The Project Gutenberg EBook of Blackwood's Edinburgh Magazine. No.2: Vol 58, No.357, July 1845. *www.gutenberg.org*

Constance Garnett - A Heroic Life, by Richard Garnett. Sinclair-Stevenson. 1991

Eugene Onegin - A Novel in Verse, by A S Pushkin. Translated by Vladimir Nabokov. Two-volume paperback edition. Volume I: Introduction and Translation. Volume Two: Commentary and Index. Bollingen Series LXXII. Princeton University Press. 1990 (first published 1964)

Eugene Onegin - A Novel in Verse, by A S Pushkin. Translated with an introduction and notes by Stanley Mitchell. Penguin Books. 2008

Notes on Prosody & Abram Gannibal, by Vladimir Nabokov. From the Commentary to the author's translation of Pushkin's Eugene Onegin. Bollingen Series. Princeton University Press. 1964

Pushkin in English. A List of Works by and about Pushkin. Edited and with an introduction by Avrahm Yarmolinsky. Compiled by the Slavonic Division of the New York Public Library. 1937. *www.feb-web.ru*

The Strange Case of Pushkin and Nabokov. Review of Vladimir Nabokov's translation of Eugene Onegin, by Edmund Wilson. *The New York Review of Books.* 15 July 1965. *www.nybooks.com*

Nabokov's Reply. Article in *Encounter,* Volume 26, Number 2. 1966

The Nabokov-Wilson Letters, 1940-1971. Edited, Annotated and with an Introduction Essay by Simon Karlinsky. Weidenfeld and Nicolson. 1979

On Translating Pushkin: Pounding the Clavichord. Article by Vladimir Nabokov in *The New York Review of Books.* Volume 2, Number 6. 30 April 1964.

Goading the Pony. Article by Walter Arndt, replying to Vladimir Nabokov, in *The New York Review of Books.* Volume 2, Number 6. 30 April 1964.

English Translations of Eugene Onegin, by Ernest J Simmons. *The Slavonic and East European Review.* Vol 17, No 49. July 1938

Nabokov and Pushkin (with Comments on New Translations of Eugene Onegin), by Edward J Brown. *Slavic Review.* Vol. 24, No. 4. December 1965

Edmund Wilson's Achievement. Article by Frank Kermode in *Encounter.* Volume 26. No. 5. May 1966, pp. 61-70.

Pushkin, or the Real and the Plausible. Article by Vladimir Nabokov, first written in French in 1937. Translated into English and with an introduction by Dmitri Nabokov in *The New York Review of Books,* March 1988, pp. 38-42.

Eugene Onegin and the Cold War Monument: How Edmund Wilson Quarrelled with Vladimir Nabokov. Article by Tim Conley of Brock University, published in: 'Studies in 20th and 21st Century Literature'. Volume 38. Issue 1. Article 4. *http://dx.doi.org/10.4148/2334-4415.1002*

Nabokov and Pushkin (With Comments on New Translations of Eugene Onegin), by Edward J Brown. Slavic Review. Vol. 24, No. 4. December 1965. *http://www.jstor.org/stable/2492899*

The Gift, by Vladimir Nabokov. Translated from the Russian by Michael Scammell, with the collaboration of the Author. Penguin Books. 1963

No Science Without Fancy, No Art Without Facts - The Lepidoptery of Vladimir Nabokov. Essay by Stephen Jay Gould from '**I Have Landed** - Splashes and Reflections in Natural History'. Vintage 2003

A Window on Russia - For the Use of Foreign Readers, by Edmund Wilson. Macmillan. 1972 (first published 1943)

A Manufactured Monument? Article by Alexander Gerschenkeron in *Modern Philology,* Volume 63, Number 4. 1966, pp.336-347.

Is That a Fish in Your Ear? The Amazing Adventure of Translation, by David Bellos. Penguin Books. 2011

Nabakov Translated: A Comparison of Nabakov's Russian and English Prose. Oxford University Press. 1977

Secret Classrooms - A Memoir of the Cold War, by Geoffrey Elliot and Harold Shukman. With an Introduction by D M Thomas. St Ermin's Press. 2002

Who Paid the Piper? The CIA and the Cultural Cold War, by Frances Stonor Saunders. Granta Books. 1999

On Translation. Selected Essays, Edited by Reuben A Brower. OUP. 1966

Russian Poetry and Methods of Translation. Article by Helen Muchnic in The World of Translation. Selected essays, with an introduction by Gregory Rabassa. PEN American Center, New York. 1987

The Prank - The Best of the Young Chekhov. Translated from the Russian and with an introduction by Maria Bloshtyn. Illustrated by Nikolay Chekhov. New York Review Books. 2015

The Chekhov Omnibus: Selected Stories. Translated by Constance Garnett. Revised, with additional material, introduction and notes by Donald Rayfield. Queen Mary & Westfield College. Everyman. 1994